An Ordinary Family
in Extraordinary Times

An Ordinary Family
in Extraordinary Times

A German Family's History
from 1933 to 1948

Margarete Roth

Dedicated to my parents,
Heinz and Isa Paulus

Cover images: (front) Cologne cathedral and bomb-damaged surroundings, 1945 (credit: Wikimedia); author as a one-year-old in a meadow in Schnittlingen, 1940. (back) Author with her father, who was home on furlough, 1940

Printed in the United States of America.
First edition 2016

ISBN-13: 978-1495493317
ISBN-10: 1495493318

Contents

Guide to Family Members and Their Friends, 1933–1948*

My parents: Heinz Paulus and Aloysia (Isa) Paulus (née Brühl)
My two brothers: Hans Bernhard (Bernd) and Karl Heinz Paulus
     Wife of Bernd: Christa (née Kink); wife of Karl Heinz: Ursula (née Paffenholz)
     Mothers of my brothers' wives, Erna Kink (Christa) and Resi Paffenholz (Ursula)

Father – Heinz Paulus

Father's parents: Edward Paulus and Marie Therese Paulus (née Suth)
Father's siblings: Marie Therese, Kurt
     Husband of my father's sister Marie Therese: Franz Heinrich
     Wives of my father's brother Kurt: (1) Resi (née Kappertz), and (2) Erika (née Gessner)
Father's maternal uncles: Wilhelm (Willi) and Franz Suth. Willi's wife: Lilly (née Adenauer)

Mother – Isa Paulus

Mother's parents: Achaz Brühl and Barbara Brühl (née Priel)
Mother's siblings: Maria, Gertrud, Anna, Mathilde (Minni), Richard, Wilhelmine (Wilma),
     Karl, Hermann, Rudolf, Hildegard, Thea (Sister Pia Theresia), Robert
     Husbands of my mother's sisters: Erich Tietze (Maria); Paul Ludwig (Gertrud);
     Joseph Fetz (Mathilde); Gerhard Baumgartner (Wilhelmine)
     Wife of my mother's brother Rudolf: Gertrud (née Wintterle)
Mother's paternal aunts and uncles: Marie, Barbara, Bernhard, Xaver
     Spouse of mother's aunt Marie: Richard Fischer
     Children of Xaver: Hedwig Pieper and Franz Brühl
Mother's uncle (half-sibling of Barbara Brühl): Xaver Priel. Wife = Walburga
     Children of Xaver and Walburga: Maria, Christel, Anton, Karl, Klara, Rosa, Otto,
     Paula, Ellie

Friends of Heinz and Isa Paulus

Msgr. Gottfried Dossing, friend from the men's and boys' youth group Neudeutschland and
     founder of Misereor
Pastor Hans Pardun, friend from Neudeutschland, godfather of my brother Bernd
Msgr. Josef Guelden, friend of the women's and girls' youth group Heliandbund, who mar-
     ried my parents
Max and Elli Pfaender, friends from Neudeutschland and Heliandbund
Hans Murmann, colleague of my father at the Allianz
Maria Hoffmann and M.E., two friends from Heliandbund (mentioned in Dr. Doerr's inter-
     view with my mother and M.E.)

* Not mentioned here or in the family tree (see below) are the spouses and children who joined our family or were born after 1948.

Family Tree

Descendants of Achaz Brühl (1873–1954) and Barbara Brühl (1879–1955)[*]

    1. Maria (1908–2007) = Erich Tietze (1903–1977)
        |—Armin (1929–) = Doris Enkel (1929–)
        |—Elinor Baumann (1931–2013)
    2. Gertrud (1909–1999) = Paul Ludwig (1909–1954)
        |—Dagmar (1940–) = Walter Böhm (1940–)
        |—Sybille Schmitt (1943–)
    3. Aloysia (Isa) (1910–1994) = Heinz Paulus (1910–1980)
        |—Margarete (1938–) = Warren Roth (1931–)
        |—Hans ["Bernd"] Bernhard (1941–) = Christa Kink (1947–)
        |—Karl Heinz (1943–) = Ursula Paffenholz (1950–)
    4. Anna (1911–1913)
    5. Mathilde ["Minni"]) (1912–1996) = Joseph Fetz (1899–1974)
        |—Günther (1937–)
    6. Richard (1914–1918)
    7. Wilhelmine ["Wilma"] (1915–1998) = Gerhard Baumgartner (1909–2006)
        |—Wolfgang (1936–2015)
        |—Susanne (1939–)
    8. Karl (1916–1943)
    9. Hermann (1918–1998)
  10. Rudolf (1919–1979) = Gertrud Wintterle (1920–)
  11. Hildegard (1920–1922)
  12. Thea (Sr. Pia Theresia) (1921–2001)
  13. Robert (1924–1944) missing in action

Descendants of Eduard Paulus (1877–1915) and Marie Therese ["Thesa"] Suth (1879–1955)[*]

    1. Marie–Therese (1904–1974) = Franz Heinrich (1904–1989)
        |—Erika Zander (1934–2003)
        |—Walther (1938–)
    2. Heinz (see Achaz and Barbara Brühl above)
    3. Kurt (1914–1995). First marriage = Resi Kappertz (1916–2003).
        |—Ingrid (1941–)
        |—Ursula (1942–)
        |—Winfried (1944–)
          Second marriage = Erika Gessner (1924–)

[*] Family members born before 1948 and therefore included in this book.

Sources and Style Notes

Sources

Diaries and Albums

Heinz and Isa Paulus (my parents)
Franz Heinrich (my father's brother-in-law)
Resi Paulus (my father's sister-in-law)
Hermann Brühl (my mother's brother)
Richard Fischer (my mother's uncle)

Interviews and Recollections

Heinz and Isa Paulus (my parents)
Erika Paulus (second wife of my father's brother Kurt)
Erna Kink and Resi Paffenholz (mothers of the wives of my brothers)
Armin and Elinor (children of my mother's oldest sister Maria)
Doris Enkel (wife of Armin)
Dagmar (daughter of Gertrud and Paul Ludwig)
Mathilde "Minni" (my mother's sister)
Guenther Fetz (son of Mathilde and her husband, Joseph Fetz)
Gertrud Brühl (wife of my mother's brother Rudolf)
Theresia (Sister Pia Theresia) Brühl (my mother's sister)
Renate Hendricks (recollections of her grandfather, Franz Suth)
Ilse (née Stein) and Henry Black (Heinrich Meier-Bende)
    (my father's cousins; talks with author during visits to their home in England)
Hedwig Pieper (my mother's cousin) and Gisela Brühl (wife of my mother's
    cousin Franz)

Letters

Heinz and Isa Paulus (my parents)
Achaz Brühl and Barbara Brühl (my mother's parents)
Marie Therese Paulus (my father's mother)
Paul Ludwig (my mother's brother-in-law)
Mathilde "Minni" (my mother's sister)
Karl Brühl (my mother's brother)
Rudolf Brühl (my mother's brother)
Gerhard and Wilhelmine "Wilma" Baumgartner (my mother's sister)
Hermann Brühl (my mother's brother)
Theresia (Sister Pia Theresia) Brühl (my mother's sister)
Robert Brühl (my mother's brother)
Willi and Lilly (Adenauer) Suth (my father's uncle and his wife)
Richard Fischer (my mother's uncle)
Msgr. Gottfried Dossing, Pastor Hans Pardun, and other friends and colleagues

Style

The material in this book consists of my translations of the documents quoted. My translations have been edited for the sake of clarity and ease of reading, but the editing has not affected the essence of the writings. Words that were underlined in the original documents have been italicized here. When no date is given for a particular document, presume that the piece is undated.

Material that appears in square brackets represents my insertion. If necessary for clarification I preface the inserted material with the word *Note*.

Chronology

Foreword

In 1993 one of my mother's sisters, a Carmelite nun, Pia Theresia (Thea Brühl), presented me with a thick album, in which she had collected photos, letters, poems, and documents of her family, with great care and love starting with her siblings, and going beyond to her parents, grandparents and great grandparents.

She chose to give it to me—as one of her seventeen nieces and nephews—in the hope that I would continue the family history and share it with others. At the time, I hadn't yet shown any particular interest in the "older generations," so I was surprised.

Her intuitions were right, however: my interest was piqued and I started to assemble anything about the family that I could lay my hands on: letters, photos, diaries, interviews with family members, anecdotes, documents, grade books, reports of relatives, military records, and obituaries. Slowly I extended the research to include my father's family. The following is therefore the merged story of the descendants, siblings and ancestors of my grandparents Achaz and Barbara Brühl and Eduard and Thesa Paulus.

During my collecting and sorting, one story grew clear in my mind: the attitudes and actions of different family members during the Nazi regime and World War II in Germany led to changes in family relationships and to changes in the economic situation of various family members.

Much has been written about this time, but I want to concentrate on three personal aspects: (1) the stressed family relationships due to the different attitudes and behaviors towards the Nazi ideology and politics; (2) the descent from wealth to poverty due to the effects of the war; (3) the struggle to reconcile one's own religious and human values with the increasing deterioration of morality surrounding them. Unfortunately much information has been lost because I started my inquiries over fifty years after the end of World War II. Members of the older generation, including my parents, were no longer alive to verify the factual nature of what I was finding. Thus most of the following narrative is based on written documents that are still available and accessible to me. Some of the anecdotes that I call up from memory may well be inaccurate since I was only seven when the war ended. Perhaps some memories were picked up from stories told to me.

I am especially grateful to my aunt, Thea Brühl, who so wisely and lovingly kept her extensive album on the family. I owe this book to her support and initial work. My Aunt Trudl Brühl, the wife of Uncle Rudolf, also helped me tremendously. Though she is a *reingeschneite* (one who marries into a family, or is "snowed in") member of our family, she turned out to know more about our family than most of us. Despite her 95 years, she still has a perfect memory and the patience to answer my questions and to translate the endless letters that were written in the old German script.

Many cousins also helped to put this kaleidoscope together. Very special thanks go to Dagmar Boehm (a German and English high school language teacher). She not only summarized the very numerous letters of her father during the war, but she and her husband, Walther (a French and history high school teacher), have added historical background to put the very personal family story into the political context of the time. They helped with many old-fashioned German expressions so that I could translate them properly. Dagmar, who had numerous talks with her mother, added family anecdotes. My oldest cousin, Armin Tietze, who was born in 1929, and his wife, Doris, have added recollections about this time period, as has his sister Elinor Baumann. Guenther Fetz, Ingrid Felten, Walther Heinrich have graciously given me access to their parents' diaries and letters and added their recollections to our family lore. Erna Kink, Resi Paffenholz, the mothers-in-law of my two brothers, all gave me much insight into this period through long interviews.

My husband, Warren, has shared with me the letters that the German relatives of his grandparents wrote after the war, when his grandmother and her sons sent Care packages to them in Germany.

Special thanks go to Dr. Margarete Doerr who gave me the transcripts of an interview with my mother that she used in her book entitled, *Wer die Zeit nicht miterlebt hat—Frauenerfahrungen im Zweiten Weltkrieg und in den Jahren danach* (roughly translated *For people who didn't live through this time—Experiences of women during World War II and in the postwar years*) (Frankfurt and New York: Campus, 1998). This book encouraged me to research my family history. Dr. Doerr has given me permission to use the content of an interview that she conducted with my mother for her book.

Special thanks also go to four readers who have read some of the drafts and provided valuable insights and comments. Foremost, Gertrud Müller Nelson, who became my "unofficial editor." She was born in Germany and fled with her parents in 1936. She has a good understanding of the cultural and linguistic differences between the two countries.

My oldest friends in the United States, Doctors Jo and Roz Hays, history professors at Loyola University, Chicago, and Dominican University in River Forest, Ill., helped in so many ways, including making sure that the historical background was solid, but interesting enough for the general public, and that the story flowed smoothly. My former colleague, Dr. Jeanne Lewis, anthropologist, gave good insights in what to stress and what to omit.

And everybody needs a friend who gives unconditional support, with remarks, like: "Everything you write about your family is so interesting; I couldn't put it down." For me, this was my good friend Pat Hynek.

It will be difficult to express the depths of gratitude to my husband, who has supported and encouraged this project from the beginning. He patiently read numerous drafts; gave me insights into what would and would not be interesting to American readers; corrected many of my "awkward" translation mistakes; encouraged me when I was tempted to give up; and took on a lot more household responsibilities to enable me to continue with my research, translation, and writing.

Many thanks to Tom Fenton, who edited this book, but did so much more as a friend to make the text more readable.

I am grateful to all who helped make this family history colorful and diversified.

Introduction

World War II started one year and ten days after my birth on August 20, 1938. Two years after the outbreak of the war, about a year after my father had returned from wartime service and one week before Germany attacked Russia, my middle brother Bernd was born on June 15, 1941. During a time of heavy air raids of Stuttgart, my youngest brother, Karl Heinz, was born on August 1, 1943. Three weeks after Karl Heinz's birth my mother and we three children were evacuated to Bad Ditzenbach, where we spent the rest of the war.

As far back as I can trace, my generation is the first in Germany to have spent our adult lives in peace. My father and eight of my ten uncles served in World War II; two did not come back and four were wounded and returned either totally or partially disabled. One of my uncles served as a civilian engineer in the munitions industry during the war, but was never in combat. Another of my uncles served in World War I as did one of my grandfathers, who was killed. My other grandfather served in the army before World War I. As far back as we can trace our family tree, males in every generation have served in wars. Thus, every generation before ours experienced the heartache of relatives killed, wounded, or missing.

It should therefore not be surprising that I marvel at the period since 1945—a time of peace for Germany—in which the children of my brothers and cousins have grown up and spent their lives in peace, so far. It is still open whether my life that began during the War years will end in peace or in a state of War. I hope to convey the idea that war extracts a very heavy price on both the military and the civilian population and should only be considered as a last resort.

The following history of our family focuses on the experiences and impressions of various family members before, during, and after the war that Germany started. It is a very personal story and shows that individuals reacted differently to the regime, and not as a group.

I am starting to type these recollections on April 2, 2002, in my quiet study in Naperville, Illinois, while the tornado and storm sirens go off during their monthly tests every first Tuesday at 10 AM. They will always remind me of the war sirens that warned of the approach of enemy aircraft. Whenever I heard that sound as a child, it meant bombs were about to fall and those who did not make it to the cellar in time were in danger of becoming another war casualty. Though seventy years have passed, I have a hard time hearing these sirens without feelings.

Before I present this family history through the diaries, letters, notes, and interviews of the participants, I will give a short biography of the main characters from the time of their births till 1933. These short biographies will put their behavior into context.

Biographies

My paternal grandmother, Theresia (Suth) Paulus, was born in 1879 in Cologne into a wealthy, well-educated, and politically active family. She was the second of fifteen children, of whom six survived into adulthood. The family owned and operated a successful carpet business. Her grandfather was a veterinarian (regional director of the veterinarian society in Roedingen, near Cologne) in the middle of the nineteenth century. Someone wrote in the family's genealogical tree next to his name: "first academician in the family."

Theresia studied to become a teacher of English and French and worked for a short time before her marriage as a substitute teacher.

My paternal grandfather, Eduard Paulus, was born in Aachen in 1877, also into a wealthy family. He was the first born of thirteen children, of whom eight survived into adulthood. He and his youngest brother were killed in World War I. His father, who had been a professional soldier for twenty years, served in the French– German War of 1870–1871. After his resignation from the military, he started a successful bridge-building business. My grandfather would have been the heir to this business, but because he was killed in 1915 the business was transferred to the next oldest son.

When my grandfather was killed, my grandmother was left with three children, ages ten, six, and a few months old. However, her financial situation and therefore her lifestyle did not change much because she received a generous payment from the Paulus business and was a silent partner in the Suth family business. She lived in Aachen in a three-story house with servants.

My maternal grandmother, Barbara Brühl, née Priel, was born in 1879 in the tiny village of Westerheim, about fifty miles from Stuttgart. She was the eighth of eight children of her father and his first wife; four survived into adulthood. Her family was very poor. They were small farmers in an area called the "rough Swabian hills." When her mother suffered a heat stroke at the age of thirty-six, while working with her husband in the fields, she was taken home in a small wooden handcart and laid out on her bed, surrounded by her surviving children, including my eight- month- old grandmother, whose twin had died right after her birth. With no access to or money for a doctor, she died after a short time. Her father later remarried and had eleven more children of whom five survived. Because his new wife had to take care of her own children, my grandmother was raised by one of her mother's sisters. This aunt died when my grandmother was fourteen. The death of her guardian meant that my grandmother was not able to finish school, and she had to "go into domestic service." First, she took care of a family with many children in Westerheim, but later she became the housekeeper for two bachelors in Ulm, where she met my grandfather. They married in 1907.

My maternal grandfather, Achaz Brühl, was born in 1873 in the small village of Schnittlingen, about sixty miles from Stuttgart. He was the eldest of thirteen children, of whom five survived. The family grew up on a farm that was by German standards a relatively large farm. By rights, my grandfather should have become the heir of the family farm, but at age seventeen he had a disagreement with his parents and started out on his own. From 1893 to 1895 he served in the army. He first learned the trade of brewer, but found the work too difficult because he had problems with his lungs. He eventually became a very successful cheese manufacturer and wholesaler of cheese and butter. From the time of his marriage in 1907 to my grandmother and the births of their thirteen children (of whom ten survived into adulthood) until 1931, the family lead the life of a relatively well-to-do middle-class family. They owned a house in Stuttgart and a large summer home in Buxheim, which later became an orphanage.

In 1931, during the Great Depression, my grandfather lost his business to the American Kraft Company, which took it over for practically nothing. From then on, my grandparents' and my mother's generation boycotted Kraft products. After the loss of his business, my grandfather and many of his children worked for his brother, whose wife's family had bought up the retail and wholesale part of the business. They were no longer wealthy, but they got by.

My maternal ancestors were very pious Catholics. Every disaster, every setback that befell them was "offered up as a sacrifice." When my grandmother died, her last words were, "As God wills."

Family legend has it that one of our ancestors, a peasant who with his wife worked very hard on their small farm during the day, would wake his wife every night so that they could pray together: "God does not want us to waste all night without praying." My paternal ancestors, while practicing Catholics, had a more relaxed attitude towards religion. However, both of my parents tried all their lives to live according to their Catholic beliefs. This was not always easy in Stuttgart. During the Reformation, entire counties and cities either became Lutheran or remained Catholic, depending on the reigning noble in the area. Stuttgart, before World War II, was a very Lutheran city. When the Allianz company hired my father in 1937, he was one of the first Catholics in its employ. The former head of Allianz subscribed to the "No Catholics need apply" policy, a practice that would be unthinkable nowadays after war refugees diversified every region of Germany.

My grandparents' siblings who figure in this story include my paternal grandmother's brother, Dr. Willi Suth; my maternal grandfather's brother-in-law, Richard Fischer; and my maternal grandmother's half-brother, Xaver Priel.

Dr. Willi Suth was born in 1881 in Cologne. He became a lawyer and was very involved in politics. He belonged to the Zentrum Party and was on Cologne's City Council from 1929 till 1933, when he was "given leave" by Hitler. In 1918 he married Lilly Adenauer, the sister of Konrad Adenauer, who was mayor of Cologne till 1933, when he was also "given leave" by Hitler.

Richard Fischer, born in 1869, was a theology student who later turned to business and became an insurance company employee in Stuttgart. His mother died when he was very young; a stepmother raised him. Apparently feeling that his stepmother's children were preferred over him, he had a strained relationship with his family all his life. He married my grandfather's oldest sister, Marie Brühl. When in 1929 Allianz bought up the insurance company he worked for, he accepted the severance package the company offered. He and his wife moved to Schnittlingen to the family farm that his brother-in-law, Bernhard, and sister-in-law, Barbara, then ran. He was much better educated than the rest of his family and was treated by the family and the inhabitants of Schnittlingen as someone special, "a *Herrle* [gentleman] from the capital, Stuttgart." Taking up Hitler's challenge to prove his Aryan ancestry, he researched the Brühl family history and made it possible for us to go back with dates and anecdotes to the late seventeenth century.

Xaver Priel was born in Westerheim in 1887 as the fifth of his father's second wife's eleven children; only five survived to adulthood. He became a carpenter and moved to Bad Ditzenbach, a secluded village about fifty miles from Stuttgart. He and his wife had nine children. He ran a very successful carpentry and furniture business

Now, proceeding to the next generation.

My mother, Isa Paulus, née Brühl, was born in Stuttgart in1910 as the third child and third daughter in a family that was at that time relatively well off. Various sisters of my grandmother were engaged as nannies for the growing family. My mother started grade school, together with her two older sisters, in Schnittlingen, where her teacher noted in her grade book: "best of five pupils." After a few years she returned to Stuttgart to continue school. She was the first in her family to enter high school, at age ten, the normal entry age for what Germans call "upper school," or *Oberschule*. She spent the first six years at a Catholic Sisters' school, and the last three years at the public school. After graduation she started her university studies in Munich, majoring in German and history. There she met my father. She stayed in Munich for two semesters. At that time Germany encouraged students to attend at least two universities to receive different insights into their areas of study. My mother therefore went with my father to Humboldt University in Berlin. There she learned in a letter from her father that he could no longer pay for her education since he had lost his business. She therefore interrupted her studies after the third semester and returned home to work in her uncle's wholesale business, before marrying my father in 1937.

At age sixteen, in 1926, she was a founding member of a Catholic girls' and women's society, Heliand. As the story unfolds below, this group will play a most significant role.

My father, Dr. Heinz Paulus, was born in Aachen in 1910, as the second child and first son into a wealthy family. At the time of his birth, his father was still working in the successful family business. My father who was not a great student in high school studied law in Munich and Berlin. Though his father had died in 1915, there was enough money from his parents' two families to allow him to finish his law studies and eventually earn his Doctorate in Law. When my parents married in 1937, he moved to Stuttgart to accept a job at Allianz where he spent forty-three years, and from which he retired as personnel director.

My father joined the Catholic boys' and men's group parallel to Heliand, called Neudeutschland, either in high school or as a university student. Membership in these two groups brought my parents together.

Since many siblings of my parents play an important part in this story, I will briefly sketch their lives before 1933.

My mother had nine surviving siblings at the time of the Nazi takeover. They ranged in age from twenty-five to nine. According to my mother, a baby was born every thirteen months. Returning from school, the older children always knew when a new sibling had arrived, because the whole apartment smelled of a special substance used for cleansing after a birth. It is said that my grandfather believed that if a new baby wasn't born every year, something was wrong with his family.

Maria, born in 1908, went to school in Schnittlingen for eight years, and then spent one year at a Catholic boarding school for girls in Bonlanden. She married Erich Tietze in 1928 and by 1931 she had two children, Armin and Elinor. Erich attended the Agricultural University in Stuttgart for three years. After his marriage he worked for his father-in-law as manager of the plant in Buxheim, where he learned the practical side of cheese manufacturing. After the business was sold in 1931, during the Great Depression, it took him some time to find a permanent job. His children, born in 1929 and 1931, were shuttled back and forth between their parents and grandparents. Before Erich had to join the Volkssturm in 1944 and then became a Russian prisoner of war, he had three different positions: in Holland, in South Germany, and in East Prussia (now Russia).

Gertrud, born in 1909, like her older sister Maria, started school in Schnittlingen and then went for one year to the same boarding school in Bonlanden. One of the stories she tells about her time in Bonlanden was that they were permitted to take a bath only if they "modestly" kept their underwear or a nightgown on! She learned stenography and typing and worked for some years at the Catholic Teacher's League. Later she worked for a Swiss firm that issued transportation insurance for emigrating Jews. In 1939 she married Dr. Paul Ludwig. After graduating from high school in 1917, he studied law in Tübingen and Berlin and graduated in 1931. After a three-year *"Referendar"* (a period of service as a clerk), he passed the Bar in 1934.

My mother, Isa, was born in 1910. See above.

Anna, born in 1911 and died in 1913.

Mathilde (Minni), born in 1912, attended school in Schnittlingen und Siessen till age sixteen. She then spent some time in Romania with an ethnic German couple, as part of a Heliand outreach program to help German farm families in that country. Upon her return she started to work for her uncle in the office. In 1934, she married Joseph Fetz, who had a business relationship with her father. Since he was Austrian, they moved to Bregenz, Austria, right after their marriage. Thus, her experience of the war differed from that of her siblings who went through the war in Germany or at the front.

The next four children were born during World War I.

After five girls, the first son was born.

Richard, born in 1914, died in 1918.

Wilhelmine (Wilma), born in 1915, went to school in Stuttgart. After school she worked in a photo shop, where she met her husband, Gerhard Baumgartner, whom she married in 1935–1936.

Karl, born in 1916, finished ten years of schooling; the first four years in elementary school, then six years in junior high school. Later he took some courses in a trade school, before being drafted into the army at age eighteen.

Hermann, born in 1918, was a trained electrician. In 1937 he worked for a year, without compensation, on the family farm in Schnittlingen. Not much else is known about his life before 1939.

Rudolf, born in 1919, was the second of the siblings to go to high school, after finishing four years of elementary school. He was only able to finish six years in high school, however, instead of the usual nine. After the collapse of my grandfather's business, the family financial situation demanded that the children had to work instead of attending school. Yet, Rudolf passed the special examination that German students take after six years of high school, and he received a degree. This allowed him to study in a trade school while he was interning with a Jewish-owned firm. (The company was later "Aryanized," meaning it was turned over to an Aryan German.) After receiving very good evaluations upon completion of his three-year internship and graduating from the trade school with a degree in business, he was poised to enter the job market. As this was 1939, however, he was immediately drafted into Hitler's civil service (*Arbeitsdienst*); from there he went into the army. He married in 1944, after many delays due to the war. His wife, Gertrud Wintterle, attended eight years of elementary and middle school and another two years in a technical school. She worked first for the police as a typist and then, till her marriage, as a medical doctor's secretary.

Hildegard, born in 1920, died two years later.

Theresia (Thea), born in 1921, began school in 1928. After elementary school she studied to be a librarian. During the war she worked in Kepler House, the Catholic press and bookstore. In 1947, she entered the convent.

Robert, born in 1924, entered school in 1930 and graduated from elementary school in 1938. He then did his three-year practicum with a firm while attending a school for tool and die making, from which he graduated in 1941. This combination of work and further study is mandatory for young people who graduate from elementary school after eight years of schooling. Learning was always hard for Robert and he was therefore very proud of having received a certificate from the trade school. Right after graduation from trade school he volunteered for military service.

My father had only two siblings, since his father was killed in World War I shortly after the birth of the third child.

His older sister, Marie Therese, born in 1905, had a degree in Library Science and worked at the University of Bonn till her marriage. A few weeks before her marriage she learned how to cook in the house of her mother-in-law since her own mother always had a cook. She married Franz Heinrich, who studied mechanical engineering at the technical universities in Munich and Aachen, where he received his degree.

His younger brother, Kurt, born in 1914, attended high school for six years and graduated with a degree (*mittlere Reife*). After completing a practical education program in the train manufacturing business, he attended two technical universities in Aachen and Leipzig. He graduated with a degree in mechanical engineering.

Kurt's wife, Resi, née Kappertz, was born into a well-educated and politically engaged family. Her father, Johann Kappertz, graduated and was certified as a junior high school teacher. He joined the Social Democratic Party (SPD) in 1918 and became a city alderman in Aachen in 1919. From 1928 to 1932 he was a state representative in the Prussian State House of NorthRhine Westfalia; in 1932 he was elected to the Reichstag (Congress) in Berlin as a representative of the SPD. In 1933 Hitler dismissed him from Congress and from his teaching position. His dismissal was based on the ministerial edict "for the restoration of professionalism of state officials of September 24, 1933" (*Ministerialerlass vom 24.9.33 auf Grund des Gesetzes zur Wiederherstellung des Berufsbeamtentums*).

Resi's mother finished high school and started her studies at a teachers' college. When she became engaged to Johann, she dropped out of school and spent a year as an assistant in the household of a mine owner to learn the art of running a household—an activity many women from "good houses" engaged in.

When her father lost his positions in Congress and teaching, Resi was a junior high school student. Since university studies were no longer an option after her father's job loss, she finished high school in half a year and also attended night school to acquire a certificate in shorthand and typing. Her plan was to start working to support her parents financially, but Hitler had introduced a year of compulsory civil service for each young person and thus she had to spend a year in a lawyer's office for minimal pay. Later, before she married, she worked as a translator and bookkeeper.

1   1933–1937

**Attitudes and Activities during the Nazi Regime:
Support, Indifference, Resistance**

An Overview of pre-Nazi German Democracy

To better understand the war years, the following short history lists some of the major reasons for the rise of the Nazi government.

Germany, before the 1933 Nazi takeover, had a democratic- parliamentary constitution. This parliamentary constitution was developed after Germany's losses in World War I. In 1919, the quiet provincial town of Weimar was chosen over Berlin as the site for the constitutional convention. Revolutionary unrest in Berlin was given as the reason for choosing Weimar, but there is another reason as well. Weimar is known as the home of two of Germany's greatest minds, Goethe and Schiller, and the constitutional convention was seen to be returning to the spirit of humanity and freedom embodied in their works. This explains why, until 1933, Germany's form of government was called the "Weimar Republic."

The constitutional convention was determined to turn away from the authoritarian, militarist Germany bent on expansion, the failure of which had just become blatantly obvious. In the convention, the three-quarters majority held by the democratic parties—Zentrum (the Catholic party), SPD (moderate socialists), and Liberale (liberals)—clearly showed Germany's will to make a fresh start for democracy. Unfortunately these efforts were completely ruined by the events of the years that followed.

Many works in the past have explored why German democracy declined in this period and the national socialist dictatorship came into power. Some of the major reasons given for the failure are these: In October 1918 the German army was exhausted; their will to continue fighting had become weaker and weaker; and the military demanded that the imperial government should negotiate a truce with the Allies. In his crusade for democracy, American president Woodrow Wilson was insisting on the resignation of the Kaiser and the establishment of a democratically ruled Germany before he would agree to a truce and a peace treaty.

In contrast to the American presidential political system, a parliamentary system, using the British model, was introduced shortly before the end of the war. One sentence was added to the constitution: "The Reichskanzler, the executive, needs the approval of the Parliament (Reichstag) for his official actions." Representatives to Parliament, the nation's legislative body, were elected by popular vote. Instead of voting directly for a president, as in the United States, in Germany, the majority party, or if no majority was reached, the party with the most votes in coalition with another party, forms the cabinet and appoints the chancellor. The executive functioned therefore like a committee of the Reichstag. The executive cabinet and the legislative parliament were interlocked insofar as the leaders of the coalition parties in parliament were also members of the cabinet.

At the end of the war, the elected representatives in parliament, though not themselves involved in the imperial war, had to accept the terms proposed for the armistice and peace, an imposed and dictated peace. The Germans felt that the enacted Versailles Treaty was a great humiliation. The Kaiser, who had in the meantime fled to Holland, and his military leaders who had advocated continuation of the war for four more years and had promised victory, could thus avoid taking responsibility for defeat. These military leaders actually blamed Germany's defeat on the Weimar Parliament, saying that the parliamentarians had not allowed the imperial army to continue the war. They further claimed that the army had been betrayed by the homeland. This stab-in-the-back reasoning impressed many Germans who could not accept defeat and who therefore felt justified in turning against the Weimar Republic, blaming the democratically elected representatives for the loss of the war. Hitler's minority party, which was insignificant until 1930, was at the forefront of this fight against the Republic, against the importance of political parties, against the parliamentary system, and against democracy. Those who opposed Hitler were portrayed as traitors and called the "November criminals" because the armistice was signed in November 1918. Hitler also accused them of being responsible for the political turmoil and economic hardships that followed the Versailles Treaty. The Nazis viewed the Weimar Republic as a political system forced on Germany by the Allies and infiltrated by Jewish elements. Since the humiliation of the Versailles Treaty was blamed on the democrats, Hitler wanted them eliminated by force. Corresponding to Mussolini's march on Rome in 1922, Hitler wanted to march from Munich to Berlin one year later. His Munich Beer Hall Putsch in early November 1923 was the first step in his plan. But the overthrow of the Bavarian government failed after a heavy gunfight with the police. Two days after the putsch Hitler was arrested and charged with high treason. Released from prison in 1925, Hitler changed his strategy completely. From then on he wanted to come to power legally by exploiting the means the liberal Weimar constitution offered: free elections and freedom of assembly, press, and speech. As a propagandist, Hitler was far superior to all democratic politicians in using these newly established human rights. Thus the constitution itself gave him the means to undermine it and finally to abolish all the rights it granted when he came to power in 1933.

Pressure on the democratic parties and the government did not come just from the right, however; the radical left, the communists (Kommunistische Partei Deutschland, KPD), wanted to use the general confusion and dissatisfaction of the people after 1918 to start their own revolution. They hoped that this would lead to the introduction of a dictatorship of the proletariat, like the communist regime in Russia. This revolution failed because the larger moderate left workers' party, the Social Democratic Party (SPD), was firmly supportive of the Weimar Constitution and fought the communist uprisings with the help of the army. The effect of these street fights was that in the years leading up to 1933, the KPD ignored the rising Nazi party, considering the SPD to be their primary enemy. Later when many KPD leaders were in concentration camps, they regretted having fought the wrong enemy and thereby strengthened the Nazis.

At the very beginning of the Weimar Republic, an unexpected but significant foreign policy defeat led to the further deterioration of trust in the new government. When details of the new Versailles Treaty were published in 1919, the disappointment was tremendous. Wilson's Fourteen Points plan for the self-rule of peoples was not extended to Germans. After the dissolution of the multi-nation state, Austria-Hungary, regions with millions of ethnic Germans and Hungarians were—against their will—integrated into the Slavic states of Poland, Czechoslovakia, and Yugoslavia, and into Italy. The reduction of the German army to a size equivalent to the army of a small country and the occupation of the Rhineland were seen as humiliations. In addition, Germany was told to accept the entire blame for the war and was assessed reparations that the country could not pay. Though U.S. troops and resources were primarily responsible for the victory, President Wilson was not able to overcome the emotions of the European victors, England, France, and Italy. America was disappointed with the conditions of the Treaty and the U.S. Senate refused to ratify it. Some observers, such as the British economist John Maynard Keynes, saw in the Treaty the seeds for another war.

The harsh conditions of the Versailles Treaty added fuel to the propaganda mills of those critical of the Weimar Republic.

Economic Effects of the War: Inflation and Depression

Germany had financed its involvement in World War I through government debt by printing money. This practice continued after the war because of the severe burden of demands for war reparations. This fiscal policy ended in the hyperinflation of 1923, which destroyed peoples' savings. Large parts of the middle class thus lost the resources for financial survival and for security in their old age. As a result, more and more people stopped supporting of the new democratic government.

In order to pay the high reparation costs imposed by the Versailles Treaty, Germany had to depend on foreign credit. In the wake of the inflation of 1923, financing to stimulate the German economy came from American banks, which gave Germany short-term credits that the German banks turned into long- term credits for industry. In 1929 the American banks called in these credits and this led to many bank failures and business closures in German and put 6 million Germans out of work. The economic consequences of the war thus weakened the middle class in Germany and strengthened the enemies of the democracy, the Communists and the Nazis.

In the years after the economic crisis in 1929, three ideologically irreconcilable groups were vying for power in Germany: the parties based on democracy, the Social Democratic Party (SPD) and the Catholic Zentrum Party; and the two extremist parties at the opposite ends of the spectrum, the National Socialists (National Socialist German Workers' Party, the Nazis: NS or NSDAP) and the Communists (KPD). Due to the economic crisis the democratic parties ended up as a minority in the elections of 1932.

Many middle-class Germans voted for the National Socialists in 1932 because they feared the loss of their property if the Communists came to power. They did not vote for the SPD, which had also fought the Communists, because between 1930 and 1933 political clashes involving two paramilitary groups, the Frontkaempferbund of the Communists and the Sturmabteilung (SA) of the Nazis, resulted in fierce street fights that left many wounded and dead. In this climate many Germans felt that the country had only one choice: the NS or the KPD. In addition, the SPD also wanted to nationalize some industries using parliamentary democratic means, but Germans by and large did not understand the SPD's intentions.

None of the three groups attained a majority in Parliament, and neither the Communists nor the National Socialists were willing to compromise in order to form a coalition government since both parties wanted a dictatorship and thus held to all their demands. According to the Constitution, in case of parliamentary failure, the power to create a new government was given to Reichspräsident Hindenburg. At age 82, Hindenburg was already infirm and somewhat senile. Monarchistic, incompetent, and conservative friends and advisors of

Hindenburg suggested that he appoint Hitler as the new Reichskanzler. As the leader of a minority government, Hitler's party, the NSDAP, had garnered only 33 percent of the vote and therefore a third of the delegates. Hitler was sworn in on January 31, 1933, by the Reichspräsident, who based his decision on his right to act "in times of emergency" (*Notverordnungrecht*).

Immediately after the takeover, the new government started its policy of intimidation and violence, first against the Social Democrats, and even more vehemently against the Communists, whom they blamed as the instigators of the fire in the Reichstag on February 25, 1933. Shortly after the fire the government passed the "emergency law for the protection of the nation and the Reich" (*Notverordnung*). This law, which annulled all important human rights, including freedom of expression and of the press, became the basis for the twelve-year persecution of dissidents and, especially, of the Jews. With the help of endless unrestrained propaganda and terror actions against opposition groups, the Nazis managed to increase their votes from 33 percent to 44 percent in the March 1933 elections. The Nazis went into coalition with another right-wing party, the German National People's Party (Deutschnationale Volkspartei, DNVP), which had garnered 8+ percent of the votes, giving the coalition a 52 percent majority. Hitler had thus become independent of the Reichspräsident. After Hindenburg died in August 1934, Hitler was declared Reichspräsident by national acclamation. With freedom of speech and freedom of the press suspended, there was no opposition candidate.

In 1933 Parliament transferred its legislative power to the executive branch of the government and dissolved the federalist structure of the country, based on individual states (Länder). In place of states, Hitler divided the country into regions (Gaue), which from then on followed his edicts. All political parties were dissolved and social and professional groups such as unions, chambers of commerce, and teachers' groups were prohibited by law from pursuing goals other than those the Nazis promulgated. With this, the dictatorship was complete.

The author of this historical summary, my cousin Dagmar's husband, Walther Boehm, has added another possible interpretation of why these events took place:

> *The question arises whether the fall of the Weimar Republic to the power grab by Hitler was inevitable. This is not the case. There were many times when decisions could have been made that would have led to a different historical outcome. On the other hand, there were confluences of events that fostered the process.*
>
> *Finally, without Hitler and his obsessive nature, his predator mentality, and his charisma, the rise of the Nazis cannot be adequately explained. The best book that was written about Hitler's personality is by the well-known and respected journalist Sebastian Haffner. It is titled: Remarks on Hitler: Anmerkungen zu Hitler.*

Nazi Writings

To gain a better understanding of the total control of daily life during this time I want to include some excerpts from a pamphlet I found among my mother's possessions. Every German citizen had to prove that s/he was descended from at least three generations of "Aryan ancestors." My family's genealogical table traces my parents' ancestry to the seventeenth century. Inside the book that describes my family tree was a pamphlet that was given to all engaged couples who applied for a marriage license. It shows the obsession with an Aryan ancestry.

The content is so shocking that I feel at least part of it should be included in this family story. It shows the enormous pressure people were put under to fall in with and agree to the Nazi ideology.

Here are short excerpts (in translation):

Pamphlet for Bridal Couples from the Federal Health Ministry

The Basic Principle of Race

The opinion rooted in the national socialistic thinking that the highest responsibility of a nation is to keep its race and blood free of all foreign influences is based on scientific research on different races (Rassenforschung)....

This is followed by about three pages defining the meaning of Aryan ancestry:

The person with Aryan ancestry has no blood of foreign races in them, especially of Jews and Gypsies in Europe, of Asian and African races and natives of America and Australia. However, as long as British, Swedish, French, Czech, Polish, or Italian people are free from foreign blood, whether they live in Europe or overseas, they are considered Aryan. But it goes without saying that a German man prefers a pure German woman.

There follow regulations for the employment of government workers, with a very detailed description of how the proof of Aryan ancestry has to be established and how the genealogical table should look.

Regulations for People Applying for a Marriage License

Good health is the prerequisite for happiness in marriage. The totality of physical and mental health guaranties healthy children who enjoy work. Marriage is not only important for the couple, but is the seed from which the descendants add to the totality of the nation.

According to the marriage law, marriage is prohibited, if one of the partners

- *suffers from an infectious disease that it is feared could lead to severe harm of the partner or the descendants*
- *is incapacitated to the point where he has a guardian*
- *even if not incapacitated, suffers from an mental disease that makes the marriage undesirable from the point of view of the nation*
- *suffers from a genetic disease as specified by the "law to prevent descendants who may get this genetic disease," with an exception if the other partner is infertile.*

Do not marry before you have ascertained that your partner is compatible to you and your family's health and that the purity of your blood will be guaranteed in your descendants. You can prove your racial purity by your birth certificate and the marriage certificate of your parents in addition to their religious affiliation. Do not rely on oral opinions, but procure written documents. Always consider your responsibility in this regard toward your family and your country.

When there is an infectious illness, such as tuberculosis, marriage is not allowed, because the partner or the descendants could be severely damaged. These diseases, however, can be healed....

If you are in doubt, turn to your doctor or the consulting agency for Genetic and Racial Hygiene. Discuss this with your partner.

However, a reminder for the people who do not follow reason and their conscience: The law for the protection of German blood and German honor of September 15, 1935, threatens jail time for Germans or non-German Aryans who marry Jews.

...If one knows that one has a venereal disease and still gets married, this will result in three years of imprisonment according to the law for the fight against venereal diseases.

Core Sayings (*Kernsprüche*)

– German Person—German Family—German Folk (nation)
– Humans are the most precious possessions of a state. (Frederick the Great)
– If one isn't strong enough to remain healthy, the right to life in this world of struggle is ended. (Adolph Hitler)
– The sin against blood and race is the original sin of this world and the end of its humanity. (Adolph Hitler)
– The victory of the genetically healthy family with many children is decisive for the life and preservation of the German folk in the heart of Europe. (Dr. Frick)
– Only German blood allows a German world outlook, German thinking, German faith, and German habits.
– We have to view each boy as the future father, each girl as the future mother of German generations. Let us educate them as the ancestors of a physically and mentally healthy nation!
– German youth, keep body and soul pure, they don't belong to you, but to the nation! (Printed by W. Kohlhammer, Stuttgart)

The following story illustrates the stress upon families and their internal relationships as their personal lives play out against the background of total government control and hatred of the "other." The narrative describes personal insights and experiences of my extended family and close friends during this time.

In Germany, the Nazis, as the National Socialists were now called, did not allow any dissension or difference of opinion; anyone who voiced any criticism of the party or the regime was threatened with arrest or even death. The Nazi ideology was based on fear: fear of the international Jewish community, of the communists, of the British (Tommys), and the French, who were blamed for the economic misery in Germany after World War I. Most importantly was the fear of German Jews who were held responsible for every societal woe. This repression turned into fear of the Nazi regime itself and the Gestapo, the state secret police. Still worse, the Nazis threatened their opponents with harm to their families. Therefore activists in the underground resistance movement and even those who criticized only certain aspects of government policies were very circumspect with those to whom they spoke. This included family members. Families divided into camps, with some denouncing other family members. Mistrust was deep. Friends and family members whom one could trust were very important for the emotional stability of the people. Family members who were hostile to the Nazis and who lived in the same household with those who supported the Nazis, could only listen to foreign broadcasts when they were alone or could talk freely among themselves when the Nazi supporters were not around. Denunciation and reporting could lead to imprisonment or execution. Some anti-Nazi individuals went underground, moving from village to village to escape persecution by the Gestapo. They revealed their whereabouts to only a few people. In many families individual members did not speak with one another for years because of their rift during the Nazi regime.

My own family, which is a microcosm of German society, included at least five categories:

- Those few who supported the underground resistance movement, including some people who were forced to join some Nazi group, but who were against the Nazi philosophy.
- Those who opposed Hitler at first, but then got swept up in the euphoria of early German victories in Poland, Norway, Denmark, and France and embraced the Nazi party line.
- Those who believed at first that the Nazis would restore order and dignity to Germany, but then became disillusioned by their human rights violations.
- Those who were neutral and apolitical, accepting everything the government said.
- Those few who supported and admired the Nazis and Hitler from the very beginning.

We know little about the attitude of many of my family members because the generation before mine chose to remain silent, and my generation began probing and questioning them too late. Parents never discussed anything political in front of their children, since "kids talk." Therefore the information that follows is based mostly on letters and diaries, together with interviews with some family members.

Open Resistance

The most resistance to the Nazi regime in our family came during the time between the takeover by the Nazis in 1933 and their march into Poland in 1939, which started World War II in Europe. Documents show that during the war years there was a quiet resistance, but no public displays. Civilians tried to survive as well as they could at home. This became more and more difficult as goods grew ever scarcer. In addition, most of my relatives had small children by then. As mentioned above, one of the most devilish actions of the Nazis was to threaten people by punishing the whole family including the children if any family member did not fall into line with the party philosophy.

The soldiers on the front lines were in an even more precarious situation. They were constantly indoctrinated by propaganda, their mail was censored, and criticism such as "We should not be involved in this war" could lead immediately to court martial and/or prison. Soldiers who opposed the regime but were not free to express their opinion were in a difficult situation, as letters from my Uncle Paul Ludwig make clear (see below). In 2009, sixty-four years after the end of the war, the German Parliament passed a law exonerating soldiers who had been convicted under military law during the Nazi regime. An estimated 30,000 soldiers had been convicted of crimes against the state under the Nazis; 20,000 of them were executed. Their "crimes" ranged from desertion, to dereliction of duty or making negative or critical remarks about Hitler, Germany, or the army itself in personal letters or conversations.

Considering these circumstances most people, including most of my relatives, could or would not openly oppose the regime. My parents and some of their women friends were exceptions to the general indifference or outright support of the regime.

A. My Mother

My parents, who were twenty-three years old when Hitler came to power, had been involved in some incidents before their marriage that could have led to their imprisonment or execution. While studying in Munich, they were both very involved with Romano Guardini, who had established a progressive Roman Catholic religious movement concerning liturgy, ritual, and social justice. In addition, even before they had met, they were both members of groups that had been formed in the 1920s by the Jesuits for the renewal of Catholic youth: Neudeutschland for men and Heliand for women. Members of these groups were to "live their lives in Christ," but the broader aims of the two groups, which were based on the current and popular Youth Movement (Jugendbewegung), emphasized a return to nature and all that was "wholesome" through group activities such as camping, hiking, folk singing, and folk dancing. Most members in Heliand and Neudeutschland opposed the Nazi regime.

Mother's interview with Dr. Doerr, in which she reflects on the Nazi years

Neither my husband nor I were ever in any Nazi organization. Our family was our first priority. Since my husband was often in a TB sanatorium—for months at a time—we didn't have much of a social life. But friends from Neudeutschland and Heliand supported us the whole time. Thank God we had this circle of friends where we could talk freely. Though Goebbels, the propaganda minister of the Third Reich, dissolved Neudeutschland, the members stayed together. They met in individual family homes instead of parish halls. And every night we listened to foreign news. [Note: Listening to foreign radio broadcasts was strictly prohibited at that time.]

According to my mother, the reason the Heliand group was never dissolved was because a civil servant who wanted to help the group interpreted the law by the letter—and not the spirit—to the groups' advantage.

From mother's interview with Dr. Doerr

During the first week in October of 1937—it was the period between my civil and church weddings [Note: In Germany a civil marriage ceremony must take place before a church wedding service. This agreement between the state and the churches was passed by Bismarck in the 1870s.]—*the mailman came to my parents' apartment with a registered letter and insisted that he had to hand the letter to me personally. (I had already moved out.) If I was not there, he explained, I had to come to the main post office the next day and pick it up personally. He did not reveal the name of the sender. When I arrived at the main post office the next day, I realized that I had forgotten my identity card, which showed my maiden name. All my protests that my maiden name was Brühl were for naught. The clerk was adamant that he could not hand over the letter. In the end I asked whether he could at least tell me who had sent the letter. As if he had been waiting for just this question, he answered me eagerly: "Yes, it came from Dr. Goebbels at the Department of Propaganda of the Reich [Reichspropagandaministerium]." My answer to this: "Ah, then send the letter back again with the note: Addressee cannot be located." He replied: "Yes, that's what I will do." He smiled; I smiled. We were of one opinion without any words exchanged.*

During the next few weeks I heard that many youth groups and clubs that did not agree with the party line faced restrictions in their free group life practices; then in 1937 they were disbanded by Goebbels. This is how a small matter of details—not carrying my old identity card—could turn into an advantage. Most probably because of the behavior of this mail clerk the Heliand association was never officially banned by the Nazis.

Another incident shows how covertly anti-Nazis had to operate. My parents were on the Gestapo list of people who had to be carefully watched. Shortly before my parents' church wedding on October 9, my mother was involved in an incident involving an open letter—called the "Goebbelsletter"—that was mysteriously printed and distributed in response to attacks against the Catholic Church by Propaganda Minister Goebbels. As my mother explained, "Dr. Goebbels attacked the Catholic Church on more than one occasion in his speeches, and he especially scolded and denounced the Catholic Clergy from whom he sensed resistance."

From mother's interview with Dr. Doerr

Then suddenly an open letter to Goebbels emerged. This letter was found in many cities in mailboxes and was being very widely distributed. Hundreds of copies turned up on the benches at Bonn University one morning. Nobody knew who the author was. The letter was duplicated by people who liked its content and distributed it to additional mailboxes. Once I was sitting next to a priest who confided in me that he had been imprisoned for nine months because he duplicated and distributed this letter. This fate was suffered by others, for example, the director of the Stuttgart Caritas, Dr. Straubinger [who later fled to Brazil], and Cardinal Galen from the Diocese of Muenster.

Eichstaedt Cathedral pastor Dr. Kraus and his secretary, Maria Hoffmann, who was a member of Heliand, together organized the widespread distribution of the letter. Kraus, who also preached very courageous sermons against the Nazis, was on the government's list of suspects, but the Gestapo did not dare to directly approach this well-known and respected priest. The Gestapo noticed, however, that in all the places to which Maria traveled, the letters appeared en masse. Her mail was therefore kept under surveillance. That's how the Gestapo intercepted a letter to her from me. I had greatly applauded her for her good work in distributing the letter. I signed it "Isa," my first name. On the eve of October 6—during the week between my civil and church weddings—the Gestapo came to my parents' apartment and searched everything. Then they asked me to accompany them to headquarters and interrogated me about my relationship with Maria Hoffmann. They showed me a copy of a letter, which I recognized right away as mine, and asked me whether I had ever signed letters as "Josef." With a clear conscience I was able to deny that. The person who copied the letter had obviously written "Josef" instead of "Isa." Thank God! During the interrogation I did not admit anything that could have implicated Maria or Kraus. But I must say that it is very uncomfortable to be interrogated so long and hard in a situation where you have knowledge and are therefore involved. I was then allowed to go home after an hour. Next day I heard from another acquaintance that when the Gestapo called on him, he admitted that during her last visit Maria had letters in an envelope with her.

I knew only one thing then: I had to warn Maria; I had to be faster than the Gestapo. The next day [the day before her church wedding] *I took the 7:00 a.m. train to Aalen, and took a cab from there to Eichstätt. Then I asked the cabdriver to pick me up again in an hour. In the meantime I went to the Cathedral parish and told Maria and Kraus of the danger. This was the only way to warn her; her mail and telephone were all under surveillance. The warning allowed the priest and Maria Hoffmann to substitute prayer cards in the envelopes and to burn the letters. When the Gestapo knocked at the door two hours later, they found only religious materials in the envelopes.*

For many years my mother who believed that the letter had been written by Kraus would not reveal who she thought was the author. She said there were still some former Nazis around. She also withheld for many years the name of the acquaintance who had revealed Maria's part in the distribution. He was a diocesan priest who implicated Maria after having been tortured.

According to my mother most of the Gestapo were not very bright. They never produced the original letter or asked her for a handwriting sample.

My mother asked the cabdriver to please not tell anyone about this rather lengthy early morning cab ride. He said to her: "Dear lady, I have never seen you." This was the way a lot of people engaged in passive resistance.

Letter from Thea Brühl, my mother's youngest sister

What was not contained in Isa's report, was added by some girl-friends. The whole Stuttgart Heliand group had prepared [on October 8] *a nice prenuptial feast and was waiting expectantly and anxiously for the bridal couple. Only shortly before the eve-of-wedding party ended, late in the evening, did they hear about the Gestapo interrogation. After the*

Gestapo agents talked to Isa, they returned with her to her parents'
house and started to interrogate her parents. They asked whether my
parents had sons whose name started with a "J." Mother told them that
they had one son named Hermann-Josef and another one, Rob-
ert-Josef. The agents waited till Hermann returned from his training and
Robert from school. Hermann was nineteen and Robert, thirteen. The
Gestapo decided that they had nothing to do with the letter. Our parents
and brothers never told anybody, so this story surfaced only much later.
They protected their daughter and made the decision that the fewer
people who knew about the incident the better… either my parents or
Isa's husband Heinz received a warning from the Gestapo: "considering
the intelligence of your daughter or wife."

One hour after Isa's return from Eichstätt, she had just enough time to
change into her wedding dress before the service, which was celebrated
in St. Nikolaus church. Josef Guelden, a priest who Heinz knew from
Neudeutschland and who was one of the leaders of the liturgical move-
ment at the Leipzig Oratorium, celebrated the nuptial High Mass. I only
remember one sentence from the sermon: "If this is a Christian mar-
riage, then the cross will not be absent."

My parents never told anyone about the incident just before the church service.

My mother's visit to Eichstätt was the day *before* their marriage, but this incident must have made such an impression on my sixteen-year-old aunt Thea that she dramatically puts it on the wedding day itself. If the Gestapo had found out that Maria Hoffmann had been warned and by whom, it could have meant imprisonment for my mother.

* * *

Fr. Guelden remained a lifelong friend of my parents, but they saw him only rarely because after the war he decided that his duty was to minister to the people in East Germany, which was occupied by the Russians. He was not allowed to leave East Germany until he became a senior citizen.

Excerpts from the interview and answers to a questionnaire
sent to my mother by Dr. Doerr prior to their interview

I read Mein Kampf. *I saw Hitler a few times, when he drove through*
the Neckarstrasse, where we lived, to give his speeches in the town hall
and be greeted by the populace with incredible enthusiasm.

I was pursued and taken in twice by the Gestapo regarding Maria
Hoffmann. Our apartment was searched twice from top to bottom. My
husband was also summoned by the Gestapo. Because I was already
married, they did not keep me, as a Gestapo functionary explained to
my husband during his interrogation the next day. Every evening we lis-
tened to BBC News.

My mother told me that at least once when she was on the way home, an acquaintance approached her but did not stop. "Don't go home now," she warned, "the Gestapo is in your home."

When Hitler drove through the city streets he was always greeted enthusiastically. Most of this enthusiasm was genuine, but some was done out of fear: people had to attend the rallies and soldiers with binoculars were stationed in every apartment and on every roof along the route.

And then there was always the strange change in people who were caught up in the mass hysteria around them. A friend of my parents was an ardent anti-Nazi. He was married to a Jewish woman and they had many children. So, he was always worried what could happen to them. But at one of the rallies, he was standing next to my mother and when she looked over at him, he had raised his arm and shouted "Heil, Hitler." When he saw her looking at him, he immediately brought his arm down, and just said: "Oh, my God...."

Many years after the war when I became aware of how the Germans treated the Jews, I wondered why this woman and her children were never taken away to a camp. Was it because she was taking care of the six young children of a Gentile? They survived the war and we continued to socialize with them afterwards.

Another example of people who fell under the Nazi's scrutiny comes from a close family member. In 2008, my cousin Armin's wife, Doris Tietze, told me the extraordinary story of her ancestors.

Letter from Doris Tietze

My maternal great grandmother, Carline Eisenhut, was Jewish. She married a Christian named Mueller. She raised her children in the Jewish faith and had no problem with either family or with her neighbors or friends. Her daughter Sofia, my grandmother, also married a Christian and converted to the Catholic faith. Her Jewish family rejected her as a result. My family never talked about the Jewish ancestors, especially not after Hitler came into power. My grandfather died young and my grandmother raised eight children [however two died in infancy and one drowned in the Rhine as a teenager]. *My grandmother sewed umbrellas at home and took in washing so that she could work and still be at home.*

So, my grandmother was half Jewish, but her sons were considered eligible for military service. They served in the Nazi army on the front. One was killed in Poland and one died as a prisoner of war.

The first time I heard about the "Jewishness" of my grandma was in 1944 when we were living with her after my mother and I were bombed out. A letter arrived instructing her to come to a certain place and bring along one change of underwear, a toothbrush, a nightgown, and a comb. My grandma went into hiding immediately; she first moved in with a daughter-in-law, who lived in a rural area. After a short time she moved in with another daughter-of-law, because she had to stay ahead of the Gestapo. Since she did not officially live at these places, the family cared for her without extra ration cards.

A few days after my grandmother went underground, the Gestapo came to our door. Another family shared the apartment with us. The husband in that family had been in a concentration camp because he was a communist. When the Gestapo asked for Sofia Krick, my mother said that she hadn't seen her for quite some time, and she had no idea where she was. I stood behind the curtain and saw that another Ge-

12

stapo man was keeping watch on the street. They conferred and then went away; we never heard anything again from them.

Later when one of my uncles came home on furlough, in the early months of 1945, he went to the Gestapo to inquire where he could visit his mother. In his naïveté, he thought if he inquired about his mother, the Gestapo would think that she couldn't be found. But when he got to the office, everything was already in turmoil. Because of the advancing Allied troops all of the office files were being transferred across the Rhine. This probably saved our lives, my grandmother's, my mother's and mine.

I was afraid till the end of the war that at any moment somebody would put his hand on my shoulder and take me into custody, because starting in 1941, I attended a special government-financed school for gifted students from families who could not afford the tuition. How did I get into this school? The principal of my elementary school strongly advised my mother to put me into this school. She eventually confided in him and told him of her Jewish ancestry. He told her, "Oh, Mrs. Enkel, that was such a long time ago, you don't know anything about that. Please allow your daughter this opportunity."

So I started the school and never had any problems. After the war, this principal found us and asked us to be a witness in his denazification trial, which he had to go through, since as a principal he had been required to be a member of the Party [the NSDAP].

My paternal great grandmother's name was Rosenbaum. I don't know anything about that part of the family, but judging from the name some Jewish ancestry was involved.

Most probably Doris' family escaped the concentration camps, because during this time no one in her family was getting married and therefore they had no need to prove their Aryan ancestry.

Mother's reflections on violence and the treatment of Jews in her interview with Dr. Doerr

This war was undoubtedly a German attack. Our adversaries were not prepared. Otherwise we could not have occupied Poland, Denmark, Norway, and France.

We had good relationships with the Jewish couple who lived below us in our apartment building. Old Mister R. came quite often to complain to us about their situation especially after he was ordered to wear the Star of David whenever he went out in public. Thank God, he and his wife managed to slip out of Germany in time to join their children in South Africa. But I believe that neither he nor I realized how inhumane the persecution of the Jews was.

After the war, we again established open relationships with our friends, but we hardly ever talked about the war. Nobody wanted to touch that sad chapter. I am deeply touched by the quiet revolution of

the East Zone of Germany. I did not think I would ever see the reunifica-
tion of Germany. That this involves difficulties seems self-evident to me.
For years I have supported the Pax Christi Movement. When, however,
a few years ago they published overly pacifistic articles, I canceled my
subscription. I wrote that for all my respect for their work I could no lon-
ger follow their attitude. For me the saying "Violence always begets
more violence" expresses only a half- truth. The other half is "Crazies
(Hitler) and criminals (Goebbels) can only be overcome by violence."
This attitude comes from experiences in my lifetime.

On my mother's eightieth birthday, the bishop of the Diocese of Rottenburg wanted to award her the highest honor of the diocese, the St. Steven's Medal, for her work during the Nazi time. She refused the honor, saying, "Whatever little I did, it was my duty as a Christian."

Letter to my mother from Walther Kasper, Bishop of Rottenburg-Stuttgart, August 29, 1990

Dear Mrs. Paulus,

I heard from M.S. of the Heliand community that you will celebrate your eightieth birthday on September 1, 1990. On this occasion I want to extend my best wishes and blessings.

On your birthday, you will no doubt look back on the past decades. You will recall many happy and many frightening hours. I hope that you will feel thankful for your full life. Important in your life was the life of the Heliand Community in Swabia. You were one of the founding members and became a talented and enthusiastic group leader. Together with your circle of friends and your late husband, Dr. Heinz Paulus, you took the trouble and made an effort to counteract the Nazi ideology. The Hilfsdienst of Heliand [outreach to the poor after the war, described be-low] *that you launched reached national importance and was recognized throughout the country. Through the program's services much material help was distributed, which you also coupled with spiritual advice and encouragement. Also, you and your family's hospitality will not be forgotten.*

Since you, dear Mrs. Paulus, do not want a public honor or acknowledgment, I want to express with this personal congratulatory note heartfelt thanks [Vergelt's Gott, a very Swabian local expression meaning God will repay you].

With all my heart, I wish you a good birthday feast within the circle of your relatives and friends. I am, with best wishes,
Yours, Walther Kasper, Bishop

B. Women Friends

At this point, a short digression to say a few words about women who were not our relatives.

Maria Hoffmann, mentioned above, was a very small, almost dwarflike person, who was also a bit disfigured. The Gestapo tortured her numerous times. She was secretary to the

Eichstätt Cathedral pastor Kraus, who gave public sermons against the Nazis and who distributed the "Goebbelsletter" mentioned above. Because the Gestapo was unable to find the author of the letter, they arrested and interrogated those they suspected of distributing it.

In the years before World War II the National Socialists launched a systematic campaign to denounce all priests as hypocrites and sexual perverts. The open letter to Goebbels was an answer to these accusations.

Maria Hoffmann was distributing the highly inflammatory letter. This is the letter that my mother had warned her to destroy before the Gestapo could find it in her possession.

Mother's diary

Maria has often told me that my lightning-speed action was of great service to Pastor Kraus and herself and may have saved them from worse repercussions. Maria Hoffmann has also, in other circumstances, shown great courage: the attacks on the churches, especially the Catholic Church, increased in intensity. They came primarily from the Secretariat of Propaganda. One day, pamphlets appeared in all church bulletins, accusing the Church and its agencies of vile things. We wouldn't have dared to rip them up. We were so cowed. But little Maria did just that at the church of St. Eberhard on the main street in Stuttgart, the Königsstrasse. Immediately a circle of spectators formed and accosted Maria. But she gave back as good as she received. She told me later that a few of the gawkers kept saying: "Is she sassy! Is she sassy!" Only with the greatest difficulty did she manage to get to the train station, that's how much her knees shook. Thank God no Gestapo agent was on the scene.

The underground work of pastor Kraus and Maria continued, but we no longer dared to exchange letters or phone calls. Later Maria was arrested—an arrest meant for pastor Kraus—and she underwent many torturous interrogations. She did not cave in, but she told me later that after each interrogation she trembled for hours in her cell. Once during an interrogation by two Gestapo agents the following happened: Maria's quick-witted answers made one of the interrogators lose his cool and he screamed: "Isn't it always the case, the smaller and more invisible these toads are, the wider they open their mouths," to which Maria answered: "What do you mean by that? Reichsminister Goebbels is also very short." The other interrogator laughed out loud and said, "You deserved that! You deserved that."

The regime [the Gestapo] wrote monthly reports about the arrests and interrogations of civilians; these documents (excerpted below) were published after the war in *The Situation of the Church in Bavaria after the Reichspräsidenten Report, 1933–34,* by Helmut Witetschek.

Excerpts from Gestapo monthly reports

In Eichstätt the parish assistant of the Cathedral pastor Kraus, Maria Hoffmann, whose hostile attitude to National Socialism is well known, is in detention for interrogation about the alleged distribution of the hate letter "Open Letter to Minister Dr. Goebbels."

...During the hearings, Kraus asked one of the prosecutors whether he could—despite his orders and directives—have some compassion and show some consideration, to which the official answered: "I am a servant of the state and therefore have to serve only the state. I have to carry out all orders without any conditions."…. To which Kraus replied: "If you see your job on this basis, then there is no difference between Stalin and Germany, since the totalitarian principle without exception reigns there also."

Mother's diary

Maria was mistreated during her imprisonment and became very ill. She was transferred to a hospital from which her friends kidnapped her and hid her in a mental institution till the end of the year. A relative of my husband who worked at the court in Nuremberg and who knew about Maria from us, allowed the papers of her interrogations to disappear—an act of silent resistance.

When researching the underground movement in 1988, Dr. Marlene Hiller made an appeal to the inhabitants of Stuttgart in the local paper. She wanted to solve a historical problem: "Who knows anything about pamphleteering in Stuttgart by local underground groups? Who received such pamphlets in their mail boxes? Who still has them today? Does anybody know whether the letters from "the White Rose" were distributed in Stuttgart? So far, we only know that one woman from Stuttgart was on the list of recipients of this organization. However, she did not accept the package with the pamphlets because somebody warned her in time."

Mother's answer to Dr. Marlene Hiller

Every time Maria came to Stuttgart from Eichstätt, she brought a suitcase full of green envelopes with the "Goebbels Letter" in it and put them randomly into mailboxes. This letter was an answer by Kraus to the mean-spirited attacks by Goebbels on the Catholic church….

How deeply my mother was involved with the White Rose leaflets or the Goebbels Letter can no longer be determined, but most probably the Gestapo visits to our parents' apartments were to look for the Goebbels Letter.

After the war, a friend took Maria in; she died in 1965.

Another courageous woman was Dr. Wendel, who was principal of the Hölderlin Gymnasium, a humanistic secondary school specializing in classical languages, which I attended from 1948 to 1957. During the Nazi regime she had openly criticized the persecution of the Jews and as a result she and the school were watched closely. One day she received an edict from the Education Department that Greek was no longer to be taught at the school. The reasoning was that German students did not need this old language. But most probably this edict was meant to hurt Dr. Wendel, whose specialty was Greek. Since she didn't want to abandon the teaching of Greek, she asked the students how many wanted to continue studying it in an informal seminar. Fifteen students registered. She then asked another teacher,

Mrs. Beyerle (who told me the story in 1998) to lead the seminar. As soon as the Department heard about it, they prohibited the seminar, because it circumvented the edict. Wendel then suggested that Beyerle teach the students at her home, in the same way that music students received instruction. That's how Greek was taught at the school until the end of the war.

Letter from Hedwig Pieper, my mother's cousin, about Dr. Wendel, 2009

After July 20, 1944, Munich came under heavy bombardment for seven days; Stuttgart for four days. After these attacks, the inner city of Stuttgart was devastated and living there was almost impossible. [Our house survived only because my father stayed in the attic and threw the bombs out on the street as they came in.] For this reason, the Hoelderlin Gymnasium was evacuated to Gingen on the Fils, with Wendel and another teacher. The dedication of our teachers was incredible. We lived with families who were forced to take us in. On Palm Sunday 1945 a meeting took place of all the principals in Stuttgart. The principals ordered all pupils to stay where they were. On Monday, during Latin class, Wendel told us, "Starting tomorrow, there won't be any more train tickets for the students." We all ran to the station, bought tickets, and took the next train to Stuttgart. Dear old Dr. Wendel had to stay behind in Gingen, since two of the pupils didn't return to Stuttgart. I remember her saying, "I am of the opinion that it is best that you are with your parents during what is going to come next." Courage! The people of Gingen were not exactly hospitable. "Those Kapitalweibsbilder shouldn't just sit around here; they should work." Wendel's answer to us: "You should be in school as much as possible." That's how we went to school every afternoon, even on Saturdays and Sundays. Mostly, Wendel was there to supervise us. We had to work very hard, because we had lost so much time during the air raids. After every attack, there had been about a two-week cleanup period.

C. My Father

Though my mother was more active in the resistance, my father, Dr. Heinz Paulus, also rejected the Nazis, because his socialization was in the Christian Zentrum Party milieu. He had planned to pass the "referendar" and "assessor" law examinations and then start a career in the state's judicial system, as the following excerpts from his letter to his future sister-in-law, Minni Fetz, showed.

Letter from my father to Minni Fetz, March 14, 1934

I have some good news. Last Saturday I passed my first law examination and am herewith finished with my university studies and will start my internship at different government law offices. I will be hired as a "referendar," which means I am a "Prussian official." After three years I will take my second examination and become an "assessor" and will then have completed my education as a lawyer.... I am the first one from my high school graduation class who finished his studies, which is quite an achievement considering my less than stellar high school graduation. I will start my career at the county court in Eschweiler or Stolberg [two cit-

ies close to Aachen].

Nothing much is known about the location or the nature of his activities until three years later, shortly before he was to take his second examination.

He did start his judicial internship, with plans to take the Bar examination to become assessor. However, since Hitler was already in power and every candidate for the Bar, by law, had to attend an intensive training/propaganda course, my father decided to interrupt his judicial career and pursue his doctorate instead. There is another version going around the family, however: because my father's attitude to the regime was well known, he had been given poor work evaluations and therefore wasn't invited to take the examination. This was the normal practice during this time: those who didn't fall in line were sidelined or their promotions were stalled. Since no letters survive from this time, the real reason why he interrupted his state judicial career will never be known.

In 1937 he was awarded the PhD in Law (Dr. jur.). He applied for a job with Allianz, the continent's biggest insurance company, and was hired. His plan was that as soon as Hitler was gone, which he firmly believed would happen soon, he would take the Bar and become a licensed attorney and possibly a judge. However, the war and his subsequent debilitating illness prevented him from achieving this goal. He stayed with Allianz till his retirement in 1975, first in the Auto Insurance Department and then in the Personnel Department. Twice, he did work as a "judge." The first time was when the Allies appointed him as a judge for the denazification program; later in the 1970s he worked for years as a labor mediator (*arbeitsrichter*). In Germany, most labor disputes are arbitrated first in front of a three-person panel, before the case goes to court. The panel includes a representative of the employee union, a representative of the employer's association (my father served in this capacity), and a district or federal judge. My father was always known as a great mediator. I can well remember when he would come back from day-long negotiations and say, "We found a good compromise. Everyone is happy." Though he could no longer partake actively in politics, he did follow political events closely and always spoke his mind freely until his death in 1980.

His own words shall speak to the events that led up to Hitler's takeover and the first years of Nazi power. This was a time of great economic hardship and political upheaval in Germany. The letters below were written to my mother while he was still a law student.

Letters from my father to my mother

March 17, 1933. Bonn, 8:30 p.m.
Yesterday I had a conversation with [...]; he is pursuing his PhD. His

---

Background notes from Walther Boehm:

* Dr. Neuhaeuser served in 1919–1920 in the German Reichs Army. After Germany's defeat in World War I, 1918, a socialistic revolution against the monarchy was started. The Kaiser abdicated and fled to Holland. The revolutionaries later split into two camps:
1. The Spartakists, later Communists (KPD, Kommunistische Partei Deutschlands), who wanted to set up a revolution based on the Russian model, a proletarian dictatorship.
2. The Social Democrats, who wanted to end the revolution as soon as possible and wanted to introduce a constitution for a parliamentary government based on majority rule and human rights. They didn't want to introduce socialism with force.

The more pacifist-oriented Social Democrats could not stand up to the militant Spartakists. The SD leaders (Ebert and Noske) therefore formed a union with the still existing, but unpopular army from the time of the Kaiser. There were warlike clashes between the two parties in Berlin and the industrial cities of the West (like Duisburg). During these riots, Dr. Neuhaeuser who fought for the Social Dem-

*thesis is about the fate of the emigrants from the Eifel region to the
United States. He is in constant correspondence with American emigrants and their children.*

Just now I had a conversion with Dr. Neuhaeuser; he served in
1919–1920 in the ReichsArmy. (We talked about this topic, because, as-
suming the MacDonald Plan† is adopted, I will have to serve soon.) He
helped put down the rebellion of the Spartakists in the Ruhr Region. At
that time he marched into the cities with the black-white-red flag [at that
time it really was only one flag]. In Duisburg-Meiderich there were violent street riots in which eighty people from his unit were killed. For me,
it is interesting to see how Neuhaeuser, exactly like myself, made a turn
from right to left [because he entered the army to be supportive of the
government], in contrast to millions, who slid from left to right. Here in
the dorm, everybody's hopes are on Dollfuss‡ (like me), that he can intervene and be successful. What distinguishes me from the others, however, is that I believe that the whole thing will end like the "Hornberger
Schiessen" (without any results), because I can't believe that the Chris-
tian-Socialists can successfully win the two-front war against Marxism
and the Nazis. Should I be wrong, I would be very pleased.*

Father's letters from after the Nazi takeover

March 18, 1933, 1:30 p.m.

Uncle Willi [Wilhelm Suth] *was "put on leave," with all other Zentrum
representatives in the Reichstag. In his place, a Nazi was appointed. I
am on my way to Cologne. Uncle Willi is prohibited from leaving Cologne; he has to be "in constant readiness to report to the Commission
mayor."*

March 19, 1933, 11:00 a.m.

I went to Uncle Willi yesterday, he is quite calm, Aunt Lilli also. He is

---

ocrats and probably for the bourgeoisie which he was a member of, defeated the left-wing radical rev-
olutionaries. Since he was fighting together with the Social Democrats, who were considered the
enemy of the nation during the Kaiser's times, the impression arose that he had moved to the left.
However, he fought under the black-white-red flag which was the Kaiser's flag. After the defeat of the
Spartikists, the Weimar Constitution and the black-red-gold flag of the Republic were introduced. The
Communists kept their red flag.

† The McDonald Plan addressed articles of the Versailles Treaty that allowed Germany an army of
only 100,000 men, without tanks, airplanes, or warships. In the same treaty, the victor nations agreed
to start disarming their military. Ten years later, in 1929, when the other nations had not begun to dis-
arm, Germany requested equality, meaning that they should also be allowed to increase their military.
McDonald introduced a plan within the framework of the newly formed League of Nations—the pre-
decessor of the United Nations—in Switzerland that would have allowed Germany to increase their
military forces considerably. This plan was not implemented because the French opposed it. Hitler
later broke off further negotiations with the League of Nations and left it. He then started to increase
the military in Germany tremendously—first clandestinely and then openly.

‡ Dollfuss was the Austrian chancellor and secretary of state who was caught in the fight between the
Communists and Nationalists. He also fought against the annexation of Austria by Germany. He was
shot by the Nazis in 1934.

prohibited from entering the Town Hall and from leaving Cologne.
Konrad Adenauer *is still in Berlin.* [In addition to his job as mayor of Cologne Konrad Adenauer was chair of the Prussian Staatsrat, which sent
him frequently to Berlin.]

*Uncle Willi will have to vacate his beautiful villa soon, since it belongs
to the city. But the worst is still to come: the government wants to deny
the representatives and Adenauer any kind of pension, so that Uncle
Willi will be without income after fourteen years of hard work.*

By the way, Aunt Lilli told me that her other brother [a Cathedral Kapit-
ular in Cologne] *told her that Cardinal Schulte lodged a complaint to
Papen in regard to Göring's speech…in which he talks of the "black
swine"* [meaning the Catholic Church] *who is aiding the enemies of the
state by watching out for them clandestinely. He also pointed out to
Papen that he is violating the integrity of the clergy.*

*Now to a point in your letter, our future: to be honest, my good con-
nections for entering the political scene are now permanently destroyed.
In addition, I believe that in the future, Catholics and especially Zentrum
followers have no chance to apply for a federal job. As far as that is concerned, I see black, but I can say: by the time that I am ready for work,
the situation will have changed again.*

*Your sister Maria's enthusiasm for the Nazis is fading more and more.
She no longer likes Göhring, whom she once liked the best. I have told
her about all the atrocities that he committed against religious groups.*

*Schulz is just handing me two pamphlets from Paderborn. Lacking in
all of them are any references to things that would be uncomfortable and
therefore unacceptable to the government.*

Uncle Willi lived quietly till 1945, first in Cologne and then later in different villages
along the Rhine river. He was prohibited from any political activity. When he wanted to
meet his brother-in-law, Adenauer, their meetings had to be clandestine. During this period,
he visited our parents a few times in Stuttgart. My parents kept a diary in which they recorded every visitor's first and last name, but Willi's last name was never written out. According to my mother, Adenauer visited them once and his son Konrad came twice during
this time, but there is no mention of either name in the diary. This indicates the extent of cau-
tion people used in their great fear that association with those who were persecuted by the
Gestapo could lead to prison sentences.

My father played a leading role in Neudeutschland, the Catholic men's group that was
officially dissolved by Goebbels. In 2003, I discovered an undated note in my mother's
handwriting, which she probably wanted to send to Dr. Doerr.

Mother's note

*When Josef Guelden was the president of Neudeutschland, Heinz
Paulus was "chancellor," which meant he was in charge of the accounts
and membership lists. The group was prohibited from meeting; therefore
we met in small groups in individual family homes. The chancellery was
dissolved and all addresses were collected and hidden. One of these
hiding places was in our apartment in the bottom of our big grandfather's*

clock in the hallway.

Because I was a friend of Maria Hoffman, Pastor Kraus's secretary, who wrote the Goebbels Letter, the Gestapo pursued us. (Twice Heinz and I—separately—were asked to appear in their headquarters.) They searched our apartments from top to bottom—once the apartment of my parents and once our new apartment on Johannesstrasse. This was during the week of our civil and church wedding. How easily they could have discovered the list of the Neudeutschland members! It was very frightening to watch how the Gestapo rummaged through all of our things. Thank God they never opened the grandfather clock! If you haven't lived in a dictatorship, you cannot imagine what that meant.

If the Gestapo had found the address list of the prohibited Neudeutschland group, it could have meant imprisonment for my parents and certainly interrogations for the people on the list.

Though Germans were in danger of running afoul of the Gestapo for some action they took, the discrimination against and harassment of all Jews, which started shortly after the Nazi takeover, was much worse, regardless of their ages, attitudes, or activities. A letter my father received from one of his closest high school classmates, who was Jewish, shows how difficult the situation for Jews had become just a few years after the Nazis came to power.

Letter to my father from his classmate Willy Kaufmann, Grand Hotel Fasano, Gardone, April 4, 1937

Many thanks also in the name of my wife for your dear letter on the occasion of our wedding, which I received here together with the announcement of your engagement. I wish for you and your bride that your dream will soon be fulfilled and that you will be married sooner than you think possible at the moment. Many things have changed in my life, dear friend. I have collected quite a few university degrees, but can do nothing with them in Europe. That's why I made the decision to go to the USA, and will embark on April 24 in Le Havre with my wife. I am hoping that in the USA they are still looking for people who are willing to work. In most of the European countries work is only possible if one doesn't express any opinion or if one wants to be a slave. This is not my way or style. The parting from my parents will not be easy, but nowadays distances are small and I am sure to return to Europe sometime. I would have liked to see you and your bride again before our departure. You are the only one who has not forgotten the old friendship. You don't have it easy either, especially since your peaceful weapons seem to be powerless.

I hope you will write to me occasionally and give me your news. I will send you my new address after I have arrived. But you can always write to my parents, they will forward all mail to me from Brussels.

We made our honeymoon trip by car to Italy, but unfortunately the weather is as bad as it was north of the Alps.

Please give my regards to your mother. And thank your bride for her

nice message and also greetings to you. I wish you everything good and beautiful.
In old comradeship, Your Willy

Willy Kaufmann arrived safely in the United States, but I doubt that my father was able to continue their correspondence after the war started, since correspondence between Germany and the Allies was prohibited. I also don't know whether his parents ever managed to emigrate or were sent to a concentration camp.

Just looking at my father's high school senior yearbook from 1930, it is obvious that there was a natural and easy joking relationship between my father and Kaufmann, his best friend.

Yearbook excerpts

Paulus and Kaufmann often fight.
Paulus: "Man, if you don't shut up soon, I'll rearrange your nose."
Kaufmann: "Too late, little man" [Maenneken, a typical Rhineland expression].

Classroom anecdotes

Kaufmann: "Shall I start from the beginning?"
Teacher Moers: "It would be very interesting to hear you start to recite the passages from the back."
Teacher Strauch: "You have used too few words in your essay, which actually is only a miniature edition."
Paulus: "Yes,… I am sorry that I didn't have time to look up the material."
Teacher to either Kaufmann or Paulus about an essay: "Too much gravy for the small amount of meat."

It seems that Willy Kaufmann and my father were comrades in mischief, but they were also the class leaders, as the following invitation shows:

The graduating class of 1930
Of the Realgymnasium in Aachen
Is honored
To invite you to the graduation celebration
which will take place on
March 22, 1930, at 8:30 p.m.
in the
Hotel Great Monarch in Aachen
Formal Attire
As representatives of the graduates
W. Kaufmann H. Paulus

Silent Resistance

Other family members were against the Nazi regime, from the beginning, but without taking overt action. These included my grandmother MarieTherese Paulus (Thesa). She had lost her husband in World War I in 1915 and raised her three children alone. She was very close to her brother, Willi Suth, who was very anti-Nazi, and she supported him all through the Third Reich. When the war broke out she lived in Aachen. When her youngest son married, he and his wife moved in with her. She and her daughter-in-law listened to BBC radio broadcasts, but they switched stations immediately when her son came home. Thesa opposed the war, because the first war had brought so much misery to her life, and she was worried that she would lose her boys—to what purpose?

My maternal grandparents, Achaz and Barbara Brühl, came from simple and relatively poor families. They did not receive any kind of political education and stayed out of the political limelight. However, a few examples will illustrate that they were not Nazi supporters.

Letter from Thea, my mother's youngest sister

I still remember very well, that as an eleven-year-old, I was in the dining room of our apartment in Neckarstrasse 73, where Dad had his famous customary nap after lunch. The radio announced: "President von Hindenburg has just appointed the leader of the National Social German Worker's Party as the chancellor of the Reich [Reichskanzler]." My father sat up and said, "Oh my, now everything is going down the drain." He stood by his opinion through the whole Third Reich, which was possible for him as a small business person. So many others felt the same way, but couldn't speak their mind. After the collapse of the regime, he told me, "I am very proud that in twelve years I never said: 'Heil Hitler' or raised my right hand in the Nazi salute."

My maternal grandmother, who had four sons and three sons-in-law in the war, was often asked why she was so nice to the French, Polish, and Russian prisoners of war. Her standard answer was, "They are sons of mothers just like me and I would want someone to be decent to my own boys." This is how I remember my Oma: good-natured and always caring about others.

Both my grandparents supported their daughter, my mother, during the Gestapo raids in their home. They never criticized her activities or told her that she was putting the whole family at risk.

Another family member, Resi Paulus, my Uncle Kurt's wife, was in a precarious position. Her father, who served in the German Parliament for the Social Democrats before Hitler dissolved the Parliament and dismissed all its representatives, remained a staunch anti-Nazi throughout the whole period. He survived the regime only by moving from place to place and staying one step ahead of the Gestapo. Resi shared her father and mother-in-law's philosophy though as a young wife and mother she was not politically active. Her husband, Uncle Kurt, was a Nazi sympathizer. After the war, she wrote a diary about this time in which she describes in detail how difficult it was to provide for the growing family in those hard economic times. She also talks about the pressures that the Nazis put on people to join the party or one of its subsidiaries. Resi will be cited throughout this story.

Aunt Resi Paulus's diary

Thanks to the date of my birth, I could avoid joining any Nazi Youth organization. It was different for my younger sister. She first had to join the

Young Girls and then the League of German Girls [Bund Deutscher
Mädel]. *She was an enthusiastic member, which I understand due to her
young age, but it was a bitter pill for my parents. At the beginning of
1945 I was put under great pressure. More than once a woman from the
National Socialist Women's League* [Nationalsozialistische Frauen-
schaft, NS] *would come to the door and tried to convince me to join.
When I continued to refuse, she would warn me that my attitude would
have bad consequences for my husband and family. I invented the most
creative excuses why I couldn't join, and it worked, because after we
were in Gunzendorf, nobody bothered me anymore.*

Involuntary Membership in Nazi Groups

While some of my family members and friends were more openly trying to resist, others
were philosophically opposed to the Nazis but who saw no way to escape some involvement
with the Party. They had to join the NSDAP or one of its subsidiaries because of their professions as state employees, teachers, or lawyers. If they didn't join they would imperil their
own and their families' lives or economic survival. Such was the far-reaching control of the
government. The father of one of our au pairs, one of our neighbors, and an uncle represent
this group.

During the Nazi regime all young people had to do civil service. The girls were often
put in families to help with small children, since Hitler was interested in large families.
Three or four of these young girls cared for us between 1940 and 1945. The last one was
during the time when we were evacuated to a rural village.

Mother's diary

*With the family of this girl, Friedl, I still have a strong relationship, and
my youngest son considers her father Joseph Weiland, whom he nick-
named "Olo," a surrogate father. But I have to laugh at our first meeting.
The au pair came with her father who wore the Party emblem on his
jacket, which really frightened me. But it became quite clear during our
first talk that he wore the emblem involuntarily. He had to wear it because he was the principal of the local elementary school. State employees had no choice but to be in the Party. Nowadays you cannot imagine
how every person you met had to be carefully scrutinized before you
could be sure what his political outlook was. I was very happy when I realized he was not a Nazi.*

The second example were neighbors in our apartment building. The couple were philosophically opposed to the Nazis, but because the husband had a managerial job at the
Stuttgart Opera House, which belonged to the Stuttgart municipality, he had to join a Nazi
organization. After the war, however, he was found innocent of collaborating.

One of the best examples of how innocent people became caught in the Nazi web
against their will, was Dr. Paul Ludwig, my parents' brother-in-law. Though he passed the
Bar in 1934 at the top of his class, he could not find a job either at a lawyer's office or an industrial firm, since at that time the Nazis had already infiltrated the legal profession. (More
on this later.) He eventually secured a job in the state judicial system, and during the war
worked for the military field headquarters. Because he was considered an employee of the

state (*Beamter*) he automatically had to go through the denazification process after Hitler's defeat. He was a devoted anti-Nazi in his ideology and his behavior as will be seen in his letters from the front and his acquittal in the later trial. His letters written during the war describe the enormous difficulties he faced in holding on to his basic human values and not compromising during the time when he was put under daily pressure and bombarded with propaganda.

His wife, Gertrud, experienced daily small-time Nazi harassment and intimidation in her workplace. When she worked for the Teacher's League as a secretary, she was in charge of organizing the reports of sick teachers. An elderly secretary who was a strong Nazi supporter constantly faulted her for misfiling the reports. Convinced that she did the filing correctly, she asked another colleague to check her work. Right afterwards she was accused again of making mistakes. Though she could prove her innocence, the other colleague was not reprimanded, because by the mid-1930s it was clear in most workplaces who was pro- or anti-Nazi. The only option she had was to find another job. Any appeal to a human resources department would have been useless, especially since all teachers had been forced to join the Party.

Vacillators

A. *Early skeptics who later supported the regime*

A distant relative represents those who did not like the Nazis when they first came to power, but then changed their minds and supported them till the end of the war. My great uncle Richard Fischer, my maternal grandparents' brother-in-law, falls into that category. According to my parents, he opposed the Nazi regime at first, because he was very Catholic and objected to the way the Nazis began attacking the Church shortly after their takeover.

As a nationalist, however, he found the Versailles Treaty and its treatment of Germany humiliating. He hated the English and the French, because he held them responsible for the harsh conditions existing in Germany between the two world wars. Accordingly, he supported the war against these two nations, and with Germany's early victories, especially the occupation of Paris, he became caught up in the euphoria that swept the country. When Paris was occupied by German troops, he sent his nephew to the nearest town, Geislingen, to buy a Nazi flag. In 1943, he himself joined a Nazi group. From our perspective it is difficult to believe that he continued to swallow the whole Nazi propaganda line after 1943, with its outrageous claims of victories and enemy casualties.

His attitude mirrored the opinions of many Germans: domestically they were not really strong Nazi supporters, but internationally they were all for the German Reich and the Final Victory. What is most difficult to understand, however, is his stance after the collapse of the Nazi regime. On the one hand, some entries in his chronicle suggest that he—of course—had always been against the Nazis. On the other hand, it took him a long time to see the true horror inflicted by the Nazis. He talks about the "so-called war criminals" and the "so-called victor countries." He became very agitated about the treatment of Germans by the Allies, but he saw no connection between this and earlier Nazi atrocities. He asks the Allies for "Christian" treatment of Germans, but nothing is written about any "Christian" treatment for the Jews or the Allies. He also had no insight into the condition of the Russian troops, who were often poor themselves and as a consequence robbed German prisoners of war and civilians in the territories they occupied. His hatred of the British and French also carried over into postwar times.

In the chronicle he wrote from 1911 to 1953, from which I quote extensively below, he recorded family activities, political and economic events, and weather-related data as these all affected the agricultural situation in the village of Schnittlingen, my grandfather's birthplace and the homestead of the family farm. (The chronicle contained no entries between 1930 and 1937; this omission was never explained.)

The following are my great uncle's own words. I have tried to translate them as closely as possible to the original, even if his style is often old-fashioned. But I believe his choice of words and even his omissions reflect his attitude. For example, he leaves out any mention of German military defeats, as for example at Stalingrad, and says nothing about the treatment of the Jews.

Uncle Richard Fischer's diary

March 11–12, 1938
  The unification of Austria with Germany was completed as the German troops marched in.

B. Early supporters who later rejected the regime

In another group of family members were those who initially supported the takeover by the Nazis because they felt that order was being reestablished and Germany was recovering some of its pride and dignity. But they soon became disillusioned with the regime's policies. Good representatives of this attitude were my mother's oldest sister, Maria Tietze, the above-mentioned Maria Hoffmann, and a member of Heliand, who I will designate by her initials (M.E.).

The following excerpts from Dr. Doerr's interview with M.E. and my mother (Isa) show the development of M.E.'s thinking over time. I believe she reflects the thinking of many at that time.

Dr. Doerr's interview with M.E. and my mother (Isa)

Doerr: *I am interested in everything that shows the mood, the whole atmosphere of the time and your personal experiences.*
M.E.: *Right after school in 1931 I started to work for the Social Security Office as a typist. Our office dealt with complaints from people who had been denied welfare, Social Security, or medical benefits. Individuals visited our office; so too did lobbyists from unions and political parties. Representatives from the Left and the Right came through our office. I heard a lot of political arguments, but I also learned a lot about the extreme poverty in Germany at that time. I was always very interested in all the political speeches: there were orators or propagandists on every corner, socialists, communists, and representatives from the slowly developing National Socialists movement.*
  And then [Heinrich] Brüning's emergency laws came into effect. The unemployed thus received hardly any help from the government; there was dire poverty. One had to work a whole year to be able to buy a winter coat. And heating materials were in short supply and expensive. Into this misery, the Nazis came with their promise of better times and they appealed to the German spirit and German ethos. We discussed this often in the office. People were yearning for the bygone days of the emperor because they felt that economically they were better off then.

Doerr: *"Was there talk about the Jews at that time?"*

M.E.: *Not at all. But personally I had a bad impression of my Jewish classmates. I was in a school where the students were one-third Protestant, one-third Jewish, and one-third Catholic. The Jews never integrated into the class; they stayed by themselves in small groups. They had their religious education in the synagogue. Whenever the grades were handed out, the Jewish students would go up to the teacher and negotiate for better grades. We would never have dared do that. That really disgusted me. There were two Jewish girls sitting in front of me and two behind me, but I was never close to them…. In many ways, the Jews tried to separate themselves from the rest of society.*

We discussed this in the office, and by around 1932, the label "Jew" was being used.

Doerr: *There already was anti-Semitism? And were the Jews really in leading positions?*

M.E.: *They were in Stuttgart. And, yes, there was anti-Semitism there. I started off being very anti-Jewish. If I had not joined the Heliand, I don't know whether I would have changed my mind. I was often conflicted before Hitler came to power. The high costs of the war reparations after World War I and the loss of the Rhineland and the Saarland—these burdened our parents. And then when [Neville] Chamberlain and the French did not stand up to Hitler, one started to wonder whether he had the answers. I still supported him when the Rhineland and the Saarland came back to Germany, but when he occupied Austria I started to question his policies. And all of sudden, the economy improved. I was susceptible to his rhetoric.*

Isa: *Because you saw so much misery in your office?*

M.E.: *I had an aunt who was Protestant and very religious. She prayed for Hitler every night, just as she prayed for her family.*

Isa: *Even in the Heliand there was a group who thought that they could influence the Nazi philosophy by joining the Female Auxiliary group of the Nazis. But it didn't last long before they came back to the Heliand.*

M.E.: *I can still visualize when there were flyers against the Catholic Church put up outside the Eberhards Church, Maria Hoffmann tore them down—in the brown uniform of the Women's Auxiliary. I know that for sure.*

Isa: *As soon as she started doing that, she was surrounded by a group of young girls who were awed that she had the courage to take this action, but also by people who were upset about what she did.*

M.E.: *Many of the Heliand girls couldn't find a job and I secured them employment. My boss told me: "I know where you stand; if they weren't such good workers." We already started to be careful around other employees. I had an assistant who was a very strong Nazi supporter; I had to watch every word. And then they assigned me a mother with a young child and I was trying to feel her out. There was an assembly that day that every employee had to attend because either Hitler or Goering or*

*one of the other leaders was speaking. When we returned to our desks,
I asked her, "How did you like it?" She replied, "You know, I was so tired
I slept through most of it." That showed me where she stood, and we
started our friendship....*

Isa: *"But you could never talk openly with people before you had ascertained where they stood.*

Doerr: *You were also involved in the underground?*

M.E.: *Well, I supported Maria Hoffmann financially, because I learned
that she didn't have much money, and I wanted to support the distribution of the Goebbels letter. So, they found out my address and my place
of work. I am grateful to my boss who knew where I stood, but didn't
take any action. He called me into his office one day and told me that
the Gestapo had warned him and that the telephones were being monitored. He was a Nazi, an old soldier, but he protected me.... I totally
switched to anti-Nazi sentiments during the Kristallnacht [Crystal Night].
I was in a meeting with my boss and two SS men came in and told us
about the night. When I came home in the evening, my mother and sister told me that they had been in the city shopping when they heard
about it, and actually saw how in a few Jewish shops in the Marien-
strasse windows were smashed. I can still visualize the two SS people
today.*

C. Unknown attitudes toward the regime

I never learned much about many family members and their attitudes and actions during the
Nazi regime. Immediately after the war, I was too young to comprehend the enormity of
what my family had gone through. Later when I dared to ask the older generation, I was met
by silence. As I reflected on what I could remember, I began to ask myself whether this silence was because of my youth? Did they think my brothers and I could never understand?
Was it denial or embarrassment on their part? Or was it simply a need to get beyond painful
memories and move on. When I approached my mother, she had a standard reply: "Honey,
let's not talk about that dreadful time." And so my generation knows only fragments of the
story.

Since my paternal grandfather died in 1915, we didn't have much communication with
this part of the family, and after my father moved to South Germany communications were
limited with my paternal grandmother's family. Therefore I know nothing about the attitudes of the siblings, nephews, and nieces of my grandfathers and grandmothers towards the
Nazis, with the exception of Uncle Willi Suth and my grandmother's other brother, Uncle
Franz Suth. According to his granddaughter, Renate Hendricks, who is now a representative
for the Social Democrats in the state government of North Rhine-Westphalia, "If you were
Uncle Willi's brother, you couldn't be a Nazi."

My father's sister and brother-in-law Marie Therese and Franz Heinrich probably belonged to the group that took no stand either way and just wanted to be left alone. As far as I
know, they were not members of any segment of the Nazi Party. Franz, while not openly
pro-Nazi, chose to go along with the military style that the Nazis pursued. It was very important to him to become an officer and to wear a uniform though he never served in the war,
but worked in the munitions industry. His diary includes his thoughts on Germany's adversaries.

My mother's siblings are a bit more difficult to classify. The sisters who were in the Heliand, Minni Fetz and Thea Brühl, were adamantly anti-Nazi, as was their sister Gertrud Ludwig, who was married to Paul Ludwig. Maria Tietze was enamored by the Nazis at first, but in time the Nazis lost their attraction for her. I do not know what position the last sister, Wilma Baumgartner, took toward the Nazis.

The brothers were all relatively young when the Nazis took over. The oldest, Karl, was sixteen, and the youngest, Robert, was only nine. Karl was drafted into the army in 1937 and was supposed to have been discharged in 1940. After the beginning of the war, all the brothers supported the war effort and became increasingly hostile toward Germany's adversaries.

The following excerpts of letters from my uncle Karl, who was my godfather, describe some of his dreams and plans for his time after his service was finished.

Letters from my mother's brother Karl

August 27, 1938, Westerheim, to Heinz and Isa

Congratulations on the birth of your girl. Please send me a photo of my godchild soon. When is the Baptism? Who will stand in for me? I couldn't write to you before because we had a regional general roll call [Generalappell vom Gau], and tomorrow we drive to Freiburg in preparation for Nürnberg, and that's why this whole week was very busy.

August 25, 1939, Ludwigsburg, to Minni

Totally unexpectedly I was commanded to report to the head of the company [Divisionsstab] in Ludwigsburg. I like it here. The building is an old nursing home, completely refurbished. Two men to a room, linoleum floor, running water in the room, in short, wonderful. Work starts at 7:30 a.m. and goes till 4:00 p.m. On Wednesdays and Sundays we stop work at 1:00 p.m. Therefore I have a lot of free time. So, I have decided to study Spanish. In a year's time when my service is ended, I want to spend half a year in Spain, and I am hoping for a good job in Germany then as a foreign correspondent.

Do you have any other advice on what I should learn so that I can make a good salary later? As soon as my military service is over, I have to earn enough money so that Father no longer has to work and can retire at long last. I want to achieve that goal by learning Spanish. I would love to visit you but I can't get a furlough soon. A few months ago the whole company was supposed to go on a field trip to Lake Constance, but it was canceled because we couldn't get buses.

When the war started five days later, Karl was immediately sent to the Western front, and shortly afterwards to the Eastern front.

While Karl's parents and many siblings did not support the Nazis, he moved to the right by supporting the military policy of the government, which constantly stirred up hatred against the war's opponents. The same can be said about his brothers Rudolf and Robert, as seen in their letters. Even their brother Hermann's letters, which showed some respect for the Russians, and those of my father, show what effect the nationalistic propaganda was having on the soldiers. Constantly surrounded by propaganda that denounced the actions and talks of the "others," makes it difficult to be critical of a policy that one knows intellectually is devilish. After a few years in the service, the difference between the interests of

Germany as a country and the politics of the Nazis became blurred for many soldiers.

From mother's interview with Dr. Doerr

To the next point: the manipulation of the soldiers. Please, no names! But the fact in itself is very interesting and should be discussed. In the examples that I personally experienced, the soldiers were not Hitler fans and certainly not beholden to him. But they often expressed the opinion: "We have to win." They could not stand the idea that they would endanger their lives daily for a useless, evil, and Satanic cause. Goebbels's propaganda exploited this situation. Shortly after these soldiers returned home they expressed completely different opinions and rejected Hitler and the war completely.

This fact becomes very clear in my father's letters, when the Germans occupied Denmark, and in my uncles' letters, which will be extensively quoted below.

D. Nazi Sympathizer

The strongest support of the regime in my family was my Uncle Kurt Paulus, my father's only brother. He was a Nazi follower who absorbed the Nazi philosophy from the beginning. He belonged to the SA, which was a Nazi paramilitary organization directly responsible to the party and not the army, which lost political clout after 1934. He was a year old when his father was killed in World War I. His mother never remarried. He was nineteen when Hitler came to power, an age vulnerable to propaganda. The Nazis understood very well how to entrap young people partially with promises for a better life and partially with threats. Though his mother, his brother, the uncle who he was closest to, and his wife all rejected the Nazi ideology, he fell into the same category as his wife's sister: he joined the movement with youthful enthusiasm. There are no letters or diaries that describe his attitude toward the Nazis, only the stories from other family members, the diary of his wife, and a decision by the Commission for Denazification. Since he was only a marginal figure, his punishment was relatively light: he had to pay a small fine and do a few weeks community service. (See below.)

Siblings MarieTheres, Kurt, and Heinz Paulus, 1914/15
shortly before their father's death in World War I

Wedding of Heinz's parents,
Eduard and Marie Therese
(Thesa Suth) Paulus, 1904

Heinz, MarieTheres, and Kurt, 1949

Wedding of Achaz and
Barbara Brühl, 1907.

Achaz Brühl's retail cheese store
in the 1920s in Stuttgart.
Family members in windows,
employees in front of the store.

Barbara Brühl with five of her grandchildren on the occasion
of Achaz's seventieth birthday in Stuttgart, 1943, few months
before the family was bombed out.

Achaz and Barbara in Schnittlingen 1950 after they had lost
five children, their business,
their apartment, and all their
belongings.

Suth/Paulus family, 1912. Middle row: Marie Theresia (Schmitz) and Franz Suth,
with their five surviving children. On the left are Eduard (son-in-law)
and daughter Marie Therese (Thesa Suth) Paulus with Heinz
and MarieTheres (Kurt had not been born yet). Willi Suth is second
from the right in row 2.

Brühl family, 1925. The ten children of Achaz and Barbara Brühl
who survived to adulthood. Second row: Maria, Minni, Trudl, Karl, Isa,
Wilma. Front row: Rudolf, Achaz, Thea, Hermann, Robert, Barbara.

Daily Life before the War: An Attempt at Normalization

Against this background of Nazi control, most people tried to live a normal life. This is shown in two reports by my parents about their wedding and in the diary my mother started for me right after my birth. The trip to Eichstätt, the visits of the Gestapo at home, and the Gestapo interrogations of my parents are never mentioned in this diary. It was simply too dangerous to put anything critical of the government on paper, because this could become a potential source for persecution. The general feeling was that the fewer people who know about your activities against the government, the better.

Though my parents' wedding symbolized to them their union as witnessed by the Catholic Church, they could not avoid having to prove their Aryan ancestry and their legitimacy of birth before they could marry civilly according to a German law introduced by Bismarck in the nineteenth century. The pamphlet that I reproduced in chapter 1, taken from my parents' genealogical book, dealt with the laws regarding race. This was the background to my parents' marriage in 1937.

My father furnished copies of his parents' and grandparents' marriage certificates to the Registry Office. These documents were marked "valid only for proof of Aryan descent."

Marriage Certificate

Nikolaus Hubert Eduard Paulus, born May 14, 1877, in Aachen;
Catholic, businessman, son of the married couple Johann Heinrich
Hubert Paulus, business owner, and Maria Katherine Hubertine Jansen.
Marie Theresia Katherina Suth, born April 4, 1879, in Cologne;
Catholic, daughter of the married couple
Franz Suth, businessman, and Theresia Schmitz.
Day of marriage: twenty-second of January 1904
Aachen, May 14, 1934
The Registrar

The original of my mother's proof of Aryan ancestry did not survive, but my father's application for a marriage license was sent back to him (signed and notarized) by the Registry Office with the following remark:

It has been decided that your application of August 19, 1937, has
been granted, since after examining the necessary documents in re-
gards to the proof of the Aryan ancestry of your future wife, Miss Isa

Brühl, no objections against a marriage are raised. The parish docu-
ments presented and the genealogical book are sent back to you. You
are requested to show me the document of the civil marriage after your
church wedding.

Researchers have wondered how it happened that the Registry Office had access to parish documents since church authorities had refused to help the Nazis by providing baptismal
documents.

Both my father and mother wrote descriptions of their wedding that stressed their com-
mitment to each other as a Catholic sacrament. I am excerpting from both reports, since they
are repetitive.

Father's account

On our wedding day, October 9, 1937, members of the Heliand and
Neudeutschland groups woke us with a morning serenade of songs and
instrumental music. The wedding was at 9:00 a.m. in St. Nikolaus. First
was the speech by our priest, Josef Guelden, from Leipzig, a member of
Neudeutschland and a good friend of ours, then the wedding ceremony,
followed by the nuptial mass. The church celebration was planned by
our friends who selected the music, the songs, and the prayers. On both
sides of the altar were the flags of the Heliand [the flags of Neudeutschland could no longer be displayed, since Goebbels had officially disbanded the group]. *The priest consecrated a special host for us. The*
nuptial blessing and the wedding ceremony were all in German [at that
time the Mass was still said in Latin]. *During the offertory, we gave the*
priest our wedding rings to be offered, and we received them back dur-
ing the Pater Noster.

Following the wedding we had breakfast and lunch for both families.
In the afternoon we invited everyone who could be in Stuttgart for only
one day to our new apartment. This was preceded by the blessing of the
rooms. Josef blessed the cross, then I read the Gospel [the sending out
of the seventy-two disciples] *and Isa read the blessing for the home* [this
prayer is still in a frame in Stuttgart]. *Then each room was blessed, es-*
pecially the nuptial beds, and at the end of the ceremony we all stood
around the dining room table and recited the prayer of thanksgiving be-
fore we ate.

In the evening we had dinner in the small hall of the Hindenburgbau
and at 8:30 p.m. over eighty of our friends joined us there for skits,
toasting and roasting, poems and songs, and dance. The whole evening
was a combination of seriousness and laughter. It was so wonderful that
we didn't leave our circle of friends till 12:30 a.m. The others seemed to
be enjoying themselves as well since the feast wasn't over till 3:00 a.m.
—an accomplishment since most of them had been up to serenade us
at 6:00 that morning. To talk about the presents that we received would
take too long, but from our friends we received a gorgeous sculpture by
Kristaller: Mother and Child. [This sculpture, which is still in Stuttgart,

was later used by my mother to hide money and jewelry in its open back.] *Special thanks have to go to our friends from Heliand and Neudeutschland who planned such a fantastic evening.*

Mother's account

Two Heliand sisters helped me with my dress and veil. They had given me the handmade garland of live myrtle and Heinz's bouquet the evening before at the wedding-eve party [the "Polterabend"; in Germany this party includes both men and women and was often just as raucous as the bachelor party is here]. *It was good that we were done with the preparations in a short time so that I had half an hour of quiet reflection before the wedding. My mother came to my room, cried a bit, and blessed me. When Heinz picked me up, he gave me a beautiful gold ring with a blue stone.*

The altar was decorated by my friends. Breakfast and lunch was at my parents' house.... Our friends celebrated till 4:00 a.m. [It seems that the women had the greater stamina!]

On our honeymoon we went first to Munich, where we had met six years before. Then we took the train to Kochel, Walchensee, Herzogstand, and Mittenwald. The weather was so great that we hiked almost all the time.

My parents received a few congratulatory telegrams, with pictures of roses, a circle of dancing children, a river or a mountain landscape, or a sailing ship on the high seas. None of their friends picked a Nazi or military scene on the front (which was very common at that time), but two of the messages had the Federal Eagle (*Bundesadler*) and the swastika on the back.

Only one telegram had a Nazi message: "To the young couple, a threefold Sieg Heil!"

The presents they received showed that at this time one could still buy anything. The gifts were, of course, mainly household items, but they also included art reproductions and books, and lots of flowers and plants.

And then life went on. They moved into their new flat on the fourth floor of an apartment building in the west of Stuttgart. Shortly after the wedding they celebrated St. Nicholas' Day with friends in their new apartment. This was four years after the Nazis had assumed power and people's opinions had solidified by then. Since the apartment's community of people was, like my family, a microcosm of the society, I insert here a description of those living in the house.

Typical Apartment Building and Attitudes toward National Socialism

In retrospect it is difficult to know what one remembers directly as a young child and what comes from the stories adults recounted around you. I was only five years old in 1943 when we were evacuated and left Stuttgart for two years, but I do have memories of most of those who lived in the apartment building at this time. There was a mixture of generations, professions, and attitudes toward the regime. I'll attempt to describe the building, our apartment, and the building's inhabitants to the best of my recollection.

The building was a very sturdy, gray, six-story stone structure with ten apartments. It was attached to a big bank, a regional credit union. It had no elevators. On five floors were apartments and storage rooms; the sixth floor, the attic, contained more storage rooms. The first level, below ground, had the laundry room and the coal cellars—till we moved in 1956, the coal distributor would come and shovel the coal directly from the sidewalk into the cellars—and below them were the potato cellars. Since our potato cellar was the biggest, it became the bomb shelter. Every family had two storage rooms on the sixth floor and two cellars. The staircase, which was made of faux marble, had a mirror on each landing. You entered the house through a rather long, wide, and dark corridor. Mailboxes were in the entrance hall on the ground floor, so at times when I was expecting mail, I would descend four flights of stairs more than once a day to check on the mail delivery. The mailman would ring all the doorbells, hoping that someone would buzz him in. Since there was no intercom system, my parents would lean out of the dining room window and shout down four floors, "Who's there?" Entrance into the apartments was through a sturdy wooden door whose top half was made of opaque glass that had within it a smaller eye-level window that could be opened to see who was outside.

The building's inhabitants had forged a strong bond, but relations were strained during the Nazi years due to the different attitudes toward the Nazis and the Jews. On the fifth floor, and just above us, lived an elderly couple, Mr. and Mrs. S. On their back balcony, they raised rabbits, which to the great horror of us children, they ate. Mr. S. was a police commissioner; Mrs. S., like all wives in the building, was a housewife. After we returned from our evacuation in Bad Ditzenbach and we children had our own apartment keys, Mr. S. was very helpful whenever we forgot our keys; as a police officer he had the tools to open our apartment. We children thought this quite wonderful. Since the couple had no children of their own, they "adopted" my mother's brothers during the war by sending them relief packages. Opposite them lived the N. family, the family of Uli, my brother's best friend.

These top apartments were small, because the front of the house on that floor was also a storage room for each apartment. These storage areas later became dwellings for refugees from the East who were fleeing the advancing Russian troops. Everyone in these rooms had to share a toilet. I don't know whether the only place to wash up was in the toilet or whether there were sinks elsewhere. I recall one family in these storage rooms: a single mother with a teenage son, probably her husband's son, and a small daughter, probably the daughter of a man whom she had met on her flight from the East. Since the rooms were very small, this family had room for only two beds and one chair.

Our apartment was large by the standards of the time and was the only apartment in the house with its own bathroom. Other apartment dwellers had to wash either in the kitchen or in the separate toilet room. Our rather large inner hallway was central to all the other rooms. The kitchen had a large walk-in pantry and a balcony. The dining room, living room, and two bedrooms were connected through doors that were hardly ever used. You entered each room through the hallway, and always closed the doors as you entered or left. The living room appeared very large to us and had a little alcove with bookshelves. The story is that when I was about one-and-a-half to two years old, I would empty all the books and pretend to read them. They say I never put them back. The windowsills were deep, and we would sit there and watch our father get off the street car and walk home in the evening. Our daily ritual was to watch him descend from the street car and wave; since he always took the same car, he knew we would be watching, and he waved back to us. They tell me that once I was sitting on the sill at the open window, four stories up, and when my mother came into the room her heart nearly stopped. She had the presence of mind not to scream, but enticed me back quietly with the promise of treats.

The apartment of course had no central heating. Only the living room and the dining room, which had wood-burning stoves, were heated. Basically in the winter we lived in the dining room. This was not without danger, since the coal-first stove sometimes overheated or the pipe that entered the wall would come loose, filling the whole room with smoke. On special occasions, and later when the economy allowed it and coal was not rationed, we heated the living room with the big *Kachelofen* (tile oven). Through a little grate in the wall the heater also warmed the boys' bedroom. The scarcity of wood and coal during and immediately after the war did not allow the daily use of this big stove in the living room.

In the dining room, on top of the stove, was a big bowl in which water was heated and used to wash dishes. Whenever my mother carried this very heavy bowl from the dining room through the hallway into the kitchen, she would always warn us to get out of the way. Since the one stove that had been fueled with coal in the evening would go out during the night, I remember waking up freezing every morning; I could see my breath and the curling "ice flowers" on the windowpanes. We always tried to stay in bed till my mother had stoked the fire. My parents' bedroom and the adjoining bathroom were always cold. Washing oneself was quick and fast! The bathroom did have a little gas heater, but this was turned on only when weekly baths were taken. Frugality was a way of life. Wood and coal had to be lugged up from the cellar—five flights of stairs! As soon as I was old enough, this became my chore. I also remember that fetching coal was a practical punishment for childish misdeeds. The kitchen and the toilet had windows to the outside and no heat. These rooms were always cold. The kitchen, with its stone floor, might warm up during cooking and baking, but washing the dishes was a cold affair. Attached to the kitchen was a balcony that was used mainly for storage and hanging out laundry. The three of us children loved the balcony as a playroom, especially building castles with blankets, under which we felt very protected.

Opposite our apartment lived the K. family, a couple with two children. The father worked for the Stuttgart Opera House. Later he was in charge of the whole makeup department. The younger son, Peter, one year older than me, became my first best friend. The wall dividing their boys' bedroom and my bedroom was very thin, and I didn't appreciate the older son's practicing his violin there. Thankfully he gave up on his musical efforts after a while. Peter and I were the best of friends.

When I was sixteen we moved to a house across the city and I never saw any of my childhood friends again. Mr. and Mrs. K. were compassionate people who were ensnared in the Nazi regime. Mr. K. could not have kept his job, if he had not joined the Party. So, after the war, during the denazification process, he was on the list of people who had to give up all their valuables to the American occupation forces. They didn't have any valuables, but knowing they had not engaged in any Nazi activities, we kept two good chairs for them till their names were cleared.

Right under us, on the third floor, lived another couple, with two sons, the L. family. The parents, who were quite a bit older than my parents, were both professional musicians. The younger son, who was already a teenager, was nice to us little ones. Because there were few cars around, he went sledding with us on the streets. The family was very patient, but every so often, the mother would come up and tell my parents that we were again being so raucous that their chandelier was swinging. Since we were the only family in the house with more than one child in our age group, our apartment was the meeting place for all the children in the building. Once Mrs. L. met my mother in the entrance of the house and told her that she had heard a loud thump from upstairs. An investigation disclosed that our Christmas tree had come crashing down because we were playing hide-and-seek behind it. From then on, a string was wound around the tree and nailed to the wall.

Opposite them lived two elderly sisters who were flaming anti-Semites. They would spit every time they passed the apartment of the only Jewish couple in the house. We hated them, but did not know why. Whenever we would pass their apartment, we ran fast and stayed quiet. Besides Jews, they also disliked children, and when we were noisy they would open the little glass window and scream at us.

On the second floor beneath us were the only Jews in the building, an elderly couple, the Rs. Their children lived with them at the start, but early on they emigrated to South Africa. I don't remember much about them because they had left Germany before we returned in 1945 from our evacuation. But I do recall that sometimes they used our phone; we had the only phone in the building. They also received phone calls on our phone, and I was sent to their apartment to fetch them. I do remember vividly one day when Mrs. R. came up to use our phone, because she was almost hysterical. Was she talking to her children? I have no way of knowing. According to my mother old Mr. R. often came to our apartment to complain and lament about the treatment he was getting from the Nazis, especially after he was forced to wear the Star of David. One day the couple disappeared. We heard later that they had made it safely to their children in South Africa. They must have fled at the last possible moment, because I certainly would not have remembered them from a time before 1942–1943. My mother mentioned in an interview that neither the Rs. nor my parents themselves had comprehended the scope of persecution the Jews were then suffering under the Nazis.

Opposite them the R. family lived the parents of my girlfriend Renate, the N. family. Renate and I spent every waking hour together before our evacuation and after the war when my family returned from Ditzenbach. Our friendship lasted until I went to high school at age ten, while Renate remained in grade school. In the German school system, children are tracked beginning at age ten. They could continue in grade school for four years, go to a *Realschule* for six years, or enroll in a high school/gymnasium for a nine-year program that prepared them to enter the university.

On the ground floor, Mr. and Mrs. S., and their three daughters, lived in very crowded conditions, because they had turned their living room into a grocery store. The dining room/living room became their office. Two of the daughters slept in the same room with the parents and one daughter slept in the little room that was the equivalent of the bathroom in our apartment. I remember going to the apartment many Sunday afternoons and helping them glue the ration tickets that they received from the customers on newspapers to hand in to the authorities. The whole family worked very hard; the parents went to the fresh produce market every morning between 4:00 and 5:00 and carried the produce home to their store on the streetcar. The mother and some of the daughters then spent all day in the store; Mr. S. was a conductor on the Stuttgart streetcar system. Though Gertrud was my age, I did not play much with her, since between school and helping out in the store, she was always busy. I did, however, go to church with her every Sunday and we belonged to the same parish group. The family was very religious and I don't think that they ever supported the Nazis.

On the opposite side of the long entrance hall lived what we children considered a very old woman, Mrs. J., whom we called the "Witch." We thought that she disliked children, and when I was very small I did not want to pass her front door alone. In retrospect, she probably just wanted some quiet time. According to my mother, however, Mrs. J. was an ardent Nazi supporter and always opened her little glass window when people went by her apartment to see who was coming and going. My parents were very wary of her and thought that she was a Gestapo informer.

The social tapestry of this community was strained during the Nazi years because it consisted of at least three strong Nazi supporters, a Jewish couple, an involuntary member of the Nazi Party, couples who were neutral or Nazi-leaning, and my parents. After the war we had very good relationships with all of them except the three single women who were Nazi supporters. They never changed their hostile attitude toward us.

From the old woman's front door on the first floor you walked down a few steps to the back door of the building, which led into the alley between our building and the one next door. That door opened up into a play lot that was our paradise, but the bane of the adults, since we were a very raucous crowd of at least six who used old-fashioned, noisy roller skates, scooters, tricycles and bicycles, wooden stilts, and the tops of our voices.

If you didn't want to go out the back door, you rounded the corner, descended a few more steps and came to the "laundry room," which meant a room with two big sinks and a washboard, no machines. Laundry was done by soaking the wash for a half hour in boiling water in a very large pot, stirring it with a long stick, and then scrubbing each item with a brush—especially the collars and any spots you could find—for what seemed to me like hours. Then you rinsed the clothes and hung everything up to dry on four laundry lines that extended out from every balcony. Since we were four stories up, I never got up the courage to lean out far enough to hang the laundry on the third or fourth lines. The two that were closest to terra firma were bad enough!

During the winter, the laundry often froze, and shirts, blouses, towels, and sheets were taken off the lines stiff. We thought it was great fun to march the stiff clothes through the apartment as if they were people. My mother did not share in our fun, since the clothes dripped water when they started to thaw.

This reminds me of another fear that I had as a child. I was convinced that our mother would plunge to her death from the very narrow ledge she stood on to wash the outside of our apartment windows. To wash the skylights, she had to stand outside and reach up—without any belts or other safety contraptions. All the women in the neighborhood washed their windows this way, of course, and I never did hear of an accident, but the thought of what could have happened still gives me goose bumps.

From the laundry room, on the same level but around twists and turns, were the individual compartments we all used for storage, particularly coal and wood for heating. I remember when my parents discovered—in 1955, as they were cleaning out the cellar before we moved to our new house—a box of soap that they had stowed away before the war. The soap could have been well used during the war when soap was rationed! One floor farther down was the room that became our potato cellar after the war. During the war this was the bunker in which we waited out the attacks of approaching enemy planes.

My mother wrote in my album that I would go down into these cellars fearlessly to bring up coal, potatoes, and whatever else was kept there. (These cellars were very cold and doubled as our refrigerators.) I do remember being very afraid when I was alone in the cellar, however. I would sing to myself, and before I rounded a corner, I would check whether anyone was there whom I did not know. Once, at the entrance to the cellars, I actually did encounter a man I did not know and who behaved strangely. I immediately fled upstairs.

Life after the Birth of the First Child

I was born at home, ten months after my parents moved into their new apartment. From then on my parents focused on their children, first me and later my two brothers. In the meantime, the Nazis extended their control over every aspect of daily life. This made it impossible to write down anything about political actions that my parents may have taken. Since they never talked about this time, it is difficult to decide whether they participated in further civil disobedience, but my hunch is they did not.

Right after my birth, which was announced with great joy, my mother started a photo album/diary that described in detail my first year.

A few excerpts from my mother's diary show how the family's life revolved around this new baby and how enamored my parents were with their firstborn.

Mother's diary

August 20, 1938

Our little girl is here! How loud such a small creature can scream! And she is kicking so much with all four limbs that I wonder whether she thinks she has to defend herself against the world. Or is it only the joy to have broken out of the small cell and the freedom to stretch and to turn. The midwife takes her from me, wraps her in a bath towel, and puts her in her cradle. After two hours of sleep, she is brought to me again. She looks very serious, and for now I call my little girl "my little wrinkly worm," to the great consternation of her daddy and others who claim that she is a beautiful baby. It is so cute to watch her arms and legs move and her mouth stretch out before a yawn and see how her dark inscrutable eyes open more every day and stare at the light.

The last eight days were very irregular. During the day, she cries at all times; at night she starts crying at 4:00 a.m. and I lie in bed trying to figure out why she cries so miserably and whether something is the matter with her. However, sometimes she sleeps all night and if I wake up, I can't stand the stillness and wake her daddy to go see if she is still breathing. But both the midwife and the doctor say she is fine.

We have many visitors and she has received so many presents that it would be impossible for her to destroy them all alone. She needs siblings! And now the hunt for a name starts. After considering many names, we settled on Margit—which won out. I hope my little girl will like her name later. I have to mention Dad's special joy. Every morning his first steps are to her crib. When she was just a day old, he picked her up and showed her around (grandma was horrified!), and he helps out a lot. I am so glad that I am enjoying these first days at home and not in the hospital. Most visitors decided that she looks like her Dad, but that her snub nose and blue eyes came from me.

I have to add a personal note here. When I was a teenager I was stopped on the street in Stuttgart by a woman who asked, "Are you a Brühl?" When I told her, "No, but my mother was a Brühl," she responded, "You look exactly like Isa looked at your age."

My parents had a very extensive circle of friends and they received 108 congratulatory cards and letters and two telegrams after the birth of their firstborn. Only one of the letters ended in "Heil Hitler," though many had swastikas on their stamps or on the postcards. I was born during the Nazi regime but before the start of the war, and I therefore received many "normal" presents, mainly toys and clothing, in contrast to the presents that I received eight years later for my First Communion.

* * *

My family has always made lists, many of which have survived. The list of about sixty baby presents, which included the names of the givers, thus followed a long tradition.

The oldest surviving of my family's lists, dated around 1880, came from my great grandfather who was a weaver and who listed all the materials that he needed to buy for his business, including their prices.

I feel compelled to insert a lovely detail here: to augment his meager income as a weaver, my great grandfather went to Vienna once a year to fetch leeches from a pond there. He sold the leeches to the local pharmacist and to a doctor near his home in Westerheim. The reason I know this is because a list of all his sales has survived! We also have a health certificate from one of his excursions in 1865. My great grandfather traveled by horse and carriage and on foot and he had to present this health certificate at every station along the way because of an outbreak of typhoid fever in Vienna at that time. He had to prove that he had not contracted the disease before he was allowed to travel on.

The next oldest family list, from 1905, was seventeen pages long and notarized with a seal. Compiled by my great aunt, the list catalogs every single thing she brought to her marriage, each with its estimated value, from handkerchiefs, to many, many different kinds of eiderdowns, blankets, comforters, and underwear, and down to the "triumph stool" (a chamber pot in a chair!).

Two more family lists describe the household goods and personal possessions of my parents right after their marriage in 1937 and the furnishings and personal items they took with them when they were evacuated to Bad Ditzenbach in 1943. The government encouraged the keeping of such lists, as these were the basis for potential payments for loss or damage after an air raid.

So, life went on quite normally till September 1939, as the following excerpts from my mother's diary about me show.

Life of a Baby: Ordinary Family Life

Mother's diary

September 4, 1938

Today is Margit's baptism. Oma Thesa came specially from Aachen to welcome her youngest grandchild. The trip is the first outing for Margit and for me after her birth. Aunt Thea gave her a big baptismal candle that shall be her candle for the rest of the life. [I don't know what happened to the candle after my First Communion when I last used it.] Her godparents are Oma Thesa and Uncle Karl, who is represented by Uncle Rudolf because Karl is in the military. Vicar Kurz asked, "What shall the child be named?" "Margarete Maria." "What do you require from the church?" "Faith." After the baptism, Dad took the child and the priest spoke the father's blessing. Then I hold my little angel in my arms and pray for her and thank God for my great blessing. The friends and relatives then sang "My Faith Shall Always Be Strong." Do you hear it, little Margit? I am glad that I could participate in this celebration. My little girl has now entered the holy church…. We were all amazed at how quiet

39

she was during the whole ceremony till the priest put some salt on her tongue. Her expression showed her displeasure, but she did not cry. She looked so adorable in her little pink dress with the veil, which a friend had made out of my bridal veil. During the joyous celebration at home, I used my good tablecloth for the first time and put a bowl of yellow roses in the middle of the table.

September 9, 1938
Our first outing with the beautiful pram made of willow twigs, a present from Oma Thesa. I am still having problems with getting the pram up and down the sidewalks. I am hoping that with time I will achieve the "perfect elegance." Our cutie looks so small and lost in the big pram, but I love her this way!

September 11, 1938
I was fetched from the kitchen today, because something grand happened: Margit smiled for the first time. I know it is a real smile, not a grimace for constipation, even if I am not always neutral and objective. What bliss to watch this first smile!

September 13, 1938
Oma, Sister Gisela, who is helping me with the baby, and I stood around her crib when Margit raised her head for the first time. What a feat!

October 2, 1938
We are taking the child to my home. Oma Barbara is overjoyed. I can't gauge whether the reaction of my siblings is based on real interest or just accommodation toward us parents. I believe that the slogan "love is blind" is not correct, rather, it's "those who love appreciate life fully."

October 5, 1938
The first real tears. The blue eyes are full of water and so you start life's journey of joy and misery. Little girl, I hope you don't have to cry a lot in life.

October 15, 1938
Margit made a pretty sour grimace when I gave her grape juice instead of her customary milk. So, she already has developed taste buds.

October 28, 1938
She is starting to make very low sounds. She seems to be astonished at these tones, but she exercises diligently, so that she adds new tones every day. I know I am no objective observer, but for me it is a confirmation that she understands my love-talk with her and that she answers me, because she accompanies the tones with a smile.

November 7, 1938

    Heinz is visiting his mother in Aachen, saying goodbye to his little daughter was very emotional. "Margit" wrote him a letter:

    Dear Vati! I am sending you a few photos of me so that you don't become homesick. How do I look? Am I not a nice intelligent little person? Please show the photos to Oma and give her my love. I am looking forward to your return next week so you can play with me. Are you still thinking of me? I am doing all right, but I am a bit lonely without you. That's why I have to cry ever so often. Mutti thinks the reason for the crying is from the milk substitute that she is giving me for my lactose intolerance, but what does she know? I don't know anything else. I hug you and kiss you, Margitle [in Swabia, my ethnic area, the diminutive is expressed by adding 'le' to a word].

And Vati did not disappoint. He wrote back (no phones then).

November 9, 1938, Aachen

    My dear little Margit, You gave Vati great joy with the photos. Vati is keeping them right next to his bed, so that he can look at them as soon as he wakes up. Oma wanted to appropriate the pictures, but I am not giving them to her because I want to show off with them. I long for you, too. I love you so much, do you love me also so much? Kisses, Vati

Mother's diary (continued)

November 11, 1938

    Today, Margit sent her doctor a pretty jug with flowers and put her photo on the card and wrote, "Dear Herr Doktor, I want to give you a bit of joy with these flowers because you have given Mutti und Vati such great joy when you delivered me. Thanks and greetings from us three, your little Margit Paulus."

Reply from the doctor:

    Dear Margit, many thanks for the beautiful flowers and the even prettier vase. Your photo shows me that you have grown nicely. Your mom had a lot of difficulty with you, because you just didn't want to appear. Most probably you didn't trust the life that awaited you. Many greetings and all the best for your future. Your Uncle Doktor

November 16, 1938

    Daddy is here again. What a celebration with his little daughter! Indescribable!

November 18, 1938

    The "conversation" between Vati and his little girl is so cute that I have to describe it here. "Ah, there you are my little acrobat. Ah, good morn-

ing little mousy mouse. Did you miss your Vati? I missed you sooo much. I think I have to eat you up; you don't mind, do you, you sweet little sparrow? Tomorrow I'll take you to the office and put you on my desk, so that I can see you all the time. Oh, oh, what was that? A little wind, a sweet little wind from my dear little mouse." Isn't that cute? I bet later we will not be so forgiving about your little indiscretions.

December 29, 1938

No earth-shaking news, but I love the daily progress. Her favorite toy is still my fingers, which she grabs so strongly that it is hard to get them back. When we approach her crib, she smiles and opens her mouth as if she wanted to start a conversation, but when we walk away, she makes her displeasure known by loud complaining. Today I taught her the first game, running my fingers up and down her arms. She squealed with joy. Though she got a lot of presents for Christmas, she was not impressed. The only thing she was interested in were the tree's lit candles [real candles that were lit only when people were singing or praying by the tree and therefore watching the tree. Just in case, a bucket of water was always nearby]. *Today she is getting her first vegetable mixture. She cried bloody murder. First she distorted her face in such a way that she looked personally insulted, and then she cried louder and louder. It's hopeless. Oh my, it will be work to get her to eat veggies!*

Uncle Richard's 1938 diary—signs of things to come

The unification of Austria and Germany was completed on March 11–12 with the incursion of German troops into Austria.

Mother's diary

January 28, 1939

What joy! I discovered her first tooth when she bit down on my fingers. I wanted to show my discovery to Vati, but the young lady did not co-operate with my request to open her mouth.

January 29, 1939

She can now distinguish between different people. Generally, she smiles right away when we, especially Vati, approach her. But when she sees strangers she studies their faces a long time before she deigns to give them a smile. She grows and develops normally, but she has very thin and sparse hair, even with all the care I give her.

January 30, 1939

She has gotten used to the vegetable mush. She does not even need the pacifier anymore, which helped her to get past the strangeness of the spoon made of horn. We alternate between carrots, spinach, and Brussels sprouts.

March 7, 1939

What progress we saw in Margit during the last few weeks: she sits, propped up by pillows all around, and plays with her toys and everything else she can get her small hands around. This leads to the ultimate achievement: putting her toys, her blanket, Vati's fingers, or the string on Mutti's sweater into her mouth immediately. She was sick for two days with the flu, had a high fever, looked pale, and cried at night—and thoroughly disliked the doctor's prescriptions of cough syrup and the compresses around her neck.

March 15, 1939

One of my girlfriends was here to visit and at first was astonished by how much we spoil Margit, but at the end of the visit, she stated: "One can't do anything else, but do what she wants." Margit already has figured that out and makes her demands. Yes, it is difficult not to spoil the first child for whom one still has so much time.

Uncle Richard's diary

March 15, 1939

German troops marched into Bohemia and Moravia. At 19:45 p.m. the Führer took over the old Prague emperor's palace, the Hradschin. Therefore Czechoslovakia has ceased to exist as an independent state.

March 22, 1939

The Memel area was separated from Lithuania and again integrated into Germany.

Mother's diary

April 27, 1939

She has now managed to put her toes into her mouth, and tries out her new teeth on her toes; she jabbers for hours, loud and strong. The most desirable object for her is Vati's pocket watch. Vati invented a new pet name for her: "Hababboubou," which first horrified me, but which I now like. Aunt Maria calls her "the little golden one"; Aunt Lisel: "the small, lovely person"; and for me she encompasses everything: "my little mouse, my little frog, my little cuddly, my little heart, my sweet one, my oldest, my best, and especially my little dear daughter."

May 10

She got her first vaccinations without crying and without any side effects.

My parents visited my mother's sister in Austria and then another sister in Tyrol while two aunts looked after me. Other siblings of my mother and my grandmother and our neighbor also checked in to see whether I was being taken care of.

Letter from Thea to my parents

[this letter was sent to Austria and then forwarded to Tyrol, all within three days!]

June 16, 1939

What a drama this morning after you left. Margit screamed, sobbed, cried, the whole gamut. I was sure the woman from next door would show up and ask what was the matter. She absolutely refused to sleep again while I was trying to get some sleep. I tried everything, but she didn't calm down till I gave her pacifier to her. Now she is content, eating her banana mush. [At this time, one could still buy everything including tropical fruit.]

Every day Marie and Thea wrote in detail about what I did and what I ate and how difficult it was to make me go to bed. They had a lot of time!! They call me Spätzle (which could refer to the Swabian ethnic food of egg noodles, or to the bird, little sparrow) and Hababaubale.

Mother's diary

June 21, 1939

While we were on vacation for eight days, Margit was taken care of very well and had lots of visitors from friends and family members. She enjoyed all the attention, but papa and I were longing for her. At least three times a day we looked at her photos and waited for mail. The last day before our return the tension rose considerably and we envisioned a joyous reunion! We had promised each other to experience this reunion together. Talk about disappointment! When we looked into her bed Monday morning—we had restrained ourselves and just saw her sleeping so wonderfully Sunday night—she gave us only an occasional look as if we were minor characters in her life. No signs of joy or even recognition. That has changed in the meantime and now she again greets us, but especially Vati, with outstretched arms and an impish smile.

Today Vati and our friends teased me mercilessly when I told them that I had gone to the drugstore to ask for a hair-growing tonic. When the druggist asked me, "How old is the lady?" I had to tell him, "Ten months old." But what's wrong with wanting to have a little sparrow that is perfect from head to toe? And for that the only thing missing is hair. [My mother probably regretted her haste in wishing I had hair. I remember many tears when she tried to comb out my very long, matted, and curly hair later—and then braid it.]

July 6, 1939

Today she managed something else that she hadn't mastered yet: crawling. And now she can't stop doing it, in the morning, when I am airing the beds, on the mattress, and in the evening just before her bath—always accompanied with loud shouts of joy. With this new activity the bath is becoming even more necessary.

July 7, 1939

*She is a very lively and active child. She doesn't sit still for one mo-
ment. When we go for a walk, she always stands up in the pram and
moves her head from one side to the other at breakneck speed—to
where there is something to see or hear.... The day before yesterday a
friend of mine visited Margit. She played so intensely and lovingly with
the child as only a very good person can do. Maria Hoffman visited us
and was astonished that Margit can't gesture: "How big is Margit?"
"What does the clock say?" Or, "Wave bye-bye." When I told Maria that
the only thing she does regularly is take off her pants, Maria grinned: "At
least some sign of culture!" Yes, Margit likes the nude culture. Maria
taught her a few games, which she enjoyed. I was amazed at my daughter's willingness to listen and learn. So, I'll try to show her more, but I
don't want to make her into a little monkey.*

July 14, 1939

*Oma Thesa is visiting us for a week. When Margit stands up in her
pram, Oma calls her "her little triumphator." She knows that Oma cannot
resist her when she crawls to her chair and stretches out her arms. And
then Oma has such wonderful shiny necklaces and bracelets and such
colorful hats, everything that Margit tries to grab.*

July 15, 1939

*Today we have to thank Margit's guardian angel. She fell out of her
bed, from a height of about one meter onto the bare floor. She can't
have been hurt badly, at least we can't see anything, but we can't figure
out how she managed to swing over the sidebars. We were all in shock.*

Poem by my mother [undated; the poem rhymes in German]

To my small daughter
How could I have lived—without you?
How could I have been happy—without you?
That I could laugh and cry
Without you in mind
That is a mystery for me today
What did I do—without you?
How did the time pass—without you?
What the sun means to the world
That's what you mean to me
How could I have lived—without you?

Judging from the excerpts above one could assume that my parents had nothing else in
mind but to dote on me and that life in Germany was normal and peaceful. This is correct in
a way: once people had children their resistance activities were decreased considerably. The
Nazi regime did not just threaten individuals, but their families. And that was too great a
sacrifice for most citizens, including my parents. But while they never mentioned the politi-

cal situation they continued their quiet resistance. Three unspoken examples may show this: Maria Hoffman, mentioned above, was persecuted by the Gestapo till she was hidden by friends in an insane asylum; when she visited my parents they became guilty by association and could have been imprisoned. They also continued to meet with small groups of members of Neudeutschland, the group that Goebbels had disbanded. And my parents had an ongoing relationship with the Jewish tenants of our apartment building till they managed to emigrate. Association with these groups made my parents suspicious and for this reason the Gestapo raided our apartment a few times.

Six years after the Nazis came to power, on September 1, 1939—my mother's twenty-ninth birthday—German troops marched into Poland, World War II began, and life changed for everyone.

Uncle Richard's diary, September 1, 1939

At 10:00 a.m. we were in Geislingen. In a radio address Hitler announced that German troops had invaded Poland.

Karl Brühl with his mother, Barbara, during his last furlough, 1942

Karl with his godchild, Margit, 1940

Karl's funeral near Orel, Russia, June 29, 1943

←Karl's gravesite. ↑Karl's death picture.

Telegram sent by his mother to her son Rudolf in France, June 28, 1943: "Our beloved Karl was wounded and died without gaining consciousness. Letter follows, Mother"

A typed version of Karl's (hand-written) last letter to his lifelong friend Alfons, written the day before Karl was killed in action.

Letzter Brief von Karl an Alfons Geiger

27.5.43

Lieber Alfons!

Entschuldige, wenn ich Dir erst heute schreibe, aber Du weisst ja selbst, dass bei uns z.Zt. allerhand los ist. Bis jetzt ging soweit noch alles gut. Leider hatte ich jedesmal Ausfälle in meiner Gruppe. Bei uns ist z.Zt. Parole Südfrankreich hoch. Hoffentlich klappt es.

Hast Du von zu Hause immer gute Nachrichten? Für heute Dir die herzlichsten Grüsse

Dein Freund Karl.

Robert, shortly after
his enlistment in 1942

Handmade prayer card, made by Thea, Sr. Pia Theresia, reads: "He was born 11 March 1924 as the youngest child in the family and has been missing in action since August 1944 near Kischinew in Rumania. Devoted to the family and true to his friends in the parish, he, like his older brother [Karl], strove to please his parents. Both had premonitions about their death. In the strong conviction that God took his childlike soul into his home and that Maria protected his last weeks on earth, we lovingly remember him."

ROBERT JOSEF

Als Jüngster in der Familie ist er am 11. März 1924 in Stuttgart geboren und seit August 1944 bei Kischinew in Rumänien vermißt. Anhänglich an die Familie und treu im jungen Freundeskreis der Pfarrei war er gleich dem großen Bruder bestrebt, die Eltern zu erfreuen. Eine wehmütige Ahnung erfüllte jedoch beide. Im festen Vertrauen, daß Gott seine kindliche Seele zu sich in die ewige Heimat nahm und Maria seine letzte Zeit beschützte, gedenken wir seiner in Liebe.

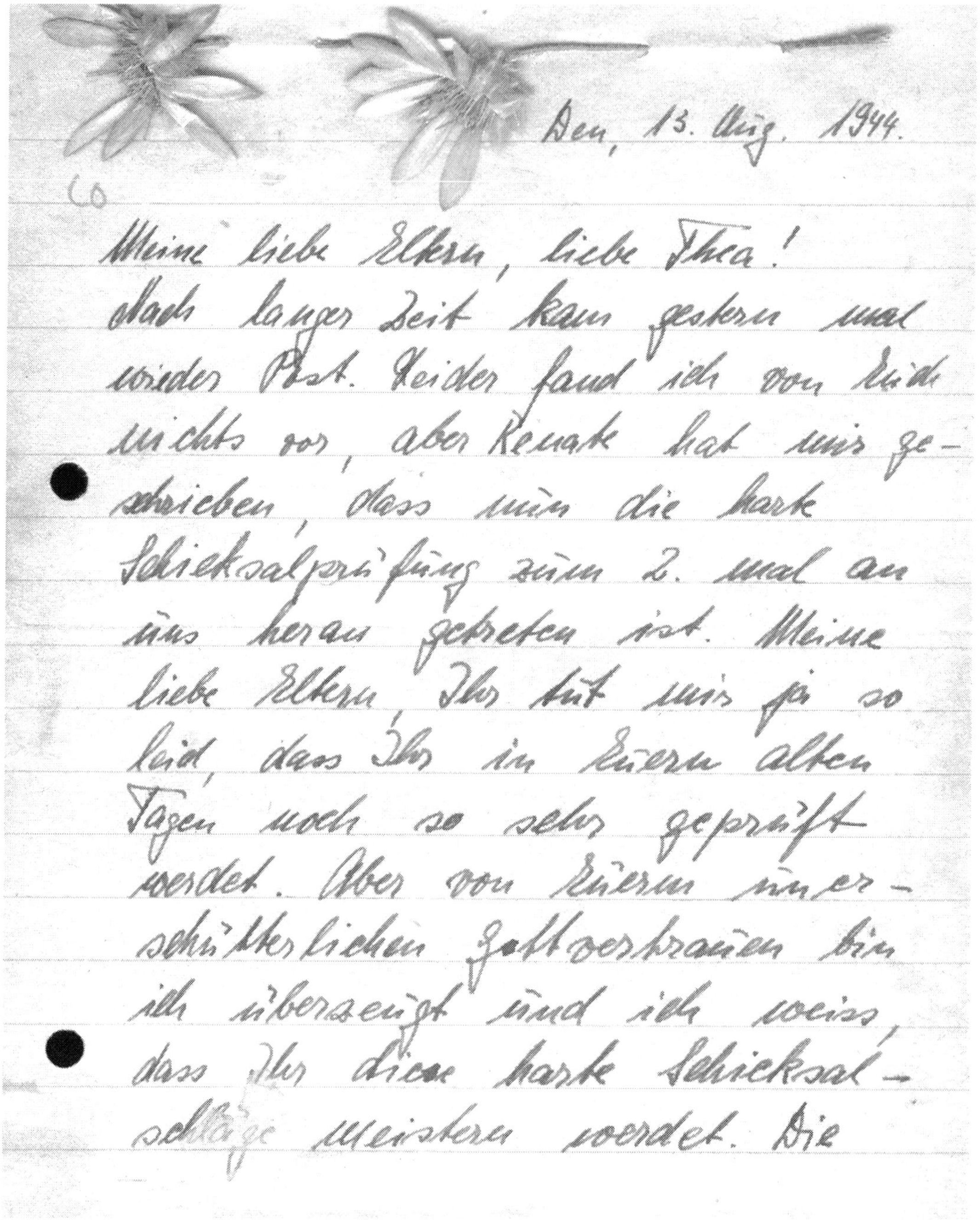

Den, 13. Aug. 1944.

Meine liebe Eltern, liebe Thea!
Nach langer Zeit kam gestern mal
wieder Post. Leider fand ich von Euch
nichts vor, aber Kenak hat mir ge-
schrieben, dass nun die harte
Schicksalprüfung zum 2. mal an
uns heran getreten ist. Meine
liebe Eltern, Ihr tut mir ja so
leid, dass Ihr in Euern alten
Tagen noch so sehr geprüft
werdet. Aber von Euerm uner-
schütterlichen Gottvertrauen bin
ich überzeugt und ich weiss,
dass Ihr diese harte Schicksal-
schläge meistern werdet. Die

First page of the last known letter from Robert, with a sprig of edelweiss pinned on the top. The opening lines of the two-page letter read: "My dear parents, dear Thea: After a long time we eventually received some mail. Unfortunately, there was no letter from you…."

Heinz, four-and-a-half years
old, in Aachen, 1914

At home on a furlough,
playing with Margit, 1940

Somewhere in France, 1940

School courtyard in Ringstedt, Denmark,
with his commanding officer and comrades, 1940

← Heinz Paulus's military passport.
↓ Details from p. 32 in the passport.

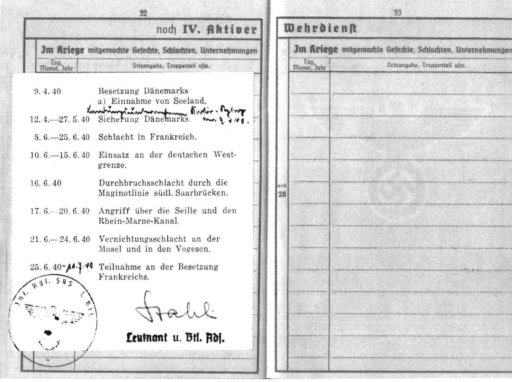

9.4.40   Occupation of Denmark
               Invasion of Seeland, Korsor and Nyborg
12.4–27.5.40   Securing Denmark
5.6–25.6.40   Battle in France
10.6–15.6.40   Deployment on Germany's western border
16.6.40   Battle of the breakthrough of the Maginotline south of Saarbrücken
17.6–6.20.40   Attack across the Seille and the Rhine-Marne-Canal
21.6–24.6.40   Annihilation battle along the Moselle and the Vogues
25.6–11.7.40   Participation in the occupation of France

3 1939–1940

From the Beginning of the War
to My Father's Discharge from the Army

General Background

World War II for Europe started a year and eleven days after my birth. When I was a year and eight days my father was drafted. My mother wrote in my album: "War is coming." And then on September 1, the Germans marched into Poland, signaling the official beginning of the war. My father had two short leaves, before he became part of the occupying army, first in Czechoslovakia, then in Denmark and finally in France. He did not return to our home in Stuttgart for some time.

My father was mustered out of the army in 1940 because after the occupation of Paris German soldiers whose fathers had been killed in World War I were put on indefinite furlough.

For our grandparents this was the second time that they were affected by war. My father's mother became a widow in 1915 when her husband was killed in France. She had three children under the age of ten. Her two sons served in the army in World War II.

My mother's father served in the army, but during the relatively long period of peace between 1871 and 1914. He and his wife had four sons and three sons-in-law in the army in World War II.

My mother wrote in her diaries about my first few years, but rarely mentioned that my father came back from the war disabled, that goods and foods were all scarce, and that the frequency of Allied air raids were increasing. Families were clearly trying very hard to raise their children as normally as possible and to protect them from unpleasantness.

In the 1980s Aunt Thea, my mother's youngest sister, wrote a retrospective of the earliest war years that highlights the conflicted emotions and attitudes of civilians toward the war.

Aunt Thea's recollections

My youth during the war

We were at the community Mass in St. Nikolaus. After Mass we generally sat together in a room in the parish hall for coffee and pretzels that one of the boys fetched from the bakery opposite the church. On this day, A.H. returned with a big bag of pretzels and said: "It is War." I went home before I went to work, and told mother: "Mother. War has broken out!" That's when mother put both hands to her heart and said: "Oh, my boys!"

This gesture—this expression of my mother's—seemed to encompass everything that war meant. These war years, these difficult and cruel years, and yet these beautiful years. It was the time when all my sisters were in the first years of their marriages, the little ones were growing up, and a few were being born in the war.

One can look at the war years from various perspectives, on the one side, from the perspective of the young and growing families, on the other side, from the perspective of our brothers, brothers-in law, other relatives and friends, who served in the war. Or one can look at it as a history of the Nazi regime. For me personally, the war period was one of the best times of my life. It was a very difficult time, and yet it was a good time, and I believe it was also a beautiful time of youth for my friends. I was still an intern at the Catholic publishing house Kepler, where I had started in 1937. My brothers Karl and Hermann were in the labor service (Arbeitsdienst, military service before the war started) when the war began; Karl was perhaps already in the army. Rudy was not yet in the military, and Robert was fifteen years old. I was seventeen when the war started and twenty-three when it ended. We were told that on this Friday Poland attacked Germany. Our soldiers told us later that they fired into Poland for a whole night before the Poles fired back.

Two days later I took the streetcar with a friend to the reservoir for a canoe trip. It wasn't that the war changed everything right away. It wasn't that we couldn't do many normal things like making visits, going for hikes, and going to concerts and the theater. While we were in the streetcar, we heard that France and England had declared war on Germany.

One of the first things that became scarce was soap. And soon ration cards were introduced. There was no more whole milk, only one percent milk; and bread and meat were rationed as was clothing. Eventually everything was rationed. Our old milk vendor, who had her store around the corner from us, often told me when I came to fetch our allotted milk ration to wait awhile and then she gave me a quarter of a liter of whole milk and said, "Here, for your old mother." She took pity on our mother: even though mother was only sixty years old at the beginning of the war, she occasionally gave her extra milk.

Letters between Soldiers and Their Families

The many letters that my father and uncles wrote from the front give us insights literally from the trenches. As soon as sons and sons-in-law were inducted into the army, an active correspondence began between those at home and family members in the field. Many letters were sent between parents, aunts, uncles, between siblings, and to the children. Sometimes families had to wait a long time before they received word. But even when soldiers were living in terrible conditions, they always inquired about the welfare of their relatives at home, and waited for mail with great anticipation. Families could not follow the fate of their relatives on the news, since the soldiers, after the first few months, could not write about where they were stationed. Their fate was determined by the random act of being chosen to serve on the western or eastern front.

In her interview with Dr. Doerr, my mother summarizes my father's military career.

Mother's interview with Dr. Doerr

On the first day of mobilization, August 27, 1939, my husband was inducted, first to Plochingen, then Reutlingen, where I visited him a few times, and he came home for short furloughs. At the beginning of November his troop was ordered to Prague. This stay in the Czech Republic was very trying: the soldiers were always cold and hungry. At the beginning of March 1940 their unit marched and took the railroad to Hamburg and Kiel via Dresden and Leipzig. On April 9, 1940, they were involved in the invasion and occupation of [the island of] Seeland and Denmark. In contrast to the occupation of Norway, not one shot was fired and no one was killed. Our soldiers had a very good life there. On June 1, 1940, they left Denmark and were assigned to the battle on the Moselle and the Vosges hills.

On July 29, 1940, a discharge from the army followed, because after the successes of the army in France, soldiers whose fathers had been killed in World War I were discharged.

The following excerpts from letters show the stark contrast between the lives of soldiers on the eastern front, who suffered tremendously from starvation, cold, horrible conditions, and long marches, and those on the western front, who had a comparatively easy life.

Most letters between spouses were numbered. This way they knew how many letters had been lost. Unfortunately, almost no letters sent to the soldiers from many family members and not many letters between our parents survived. This makes it difficult to follow the sequence of events. What is surprising is that the mail only took a few days to be delivered even though addresses had only a name and a military number. Letters were sent to a central location (Karlsruhe) before they were delivered to the soldiers. Letters coming back did not have a return address, only a stamp that said "field mail."

Almost all packages, many containing food, made it to their destinations, even though toward the end of the war package sizes were limited and one had to buy special, scarce stamps. The packages were longingly awaited by the soldiers, especially the ones on the eastern front. Extended families divided the care packages. For example my mother sent things to my father; my grandparents sent packages to their unmarried sons; the unmarried son with a fiancée received his packages from his fiancée and her family. All soldiers received occasional packages from their aunts and uncles, who lived on a farm; after my father's discharge, my mother sent packages to her brothers.

Uncle Karl, my mother's oldest brother, started his military service before the war and was to be discharged in 1940 after having served his two years. At the start of the war, however, he was immediately sent to the western front. His letters from that time were still full of hope that the war would be short; his letters were full of his plans for the future after the military. His three brothers were drafted into service later, as soon as they came of age.

Uncle Kurt, my father's brother, was also drafted right at the beginning of the war. At first the soldiers could reveal where they were stationed. My father was sent to the east, to Czechoslovakia. Unfortunately only postcards survived from this time. His later letters from Denmark, in which he described the harsh winter in Czechoslovakia, are lost. Recurring themes in all letters from soldiers are loneliness, homesickness for loved ones, and the hope for letters from those at home.

Soldiers carried on a regular correspondence with their relatives at home, writing about how they wished to partake in the daily lives of their families. Their letters also show how much they were brainwashed by incessant propaganda about the "glory of the German Reich" and how they were taught to hate the others—the enemy.

Letters from my father from Czechoslovakia, Austria, and Denmark were written to my mother, unless otherwise noted below. (My father's handwriting was notoriously difficult to decipher. Spaces in the excerpts that follow mean that I could not read a particular word in the original.) The letters and cards from 1939 to the beginning of 1940 are from Vienna and the Czech cities of Bruenn, Pilsen, and Prag. The German names of these Czech cities are used, because Germany had "integrated them into the German Reich" in March 1939. The letters and cards are just greetings from coffee houses where the soldiers were spending their time.

In one card, my father wrote, "Please send me painkillers for my headaches." A friend wrote, "Greetings. It doesn't matter where you greet from, the main thing is that you *can* greet."

Early on, when the soldiers were scattered in all directions, life at home was fairly normal. Clearly parents wanted to spare their children the upheaval of war, especially since many of their fathers were absent.

In written correspondence nothing political was ever brought up, not even in personal diaries: political attitudes or actions were never mentioned again. Everyone lived under threat of household searches, which the Nazis could conduct without warning or warrant. When people were harassed by Gestapo raids—as were my parents—this information was not safe to enter into diaries. The same can be said about letters from the soldiers. Some American friends who read an early draft of this family history wondered why the soldiers never questioned the authority of their superiors or the legitimacy of the war, as American soldiers did. For German soldiers any criticism would have been very dangerous. As mentioned above, recently released German government documents reveal that 30,000 soldiers were accused of war crimes and 20,000 were executed by the military. These "war crimes" included simply writing anything critical of the government in one's diary or in a letter.

My mother's detailed diaries about her three children offer insights into life at home.

Mother's diary

August 28, 1939

Our dear Vati was inducted today. War is just outside the door. He touchingly said goodbye to his "Pippifraetzchen," as he calls Margrit lately. Hopefully we will have him back with us soon—and forever.

August 30, 1939

Margit took her first steps today, from Marie to me. What a pity that Vati could experience this with us!

September 2, 1939

The child is a great solace to me in these trying days, but I would like to see her spend time with Vati.

Letter from Karl (from the Western front) to Isa

[Note: Karl had moved from the *Arbeitsdienst* to the military on the first day of the draft.]

September 8, 1939

Many thanks for the package, which I was very glad to receive. The sweet little stones that fell from your heart [chocolates] are a great solace for my sensitive stomach. In case these little imps should oppress you in future, send them to me posthaste. Out of love for you, I will digest them. I cannot write where I am stationed, but I am leading a quiet life without much worry. Sometimes I think that I am here on a summer vacation. It's a pity that this easy life will not last much longer, in my humble opinion, because in about two weeks these glory days will be over. I am pleased that Heinz was assigned to my branch of the service, the royal infantry. I hope he will have more opportunities to earn the Iron Cross than I. At the moment this is my only concern. Dear Isa, aren't you a bit scared? What has to be, has to be; from nothing comes nothing. And in fourteen days everything will be over anyway.

Mother's diary

September 10, 1939

Heinz was here today. Margit immediately laughed and played with him. Even with his uniform she recognized him after a two weeks' absence.

September 17, 1939

Today Vati came again home for a furlough. At first, when he still had his coat and cap on, [Margit] acted as if he was a stranger. But after a very short time the deep friendship between them was reestablished. When I talk about Vati, she immediately looks to the apartment door and expects him.

September 21, 1939

Lately, Margit has a lot of joy in walking. It is also cute when she manages to get hold of a mirror. She laughs and plays with her mirror image and does gymnastics in front of it. When she gets a handheld mirror, she turns it around and tries to figure out what's in the back.

October 15, 1939

Margit runs cheerfully through the whole apartment. She doesn't speak much yet, but she points to all the things and persons that I ask her about. She knows her environment now. It is so wonderful to experience how her little soul awakens more each day and is able to form thoughts in her little head. "All first impressions stay in a child forever." A serious task is to impart the first impressions to a child. I am very happy about this, but would like Heinz to partake in this process too. I am going to close this first diary of Margit with the sincere wish to have our Vati with us soon permanently.

Experiences of Civilians versus Soldiers

While at home everything proceeded normally, though husbands and fathers were absent, war-time letters from the soldiers tell a different story. My mother received letters from her husband and her brother Rudolf, who were serving mainly on the western front, and from her brothers Karl, Hermann, and later Robert, who were based mainly on the eastern front. These letters show that the soldiers completely misread the military situation. They believed that the war would be over in a few weeks and that the citizens of the invaded neighboring countries would offer no resistance and would welcome the German occupation joyfully.

Soldiers stationed in the west encountered few difficulties or hardships in general, as the letters make clear, but the situation in the east was heartbreaking. Conditions on the eastern front were shocking and deeply moving: the occupied populace was very poor, the winters long, snowy, and freezing cold. And the letters often describe how heavy the resistance was as well.

Shortly after soldiers were inducted, their spouses were informed about the compensation they would receive:

Mayor's Office, Department of Women's Welfare,
Stuttgart, November 14, 1939
Notice regarding family compensation for induction to the fulfillment of the active service duty.... [Bescheid über Familienunterhalt anlässlich der Einberufung zur Erfüllung der aktiven Dienstpflicht.] Spouse Aloysia [Isa] Paulus will receive a monthly maintenance fee immediately of 232 RM from November 1, 1939, to November 30, 1939, and 276 RM from December 1, 1939, on. This compensation will be paid as long as the military service of Heinz Paulus is in effect and her maintenance cannot be secured in any other way.

Rationales for the War

My grandaunt's husband, Richard Fischer, was not a Nazi supporter in the beginning. He especially disliked the Nazi's stance toward the Catholic Church. He was a strong nationalist, however, and once the war started he became a Hitler supporter and began to equate Hitler with true German nationalism. He also developed a deep-seated hatred of the English. In his diary (excerpted below) he describes the beginning of the war.

Uncle Richard's diary

September 1, 1939, 10:00 a.m.
We were in the dentist's office in Geislingen and heard on the radio that German troops had marched into Poland.
On September 3, 1939, England announced that as of 11:00 a.m. they are at war with Germany because they had a mutual defense agreement with Poland, and Germany refused to heed the call for withdrawal of its troops from the area. France gave the same reason for declaring war on Germany at 5:00 p.m.

When my father was gone, my mother wrote to him regularly, including letters that she composed as if they were written by me. Only a handful of these letters have survived. I presume that my father brought them back with him when he came on furlough.

Letter from "me" to my father
(the third letter), written sixteen days after he left for the first time

September 14, 1939
Dear Vati,

It's time that I write you a letter. And it is only 6:00 a.m. I just couldn't leave mama alone. You would be surprised how well I can walk already. Therefore I follow Mutti all day long, to the kitchen, the balcony, and to the room of the nice lady who rents a room in our apartment. I know my way around and know which drawers are interesting and where the keys are kept. I often look for you, in the dining room on your chair, and in the bedroom in your bed. Why aren't you coming home? I still know you very well. Mutti shows me your photo often. Every day she and I have cuddling time. I sit on her lap and we play. Mutti always says, "You are such an imp." And then I laugh.

Yesterday Mutti photographed me in my playsuit. It was hard work. Mommy pesters me a lot. I don't want to stand still in one spot, even for a few seconds. Mutti is waiting longingly for a letter from you. Write a long letter. That puts her always in a good mood. So, now you pick me up in your arms and I give you many hugs and kisses, I love you so much.

Your little daughter, Margitle

Letter from Karl to his brother Rudolf, October 11, 1939, at the front

You might be right that you still have to serve at Christmas. I believe now that it is taking longer than we thought. Whether I am at the base or here at the front makes no difference to me. On the contrary, here I get extra compensation for front service and twice my base pay. In addition, cigarettes, cigars and tobacco are still plentiful. I haven't seen any wine yet! By the way, I haven't seen a movie in half an eternity. It's time that the war comes to an end so that I can rectify this situation.

All the best, your brother heart [Bruderherz], *Karl*

Recollections of the Early War Years

After the war Resi Paulus, Uncle Kurt's first wife, wrote a detailed diary from memory that gives insights into the way of life in those times. She moves between verb tenses, as if she was reliving the events. I have left the changes from present and past tenses in her narrative.

Aunt Resi's diary

When Kurt and I got engaged in 1937, we decided to get married in 1939, but that date became questionable. August 1939 saw the intro-duction of the rationing cards for groceries, and on September 1 the troops marched into Poland, the so-called campaign of eighteen days. Kurt is part of it and returns safely. On September 20, the rationing cards for clothes are introduced. Kurt is ordered to a unit in Luxemburg and is not discharged from the army as planned. Therefore we decided

*to have a war wedding. Because it was becoming more and more diffi-
cult to get the ingredients for a wedding meal and the other accessories
needed for a wedding with ration cards, we decide to celebrate our wedding on the same day as my parents' twenty-fifth wedding anniversary.
They also got married during a war—World War I. Everything was prepared, but then Kurt sent the message that the army would not grant
him a furlough and that the wedding had to be postponed indefinitely.
We celebrated the silver wedding anniversary with just a few family
members, and the food that we had already managed to secure was
stored for later use.*

*On Christmas Day, my mother woke me with a telegram from Kurt:
"Wedding can take place December 29, [1939], will arrive December 27,
evening." I immediately sent out the announcements. We married December 29, but only with a few family members and friends, because
many could not come on such short notice. I sewed my wedding dress,
lilac, and my coat. We had a short honeymoon in Düsseldorf and Kurt
had to return to the front on January 4, 1940.*

The following excerpts from the diary of Uncle Franz Heinrich, the husband of my father's sister, illustrate how important status and acceptance by the military was. He wrote
these memoirs in 1969–1970 about his war years (1937–1945).

Franz Heinrich's diary

*In 1937 I accepted a job as the leader of the "technical department" of
the army service agency in Cologne, which had as its goal to prepare
and equip the German industry for a potential war. However, when the
war actually broke out I had already switched to a private firm, Dynamit
Nobel, because the army insisted that the employed engineers would
become civil servants after a probationary period. However to qualify for
the status of officer, employees in uniform had to undergo military training to become at least applicants for group leader. If we passed, we
would receive the title of Regierungsbaurat. I applied for this training in
1938, but the required medical examination resulted in my being rejected for military service because of a previous operation for varicose
veins that left a big scar on my leg. I would have liked my work there,
and was interested in becoming a civil servant, but since this was not
possible I decided to forgo a career in the military and to return to the
private sector.*

*I resigned on October 1, but since the war had started in September
all my plans were upset. The military told me that my resignation at this
point was not possible and I had to stay in my position. They would inform the private firm, which had to agree. After the war started, the military was even more interested in giving us military status and putting us
into uniforms. However, we still had to pass the basic military training.
My boss signed me up for the next available course—without a medical
examination—and so I started my eight-week training in Berlin-Spandau*

in January 1940. This was an especially harsh winter and the training in snow and ice was very difficult for me, but in July of 1941 I was promoted to Regierungsbaurat and became a civil servant with a military uniform. Since the whole defense agency was run by officers, this military garb was important. Even though I served a time as a private, I was promoted to major, which at least outwardly equated me with the staff officers. In reality, this equality was based on my technical knowledge, which many of them did not possess. However some looked down on the civil servants in uniform, which did not bother me.

Mother's diary, December 1939

Our Vati is now far away. In Bruenn [Brno]. But Margit still remembers him vividly. His photo is on the desk and she points immediately to it when she is asked about him. If I give her the photo, she pats it gently. What solace the child is to me since she fills the apartment with her liveliness all day and keeps me busy. And how bitter it is that Heinz cannot experience this developmental stage where every day brings new, amazing things.

Letter from "me" to my father, Advent 1939

My dear Vati! I am sending you many, many Christmas greetings. I will pray to the Christ Child for you often. Mutti always tells me much about you. But you really have to come home soon, because nobody can play with me as well as you. Then I will show you my Christmas present that I have for you: I am sending you myself again, first here in the photo and in a small 8-mm movie. You'll like that, won't you! I now put my small arms tightly around your neck and send you lots of love, Margritle

Mother's diary, December 23, 1939

Today Margit, an aunt and an uncle, and I celebrated Christmas. My wish was that the child would see her first Christmas tree in our apartment. The lighted candles and the bulbs made a big impression on her, but the best was blowing out the candles. After we sang in front of the crèche and prayed for our Vati, we opened our many presents. It was a wonderful evening with a blessed Christmas mood. We know that our Vati was with us in thought and spirit.

Letter written by my father on December 17, 1939,
on the assumption that it would arrive after Christmas

My darling little Margitle!

Now the Christ Child has brought you so many wonderful toys and Vati can't even look at them. You don't know how much I regret that I cannot celebrate Christmas with you and Mutti. It would be so nice if the three of us could play with your toys, light the beautiful candles on the tree, and sing songs together. You would sit on Vati's lap and accompany us and admire the lit candles with your beautiful blue eyes. Now since Vati is not there, you must sit on Mutti's lap—which you prefer anyway. You dear child! Vati loves you very much; do you love your Vati too? Do you think of him sometimes? Do you even still remember him? Vati thinks of you and our good Mutti often. Surely you are an obedient child and don't give Mutti any concerns. You know, you are Mutti's sunshine and therefore have to give her only joy. Mutti writes a lot about you and that gives me great joy. Hopefully Vati can visit you soon. Write what you got for Christmas.

Unfortunately Vati can't give you any presents this year; Mutti will do that for him: Come, let's play "gucki-bumbi-bambi" or "airplane" and "cuckoo." Do you still know Vati's games? Vati gives you many kisses and holds you up, and shows you the little lights and the beautiful toys that the Christ Child brought.
Your Vati

Letter to Heinz from his brother-in-law Erich

Dear memories of our beautiful Christmas celebration. It is a pity that you could not celebrate with us. Margit was overjoyed with all her presents. She can distinguish them all and brings them to her Mutti. I wish you also "Gemütliche" hours for the holidays.

Letter to Heinz from Maria, my mother's sister

We celebrated a wonderful Christmas and it is extremely sad that you couldn't be here. Isa's tree is wonderful; a thick white pine tree. Our Margitle was of course totally enthralled. She didn't know which of the many presents to open first. The surprise of your photo was perfect. Many heartfelt greetings.

Mother's diary

December 30, 1939

Yesterday we experienced a miracle. Heinz was at the door at 1:30 a.m. Margit immediately woke up and reached out her arms to him as soon as he came into the bedroom.

A New Year starts and Germany is still at war.

January 1940

We three just spent ten marvelous days together. That makes the "being alone" so much more bitter. Margit seeks Vati behind every door. She runs through the whole apartment and asks so lovingly and seriously, "Vati?"

Aunt Resi's diary, 1940

February 3

I moved into our two-room apartment on the second floor in the house of my mother-in-law in Aachen (Friedrichstrasse). I furnished the formal living room and the bedroom. The bathroom was shared by us and my mother-in-law. The toilet was halfway between the first and second *story. I moved in all my personal belongings in suitcases by foot from my parents' house. In order to avoid the army confiscating my room, which was now empty, my parents rented it to a student. I continued to eat my breakfast and lunch at home and only ate dinner with my mother-in-law. Her housekeeper insisted that I not have access to her kitchen, otherwise she would leave. My mother-in-law was dependent on her.*

April 27
Kurt has an unexpected furlough, but has to cut it short on May 10th because of the invasion of Holland and Belgium. He visits me again from May 26 to 28 on the way to the front.

Letter from "me" to my father, February 5, 1940, Stuttgart

My dear Vati!

First I am going to lay my little head on your shoulder and pat-pat you with my small hands and give you many kisses, because it is your birthday and I love you so much. I wish you all the best. But you should really come home to Mutti and me soon! I pray every evening for you and send you greetings through my little angel. Did you feel it yet?

And now I want to tell you about me. I'll describe my whole day so that I don't forget anything. I wake up at 7:00 a.m., but Mutti still sleeps tight then. You know, I have to tell you something, she goes to bed so late every night, at about 11:30 p.m., because she reads and writes letters. That's why it's no surprise when she can't get out of bed in the morning. I make allowances for that for a while and talk very quietly to myself. When my voice rises a bit, Mutti yells very loud: "silence." I will stay quiet for a while, but when it gets too boring, I start babbling again. At 7:45 a.m. Mutti turns on the light and then we talk a bit from bed to bed. So, Mutti relies on me to wake her up because at the moment she doesn't have a clock, and it is completely dark in the bedroom, because we have darkened all the windows so well that we don't know when the day begins.

After I am dressed I get my bottle of milk and when Mutti eats breakfast, I sit on her lap and eat a piece of bread with butter. Then we straighten out the rooms together. I already know my way around and when Mutti says we are going into the kitchen, I run ahead, so that I am the first one there. And when somebody rings the bell, I run right to the door, because I am no longer afraid of strangers. What I like especially well is to make the beds. I puff up the pillows again and then smooth them out. When Mutti wants to start the heat, I bring the paper basket and the basket with the kindling wood. I stand right next to her and when the flames have caught, I blow strenuously. But you don't have to be afraid; I don't go too close to the heat. I know it is very hot.

When we work in the kitchen, I rearrange Mutti's kitchen cabinets: the clean pots come out and the dirty ones go in. Sometimes I have to toil a lot, because the pots are so heavy and I have to sigh heavily, but I take my job very seriously. I also close all the doors and drawers wherever I am. And I pocket the keys wherever I find them.

In the bedroom I immediately go to Mutti's makeup table. There are so many fine things: comb, mirror, and a box with cotton. Mostly I take the cotton and make little piles on the carpet through the whole apartment. She doesn't like this at all. Anyway she has different tastes. But when she is upset and starts to scold me, I stroke her immediately, and then she cannot scold anymore. I learned that a little while ago. But she is not really that upset with me anyway, because she knows I got it from you. I mean my lively personality.

Now back to my day. Around 10:00 a.m. we are generally done with the rooms, then I get my vegetable and fruit porridge, and then I play in the playpen by myself. Mutti is busy in the kitchen and only checks on me occasionally. And then comes the best part of the day: Mutti plays with me or we both look at my picture books. I am very quiet then and well-behaved, and she can't show me the pictures often enough. I know all of them very well, and I can also speak a bit more. I think nobody besides Mutti understands me, but that is enough for the time being. I learned all kinds of words, but I speak mostly about you. And I ask many times for your photo so that I can pat it and hug it. I won't forget you, darling Vati, but you really, really have to come home soon. After all this work, I get tired and entertain myself quietly with my toys. I have to tear up the old railroad schedule, undress my dolls, and take apart my animals that are made of fabric.

At noon we have lunch. Even though I am more like you in most things, my taste for food is clearly Swabian. I love Spätzle. Really, I like a lot of food that you wouldn't touch: sauerkraut and rice. I always eat the same as Mutti; I even like spicy food. The other day I started to cry while I was in bed already, and so Aunt Maria took me up and I sat next to the adults who were eating liverwurst, fried potatoes, and red cabbage salad. I ate along with them as if I had just come off an eight-day hunger diet. Aunt Maria kept on saying, "The child will not be able to sleep tonight." But of course I slept soundly. After lunch we both take a nap. And then, when the weather allows, we go for a ride in the pram. Sometimes we go shopping and we leave the pram at home, which Mutti always has to carry up four flights of stairs. At 4:30 p.m. we have to settle down for a coffee hour.
Please come back soon to your little girl,
Your Margitle

Reply from my father, February 8, 1940

My darling little daughter!

You gave me great joy with your "daily schedule" and with the gorgeous photos. I am interested in all that you do, how you spend your day, and how you develop. Due to your report I now know precisely how your day proceeds. It is so good of you to pray every day for Mutti and

Vati. The Good God will surely listen to the prayers of a little child for her Vati. Yes, child, Vati has to come again soon! But who knows when that will be?

I love you and Mutti so much that I would walk home if I could. I'd love to play with you on the floor, dance in circles, play peek-a-boo, go for walks with you, hug you, give you kisses, and tell you that you are my only and best little girl. That you like Vati even more than your dolls gives me great pleasure. I hope you will still remember Vati, even if he stays away long. Vati bought you shoes, but you have to grow into them. I hope you and Mutti like them. My dear little Margit, come sit on Vati's lap, hug him tightly, and give him a kiss. We both love each other so much.

Many kisses, also for Mutti,
Vati

Letters from my mother to my father

February 18, 1940, Sunday, 5:00 p.m. (fourth letter)

I went for an hour-long walk with Margit. We went to church; the pastor was there and asked about you and made a little cross over Margit. She prayed devotedly for you; she immediately puts her hands together; of course she also talked incessantly and kept on asking: what is this? Of course only insiders could understand it. I am astonished how intensely she asks about all the things that she can't pronounce. She jabbers constantly; it is lots of fun. I could report to you all day about the child. It is one of the most bitter disappointments that you can't follow this cute developmental stage of your daughter. And nobody can alleviate this sacrifice for you. I wish so ardently that you would show up one Sunday afternoon and experience her. I am sure the two of you would spend all afternoon playing on the floor. You know, she can be very loving now—like run to me and clasp my legs. Sometimes when I come home we have a giant welcome. And her facial expressions! It would make a great movie. Often when she misbehaves, she waddles toward me bent over like a little dwarf. I have to first turn around to smile before I give her the deserved paddling. An endless topic such a child! And I can only give you a tiny impression of her. But Vati is clear in her mind. She recognizes you in all photos.

February 21, 1940 (twenty-sixth letter)

Many thanks for the three towels. I can use them very well. The book also came, but I am still waiting for the things for the child. Hopefully they will arrive soon. Your twenty-seventh letter arrived tonight. The twenty-fifth letter is therefore lost. Paul [brother-in-law] was declared fit for combat during a special examination. He did not request a special unit and therefore will probably also be inducted into the infantry. I am really sorry for him. These marches will be impossible for him. He told us that he read in the Dutch newspapers...there is a silver lining on the

59

horizon. My God, the joy would be overwhelming.

How are you doing with sweets? Shall I send you some? You have no idea how often Margit speaks about you—totally unexpected. In the bedroom she always runs to my nightstand where your picture is displayed.

Letters from my father to my mother

March 9, 1940, 2:00 p.m., Prag (Prague)

In half an hour we are off to the railroad station; when we will leave, we don't know. Everybody is in good spirits and glad that we will leave here. Our hope is for the West. Tomorrow morning we will know at least the direction. Last greetings from the Protectorate!

March 10, 1940, 7:00 a.m.

We are at the Czech–Saxonian border. At 1:00 a.m. we passed through Prag. We departed at 7:00 p.m. last night. Where it will lead… uncertain. Thank God, we sit in a well-heated compartment, third class.

March 10, 1940, 8:15 a.m.

We are just passing under…. The German border…and again German people. Now, presumably, we are headed for Dresden!

March 10, 1940, 10:00 a.m.

And now Bodenbach, the first German border city. The ride along the Elbe is simply marvelous. Everywhere we are greeted with cheers. Mood: first rate! The question: where to?

March 10, 1940, 11:20 a.m.

Now we will soon reach Dresden. We already passed the Bastei.

Letter from Thesa Paulus (my grandmother) to her son, my father, April 8, 1940

Today I received the letter you wrote before you shipped out and I think you can well imagine how I feel. It seems that I won't be saved from anything. Now I have to worry about you two [my father and his brother, Kurt]. But I cling to the hope that God won't allow the sorrow that has already hit me once to hit me again. He will protect you and accompany you and will bring you back healthy again. If this hope wasn't possible, I wouldn't know what to do. Now I could not endure another one of these blows. And one can't do anything else but pray for you, that the Lord may protect you.

I can very well understand your plea in regard to Isa and Margit. But you can be assured that in case something should happen to you, Isa and the child would be a holy legacy from you, even without your plea. I have no more ardent wish than that the two would come here and that Isa and I could bear our worries together. Send news as soon as you know where you will be stationed. It might be possible that you would be in this region.

When I hear from you again, I might be more tranquil. And then: write as often as you can, even if only a short greeting. You have no idea how trying it is when you wait for news. I will also write to you often; I will be with you in spirit all the time anyway. You can take the thought with you into the field that nobody, besides Isa, can love you as much as I do. This may be a beacon of light for you in the difficult days that are probably ahead of you. I wish for you all the best and God's protection and beg you again, to send news often. Heartfelt greetings and kisses from, Your Mother.

The Invasion and Occupation of Denmark and Its Aftermath

Letter from my father to my mother

April 8, 1940, 2:00 p.m. (sixty-second letter)

This letter can only be sent to you when the whole enterprise is successfully completed. However, I want to describe everything in sequence, so that you can partake in it after the fact. Yesterday morning we were loaded into freight trains in P.[?] and rode—accompanied by the most wonderful weather—via Hamburg directly along the Alster to Kiel. We disembarked there and bunked all night in a waiting room, ready for action. To be precise, we "sat up." At 7:00 a.m., the alarm was given. Then we boarded, both "men and mice," a large commercial ocean liner. I am lying on the second deck [on a straw sack]. The ship is surrounded by numerous similar…ships and from…boats. We have to stay below deck all the time in order to avoid discovery and recognition and can only go on deck to use the bathroom. We are lying in the water motionless for hours—about 8 km from Kiel. When, where to, and how long we'll sail is the interesting question, which cannot be answered by anybody. Norway or Denmark? The light from the deck is gorgeous. The ships next to us, behind us and in front of us enhance the picture even more. My only worry is that you do not worry about me.

April 9, 1940, 4:15 a.m.

In exactly an hour the conquest of Denmark begins! Our ship will be the first one to anchor. At the same time our comrades will occupy Norway, Holland, and Belgium. I will stay on ship till everything is unloaded. I hope that the occupation will proceed without any bloodshed.

The mood among the troops is very good. We have the order, to occupy one coastal town immediately and to keep it.

April 9, 1940, 5:00 a.m.

The Danish coast is fully illuminated, proof that the Danish people don't suspect anything. At 5:15 a.m., with the landing, the German ambassadors will contact the head of state. The Reich is prepared to pay for all damages. Extra money was printed for the occupying troops.

April 9, 1940, 8:00 a.m.

   The occupation proceeded without resistance. I am in charge of unloading the food. Now we'll proceed to Copenhagen. I am writing this on the lowest deck.

April 9, 1940, 12:00 p.m.

   The ship is almost unloaded. The population of Korsør is very friendly and cheers Germany's step. Our comrades who had to conquer Norway, fared less well. One ship was sunk by a British U-boat: 150 dead. Belgium and Holland also were occupied. The Mediterranean and the Black Sea are sealed. The English are lost! In a few minutes, we are off to Foeroe [a small town in Denmark] *by truck.*

April 9, 1940, 7:00 p.m.

   Now I am in Foeroe. As a consequence of a misunderstanding between H. and F. our car drove on, which led to a dreadful scolding by H. and a forced night vigil of F. This doesn't shock us old seamen any more.

   The population is exceedingly accommodating.... It is wonderful here. Add to it, gorgeous weather; the crew had no idea, but everybody thinks it was the right thing to do, because if the English had landed in Denmark it would have come to a fight. Tomorrow, we'll drive farther, probably to Copenhagen. The statements in regard to Belgium and Holland do not seem to be correct, at least to be premature.

   Tonight I have to organize the sleeping arrangements for the whole village. This day was an experience!

April 10, 1940, between 8:00 and 9:00 a.m.

   We are presently in the hotel where we are quartered in a huge room. For breakfast: wonderful coffee, milk, white bread, butter. And all of that for a few pfennige [cents]. *Here, you can still get everything: chocolate, soap, etc. The mayor of the town, with whom I negotiated last evening, was very friendly and welcomed the official step. It is truly wonderful here.*

April 10, 1940, 12:30 p.m.

   We have reached Ringstedt now. F. and I drove with the food truck. After moving in and lunch, we enjoyed a nice day since H. will only arrive tonight. I bought Palmolive shaving cream. I am anxious to find out when the first mail arrives.

April 10, 1940, 4:00 p.m.

   I have now slept and am sitting in the courtyard of the school in the sunshine. I have to wait for H., who probably will only arrive tonight. I am therefore presently leading a very quiet life. If I could only communicate with you!

*During the Norway transport, two ships (Blücher and Karlsruhe) were
sunk. We have to thank God that everything went so well for us and is
still going well.*

April 11, 1940, between 1:00 and 2:00 p.m.
   *Now, I drove with F. on a truck to Copenhagen and am sitting—after
we unloaded the food rations to be kept in the local military barracks—in
a cafe near the railroad station. In a moment, we'll return to Roskilde,
where the troops are stationed for tonight. Tomorrow we'll probably
march to Copenhagen. Such wealth as in Denmark is unimaginable in
Germany. We are even getting the first (though a few days old) newspapers and learning some news about world politics. Copenhagen is very
big and surrounded by beautiful countryside. You can literally buy everything here!*

April 11, 1940, 9:40 p.m.
   *Returned to Roskilde and received the order to drive immediately to
Copenhagen tomorrow morning, to reload the food rations and immedi-
ately bring them to Helsingør (by truck). The troops are going to
Helsingør instead of Copenhagen.*

[Note: The people at home were constantly waiting for mail and news of their loved ones,
even if by modern standards they sent letters back and forth quite often. They knew that big
troop movements were in progress, but they didn't know where to and whether their relatives were part of them. The next letters are from my mother to my father.]

Letters from my mother to my father

April 10, 1940, 11:00 a.m. (sixtieth letter)
   *This constant waiting is terrible. I walk around all day as if I were in a
daze, and wait for news on the radio. If I would at least know that you
are close by. That would calm me down. I can't deal with the thought
that we won't be able to see each other now for a very long time. I just
wish that you are fine and that life is bearable up there in the north. This
morning after Margit and I played for an hour, I put her in bed with me
that she may console me. And truly in this dark time of waiting she is
like a gift for me from God.*

April 11, 8:00 p.m.
   *Again another day of waiting has passed. This is now my new timeta-
ble. Today I feel a bit happier and calmer. I so hope for a good end and
that I will see you again sometime. Your mother wrote and asked
whether I wanted to visit with the child. But I first want to go to
Schnittlingen* [the home of her father's relatives], *but I will not travel anywhere before I have heard from you.*
This afternoon a small package arrived from you with five [indicipher-
able]. *How well you look after us. I treated myself to one immediately to-*

night: a rare treat. How are you taken care of? Oh, I could write a letter full of questions, but I hope you will answer all my questions in your next letter.

...that the child speaks Swabian cannot be avoided. Maria and her playmate HansPeter make sure of that. Mrs. S. [who lived above us] told me that she sent a package to you. Did you get it? You should see and hear how Margit prays; she likes to do it: Maria, bait dein Mante aus; mach fuer Papi Utz und ild aus [translated from baby talk: Mary open your coat and use it as shield for my Vati].

Continuation of my father's letter, still unsent

April 13, 1940, between 4:00 and 5:00 p.m.

We will stay for the immediate future in Helsingør. Last night we feared a counterattack of the English. But it did not materialize. We live high on the hog at the moment. We live in the best hotel (on straw in the Great Ballroom) and eat there at our own cost. Unfortunately, I have almost run out of money and...is impossible. Denmark is indescribably rich! [Note: It seems that my father was the quartermaster for the unit, and/or the paymaster, though he never talked about it.]

April 14, 1940

Today is a wonderful day. The treasury is in a wonderful room, one side of which has enormous windows. You may be wondering why I am writing on this paper. The situation is this: Only the so-called Squadron 1 came here to Denmark, while Squadron 2 remains in Germany for the moment, but is now following us. All our luggage is with Squadron 2. We were only permitted to take precisely allocated things with us. Squadron 1 includes only the fighting troops and the paymasters. Squadron 2 has all the vehicles, drivers, clerical equipment, and supplies, etc. I am very glad that I am with 1. [Squadron] 2 is following with the ferry. They are lacking the experience that we had this week: we receive as of today extra pay for service at the front, 1 [Deutsch] mark a day. I am afraid that I can't send this letter now, but I have to wait, till the operation has solidified and I can write freely about everything. And what are you doing today? How are you two doing?

The time will come when you can read the letter and the report about this interesting week. Hopefully soon.

May 7, 1940, 1:00 p.m., Helsingør (eightieth letter)

Presently I have to drive to Hillerød with the car, to pick up oats; perhaps tomorrow I'll drive with H. to Næstred, 80 km south of Copenhagen. You can see I lead a rather turbulent life, but I like it that way, because I have always appreciated responsible work.

I am waiting with greatest longing for a letter from you and I hope it will arrive this afternoon.

May 7, 1940, Hillerød, 4:00 p.m.

After having completed our official business, I have dismissed the five men from my work unit for an hour "on their word of honor," and am now sitting with a glass of beer. Yesterday in Copenhagen I had ten men with me, whom I granted 1.5 hours "furlough on their word of honor." I myself select the men for the work unit. Also the trucks. H. gives me a 100 percent free rein. You will think, Heinz is living the good life, while we have to cut back on everything. Yes, that's the way it is, but I would so like for you to share in my life here. You can obtain everything here. After a while, though, even this good coffee and the best cakes get boring. You can even buy a great variety of fruit here. If I could only send you or Margit a Toblerone chocolate or some fruit or something!

Did I already write that I am sharing my pad in the kitchen building, over the cafeteria, with F. And that we can buy milk there (a whole bottle) for ten pfennige, cake for four pfennige, whipped cream, etc., because of the proximity of the cafeteria. Of course we get plenty.

I consider this time as compensation for the gruesome time in.... Hopefully something like this will not be repeated! ...I am socializing with a lot of marines. Very interesting. Now, I am looking forward to one thing: mail from you; I am counting on it today. I hope that I am not disappointed again.

May 7, 1940, 7:00 p.m.

Oh, the disappointment! Again no mail from you! I'll have to wait till tomorrow.

May 8, 1940

Private B. will take this letter to Stuttgart

Some of the above comments of my father in the letters above are astounding, considering his involvement with the anti-Nazi movement before the war. They also show a total lack of insight into the feelings and attitudes of the occupied population. Because the inhabitants were polite to the occupiers, he assumes that they supported the German invasion. Like so many others, he succumbed to the propaganda and to the euphoria of the first German successes.

Those who stayed home could not express their surprise about the soldiers' change of mind, since all correspondence was censored and the soldiers could count on nasty outcomes if their loyalty was questioned. Also the secrecy had started. When the troops marched to another part of Europe, the families at home were not allowed to know where they were.

Uncle Richard's diary, April 9, 1940, 5:15 a.m.

German troops crossed over the Danish border. At 8:00 a.m. Copenhagen became German property. In the morning of the same day the Germans occupied the most important strategic points on the western coast of Norway. This starts a new phase of the war between England/France on the one side and Germany on the other side. The whole world is watching its outcome. If it should result in England's defeat, the world would sigh with relief that England has after all found its master.

Aunt Resi's diary

April 27, 1940
  Kurt comes home unexpectedly for a furlough.

May 12
  Kurt has to interrupt his furlough—invasion of Holland and Belgium.

May 26
  Kurt visits for two days on a military trip.

Letter from Karl to my mother, May 1, 1940

The cake was fabulous and very timely. We are now on a location where we can't go to the field kitchen for extra rations. Because my stomach has a big capacity, I feel pretty hungry one hour after each meal. It was especially bad during the first day when due to a logistical problem there was no food available. Imagine, after a 60 km night march, no food all the next morning! And then your cake arrived. Before I had the package completely open, I already had eaten it all. As an explanation: from our old base to this new base, we marched during four nights about 180 km. I have only two cigarettes left. As everybody knows, I'll smoke everything. If the war drags on, I'll start chewing tobacco! The landscape here is gorgeous.

Mother's diary, April 5, 1940

Today Margit managed for the first time to give a real kiss. Till now, when she wanted to "honor" somebody with a buss, she offered her lips without the accompanying smack [schmalzerle]. I was therefore quite impressed how she kissed her Vati's photo tonight properly. Vati is very much in her memory; she recognizes him in all photos.

My mother sent a photo collage of me to my father and he responded.

Letter from my father to me

Easter
  My darling big daughter! Your Vati is so lonely for you, but he cannot come to you; first he has to defeat the bad enemies. But then he will come home to you and your good Mutti. For a while, however, Vati has to be content with your photos and Mutti's reports about your life and your hustle and bustle. The photos show me that you have grown into a fine little lady. Mutti's reports tell me that she is generally satisfied with you, since you are a darling and well-behaved child. But sometimes, Mutti says, you don't want to obey. Is that right? If she is right, you will probably be better in future. You have to be now, that Vati is not with Mutti, twice as obedient, because you are her sunshine and her only so-

lace.

It is good that you still think of Vati. Never forget him, then Vati will come home soon and the three of us can love each other as much as you love Mutti on the last photo. And you can already give a real buss. How much Vati wishes to have just one little buss from you. Later, when Vati has returned, we have to make up for it. You have to show me your toys, have to explain everything, and have to give me thousands and more kisses. My darling little daughter! Vati thinks of you all the time from afar. He has only one wish –to have you and Mutti healthy and cheerful and close to him soon.

Pray always for your daddy! Blessings to you and Mutti, Your Vati

Mother's diary, May 1940

Something needs to be said. Margit is not one of the most obedient children. She has now discovered that she can do things differently from what the adults want her to do. And she practices it keenly. She doesn't respect anything or anybody. Even the threat of a "paddling" doesn't make much of an impression, only perhaps in the last minute when it is given. But she doesn't linger over it. The biggest punishment is when I tell her: "Mama doesn't love you anymore." Then she sobs and does everything that I want her to do and starts to flatter and beg: "Mutti lieb, Mutti lieb," till I make up with her.

Uncle Franz's diary, 1940

The war was still tolerable at this time. The air attacks were limited. With the beginning of the offensive against France things became livelier. My brother Wilhelm was legal counsel [Kriegsgerichtsrat] to a military division that was kept in the Cologne area in reserve. He survived the campaign against France, and returned with lots of looted goods from there.

Letter from my grandfather to his son-in-law, my father, who was probably still in Denmark, May 13, 1940, Stuttgart

We are very pleased that you are doing well considering the circumstances. However, the best would be if we had our sons-in-law and our sons among us again with their families.

During the time that the action in the north started, we were very worried about you, as we are today about Karl. This war is becoming more and more like the World War, if not worse. We think of you every day and pray every day, especially in the morning and evening and on Sundays. We think this is the best service that we can give you. Rudolf is still at home. Hermann will be inducted soon. We hope to get a long letter from Karl once the letter prohibition [Briefsperre] is lifted. We know nothing about his actions. I wish you all the best and a healthy return soon.

P.S. [added by Barbara] Still haven't had time to write a letter, but I pray every day for all my sons and sons-in-law.

The Campaign against France

Letter from Karl to Rudolf, May 7, 1940

[In handwriting] *For your information: I am at the front again* [in northern France] *and was assigned to the communications unit. We have already spent three days in combat, but now it is quiet, that means there is a break in enemy artillery fire* [Kriegsruhe]. *At the moment three French fighter bombers are above us. We have sustained heavy losses. We marched during the last ten days 500 km and then were immediately involved in combat. In the last three days I wouldn't have bet my life for a cigarette. When I look at the bloody, mutilated bodies of my comrades, I feel sick. With the dangerous enemy tanks against us, our simple infantry is powerless. Yesterday I faced one of these things about twenty meters away. Thank God right next to me was a dirty open sewer into which I jumped, covered all the way to my neck. I had to wait two hours till I could get out of it.*

What is going on at home? We are completely cut off from news. I am sending this letter to your fiancée, Trudl, so that the parents do not worry. I will let them think that I am still far from the front. I hope that you, Hermann, and Robert, know your responsibilities toward the parents should I not return.

[Typed the next day] *I wrote a letter to the parents today. They will probably give it to you to read. Father is always a bit suspicious and believes that I lost my position at the purser's office, so I borrowed a typewriter from our office. Please tell me whether the parents are still worried about me after receiving my letters.*

We just experienced another wild night. Yesterday, as I wrote to you, three planes were above us, most probably reconnaissance planes. At night we were in a fine mess. Artillery drum fire! For seven hours I lay flat in a field of stinging nettle. Only at dawn could we start to give first aid to our wounded. One of my comrades, who was lying ten meters from me, had his left arm ripped off. He has died in the meantime. I hope we will have a quiet night today so we can recover a bit.

I am glad that you are still at home and can help the parents. Please don't forget to send my watch and I desperately need a soap dish. What's new at home?

Letter to Rudolf from Karl, June 2, 1940, in the field

We are at the front again. For hours I have been lying under enemy fire. However, we are shooting back quite heavily too. This morning I rode on a captured French moped. While it was relatively quiet, I rode a horse. I did quite all right. Nothing else new!

Letter from my father to me for my feast day (June 10), June 6, 1940

You will celebrate your feast day in a few days. [Catholic families celebrate the birthday of their patron saint, in my case Margaret of Scotland.] *Vati sends his best wishes. I hope that the small presents from Vati*

reach you in time and give you joy. Vati would like to see you in your lit-
tle apron and shorts. I just hope that the clothes will fit you. Vati thinks of
his dear little daughter and of dear Mutti all the time. He longs so much
for you and looks forward only to one thing: to see you very soon! I am
glad that you enjoy your time in Schnittlingen. Stay there for a while and
relax. Think of Vati, pray for him and love him a whole, whole lot—as
much as he loves you

Letter to my father from Aunt Thea, June 7, 1940, Stuttgart

One should never give up hope, I mean especially for mail from one's
young cheeky sister-in-law. I only know that you are in the West and
could see combat daily. I have no news from home, because I am at-
tending a ceramics course…. Two days ago I received a letter from my
Irish pen pal. She is so cute. She wrote six pages in English and three
pages in French; she is very talented, linguistically. She wrote among
other things: this year saw a real influx of people in Ireland; all of a sud-
den everybody loves Ireland, even the British, this is strange. She does-
n't like the British very much and was never in London, but as soon as
the war is ended, she will visit her friends in Stuttgart. At Pentecost she
prayed in church that God bless my relatives and my fatherland.

Karl is in France, but not on the front. Once he wrote that they re-
ceived a baptism by fire [Feuertaufe]. Hermann was moved, but we
don't know where to. Gerhard [husband of sister, Wilma] had a car acci-
dent in the army. He drove down an embankment and the car rolled
over. But he and the other occupants of the car were not seriously hurt.
We have no news from Paul [husband of sister, Gertrud]. A letter that I
sent to Ireland two days ago was returned because mail delivery is can-
celed. But soon we can write to Belgium again. I—and all the others—
wish you all the best. You know, mother will most probably not manage
to get a letter out to you, since she writes regularly to Karl, Hermann,
and the other children. She hopes Isa will give you all the news. Even if
we are quiet for a while, our good wishes are always with you

Letter from Karl to Rudolf, in the field, June 13, 1940
(sent in care of Trudl, Rudolf's fiancée)

Please give this letter, like the other, to Rudolf. Since we started ac-
tive combat, we always lie close to the enemy. Our regiment is the for-
ward party, so that the troops following have an easier way through. So
far we have counted a 70 percent loss. Today we took the first black
people prisoners. We, the survivors, hope every day for relief of our du-
ties. Last night when I fetched water alone for my comrades, I was shot
at by a French mounted reconnaissance patrol. I was just traversing a
meadow and therefore couldn't take cover and couldn't defend myself
because I had left my rifle behind so that I could carry the water bottles.
Thank God I received help from a machine gun that had been mounted
in the vicinity. Otherwise I would have been a goner. When I return, I will

give you the details. Please send me a good watch band for the watch
that you sent. The old one was destroyed in the last fire storm.

Letter from my father, written from an unknown location
sometime after the occupation of Denmark in May–June 1940
[none of my father's other letters survived, though he had been sent to France before his discharge]

June 13, 1940, 1:00 p.m.
In three hours we are moving. But don't become concerned. I was just
visited by S.T., who is in my unit and in the telephone agency. He is tak-
ing this letter with him.

Note: On the reverse side of the card was this note to my mother:
As soon as I found Heinz's address, I went to see how he was doing.
Now we talked for an hour about old times and in solidarity about our ex-
periences, about home, and about old friends. Heinz looks fairly well.
Probably we will be able to meet again. That's great!
Many greetings and continued good development for the little girl, H.S.

Increasingly the war also affected those at home. Goods had started to become scarce as early as 1939 and became scarcer every year. My mother wrote: *"I bought boots for Margit today. That wasn't so easy, since I first had to fetch a ration card."* This was surprising to my father who could buy everything in Denmark while he was with the occupation troops there.

I can still recall three events that would not be remarkable during normal times, but which became major crises in the war years.

- I carried a stack of plates from the kitchen to the dining room through the rather long hallway in order to set the table. While I tried to heave them onto the table, they fell and broke. These were rather ordinary everyday plates, but my mother scolded me severely, because she said that she could not find new ones.
- Shortly after this incident my mother caused a similar "catastrophe." When one of her brothers came home on furlough, she invited all the family members in Stuttgart to bring ingredients for a cake (sugar, flour, raisins, milk, all on ration cards) so that the family could feast. In the excitement of greeting the returning soldier, she forgot the cake in the oven. When it was discovered it had burnt to a crisp.
- After the war, our parents found a whole box of soap in the cellar that they had hoarded but forgotten. How well they could have used it during the time when real soap was very scarce, since it was one of the first items to be rationed.

Aunt Resi's diary
On June 16, 1940m I was told by phone that Kurt had been wounded.
The dumdum shot had gone through his upper right arm. He was in
Alzau in the hospital. Our cousin Hedwig Paulus, who worked for the
telephone company, connected me with Kurt whenever a line was open
and at no cost. [Note: It was common during the war that every
wounded soldier was nursed by a BDM girl (Bund Deutscher Mädel/
League of German Girls, a Nazi association for young girls). Many ten-
der bonds were forged that way.]

Letter to my father from Lilly Suth, my grandmother's sister-in-law

To Heinz Paulus, 19321 A, June 30, 1940, Bad Wiessee, Hotel

...and now, my dear Heinz, where are you? We don't hear anything from you or your mother or Isa. We hope that you will continue to be lucky and will be spared the worst. My nephew Max [son of Konrad Adenauer] is in the field hospital in.... It is terrible in Cologne; every night enemy attacks. For the last week they seem to be indifferent to where they fly. Even in our neighborhood [five km away] they have razed houses. I hear that it is not as bad in Aachen.

I have recovered nicely here; it is so wonderful and peaceful. I am not looking forward to returning to Cologne as you might imagine. I wish it would stop soon, but what will come afterward? Here you hardly notice there is a war. It must be the land of milk and honey. One can hardly imagine that hell has broken loose in other parts.
Your Aunt Lilly and Uncle Willi

Letter from my mother to my father, June 14, 1940, Schnittlingen (one-hundred-and-first letter)

My dear, dear Heinz!

I have seldom taken anything so hard as the news of our troops marching into Paris. I ran away from the lunch table and cried in my room. On the one side because of my concern for you and on the other side because of my pity and compassion for all who had to sacrifice their lives for such a.... I believe that the situation in the combat zones is terrible. And what a hard lot for the women at home who have to sit at home and wait for news. If I receive you back in good health, what wouldn't I do for joy and gratitude? Are you thinking of us always with great love? Thank God I received another letter from you today. That was a great solace. I still have no news from home. I don't know anything more about Paul.

Mother wrote today how much she appreciated your phone call. If I could only hear you myself! But I probably couldn't say anything because of my excitement. H.P. sent me a delightful letter today. If I have some worries, I should contact him. He asked whether the child and I had enough to eat and whether he should send me something. I am going to ask him to find some shoes for Margit. I have to say, our friends and acquaintances are wonderfully supportive. We will still stay in Schnittlingen for a while. The farm has a few small chickens. When you come back, one of them will be sacrificed. You have to take care that the war is over soon.

Many heartfelt greetings and kisses from your Isa.

Letter from Karl to Rudolf, in the field, June 29, 1940

As an aside: After a long time I hear German music on the radio. Marvelous. I just heard that my troop leader [Meldestaffel-führer] has been killed. I was of the opinion that he was only slightly hurt and recovering in the hospital. Here is how it happened: the evening before, we stormed the Malmaison fort. The next day the French fired their artillery directly into the fort. Shortly before that I received the order from the leader to carry a comrade who had been wounded to the first aid station, which was set up in the fort. The trip did not take long, because the wounded soldier was lying nearby. When I delivered him to the station, the artillery fire started suddenly and I couldn't return to my communications troop. As soon as it was a bit quieter, I started to go back.

Our battalion just started to launch a counterattack over a high plateau. Because the battalion commander of the communication troop is mostly in front of the other troops, I tried to reach the front as fast as possible. But in a short time we got more machine gun fire from the left and this time directly on the high plateau that we traversed. To the right and in front on a hill was a small forest to which we sped. Luckily for me that I was so much in front, because the artillery fire caught most of the soldiers in the back of the company. My troop leader must have been farther back because his abdomen was ripped open by a grenade. A communications soldier who was with him administered first aid and then returned to the fort to get the paramedics. Because of the heavy fire, he could not be rescued in time and bled to death. He managed to write on a piece of paper: "If the paramedics come back here soon, everything will be OK. It is 9:00 p.m. Many greetings to my dear mother and my siblings. All for Germany. My last wish is to be buried in Botnang [part of Stuttgart]." I only heard about his death today. He was a first-rate chap with whom I had a good relationship. I have seen many comrades die, but none of the others upset me as much as his death. It's always the best ones who get killed.

In the meantime it is quiet here and I am working again in the purser's office as a clerk. There is not much else new here. Incidentally, I am yearning to wear a blue suit with a tie.

P.S. Any news from home?

From May 1 to July 16, 1940, I spent time on the family farm in Schnittlingen, where two sisters, a brother, a brother-in-law, and a nephew of my maternal grandfather farmed—a paradise for kids, huge gardens, many animals, close to forests and meadows, with five childless adults to spoil me rotten.

Note in mother's album

"This is a time devoted completely to eating and getting fat."

Letter to my father from "me," July 5, 1940, Schnittlingen

Many good wishes for you on your feast day. My special wishes from me are that you return to us soon. So you can see how much I have grown, I am sending you an illustrated letter today so that you can see what I do all day.

Mama says that I turned into a lazybones because I prefer riding over walking. When you come back, will you be my horsie?

"The little miss likes to ride in her cousin Franz's self-made cart or on the hay wagon. Her playmates are Hektor, the dog, the mulle-kitten, the quack-quack ducks, and the peeping chickens."

Animals give me great joy. You already know our dog Hector. We also have teeny new kittens. And I love to feed the tiny chickens so they grow fat for a good roast when you come home.

If I am not outdoors, I spend most of my time at the window, and I shout at the people and farm carts that come by.

My favorite activity is to ride on the hay wagon. I sit on top of the hay wagon, which is very soft. I always pay attention when Uncle Bernard harnesses "Brown" or "Fox" and tell him not to forget me. I beg and beg "Margele up; Margele up" till he can't resist and takes me with him.

One of my favorite things is playing with water in my little pool. If Mutti is anywhere near, I spray her with water. If not, I wash myself from head to toe and water the flowers and the grass. Mutti is OK. She plays with me a lot; I may pull her nose and climb all over her as much as I want. That's why I love her so much.

But of course I love you still more. I plant little kisses on your photo. And when you come home, you'll see how well I can pat you and give you busses. But Mutti and I are really sad that you are not coming home right now. We had been counting on it very much and I already learned a short welcome speech. So, I will continue to pray for you and that the war will be over soon. Now I have told you much about me. Come back to us soon, then I will tell you much more. I can now speak quite well. Auf Wiedersehen, darling Vati, I send you many kisses and wish you much luck. Please think of your small daughter, Margit.

Mother's diary, 1940

July 5

Margit can now speak very well. As soon as she hears something, she repeats it. I think she thinks aloud, because all her play and activities are accompanied by words. She speaks very fast, which shows me that she is half Rhinelandish. Her voice can be so sweet and soft, for example when she says: "Auf Wiedersehen, Mutti," but also very loud and strong when she gives her orders: "Hello, go away" or "Uncle Bernhard, stay here." Sometimes the volume of her voice is so loud that everybody all over the neighborhood can hear it. In our city apartment we couldn't allow her to speak so loud. When you ask her name, she politely answers, using the diminutive form: "Margitile Ballus."

July 13

Totally unexpected, Vati stood in the middle of the living room when we returned from our afternoon walk. The first few minutes we were speechless, so big was the surprise and the joy. Margit, surrounded by all the relatives, who wanted to watch her reaction to this enormous event, was a bit standoffish. But after about five minutes she was best friends again with Vati, and played and roughhoused with him. However, the idea of "Vati" took some time for her to understand. She talked about "Uncle Vati" and every soldier in uniform gets greeted with "Vati." It was therefore important that Vati should show up again in person.

My father had marched with his unit to France. But as soon as Germany occupied Paris, he and his brother Kurt were put on temporary leave, since their father had been killed in World War I.

The following excerpts show my father's military career:

Military passport

Eagle with swastika [on all documents]

Army

Active military service

August 27, 1939, inducted 9136; Infantry Reserve Battalion 435

Service counts from August 27; sworn in September 3, 1939

Training [also during the war]

Rifle 98 L.M.G. 08/15

Other training as controller/paymaster

Promotions and honors [also during the war]

July 1, 1940, promoted to private first class

Discharged, July 27, 1940, as private first class to Stuttgart

Type of discharge: ready for reenlistment

Medical evaluation: ready for discharge, no medical treatment necessary

Instructed about espionage, espionage defense, high treason, preservation of secrets of military service and military surveillance on July 29, 1940, by military unit in Stuttgart

Involvement during the war in military operations, battles, and enterprises

Month/Day/Year Location, troop unit, etc.

April 9, 1940. Occupation of Denmark

   – invasion of Seeland

   – naval landing Korsør-Nyborg

April 12–May 27, 1940. Securing Denmark

June 5–June 27, 1940. Battle in France

June 10–June 15, 1940. Deployment on the German west border

June 16, 1940. Battle to penetrate the Maginot line south of Saarbrücken

June 17–June 20, 1940. Attack via the Seille and the Rhein-Marne canal

June 21–June 24, 1940. Annihilation battle on the Moselle and in the Vosges

June 25–July 11, 1940. Participation in the occupation of France

July 27, 1940. Given leave into the reserves.

Given to soldiers as they are discharged:

Gas mask; steel helmet; cap; boots;
Blood group A
Severance pay RM 50.-
Salary RM 14.40
Ration supply RM 16.80
Total = RM 81.20
Paid October 17, 1940 in Stuttgart

Certificate of Reserve. July 30, 1940. Stuttgart
Preparedness Certificate [Bereitstellungsschein]
This certificate is your identification card for your temporary discharge
from the service. You will herewith be available to the military office that
is responsible for your residence and you are required to contact them
personally or in writing within forty-eight hours of your discharge. You
must keep this certificate with your military passport in a safe place and
present it to the head of the employment office or his representative. If
you are required to report for military service again, you must mail back
this certificate immediately. If you change your residence, you will have
to inform the appropriate military office within three days.
Ration cards for the period of July 28–August 25, 1940, given to Heinz
Paulus by the Office of Nutrition.
Discharge Certificate [Entlassungschein]
Private first class Heinz Paulus was discharged July 29, 1940, to his
residence in Stuttgart, Johannesstr. 92. All his military papers will be
sent to the appropriate office.

On the day of his discharge my father received: his military passport; his salary till August 12, 1940; room money till…[?]; food allowance till July 29, 1940; maintenance money till August 12, 1940; as his property: one shirt, one pair of pants, one pair of socks or leg wrap, one handkerchief; for a price of RM 10.00 one pair of laced shoes; as a loan: march equipment, including field cap, field shirt with tie, long cloth pants, string [*koppel*] with lock, laced shoes [bought]; severance pay RM 50.00.

A year after his discharge my father was diagnosed with tuberculosis.

From my parents I learned that the soldiers, when in the east—in the Czech Republic—were quartered in primitive barracks and suffered terribly from the cold continental climate.

In Denmark they had good quarters and enough to eat, but were freezing, especially when they were quartered in Helsingør, "Hamlet's Castle." It is therefore not possible to determine where and when my father was infected with tuberculosis.

Uncle Richard's diary from the beginning of 1940 to my father's discharge

May 10, 1940
The Germans marched into Luxemburg, Holland, and Belgium, as
Germany could ascertain without a doubt that Belgium and Holland did
not honor the neutrality pact, but had allied themselves with France and
England. I heard about the invasion during a day trip with Isa in
Donzdorf.   The mood there was pretty excited.

June 4, 1940

    The battle that started on May 10 in Flanders, in Artois, and northern France was completed with the destruction of the last fort in Dunkirk. This battle against the enemies became Germany's biggest annihilation fight. The Allies lost more than 1,200,000 prisoners of war. Weapons and ammunition from 75–80 divisions were either destroyed or captured. Around 3,500 planes were shot down.

June 5, 1940

    The fight in northern France commences. On June 14, the German Army marches into Paris.

June 16, 1940

    Italy declares war on France and England.

June 17, 1940

    The French prime minister, Petain, addresses the French nation, telling them to give up their arms.

June 22, 6:50 p.m.

    The German–French truce is signed in the forest of Compagnie.

June 24, 1940

    The truce between Italy and France is sealed. Six hours later, both truces become operative.

Wedding couple, April 1944.
(The bride's trousseau is
described on p. 151.)

Wedding party. On the left are Thea and Robert Brühl
on his last furlough before he was declared
missing in action.

The wedding
of Rudolf and
Gertrud had to
be held in a
temporary cha-
pel of St. Niko-
laus church in
Stuttgart be-
cause the
structure had
been seriously
damaged in an
Allied bomb-
ing attack.
The photo to
the left shows
the church in
1937 on the oc-
casion of Isa
and Heinz's
wedding.

Family farm house in
Schnittlingen in the 1940s

Backyard of Schnitt-
lingen farm, 1930, Richard
Fischer, four Brühl sisters,
one Brühl brother, a cousin
of the Brühl sisters, and
a son of the oldest sister.

Ride on a hay wagon, aunts Maria and Thea,
cousins Armin and Elinor Tietze, and Margit, 1942

Margit playing in endless meadows
of flowers, 1940 – a child's dream

Xaver and Walburga Priel with their children. (Three sons were in the war.)

← In Bad Ditzenbach, 1944
(author is second from the right)

↓ The carpentry shop's outdoor
storage area offered ample opportunities for play

My brother Karl Heinz,
one-and-a-half years old

The winter of 1944 was extremely cold:
Margit, Bernd (Hans Bernhard), Karl Heinz

Our village did not have
a restaurant. During my
father's weekend visits,
we walked to the next
village for lunch. Heinz,
Isa, Margit, and Bernd.

Bernd and Karl Heinz in front of our birthplace in Stuttgart. The building miraculously survived the war while almost all the houses around it were leveled in Allied bombing attacks.

First day of school, September 1944, while evacuated in Bad Ditzenbach.

Back in Stuttgart, 1946 – no longer internal refugees. Bernd, Karl Heinz, Margit.

First communion, 1948,
a few months before the
beginning of monetary reform.

First passport picture for a
children's passport to allow
travel to Switzerland, 1948.

Richard Fischer with his wife and sister-in-law in Schnittlingen, 1906

← Franz Heinrich and wife celebrating their twenty-fifth wedding anniversary in Cologne, 1957. ↓ Hermann Brühl with his sister, Thea, in Konstanz, 1996.

Resi (Kappertz)
and Kurt Paulus

Paul Ludwig's official pass as a federal judge 1949 reads: "The offices of the Federation
and the States are demanded to support the owner of this pass in all his official jobs.
Especially, all police stations are directed to allow him to circumvent barriers
and to grant him protection and help."

Wedding of Isa Brühl and Heinz Paulus, 1937

Der Oberlandesgerichtspräsident   Köln, den 24. August 1937.

    XII P 210

                        An

          den Referendar Herrn Heinz P a u l u s

                 in S t u t t g a r t

                    Neckarstraße 56

Anlagen: Ahnenpaß u. 2 Urkunden.

      Auf Ihren Antrag vom 19.8.1937 werden Sie
beschieden, daß nach Prüfung der erforderlichen
Urkunden Bedenken hinsichtlich der arischen Ab-
stammung Ihrer zukünftigen Ehefrau, Frl. Isa
Brühl, nicht geltend zu machen sind.

      Die vorgelegten pfarramtlichen Urkunden sowie
den Ahnenpaß erhalten Sie in der Anlage zurück. Die
erfolgte Eheschließung wollen Sie mir unter Bei-
fügung einer standesamtlichen Urkunde demnächst
berichten.

              In Vertretung
              gez. Forschbach
              Vizepräsident

Official letter of the circuit court in Cologne, August 24, 1937. Translation: "After examining the necessary documents of your application of 19.8.1937, there are no objections about the Arian descent of your future wife, Miss Isa Brühl.

The parish documents and the ancestry pass are returned to you. You shall supply me with your marriage documentation."

Official letter to Isa Paulus from the public prosecutor in the court in Stuttgart, August 28, 1946. Translation: "According to the information in your document you are not affected by the law of 5.3.1946 for the liberation of National-Socialism and Militarism."

Auf Grund der Angaben in Ihrem Meldebogen sind Sie von dem Gesetz zur Befreiung von Nationalsozialismus und Militarismus vom 5. 3. 1946 nicht betroffen.

Datum des Poststempels

Der öffentliche Kläger:

Isa and Heinz Paulus at a family celebration the the 1960s.

4   1940–1943

General Background

My father was discharged because Germany had "secured" Denmark, the Benelux countries, Norway, and France. Civilians in those countries were already affected by the war since they were occupied and had to do the bidding of the occupying forces and administration. Meanwhile, in Germany in 1940, after my father's discharge from the army, life for civilians proceeded more or less normally at first. Every day we went for walks in the woods and I played with the neighborhood kids in the street, since there were hardly any cars to disturb us. I attended the Catholic kindergarten, which was two blocks away.

In June 1941, about two years after the outbreak of the war and about a year after my father's return, the first of my two brothers, Bernd, was born. My father was back working in the Allianz insurance offices in Stuttgart, where he had started in 1937. He had switched from the automobile division to the personnel department.

During this time food was still readily available and bombing raids were limited. One of the reasons for Germany's relative well—being was the fact that it extracted goods and personnel from the occupied territories. Hitler was determined not to repeat the situation of World War I when a few years into the war the population suffered from a scarcity of goods. While Germany held control of the occupied countries, it exploited their wealth. The troops paid for goods with printed money that was not of much use, or they just helped themselves to crops, fruit, and vegetables in the fields. In addition, the German government imposed forced deliveries from the farms in the occupied countries, and their industrial firms were forced to produce for the German military. This was especially true for France.

As the war continued, however, life became more difficult for those on the home front. Food became scarcer and the bombing of German cities began. My mother gave birth to my second brother, Karl Heinz, in August of 1943, during heavy air raids on Stuttgart. Three weeks later my mother with her three children had to leave her husband in Stuttgart. We were evacuated to a rural village, Bad Ditzenbach, about fifty miles from the city, where we spent the rest of the war. By the end of the war, I was almost seven years old and the only kind of life I could remember was war.

My father's job during the war years changed from writing insurance policies and supervising personnel to becoming caretaker of the building. Since many of the company's employees had been drafted as soldiers, people were needed to take care of the building and to make sure that company property was not considered abandoned. The Allianz company, which was located in the middle of Stuttgart, had good bomb shelters. Whenever the air raid sirens howled, the employees all ran into the cellars.

We stayed in our apartment and my father came home every day for lunch if there was no attack.

Meanwhile the war was not going well for Germany, as is clear from the letters of soldiers and the entries such as the following:

Uncle Richard's diary, October 28, 1940

The Italians marched into Greece. Greece did not honor the promised neutrality, but allied itself with England. On November 9 in the evening, Neville Chamberlain, who was mainly responsible for the beginning of the present war, died in London.

Letters from the Front

The following is the first letter that my Uncle Karl wrote to his brother Rudolf in the field, somewhere on the Western front. All the previous letters were sent to Stuttgart since Rudolf had not yet been inducted. Karl was stationed in the barracks at that time near Stuttgart, and his brother Hermann was on furlough in Stuttgart. His youngest brother, Robert, who was only sixteen, had not yet been inducted into the army.

Letters from Karl to Rudolf

November 9, 1940, Stuttgart

Hermann left again yesterday. At about twenty minutes to 9:00 p.m. he put on his coat when the sirens started to go off. As we were instructed, we went down into the bomb cellar and there deposited our bodies on the floor till early morning. The all clear came at 1:00 a.m. Robert and I took Hermann to the station; his train left at 2:52. Thank God I caught a streetcar for the ride back, though it was already completely filled with people. With both hands I grabbed an outside handle (I looked like a South Pacific Islander climbing up a palm tree) and I rocked myself back to the barracks. At the top of Heilbronner Street, my innocent rear end knocked over a warning light—construction was going on right next to the tracks. Since the warning light did not consider being knocked over was fun, it took a huge triangle out of my pants and kept it as a souvenir. So, little brother, many greetings and do write.

November 27, 1940

When I think how much free time you have without much to do, since you are hiding out in such a godforsaken village, I think it is catastrophic how little you write. When I was still serving on the western front, I wrote home almost every day. You have adopted the role of the Great Silent One. This has to change. I can't compromise my good reputation for a ne'er-do-well brother! That it is lonely to keep watch on a solitary post I can understand. Are you practicing the art of "visiting your beloved through the window" [Fensterln].

Back on the Home Front

As sticklers for law and order, the Nazis were also quite willing to bend the rules when they wanted to, as the following diary excerpts show.

Aunt Resi's diary

After Kurt's wounds healed, he had a short rehabilitation furlough, but on December 1, 1940, he was to return to the front. I was not happy with this short stay; I wanted to change this to a permanent discharge. I tried many different venues. One of Kurt's cousins helped me. I managed to get an invitation to an officers' "party" in a villa in Aachen-Soers and Kurt's cousin escorted me there and introduced me to the responsible officer. I was allowed to visit him again the next day and express to him my concerns and worries, and he arranged everything.

On December 19, Kurt told me on the telephone that he had received an indefinite furlough. We celebrated Christmas very happily in our apartment in Aachen. Kurt then traveled to Stuttgart to start his new job at Bosch.

Mother's diary, August 16, 1940

Oma from Aachen was here for three weeks. For Margit she was the most devoted and patient playmate. She "paid for" that little village she brought as a present. Early in the morning, Margit crawled into Oma's bed to "build little houses," and every night before going to bed another village had to be built. Margit also takes her role as helper in the cleaning of the apartment very seriously, especially when clearing the table. She proceeds with the slow pace that she adapted in Schnittlingen, hanging on to the big wooden bread plate for dear life. She props the plate on her stomach, which she extends out. When I work in the rooms or the kitchen, she is always with me. She pushes up the sleeves of her dress, fetches the dust cloth, and dusts and cleans everything in her sight: the chairs, the floor, her dolls, and her Papa. But best of all she likes to wash down the apartment stairway to the floor below. This way, she can swish her little brush in the water with gusto.

One of the quirks of the Swabian Hausfrau culture that the rest of Germany thinks is "bizarre" is the "Cleaning Week" (*Kehrwoche*). Every Saturday two jobs had to be carried out: (1) Washing down the stairs from one's own apartment to the floor below. This meant alternate weeks, since there were two parties on each floor. (2) Sweeping the sidewalk in front of the house in the summer and clearing it of snow in the winter. Since our apartment building was a corner house, the sidewalk was quite extensive. This job, however, only had to be done once every ten weeks because there were ten parties in the building.

I do remember that certain women in the house monitored very carefully that every party "did their duty." When we children got old enough, this was our job, and I always let it slide till Saturday afternoon, which would lead my mother to remark: "Do it now! What will the neighbors say?"

Mother's diary, 1940

October

Margit has developed her own way of talking. She is a real Swabian. How could it be different with the daily company of her Swabian Mutti and her little friend Hans Peter, who speaks pure Swabian. Vati's High

*German hasn't a chance. On the contrary, he accommodates his speech
to that of his little daughter. The two of them are united in a deep friendship. She knows full well that Vati plays the best games:
Jucki-bimbi-bumbi! Ri-ra-rutsch!" And that she gets away with a lot with
him. When Vati tells her: "You are a big ragbag [Lumpensack]!"she runs
to me and makes sure that she is a good Margit, and then she runs
back to Vati with an impish grin on her face and pointing a finger says:
"Vati, you are a big* Lumpensack*." As cute as this sounds, we are worried that our parental authority is being undermined. We have to admit
often with a sigh that we thought that raising children was easier, because it is difficult to overestimate how much power such a little person
with these impish eyes has over adults.*

December 26
   *She doesn't show much interest in building anything. She loves to tear
things down and break them up. Even her most precious picture books
are not safe. She asks innocently: "Mutti, can I make the book kaput?"
which we parents already see as progress since till lately she tore them
up without asking permission. St. Nicholas who unexpectedly made no
great impression even with his stick and his very deep voice, brought
her a set of beautiful little village houses. She played with them with real
concentration all evening, but just when I wanted to express my joy
about it to Vati, we heard a suspicious noise from her play corner. When
we inspected the little village, we were shocked: she had either
smashed in all the roofs or torn them off. A "banschi" [paddle on the be-
hind]* was unavoidable. St. Nicholas took the toy back that evening, but
the angels in heaven took pity, glued it together again and gave it to the
Christ Child to return to the naughty girl. After these pranks we wonder
where this tendency for destructive rage comes from. It would be easier,
if she were a boy. One would say he will be an engineer. But a little girl?*

The first page of the next letter sent to Rudolf in the field is missing; it is clear that it was
sent before Robert was inducted and when Karl was on furlough.

End of December
*Thea: We sit here together comfortably at home. Everyone wrote out his
or her wishes for the next year.* [Note: This was a tradition the family followed every year; at the end of the year they read what they had written
the previous year.] *I am curious. I have just read what we wrote last
year. Some of my wishes were fulfilled.*
*Oma Barbara: I hope the New Year brings what I wrote out: my three
boys back strong and healthy. God bless you, my son Rudolf. Love,
Your Mom.*
Opa Achaz: My best wishes for the New Year. Your Father
Karl: Take care, old fellow. Your brother, Charles.

Mother's diary, January 1941

Margit is becoming an independent person. Until recently, she talked about "Margiti" and "me" when she talked about herself, but now she uses "I" correctly and independently.

She has discovered herself as a person. I heard it for the first time when I was putting laundry away and she ran to me and said, "Mutti, I help you." Her independent thinking and emotions are often expressed. We are preparing her for the birth of a sibling, and asked her, "Would you rather have a little brother or sister?" Her answer, "a little sugar cube."

Aunt Resi's diary

Kurt was transferred to Bamberg, which was attractive to me with its cathedral and its location, but especially because it had not been bombed. Kurt was looking for an apartment, but without success.

Then things became uncomfortable. Kurt thought that the bomb shelter near his mother's home was safer than the one in the Karlsburgweg. My mother-in-law's housekeeper insisted, however, that I not use her kitchen. I had breakfast in my apartment and nursed Ingrid. But I had to go to Karlsburgweg to bathe her, which meant during the day I had to stay with my parents, because I couldn't cook in the kitchen. Then I got an infection in both breasts and had to stay in bed. My poor mother had to commute daily between my mother-in-law's house and her own house to pick up Ingrid for bathing. Each way was about half an hour. She brought me all meals, looked after me, and did all the laundry. But then I got worse and the doctor admitted me to the hospital. After my discharge I moved—over Kurt's protestations—into my parent's home because I was too weak for the daily commute between the houses. This way my parents had their first grandchild close by and were very happy.

In the meantime, Kurt was living in a hotel while we waited for our new apartment. However, the owner refused to allow Ingrid to be with us till we could move into the apartment. I telephoned a professor in the women's clinic in Bamberg and he agreed to take care of Ingrid in the hospital till we could move. But when we arrived at night the town had been completely darkened and the route from the station to the hospital was quite a distance. The night nurse admitted Ingrid only after a long discussion and many tears. When I arrived the next day at 6:00 a.m. to nurse Ingrid, the same nurse was very relieved, because she thought we wanted to rid ourselves of our baby. The professor had forgotten to inform her about us.

I am now the happiest person in the world. We have a sweet child and Kurt doesn't have to go back to war. We have a beautiful apartment in a good location and a large garden, but most importantly we don't have to run every night to the bomb shelters and fear what will greet us when we come up.

Mother's diary, 1941

February

Vati is in the hospital with a stomach ache. That's all we are telling Margit of Heinz's appendix operation. I have never seen the child sob as pitifully on this first night when Heinz was gone. It was not a tired or stubborn child's crying, but a really heartfelt sobbing. What kind of notion about hospitals must she have? In any case, she misses her Vati tremendously.

At the same time, she developed whooping cough, which she caught from a friend. The doctor gave her two shots of Petein, which she accepted without a peep because, as she said: "Doctor has to clean my little behind." We spent a few weeks at a spa in the countryside for her to recover. There was just one relapse with a heavy cough, high fever, no appetite, and great mood swings. The last ten days have been very good and we used it for long walks in the spa park.

March

Margit shows a tremendous interest in everything that is happening around her. She is developing interesting connections of ideas. She wants to know precisely who made all the things: the houses, the ground, the snow, the air, Mutti and Vati, and the good God.

With great joy she plays hide-and-seek and "shopping." In the hide-and-seek game she is on the one hand not clever enough to change her hiding place, so she hides in the same corner where she was found before. On the other hand, she takes her time to flush out the person who is hiding even when she has already discovered them in order to prolong the game. When playing shopping, she addresses us with the polite form: "Sie, Papa was wollen Sie?" She then spends some time to wrap the requested goods—in the form of little blocks, in paper—and then hands them to the buyer, always at the same price of five marks.

During the war, families with young children were assigned a young girl as a household helper, like a nurse, nanny, or au pair. While the young men were in the military, the young girls had to serve a year in community service. They were assigned to families, hospitals, and old age homes. Our second au pair girl was Gretel, who became a photographer after the war.

Mother's diary

Margit is the most obedient when she can play on the balcony with water. She has discovered nudity. She is going through a "nude phase." Every night we discover her in her bed without any clothes. Gretel had taken her to the playground and before she could intervene, Margit had taken off her summer outfit and ran—in her birthday suit—down the street. This to the great joy of the people on the street and aboard the street car who watched Gretel chase the "little frog." What a glorious time of no cultural restrictions where everything still is allowed!

April 1941

Margit isn't much for caressing except in the evening. The ritual has one goal: to postpone bedtime as long as possible. During the day, when we ask her for a kiss, her laconic answer is "Have already given kisses." "When?" "Last Christmas." Her biggest joy is to roughhouse with Vati. She shouts with joy and is convinced that his job in life it to play with her. When he comes home, she greets him with: "My darling Vati is here again; my darling Vati is here again"

Note from Karl to my mother, April 1941

"I am convinced that the war won't last much longer."

Mother's diary, May 1941

We spent two-and-a half weeks with Heinz's mother in Aachen during which time Margit showed her best side. No moodiness or temper tantrums. That was quite astonishing considering our rather spoiled "sparrow." Even with all the visitors every day she was well-behaved and played quietly with her toys in a corner. She loved the big house and the large garden. The visitors and family members who live mainly in the Rhineland were enamored by her Swabian idioms and accent. [Note: This must have been during a lull in the bombing of the Rhineland.]

Birth of My Brother, Hans Bernhard (Bernd)

Mother's diary, Sunday, June 15, 1941, 3:03 a.m.

We have a little brother!!!

Sunday morning, June 15, 1941, Daddy fetches Margit and lets her look into the crib. Her first words, "Give it to me," end in big disappointment when she can't take him in her arms and play with him like she does with her dolls, because we promised her for so long: "You are going to have a little sister or brother." In general she is very affectionate with the baby, and we haven't seen any signs of jealousy yet, thank God. The first few days Bernd's constant crying was a special grief for her. She approaches us and says with trembling chin: "Mama, he's crying! Why don't you give him a little piece of sugar." She has already tried to feed him her bread and brought her building blocks for him to play with.

Excerpts from the marriage book written by my mother

Hans Bernd: "Your desired son is here," announced the midwife, even though we had not concentrated on the sex. If it had been the third birth, the situation would have been more ticklish. Heinz came into the room right after the first cry and acted like an experienced father. These were such glorious days when I was in bed and I became very conscious of a friendly world, which made me very happy. Considering that I recovered well and looked healthy in no time, everybody said: "The boy was good for you."

Note: Though the war was raging on three fronts—west, north, and east—the civilian population in the south of Germany at this time did not suffer much.

Excerpts from letters and cards for Bernd's birth show the general attitude toward the birth of boys versus girls.

Note from Kurt, my father's brother

"…since you have won the competition for the first boy, I wish for ourselves that our second child will also be the desired son and heir."

Note from the priest who married my parents

"Congratulations that this time according to plan a boy was born.… I will probably not have to serve in the military for the foreseeable future.… Our prayers and thoughts go to the many friends on the Eastern front, so far away from home. May God protect them."

Note from H.S. and wife, M.

"Heil, and victory! When I returned from a trip I found your promising announcement."

From an Allianz colleague
[fourteen colleagues signed this note]

We rejoice with you and your wife on the birth of Margit's brother. May Hans Bernd become a soldier in the future, but not a warmonger, but devote his time to the great works of peace, which will fall on the coming generation.

Letters from Hans Pardun, a priest friend of my parents
[a pastor in Düren, near the Belgian border, he became Bernd's godfather; the first letter below was written after he surfaced from the bomb shelter]

Dear four happy earthlings!

…here the situation is so dire because of the constant alarms. The last nine days we had to go into the bomb shelter every night while the bombs above us whistle loudly. Dreadful for the small children! This moment Radio Luxemburg has stopped broadcasting, which means there will be an alarm here in about fifteen minutes.

Dear young happy family!

I hope I can still say that, because the war brings so much misfortune and misery. I want to tell you that I was with you in spirit during the baptism. I put on a new shirt, thought appropriately about my godchild, and then went to a friend in Kempen in order to be able to drink a good cup of coffee in his honor. I can't tell you when I can come to Stuttgart. There is a new regulation that we may not leave the parish on Sundays. Last Sunday I was in Aachen. You have probably heard the worst from your mother. We have been lucky. The Kaiser Wilhelm High School was totally destroyed, engulfed by exploding and incendiary bombs. We had an unexploded bomb on our roof. Your mother's house was not damaged. Here, it is also terrible. Every night we spend in the basement. We have lost quite a few windows. In the last few days, there have been thirty-six dead in Krefeld, five of them parishioners.

So, now a big bow to the four persons: The happy mother...the proud father...the little daughter Margit...and my dear godchild, Hans Pardun (pastor)

Note from a colleague and good friend, who was an ardent anti-Nazi, from Breslau, East Prussia, now Wroclaw, Poland

Now we both have wives whose name is Isa, my son who I expect after a peace treaty will also be named Hans, we were both born in 1910, work at the Allianz, both keep a diary, and are devout Nazis! Considering the circumstances, mother and son seem to be doing well. During these times of excitement we would like to celebrate a community of four with you, if Heinz doesn't have to go play rough soldier again soon.... I am glad that the decision in the east has been made. That constant waiting was too trying. During the first night there were no Russian fighter planes here. I am an optimist and think they won't come, but lots of citizens of Breslau are so nervous that they are pissing in their pants. However, I find it better not to write about politics in a letter, but I yearn so much to sit down with you and talk for hours. We are still planning to go on our honeymoon trip that had to be scrapped so far, and we would like to come to south Germany and hopefully rendezvous with you.

We have a lot of work at Allianz. The salespeople run around wildly and insure everybody against everything, and we then have to do the work.

Being married is wonderful, but we live in uncomfortable circumstances. The lack of decent housing—like everywhere in Germany—is severe. We live in two rented rooms whose furniture leaves much to be desired. Even the landlady's title of nobility cannot change that. Everything is dirty. We do not like Breslau; even the opera is ugly. You hang your coats on the wall because there are no coat checkrooms, like in school. We are hoping that within two years after a peace treaty we can move. But since I am not convinced (nor is my wife) that the war will end soon, we'll probably have to be here for some time. I spent the week before in Berlin and was surprised how poor the food in the restaurants was. It seems to be better here, but Isa complains about the bad treatment in the shops. It is difficult for her since she is a newcomer and has to be registered in each shop before she can purchase anything and nobody knows her.

Note: While food was scarce, it was good to have a close relationship with merchants who occasionally handed out some extra rations. See Thea's letter about the milk.

Note from Isa's brother Hermann, January 30, 1941
Military mail (printed on a postcard that read
"Wherever we can defeat England, we will defeat England. The Führer")

Received your birth announcement and was pleased to hear it. Too bad, that Heinz was inducted again shortly before that. [This is not clear to me. Perhaps my father had to go to the authorities to prove that he did not have to serve again because of his TB.] *Anyway heartfelt greetings on the birth of your son and heir. I am doing well, am happy and cheerful. Greetings, Hermann*

Military letter from Dr. K. 11806 A, July

I have just received the birth announcement of your son, because I am deeply embedded in the East, beyond Smolensk. Is Heinz still at home or is he a soldier again? Since March I am the battalion doctor of a motorized infantry regiment; since June 22 we have been marching and fighting. The war in Russia is terrible; Poland and France were easy in comparison, Greetings, T.K.

Mother's diary, 1941

June

At Hans Bernd's baptism, June 29. How dreadful Margit behaved at the baptism! She was dressed like a little angel and behaved exactly the opposite. Obviously the ceremony was too long for her; she constantly shoved her obedient cousin Wolfgang. At the mother's blessing, she sat down on the kneeler next to me, but turned around to the praying parishioners and observed them all, which amused the group.

July

Every visitor gets greeted with the same two questions: "Have you seen my little brother yet?" and "Have you seen my new room?" She is very proud of her new room, but she doesn't like to play there by herself. When I care for Bernd, she is always right next to me and imitates my actions with her doll. She has also started to lord it over him from her three-year-old point of view and to mother him: "Be quiet, little one, Mutti will bring you something soon." But she also scolds him: "Now it's really time to sleep; I want to have some quiet time." Every morning she greets him with enthusiasm and then tells me excitedly: "He laughs because his sister comes to see him." And I believe that he likes these rather rough endearments of Margit; he laughs at her even if he just "cried terribly," as she maintains. She has reached the age of eternal questions: "Why? Why? Why?" all day long.

In Gretel's room she found a picture of the resurrected Jesus and asked what that meant. Gretel explained, "That is dear Jesus who ascended to heaven [the German word for "ascended," "auffahren," is related to "fahren," driving a car]*." Margit therefore wanted to know precisely: "With what kind of an auto?" We always threaten that if she* *leans out the window and falls down, she will be dead. When Gretel told her that she doesn't have a father anymore, she asked, "Did he fall out of the window?" Aunt Paula visited us. When she told Margit that she had no children, Margit thought about it, and then announced happily: "You know, auntie, I am going to ask the Christchild to bring you lots of children." But she was not done yet. She looked at Paula's glasses and then declared: "And I'll ask for glasses for them too." What primitive ideas about genetics!*

More Letters from the Front

In the letters that follow one sees a disturbing development of hatred and of dehumanizing "the other." The Nazis brainwashed the soldiers with their ideology so that the fighting men would find purpose in risking their lives. One enduring topic of all letters is the desire to get something to smoke. One of the few pleasures that my uncles had when they were growing up poor after my grandfather had lost his business was to have an occasional smoke. And now it was also one of the only treats they had at the front.

Letters from Karl on the Eastern front, 1941

July, to Rudolf

You can probably guess where I am. Wretched location, miserable roads. My mood is appropriate, little sleep, great strain, and sometimes nothing to devour.… We are driving out again. As you know that is often worse than marching, considering the bad road conditions. Can you send me a nail clipper?

August, to his sister Minni in Austria

Thank you so much for the cigarettes. I received them while I was lying in a foxhole, covered with dirt from head to toe, and was just saying to a comrade: "My, what I would give for a German cigarette." You can imagine how great my joy was. It was literally the straw for a drowning person, because at that moment, things were very bad. In the meantime luck has changed for this soldier and luck is smiling on me. I just ingested a twenty-egg pancake, but, who knows, tomorrow I might be glad if I get a piece of dry bread. Things are that unstable.

Middle of August, to his sisters Isa and Minni

Since the day before yesterday I have been in an Army hospital. While chasing a "Red Commissioner," I received a graze wound on my neck. None of my inner organs are affected. I hope to join my troop again in a few days. Write, but don't tell our parents.

August 30, to his brother Rudolf

Think about it. Absolutely nothing to smoke! I have told Thea—for whose sake I severed ties with three girls (she gave me a moral sermon!)—that she at least should provide me with smokes. And what is the result? After about three weeks a skimpy package of Ecksteins arrive! Catastrophic! Unfortunately I have also lost my pipe, so that I can't even smoke my fingernail clippings. And how are you doing, brother heart? Do you have a lot of planes flying over you? My wounds are healing well. I joined my troop a few days ago. I hope Hermann's wounds are not so bad also. Will the three of us see each other on Christmas?

September 24, to Rudolf

I don't have the G.K. [meaning unclear; "K" probably stands for Kreuz, cross, a military decoration] *and will never receive it since our commander thinks that a member of the administrative staff never merits it, even if he accomplishes heroic feats. I feel pissed upon here just as much as in France, constantly lying in shit, but I will never get any recognition. We can talk about it when we are home and healthy again. How are things with you? Do you experience as much upheaval? Write a bit more in detail. Otherwise, I am doing well.*

October, to his sister Isa

Thanks for your package, the letter, and the Pralines (which arrived safe and sound). Please start the process for my dismissal from the army, so I may enter the family business. But most probably it will not be granted. Anyway, Dad can carry on till I come home, since in my opinion the war will be over soon.

November 1, to Rudolf

Thanks for the letter of October 30 and my sincere thanks for the cigarettes. Perfect timing, I haven't had any cigarettes for days. Could you buy a watch for me? Urgent, urgent, my boy!

November 2, to Isa

Thanks for the cigarettes. Since we always lack any kind of smokes, you can imagine with what joy I opened the package. Now the mail is getting through faster, after we hadn't received any in four weeks. Did you send the toilet articles already? If possible, send me a whole travel toilet kit; you can send packages up to one kg. We are experiencing real, wet cold; miserable fall weather. Snow and rain mixed! The streets look like cabbage fields.

Did Heinz get redrafted—again? As I heard from mother, you have to run into the cellar more often lately. In that sense we are better off: we lie down flat and everything is fine. At night we don't worry anyway.... I'll send you money in the next few days to get me wash and shaving things. If the twenty reichsmarks are not enough, let me know.

November, to Isa

The rolls were wonderful. During the last few weeks, I am crazy for things like this. We live in halfway sane quarters and will march the day after tomorrow to.... Most probably, new fighting. When the operations

have been concluded, we should expect some furlough.
[Signed] *Obergefreiter* [a small promotion to private first class]

November 22, to my parents
   *"...the town in which L.R. was killed, is well known to me. We were
stationed there during one of the first attacks on our regiment. The first
one of our division who got it, was our boss, who, exactly like me a few
weeks later, went on an exploratory drive with the motorized bicycle and
got caught unawares in a Russian ambush. The two technicians whom
he had with him, escaped at the last minute; however one of them had
to leave his bike behind. The second, our adjutant, was killed on the infamous runway ("infamous" because of the often daily air attacks by the
Reds; therefore we also call it bomb runway). While we were driving in a
convoy, to follow our tanks, we were shot at from the forests, which
reached all the way to the edge of the road. And we had some deaths.
We of course immediately got down from our vehicles and attacked. The
SS that followed us cleaned out the woods a few kilometers deep on
both sides, but sustained heavy casualties. Mass grave with sixty men,
etc. Whoever at that time was left behind alone to guard his disabled vehicle was a dead man. How often did we come upon vehicles that had
been disabled the day before and that we wanted to tow in, but found instead the whole crew dead.*
   *Only two days ago, we had two more dead soldiers who were slain by
partisans behind the front. Of course the next day we immediately sent
a punishment expedition and shot any Russians who happened to be
near the crime scene, after we made them dig their graves first. In Russia, you are not safe anywhere. Therefore our side is especially severe
in our outings. In the local market place you can see partisans every
day, who—to deter further attacks—have been strung up on a tree limb.
Actually it is good, when in times of doubt, that one kills more than less.
I believed very differently before, but since I was ambushed myself by
one of these cunning dogs, I have become very cautious....*

In November 1941, my mother started a diary about Bernd.

Mother's diaries

   *What joy! Sunday, June 15, 1941, at 3:03 a.m. the little brother ar-
rived. "The longed-for son," said the doctor proudly. He is like all babies
a little wrinkled worm—mostly with his eyes shut tight. It took about eight
days before he slept through the night. At five weeks he smiled the first
time; this time I was the recipient. What bliss; the baby's first smile. I
nursed for five months, but added fruit juices and vegetables after three
months. Unfortunately we don't have much choice in fruit and vegetables. That's war. There are no oranges or bananas. So, it is carrots every day. Bernd already looks yellow from it.*
   "Our little one," as Margit calls him condescendingly, is very interested

in his environment. Vati is his favorite.

November

   How good Margit is with her little brother! She insists on being present at his daily bath. She "pours the water in." A few weeks before the birth we watched how she pushed the empty pram back and forth for half an hour. When we approached her we saw that she had piled all kinds of toys in the pram, something that was strictly forbidden. But we couldn't be angry when she told us innocently, "But I want to give all this as a present to my little sister." She and we were expecting a girl. Margit sometimes still insists: "Now I want a younger sister, but a big one." Her favorite activity is helping others. She feels really important and irreplaceable then. The other day she told me: "You know, Mutti, I have a lot of work, but it is nice of you to help me so much." And when she is all grown up, she wants to do everything for me. She mentioned that there would be no more work for me. Yes, when you are grown, dear daughter....

   Did I already mention that she wants to be known as a girl from the Rhineland like Vati, in contrast to her Swabian Mutti and nanny. She finds an excuse in any sticky situation she gets into: "But I am only a little girl" is her standard answer when she gets scolded for her misbehavior. And she takes full advantage of the "rainbow mood," the first heavenly minutes after a bad emotional thunderstorm.

   She has no sense for money. After she tore up twenty marks in seventeen little pieces, which took two hours to glue together again, I found my streetcar pass today like "chopped vegetables." When I sigh about money problems, she advises me to buy money in the city or to order what I need from the Christchild.

December 6

   Yesterday St. Nicholas visited us. Margit accompanied me to the glass door. I could feel from her trembling hands how much this encounter with this imposing Holy Man meant to her. But she wasn't cowed. Very cute; with what seriousness and enthusiasm she answered his questions, quite loud and clear, as I had advised her: "Grüss Gott, dear Nikolaus." She then introduced everyone: "This is Vati; this is the little brother; and this is Gretel [the au pair]."

   First Vati and Gretel were interrogated while Margit watched without moving and with great interest. When Vati was asked to sing a soldier's song and he constantly tried to make excuses, she whispered to him with great excitement: "Vati, you have to sing." She herself sang with the loudest voice and as off key as possible. To the question why she destroyed the camera, she answered: "Because I can't take photos yet," and when St. Nicholas wanted to know why she made such a fuss every night when she had to go to bed, her answer was: "Because then I am always allowed to stay up a bit longer."

The contrast between life at home, as my mother portrayed it in her diary, and what was heard about in letters from the front was striking. It was clear by Christmas 1941 that the war was not going as Hitler had planned and it was going to last much longer than expected. The cruelty of killing and the dehumanizing aspects of fighting were becoming increasingly apparent, especially for those who were in the east. The deplorable conditions that the soldiers on both sides of the conflict endured might best be described in the words of Uncle Karl who wrote regularly.

Letter from Karl to Isa, December 6, 1941

I was pleasantly surprised and overjoyed about the cooking skills of my godchild. Unfortunately I ate it all up at once, so that today, I am sitting here empty. To be honest, I was really counting on mail today. But, as usual in Russia—it seems to be the routine—the trucks with the mail got bogged down again in the snow (as an aside: so far, they have gotten stuck every day, so this is perfectly normal). I can already imagine a sad Christmas, in a dirty hole, full of lice, without mail, and no light. But perhaps we'll be marching by then.

But to make sure that the completion of my first quarter century does not pass unnoticed, I procured a samovar for us, in which our old woman has to cook the tea tonight, and we will have fried potatoes to go with it.

It is truly cold here. Minus 32 degrees Celsius [-25 Fahrenheit]; accompanied by an icy wind. Normal temperatures range from minus 40 to 45 degrees. The snow is one to two meters high. Today an express courier (three men because of the danger of partisans and wolves) returned without having fulfilled their mission. The men were sent three days ago with a sled and our two best horses; they have been walking in circles since then. They couldn't use the map, since everything had been snowed over and they could only orient themselves with the compass. Their nostrils were frozen and the horses had long icicles hanging from their noses.

…Just returned from a festive dinner. What was lacking in quality, I made up in quantity. At least my stomach is almost full. I can't say that I am not hungry, because in the last few weeks I have developed a hearty appetite. Why don't you ask mother for some of my money and buy Margit a nice Christmas present. When you have the time, you can tell me what you bought.

Letters from Karl

To my father, December 13, 1941

What is the status of your reclamation? Are you completely free now or only for the time being? Hopefully, they won't send you to England. What can we expect in 1942? Iran; Iraq; Suez Canal; Egypt; or the Island?

To my mother, December 1941

Your package with the washcloth was received three days ago already. We were marching, that's why I couldn't write before today. Ev-

erything arrived in good shape. I am sorry that the purchase of the items created so much work for you. If I had known that you can't get these items any more in Stuttgart, I wouldn't have asked you to buy them for me. That you also sent me toothpaste, and your own toothbrush, is really nice of you. I am now blaming myself, because I could have continued to clean my teeth—as I have done for a while—with my handkerchief. If I am lucky, I can clean my teeth every two to three days.

The people in Stuttgart will have bought everything up for Christmas so that nothing is left in the stores. I sent you the money a few weeks ago, I hope you got it. What we feared seems to have become reality. In a few days we will see more action and most probably we'll be in the middle of shit during Christmas. We envy our buddies who are in the hospital because of dysentery, jaundice, or pneumonia. Comically, I am always healthy.

Our quarters are truly catastrophic: all wretched hovels. I established my "quarters" in a drafty hovel. Where a window is supposed to be, straw bales fill up the frames. On an incredibly dirty bed frame lies a ninety-year-old man, who sighs all day and all night long. He stands with 1¾ legs already in the grave. I did manage to eject a two-ton sow from the room by grabbing her hind legs and positioning my rifle in the vicinity of her main artery. Grandmother, mother, and the four piglets erupted—as if on command—into a wild shriek. They congratulated themselves afterwards that they were successful in saving their one pride from my murderous hands. I achieved my goal, but the odor will stay with us for a long time. When the youngest child this afternoon started to poop in the middle of the floor, I screamed at him so loudly that he fell onto his behind.

The people have no night pot, and to go outside is too cold, therefore they always shit on the living room floor. The young mother also has the habit of spitting as long and as much as possible onto the floor; but she has ceased doing that since I arrived. My application for a discharge will probably not be granted, because for the eastern front the rules are especially strict.

Mother's diary, December 17, 1941

Margit is in high anticipation of Christmas. With the help of Vati she wrote a long wish list to the Christchild. She has a darling little gingerbread house on which she finds every morning a tiny figure, which gives her great joy. And every night she is allowed to open a new window on her Advent calendar and sing carols with Mutti and Vati: "Ihr Kinderlein, kommet," "O, Christkindlein, komm," and "Auf dem Berge, da geht ein Wind." I hear her also singing these songs during the day. Unfortunately she is completely unmusical. The text is always right, occasionally she changes the words to better fit her grammatical sense, but the melody is created completely anew. A few days ago, I told her the whole story of Christ's birth with the help of pictures sent by our priest friend Hans, who *was of the opinion that she needed some religious instruction when she told him after he said that God was in heaven: "Oh, I didn't know that yet". Margit listened very carefully.*

Letters from Karl to Isa

After Christmas, 1941

I received your two packages with the egg liquor on Christmas Eve. Both were excellent and were imbibed promptly in honor of the day. I have also received the package with the cookies, the comb, the face cream, and the little cup for shaving cream.... I ate the cookies today for breakfast, because today we didn't get any troop food. We are still on patrol…have little time….

End of December, 1941

I am enclosing the tin box. I have also enclosed two pairs of socks. Please give them to mother and tell her, if they can no longer be darned, to unravel them and use them for the wool yarn. Nothing new.

In 1941, households were asked to make an inventory of their belongings in case they lost them in the war. Items were written on a preprinted form: "My Possessions and Belongings."

Proof of the belongings of the household of Dr. Heinz Paulus. "To be filled out carefully and conscientiously! Proof for the acquisitions' prices, like bills and receipts to be put into an envelope, if possible photos of the furniture and the most valuable appliances should be included. For bigger purchases special lists should be made. Two witnesses are necessary to notarize the veracity of the claims. Two copies must be made, one should be taken to the bomb shelter during an air attack in the air protection suitcase while the second copy should be deposited somewhere else."

The individual items were preprinted and the owner added the numbers. Short excerpts follow (the original list is seven pages long):

A. Furniture and appliances: All furniture was listed with the purchase price, the year of purchase, and the kind of wood from which the furniture was made.

1. Bedroom: from furniture to linens, carpets, curtains, baby outfits, lamps.

2. Living room: same as above; books, desk accessories, wastebasket.

3. Dining room: same as above.

4. Hallway, bathroom: same as above, bathtub, sink, gas heater.

5. Kitchen, pantry: same as above, pots, pans, iron, cutlery, stepladder, kitchen scale, coal bins, plant stand, gas stove, no refrigerator or record player.

6. Children's room: children's furniture, beds, changing table, curio stand.

7. Balcony, cellar, attic: nothing was filled in.

8. Miscellaneous: four suitcases, vacuum cleaner, one radio, camera, tool kit, sewing machine, musical instruments or hair dryer.

B. Paintings, other art pieces, antiques: Original paintings and etchings with names of artists and purchase price; prints, pottery items, Japanese silk screen, crucifixes, crystal plates.

C. Jewelry, gold: man's gold watch (family heirloom).

D. China, flatware, crystal: China for twenty-four, flatware for twenty-four, coffee cups and saucers for forty, crystal bowls, fruit bowls, beer glasses, serving spoons and forks, eighteen vases, twenty-four wine and champagne glasses.

E. Linens: twenty-two tablecloths for dinner and coffee, thirty-six napkins, thirty-six wash, hand, kitchen towels, seventeen sheets for adults and children, blankets, three eiderdowns, baby crib.

F. Clothing: *Men:* six suits, one winter coat, two lighter coats, ten shirts, five pajamas, five sets of underwear, ten ties, four pairs shoes/boots, two hats, two pairs of gloves, two sweaters, twenty pairs of socks, two shawls; no uniforms. *Women:* one ski outfit, one formal dress, two suits, six wool dresses, four silk dresses, one leisure outfit, two robes, underwear worth 120 marks, six shoes, two skirts, five blouses, twenty pairs of stockings, three handbags, five umbrellas, six pairs of gloves, three winter coats, two lighter coats, seven pullovers and sweaters, one fur stole worth fifty-five marks. *Children:* five winter coats, three summer coats, four wool dresses, two wool jackets, six baby wool jackets, three leotards, eleven pairs of stockings/socks, six pairs of boots, five pairs of sandals, three training suits, seven panties.

G. Special: The only thing mentioned here was that the apartment had been renovated. Year not clear.

Two witnesses:

> *I certify that I have verified that the main items in this list exist and I am willing to swear under oath to its veracity if an insurance claim is made.*

[Note: This list was never witnessed and was never used since my parents' apartment survived intact.]

Uncle Richard's diary, an overview of 1941

Bought one-year-old horse, "Hans," in Steinekirch, March 5, price: 18,000 marks.

Since March 2, 1941, the Catholic Weekly has not been allowed to be published. Also, on this date, Germans march into Bulgaria.

April 6, this morning, German troops crossed the Greek Border. Belgrade was heavily bombed. Italian troops also marched into Yugoslavia.

April 17, the whole Yugoslav army capitulated.

From April 25 to 29, our niece Maria and her two children were here before they joined her husband who had been transferred to Prussian Holland.

June 4, the entire population of Schnittlingen was X-rayed to detect tuberculosis.

The war with Russia started June 22.

On July 21 the Cistercian monastery Mehrenau, near Bregenz, Austria, was closed by the authorities, and on July 31 the Cistercian abbey in Birnau near Überlingen followed suit.

On December 7, Japan declared war on the United States. The fight-

ing started in our time zone at 10:00 p.m.

1942—The Third Year of War

The experiences of the soldiers and their families at home were worlds apart, as the diary entries below make clear.

Mother's diaries, January 1942

[Bernd] still does not like to be alone, but likes to be entertained. He is watching Margit at play from his bed. She came running to me excitedly the other day, pointed to her rear end and said: "The little one has his head there," meaning he had turned completely around in his bed. His head was—Margit thought—where his rear end should be.

* * *

Little girls are a combination of naivety and ingenious manipulation. Margit has taken all the sheets off her bed again. To my question, Who did that?, she answered, "the seven dwarfs." And once she didn't answer at all when I asked her about something bad that she had done. When I insisted with my question: "Who did this?", she hesitantly asked, "What will you do, if I tell you?" She has also developed the bad habit of asking every visitor: "What did you bring me?" I have strictly forbidden her asking this question, and she formally followed the order by asking the next visitor: "Auntie, what do you have in your purse?"

Letter from my mother's sister Minni to her brother Karl

[one of the few surviving family letters written to soldiers at the front]

Lochau, February 1, 1942

First off, my heartfelt congratulations on your promotion! Did you do anything special, or was it for your long and loyal service against the dreadful Russians. On January 5, I sent you a small package of pralines. On January 12, I sent a small bottle of liquor and cigarettes, but the package came back after a few days. Most probably it became a victim of the new package restrictions. I will wait till the restrictions are lifted before I try again.

And what are you getting from the wool collection that took place in the whole Reich? By the way, how are you doing? Do you have enough pencils, writing paper, and fountain pens? Can you use fountain pens? Are you still in the winter quarters that you furnished on December 25 or did you have to move again? Hermann wrote me saying that our parents were informed, at some point, that you had been "killed in action."

Do you have a paperback to read? Do you want one? Perhaps I can scrounge one up. Paul has now also been called up. It's going to be hard for him. Being older and with a family makes it so much harder. My eternal hope is that you will be sent back. That's my hope. When we sit safe and secure in our homes, lie in our warm beds, and eat ordinary meals, I would like to share my riches with you. Our concern for you courageous ones weighs heavily and oppressively on us. All our good wishes for you are included in my daily prayer.

Günther [her five-year-old son] *is very cute at the moment. This morning he was musing: "Mammi, I was wondering what kind of car I should buy when the war is over. Buying a truck doesn't make sense, because you have to load it with stuff. I think the best car would be a taxi or a children's bus. But if it is still winter and if it snows when the war is over, how will I make it down from the mountain with my taxi?" Those are Günther's worries and considerations.*

Peppi [her husband] *is pretty sure that he will not be drafted. As long as we are healthy and keep our nerves, we are satisfied.*

Heartfelt greetings from your Minni, Peppi, and Günther

Difficulties Intensify on the Eastern Front

The following letters show that the situation in the East was becoming more dire and that the soldiers had completely dehumanized the enemy.

Letter from Karl to my father, January 11, 1942

Already greetings for a happy birthday. I hope you are still at home and aren't running around somewhere in the world. Everything is the same with us. Lots of lice and no mail.

Letters from Second Lieutenant Karl Brühl [another battlefield promotion]

To Richard Fischer in Schnittlingen/Alb bei Geislingen/Steige, January 22, Russia

The rolls were first class and I devoured them as rare delicacies and with great gusto. Not much new to report from here. Our unit is quiet with the exception of occasional shootings and skirmishes. The cold will have reached its lowest point. Last night it was -48 degrees Celsius [about -54 Fahrenheit]. *We expect this to last till the middle of February and then it will improve. In general I feel fine and my lice seem to like it too, since they are reproducing faster than rabbits.*

To Minni, January 24, Russia

The letters that I wrote in November arrived so fast, because I had the opportunity to post them at an airport. The next ones will probably take four weeks again. Here, two brothers, two lieutenants, were killed in action the same day. In this respect, our family has been spared so far. But perhaps we'll have to pay the "blood tax" also. In our unit, with the exception of a bit of a skirmish, everything is quiet. When I think of the Christmas packages, my mouth waters. That doesn't mean however, that you should send me more, I just wanted to express my appreciation and thanks.

To Rudolf, February 10 [sent to France]

Enclosed is yesterday's army report. This should give you an idea how things stand here. In front of our base there are hundreds of dead. None managed to slip through. What do you think? You know, where

there is a Swabian on patrol, the Russians break their necks!
P.S. By the way, I received the Iron Cross this winter.

To Rudolf, February 16
Boy, you were lucky with your furlough. I can't even imagine what it
would be like to have a free Sunday, let alone a vacation. I'm just happy
if I don't have to lie in shit all day and half the night. I don't agree with
you about getting a pocket watch. The most practical thing here is a
wristwatch, because we can't take our pants off and put the pocket
watch on the nightstand every night. Here in Russia, I haven't taken off
my clothes more than twenty times. I sleep in my day clothes. I would
have long since lost a pocket watch or would have crushed it. And at
night when I am called to stand guard or go on patrol duty, how would
that work? Or when I sit on our moped, with that long coat wrapped
around my legs and buttoned up, how could I reach my pocket and extri-
cate my watch in a hurry (and speed for us is the alpha and omega).
Hey, young fellow, you are still a young and green trooper. You have no
idea about the nuances of a month-long nomadic life in the most primi-
tive conditions! I did survive, however, the last few very hard days (you
did read the report) and I hope that the winter will pass well.
P.S. Do you honestly think that with the tremendous piles of snow we
could still use mechanized transportation? We do everything now with
sleighs and horses.

To Isa, February 25
I was very pleased that you wrote to me in such detail. News from
home interests me enormously. I am doing fairly well. Since the last de-
fensive fights, I spend most of my time inside where it is warm. Also, it is
not so cold anymore. Only the lice are still with us. I just can't get rid of
these pests. I now have nearly all my things together. Your toiletry bag
has been especially practical. It's always a pleasure when I take it out.
You will have thanked Maria in my name for her washcloth. I am glad
that I have it, because I mainly wash myself from water in a narrow, cy-
lindrical pail.
I developed my enormous appetite only since I arrived in Russia.
There must be an underlying illness, because, as you know, I was a
very picky eater at home. But when I return home, I will eat every night
an extra portion of Spätzle. That is the only hope that carries me
through.
What is the news from Robert? Will he be commissioned soon? Do
you know where Paul [his brother-in-law] *was transferred? We hear a*
rumor that we will spend the next winter in Russia as well. Lovely expec-
tations, aren't they?
To Heinz, March 5
You will have heard the result of my application for a furlough.
Negativ!

Everything is the same here. The usual gunfights, occasionally visits from planes, that's all. But our life is distinctly primitive. After we have completed our second year in Russia, we will have gotten used to it, I hope. Now we have lived nearly a year without Sundays. Strange! I cannot even imagine a normal life. At the moment I am involved in digging ditches and building bunkers.

To Minni, March 30
The expected Spring has not arrived. During the last change of location, we needed twelve hours to go three kilometers [1.4 miles]. Our field kitchen literally sank into the snow. We live in bunker cellars at the moment. No heat, no light, no water. There is not a house left in the village. Fortunately, it isn't so bitter cold anymore. The feared Spring outbreaks are making their appearances: boils, pus abscesses (lice), etc. I have to go every day to the district office to get new bandages. An increasingly smaller percentage of us are being granted furloughs. I reckon it will take another ten years till it is my turn. As soon as the swamp period is over, we will probably start new attacks. No word about replacements for us…. As long as I am in Russia's shooting gallery, I don't have to think of these things. When I come home, I'll first cure my rheumatism.

Did I write you already that a few weeks ago, we got some thirty- to forty-year-old men as replacements? They arrived the day before the big mess. Today, none of them are alive. The poem [not attached] *is not mine, but from a buddy. He composed it on Christmas Eve, shortly before he went out on an exploratory expedition. He was a corporal and the leader of the troop, and was ambushed by the Russians.*

Mother's diaries, 1942

February 14
Tomorrow Bernd will be eight months old. He doesn't like to lie in his bed anymore; he works his body so long till he can sit up, stretching his legs through the slats…. He has learned how to cuddle. He distinctly says: "ba-ba," which endears him to Daddy. How poor are these notes about the child's development in relationship to the reality. It is indescribable how much joy and elation we experience every day from such a sweet little boy.

March
This winter with its endless snow was a delightful time for the children. Margit always plays outside; she helps with shoveling snow, rolls around in the piles of snow, and is sassy and independent enough to join other older kids in sledding.
Margit does not like to go to bed anymore. She uses all kinds of ruses to extend her staying up time: "I'll check the thermometer what time it is," and then she announces with a serious expression: "It is only 3:00 p.m." I read to her every evening from a fairytale book that she got for

Christmas. She doesn't understand the whole story yet, but is very impressed by certain points: "Why does the star child [Sterntalerkind] not have parents anymore? Why did they die? Will it get a new pair of parents?" When I asked her: "Do you have a good or bad Mutti?" she didn't answer, but caressed me so lovingly that I was very touched.

She has gone to the theater three times. She enjoyed many individual scenes, but couldn't grasp the whole story. In the morning before one of the performances I washed her especially well and told her that only clean children could attend. When we entered the theater, she declared loudly: "Yes, all the kids have been washed."

On Opa's sixty-ninth birthday, her performance was not a total success. She was dressed as Red Riding Hood, but she immediately stormed back to me after she had given Opa her little basket. She would only recite her little poem after a lot of talking to:

> I am Little Red Riding Hood
> > and I come walking from the wood.
> Today I am not going to Oma,
> > Instead I am visiting Opa.
> I bring a cake and some wine to your fest
> > and I wish for you all of the best.

April

It "smelled" again. Margit's expression when somebody passes gas. My question whether she was responsible was emphatically denied. Her counter question: "Mutti, did you do it?" was also denied. But Margit wasn't done yet. She shook her head pointing to the picture of the Holy Family and said, with no emotion, "Perhaps it was them."

As an excuse for misbehaving, lately she uses this answer: "Because I am such a big imp" or "Because I am so dumb." She does this while smiling so innocently that our initial anger dissipates and she escapes the planned punishment. I have talked a lot about her misbehaving and our inconsistent behavior in punishing her, but to tell the truth I have to say that she gets paddled quite a bit, especially from me. The good thing about her is that she does not sulk or bear a grudge. After the storm is over she has only one worry and that is that one dries her tears and loves her again. Easter was especially nice. With great patience Margit searched the apartment for the tricycle that had been promised her. At long last she found it on the veranda. Her joy was without limit.

March 15

The three-quarter-year-old young son is sitting up and kneeling the whole day in his bed. He is in a period of good behavior. Visitors remark that one cannot imagine him crying. Like a little philosopher he greets the world: first he takes his time to observe his surroundings and then he smiles.

March 15

It is so nice when the little one crawls through the whole apartment in his training pants! What Margit only learned after she could walk, he grasped in three days: to crawl and slide in all directions. When it comes to eating, he is a champion. He eats lunch together with us now: soup, potatoes, vegetables, or a soufflé. He eats everything in sight, oranges, dates, and chocolate. [My mother wrote before that tropical fruits were no longer available?!]. *He loves to chew on bread crusts. He and Vati have a special relationship. They can talk to each other for hours: Vati starts with a few sounds and Bernd answers, "bababba, mamama," back and forth with both of them having a good time and perfect understanding.*

The next letters from Uncle Karl seem to show a growing lack of empathy in the soldiers for their comrades. Were their feelings muted because they hadn't been able to afford to feel all that they had experienced?

Letters from Karl

To Minni, April 2

....when we returned to our so-called lodgings, I received your two peppermint packages. We attacked for thirty-six hours. Of course victorious! —Have pushed back the Russians again a good piece. I operated as the leader of the communications staff. Two of my operators got it. One received a shot through his steel helmet, the other a grenade at full force. Myself, I lucked out again. Only received a grenade fragment to my rifle. But I am still frozen through and through. Will ask the doctor later for quinine. At the moment I lodge with my squadron in a domed cellar. Here again, the Russian artillery did not leave a house standing. —I need to close here hoping to sleep a few hours before the next dance.

To Family Fischer-Brühl [three siblings of my grandfather and Uncle Richard, who was married to one of them], *April 12*

A thousand thanks for the two packages with the cured meats. It was a great pleasure to enjoy this greeting from home. The snow is starting to melt quite a bit. Of course, it will take a while till all the snow is gone. At the moment it is fairly quiet here. The Russians seem to be preparing for their defense. Do you still have the Polish guy? [Polish and Russian prisoners of war were put to work on farms and on construction projects.] *I am sure you are going to have a lot of work.*

To his family, May 15

Thanks a million for the two packages of cigarettes. I had just reached the lowest point and was therefore pleasantly elated. I joined my troop again yesterday. The beautiful days in the convalescent home passed too fast. But I took full advantage of them and avoided any unnecessary movement. And now I will savor them as long as possible. The roads are slowly drying out. Perhaps we'll see action again soon, as in the South. Marvelous, how the Reds get their thrashing, isn't it? For sure, there will be another surprise in the near future, because this time we can't allow these guys to escape again. Otherwise we will still be here next winter and for that I have no desire whatsoever.

In the meantime the effects of the war affected our nuclear family directly. In her interview with Dr. Doerr, my mother described my father's tuberculosis, which changed his and our family's life forever.

Mother's interview with Dr. Doerr

In May 1942 Heinz was diagnosed with tuberculosis, which led to six lengthy stays in TB sanatoria: Brilon/ Wald; Berlin; Schömberg; Schönblick near Schwäbisch Gmünd (twice); and Wehingen-Oberhausen.

Shortly before Heinz was drafted into the army, his X-rays showed that his lungs were healthy. Therefore he developed TB during the first harsh winter in Czechoslovakia. The army immediately accepted the verdict and gave him a 100 percent disability classification. That's why he was not redrafted when the war continued.

In May 1942 my father went to Berlin for a thorough examination by a specialist and with the hope of being cured of his tuberculosis. This was not possible because at that time Germany did not have penicillin or any other antibiotics that could cure the disease. He suffered his whole life from TB and was sent to a sanatorium when the TB was contagious. Every year he could do fewer things like walking uphill or walking for any length of time because his breathing had become more labored. One of his lungs was collapsed and could not be restored. Till we three children moved out of the house, we had to be X-rayed every half year to make sure that we had not contracted the disease. We also did not use the same dishes or cutlery as my father when he was suspected of being contagious.

Mother's diary

May 1942

Vati is on the way to Berlin and Margit is spending some time with me in Bad Dürrheim. She had many colds this winter and a bad case of the flu in April. The plan was for her to cure herself out in the good air of the Black Forest. Because I was worried about Bernd, due to the many air attacks, I went back to Stuttgart after two days. Margit stood outside the bus and smiled and waved, not a trace of homesickness. The Limburger family and their two children, around Margit's age, gave her a wonderful home. After I returned in three weeks to pick her up, she greeted me at the train station, tanned, with rosy cheeks and a little flower garland in her hair. She obviously was very pleased to see her Mutti again. These were three wonderful weeks for her, since she could spend almost all her time outside. If we had only a playground or park near us in Stuttgart!

May 16, from Bad Dürrheim [a card written by an adult in the old German script]
Dear Mutti,

My best wishes for Mother's Day and many dear greetings from Margit. Greetings to the little brother.
Margit

Letter from my mother to Karl

I am sending you this little package that I received for Mother's Day. Your hunger for sweets can never be filled. Thanks for the greetings from the convalescent home. What kind of strange situation is that? I hope that you were not sick. I am very worried about Heinz. The TB that he brought back from the military broke out again a little while ago, on a small scale. It is good that it was discovered immediately. He can't be in the fresh air much and he does not receive extra rations of milk or eggs, all of which are scarce. Right now he is with a famous doctor in Berlin, who promised to cure him again shortly. I hope he meets with success. Heinz feels OK; he does not notice any effects of the illness. They found the spot during a routine X-ray. His last X-rays in March had shown nothing. So, we are hopeful that the illness was recognized at its beginning.

Letters from Uncle Karl deal more and more with the lack of food for the troops, either because of logistical or transportation problems or because the German government was running out money.

Letters from Karl

To the family in Schnittlingen, June 9

The cured meat was wonderful. We moved our position again. The Russian here is very active. Every night we get strafed by planes. And we feel the artillery also. Besides these minor trivialities, I am doing fine. Weather is gorgeous. I am surprised that you can't get any farmhands to help out. Can't you get a prisoner of war? After all, we have enough of them.

For the first time, Uncle Karl uses the expression "the Russian" (*der Russe*), instead of "the Russians" (*die Russen*). This was the pejorative term German soldiers used for the enemy, the Russians. Later, the word "Ivan" was also used with the same connotation.

To Isa, June 11, Eastern front

Many, many thanks for the box of chocolates. The thing with the convalescent home was this: I was not sick or wounded, I just relaxed for eight days behind the front lines. I am doing fine, but at the moment Russian planes are over us again.

Mother's diaries

August 8, 1942

Today Bernd walked by himself for the first time, a few times half the length of the room. Heinz and I marveled at him like the greatest miracle in the world, and kept on sending him back and forth between us. His sudden accomplishment of walking astonished us since Margit learned it step by step, every day a few more. We are not amazed at his liveliness, considering how much he eats, but it is becoming dangerous. The last few weeks he dived out of his bed with two perfect headers. My shock was surely stronger than his pain, but I have to get used to the idea that I no longer have a baby but a growing boy.

September 1942

Our "Butzimann" [Bernd's known and beloved pet name] *is popular with everybody due to his sunny and happy disposition. He hardly ever cries, makes his rounds of the whole apartment, often falls down, but never minds, and always smiles at everybody. Oma Brühl looked after the two kids together with Gerda* [our third assigned au pair] *when we went for an eight-day trip. Oma declared Bernd the most well-behaved of her six grandkids, and said she would be willing to take care of him more. Good thing, you little man, that you don't understand praise yet, you would become too proud! His favorite play partner is still Vati; he loves the rough and tumble, which I consider too wild, and he shouts for joy—the rougher the better. He generally loves his sister and caresses her, but sometimes shows real signs of jealousy.*

September 1942

Margit is in kindergarten. She loves it there and tells me every after-noon what they have done. It was cute when she answered my question about what role she played in the performance of the Dornröschen with: "You should know, I played the circle." She also participated in the Cor-pus Christi procession in church and was obedient during the whole long ceremony. Her favorite activity is pretending to be the grocer. She imi-tates our grocer and wraps the biggest bags of vegetables and fruit. It is great fun to listen to her incessant chatter with phrases that imitate the adult salespeople. She is very condescending to her young brother, which she expresses in her punishing, scolding, or instructing tone. The other day, I told her about our wedding. She then turned around and said to Bernd: "You know, little one, at Mutti's wedding you weren't born yet!!"

October 1942

"Sassy as street dirt" [frech wie Strassendreck], *that is the only de-scription that fits Margit at the moment. There is no way to change her behavior right now: being kind to her hasn't worked; she hasn't yet de-veloped an honor code to fall back on; but even strict punishment includ-*

ing paddling with a stick does not work. Oma, who called her an urchin child, was told: "And you are an urchin Oma." When I really scold her severely, she turns into a corner and calls: "Devil, come out, and eat my Mutti." And she told her Vati, who wrote a letter to St. Nicholas: "You know, I have paper, too; I can write my own letter." We seem to be powerless and often don't know whether we should be angry or should laugh.

Letter from Robert to Minni, October 20

[Robert, the youngest brother of the Brühls, was still at home finishing his internship]

We received our first mail from Hermann [their third brother, who was then serving on the front]. *But he does not have an address yet. Among other things, he writes that he is traveling the countryside in a hay wagon. They haven't reached their destination yet, and expect another ten days of traveling.*

[Added note from their mother, Barbara Brühl: "Karl gave up his furlough for three weeks in exchange for a buddy's who had word from home that his house had been destroyed by planes. We will write when he comes home."]

Stuttgart, October 20 [before Robert joined the army]

Now at last it is my turn. The day after tomorrow, I have to show up at the artillery in Ludwigsburg [Ludwigsburg could be considered a suburb of Stuttgart. Its large castle was the original seat of the Württemberg kings when Stuttgart was still considered difficult to access because it was surrounded on three sides by hills]. *I hope that I will receive training there, so that I will be lucky enough to return home a few more times. Where are the Schnittlingen draftees assigned to? A buddy from our parish will also be in Ludwigsburg.*

Family lore has it that Robert volunteered for the army. Due to his young age, 18, and the fact that he had three brothers already in the war, he would not have been drafted at that time. My grandpa Achaz apparently got very angry when he heard that Robert had volunteered, but he had signed up before he told anybody. He told some friends that he felt he couldn't stay at home when all his brothers and friends were at the front. Robert was in Ludwigsburg for six weeks, in Marseille for six weeks, and was then shipped out to Russia.

Letter from Canonier Robert Brühl to Brühl-Fischer, November 1, Ludwigsburg

[Robert was then on the Communications Training Staff, Queen Olga Barracks]

Today I have a short rest period and I don't want to miss sending you some greetings. I have already spent one-and-a-half weeks in the military and am getting used to the life here. I am receiving training as a truck driver and radio operator. Our service is very interesting and eventful. As far as I can tell, we will be in training for twelve weeks. During this short stint I have to learn a lot. Often we work till 8:00 p.m. Tomorrow we will take the oath and later they will send us out. Some of us will be sent to France. Whether I will be among them, I don't know. The food is good. I get along with the other guys in our room.

In the meantime, it became clear to the military and the regime that the easy wins of the first few years were not going to continue. Therefore the soldiers who had been granted discharges when Germany was victorious in France, were redrafted.

After a routine medical examination verified that my father had a severe case of incurable tuberculosis, he was discharged from the army permanently. After the war was ended he received a "War Disability Passport." In 1942 he received his discharge papers.]

Letters from Karl
[Karl was at home on furlough in October or November 1942.
He wrote the letters below after his return to Russia.]

To Minni, December 1, 1942, in the East
Almost no day passes that I don't think with great longing about the "gemütliche" days in Lochau [Austria]. Every time I scoop up my stew, I think of the grilled chickens and the chocolate cake. And then the cozy fireplace! It was beautiful to be at home with you, but it's over. My mood is still very miserable. In my hole I freeze like a schnauzer. At the moment I spend all night outside. These eternal winds and snowstorms give me a lot of grief. At least we occasionally get a bit of schnapps.

To his parents, December 6, in the East
I have re-accustomed myself to life here. To celebrate today I even caught my first louse. My lodgings are more or less furnished, so that I can live in them. Only our self-made stove does not want to work properly. Except for the daily shootings, our front is relatively quiet. Hopefully it will stay that way for the rest of the year. I wish you a happy and merry Christmas.

To Isa, December 22
I take every day as a gift from God and rejoice as much as a child when I can get to lie down on my wire bed. One never knows from one day to the next when one will have to account for all the good and beautiful things on this earth. I must admit I am pretty careless in this regard, perhaps, because so far everything has gone so well. But why worry too much about it, when it is all fate and predestination anyway? When the shot is destined for one, it will meet its target one way or the other. But why do I send these thoughts to you? Disregard them and don't think about it. Be happy and take life as it comes; I feel really good at the moment.

To Thea, December 24–25
I just devoured a goose leg. Yes, we had roast goose. So different from last year, when we didn't even have bread. I sat with the officers yesterday and discussed with them the deeper problems of life; it was a lively discussion. In general I can say that it was a good feast. Now it is 7:00 p.m. and I'm imagining what it is like at home.

Already in 1942, people who lived in major cities, like Cologne, had started a nomadic life after the air raids made living in the cities impossible, as Uncle Franz's diary illustrates.

Uncle Franz's diary, end of 1942

The war at this time was still bearable. The air raids were limited. As the fighting with France began, however, things livened up. With the progress of the French war the air raids on Germany and Cologne increased dramatically. Cologne experienced the first major bombing attack in May 1942. Our house was heavily damaged because the corner house received a direct hit. The wall between our living room and master bedroom collapsed. All the windows were blown out due to the air pressure and all the rooms that faced the street were totally destroyed. The children suffered tremendously during this attack, which we survived in our not-too-fortified basement. They were especially frightened to be surrounded by fires that burned for some time.

We decided therefore to find some temporary accommodations for the children somewhere else. My brother, who at that time was still living far from the war front in Wittlich, agreed to take in Erika for a few weeks. We brought four-year-old Walther to my parents in Trier after a very hazardous journey. The bomb damage was repaired relatively soon. As far as I can remember Italian prisoners of war rebuilt the wall. We fetched our children back and hoped that the worst was over. But that turned out to be an illusion....

Aunt Resi's diary

After the birth of my second daughter, Ursula, I developed a minor breast infection. At the same time, the wife of a colleague of Kurt, had a baby and developed such a severe infection that the breast had to be operated on. A little bit later her baby became critically ill due to an intestinal infection. The doctors told her that only mother's milk could save her baby, but the woman could not nurse. There is no milk bank in Bamberg. So I decided to increase "my production." I drink a lot of malt beer and pump the extra milk aggressively. This way Kurt can take two milk bottles every day to his colleague—for eleven months. The little girl survived.

Uncle Richard's diary, 1942

On Pentecost Sunday, M.M. from Hexkoxobo in Russia started her service with us. She gets a weekly allowance of RM 6.50.
July 31, the Polish girl A.T., born in 1902, started her service with us.
December 24 at 3:00 p.m. a French general was murdered in Algeria. He was the confidant of the American President Roosevelt in North Africa and was an enemy of England. The general opinion is that the English Secret Service ordered the assassination. The murderer, a young man of twenty, was executed the day after the assassination.

Letters from the Eastern Front begin to increase in frequency.

Letters from Karl to his uncles and aunts on the family farm in Schnittlingen

January 23, 1943

I just received the two packages with the cured meat and the cookies. We are in the middle of a march and have pitched our tents for the night. It is fiercely cold. Thank God I have enough blankets with me. The meat was a dream. And on a day like today, a gift from heaven. I am doing fine. Main thing is that I am healthy. Did you get enough laborers for the farm?

To Isa, January 31

Thanks for your letter that was sprinkled red for love. The question of support for the parents is clear. I already wrote to you that I consider it my duty and that I will gladly do it. I would be a dog if as the oldest son I would try to avoid that duty. I am actually proud of this role. In the event that I do not return, I have informed my brothers. And in addition I didn't sign a life insurance policy for nothing. I have to end now. It is 11:00 p.m. and at 3:00 a.m. we expect a major attack by the Russians, and I have to be fit then.

Letter from Robert to his family, February 12

I want to send you my first greetings from Russia today. We arrived here January 26. We marched for three days and three nights to reach our designated location. I was of course not used to the climate here and therefore my two big toes were frostbitten. Thank God, only slightly. I hope that I won't have any problems with them in my future life. Otherwise I am healthy and in good spirits, and I still have my old sense of humor. How are you doing? I hope you are all well.

The Nazi propaganda must have reassured the soldiers that Germany was advancing, thus they deluded themselves into believing they were winning.

Letter from Karl, February15, East

I just received your package with the cigarettes, which made me very happy. Thanks. I am savoring one of them right now. With the exception of the total lack of tobacco I am feeling fine. I am in a good mood. Last night we taught the Russian a lesson, which was marvelous. With tricks and cunning we crawled to his position, broke into his ranks, and totally surprised him with a great Hurrah. We squeezed the lads against the wall. Of course, we took advantage of the situation and have advanced quite a bit. The Reds were totally taken unawares. Some of them ran like hares. Only a few could save themselves. At the beginning we were surprised ourselves about the weak resistance, till we found out that they had already pulled back their main troops in order to launch an attack farther south. We blew up their remaining battalion of course. But a bad sign for the lad that he allows his front to be so exposed.

They are running out of people slowly. I am convinced that by fall *they'll be lying on the floor. Till a few days ago, we had expected a major offensive from them. By the way, the Russian drafted anybody they could find. Can you imagine, fifty-five-year-old men! In the front line! The fellow whistles out of the last hole. In the south he is bleeding to death. His wins at Stalingrad are in reality his biggest defeats, if one counts his enormous losses. Because he did not break our power, his is going into the bucket. Perhaps I have drunk too much, but even sober I have the same opinion. By Fall there won't be a Stalin<u>grad</u> left, only a Stalin<u>grab</u> [<u>grab</u> means <u>grave</u>]. So, now I'll drink the rest. My storm troop did, you know, receive an extra ration.*

The German troops who survived the battle of Stalingrad surrendered on February 2, 1943. This is often considered the beginning of the end for Germany's army.

Karl's letter to Minni, February15, East

Did you hear the military report? Listen, that was our division! I am…proud of my group. While everybody else retreats under field pressure, we attack and break through. The strain is very heavy at the moment, but otherwise I am fine.

Celebrations at Home Continue

On March 1, 1943, my mother wrote a detailed description of her father's seventieth birthday to my father who is in a sanatorium. In the first part of the letter she tells him how happy she is in her marriage—she obviously misses him a great deal—and that none of the daily unpleasantries, like air raids, ration cards, or scrounging for food, matter.

Mother's diary

Opa's seventieth birthday was very, very nice. The children conducted themselves well. I made the three boys long sticks decorated with flowers and the three girls, little flower baskets. The six marched in together and sang: "What do we want…." Bernd also participated in the singing. When everyone else was finished he continued loud and clear. Margit was the first one to recite her poem [written by one of the relatives; rhymes in German]:

> *What can I tell you,*
> > *what can I bring you,*
> *I am so young,*
> > *but I have a young heart,*
> *that thinks and says:*
> > *I love you, I don't know anymore.*

She had been told to give Opa a kiss after she finished, and she carried out the order by going up to him straight away, said "kiss," gave him a small kiss, and came back to me. You needed to be there to appreciate the humor, when she said "kiss" so militarily and cute. It was so original that everyone laughed. She was dressed very nicely as a beautiful Swiss girl with a dirndl, and during the evening celebration we had lots of cakes. I brought a punch torte. Minni made a gorgeous chocolate torte in our apartment. In the evening we ate an Italian meal.

We did a lot of singing and took lots of photographs. Father was very touched with all the honor. It really was a nice day and everybody agreed that the grandchildren gave nice performances, and how great it was to watch them being well behaved and modest.

Yesterday, Bernd was also well behaved, but generally he is not a model of obedience, especially at night. The few hours of sleep that we have (five to six hours at the most) are interrupted by his cries. That's why I am very tired, I can't wait till you come back.

The celebration was attended mainly by women: four daughters and one future daughter-in-law, the mother of a daughter-in-law, and a niece. The lone male celebrant was my Opa's sixty-four-year-old brother. The four sons and two sons-in-law were on the front and my father was in a TB sanatorium.

Another planned celebration of my grandfather's birthday did not come off as well.

Note from my cousin Elinor, who remembers the following

While we were evacuated with my mother and brother Armin in Donzdorf, around 1943–1944, we often visited the grandparents in Stuttgart. Most of the time we got caught in air attacks and had to spend hours in the bomb shelter. Since Opa's seventieth birthday fell in this period of time, we wanted to surprise him with a torte. We hoarded some ration cards for months to be able to buy flour, sugar, etc., borrowed some ingredients from friends and baked a wonderful torte that was just completed when the sirens went off. When we returned from the shelter after a few hours, the torte was full of glass splinters since a bomb had hit in the area and had broken all the windows. No big celebration for Opa.

Mother's diary, March 1943

Since Margit was sick for a rather lengthy time [mumps and angina] *and did not recover in Stuttgart due to the constant air attacks, we took her to Schnittlingen, where she recovered fully. She was there a quarter of a year, and the reports were always the same: "Margit is becoming more lively and wild every day. No signs of homesickness." She participates fully in the country life and shows great interest in Uncle Richard's books and albums.*

The War Reaches Civilians in Western Germany, close to France, Belgium, and Holland

Uncle Franz's diary

The bombing raids were repeated in intervals, but the Deutzer suburb of Cologne was spared for some time. Then during the Spring of 1943 a major attack rolled over Cologne and this time a bomb landed in our house. We did manage to survive in the basement without personal in-

jury, but the lights went out, coal dust raced through the cellar, and everybody screamed; then total silence. When eventually we made our way upstairs, cautiously, there were some surprises. Obviously, a smaller bomb had come through the roof into the fourth floor, then through our children's bedroom on the third floor, and exploded under this room on the second floor. There was a huge hole in the floor of the room and all furniture had been destroyed.

Due to the power of the explosion the floor of the hallway was bumped up by twenty to thirty centimeters. It was held in place only with some iron beams on the sides. After an inspection the authorities declared the apartment uninhabitable and we received a receipt. Theoretically there was some arrangement made for "bombed out" people, but compensation and/or relocation often took so long you didn't know where you would end up.

I therefore decided to find a new place on my own. Because of my work in the defense industry, I knew a lot of business people. I found through these connections a temporary home in a small inn, "Jägerhof," in Overath relatively soon. This was the beginning of our war and our adopted home in Overath. The apartment that lay opposite our destroyed apartment in Deutz was not occupied at this time. It belonged to a young couple without children. The husband was in the military and the wife lived with her parents in Dresden. They offered us the use of the apartment, which was barely furnished. We moved what we could from our apartment into that one, whatever we needed for our daytime stays there.

For a while we lived practically in two apartments. At night we took the train to Overath, and in the morning we took the train to Deutz, where I had to continue working. During this time the air raids were only at night, so that it was relatively safe for Marie Therese and the children to be in Cologne. This back-and-forth commute was in vogue at that time and whole hordes of people rode each day from all sides to Cologne and back to the countryside at night.

The accommodations in the inn were very primitive and a stay in an inn at the expense of the government was limited. But we enjoyed the life in the countryside with its quiet nights, so we decided to look for a more permanent home in Overath. We found it in a little building with two small attic-like rooms in the courtyard of the inn. We rented them from the owner and paid for clearing them of the junk that had been stored there and furnished them. We put in two double bunk beds, the bottom ones for us and the top ones for the children. The living room, which faced the garden, we furnished in a country style. The furniture was manufactured according to my plans by a firm with which I had connections.

We started to become acquainted with other people from the village and though the war dragged on and its outcome became more and more uncertain, we spent many quiet days in Overath, which almost *made us forget the horrors of the war.*

Aunt Resi's diary

We had many houseguests again in 1943.

My father is again employed as a teacher. He first worked at the rural school where children from Aachen were evacuated to the castle of Monschau. He and my mother rented a room in Hofen, to which they transported some valuables from Aachen in the hope that Hofen was more secure. Hofen was never bombed and was spared during the war; however, all their belongings had disappeared—were stolen. Then he was transferred with his pupils to Zwiesel in the Bavarian Forest. This is how he escaped the concentration camp. His transfer was arranged through the efforts of my mother; he knew nothing about this transaction. She even went to the cave of the Gauleiter [party leader]. They agreed that the law was not applicable to him. But he did not get compensation for all the goods that he lost till after the war.

My mother's third brother, Hermann, who also served on the Eastern front, did survive, but was permanently disabled after being shot in the leg. Like his brothers he talks about his burning longing for mail and about the poor living conditions in Russia. He shows more insight into the daily life of the Russians, however; he views them not simply as the enemy, but as fellow human beings caught up in a war not of their making. He tries to make the best of a bad situation. After the war he became a sculptor.

Letter from Hermann

To Isa, April 19

Perhaps you can still remember my furlough last year when we spent the last few hours in the waiting room of the train station. Over the past year I have often thought about these hours and my furlough in general. These are memories that I can come back to for a long time. Every time I revisit them, I get really homesick. Then I turn around, shake these thoughts out of my brain, and believe that I have overcome them. However, I don't succeed in this since I link everything that I see in Russia with home, and compare. It happens every time, and I start dreaming. Today is a gorgeous day. The sun shines brightly. The bees and the flies hum and there is a light wind in the air. There is a comforting stillness (I generously ignore the thunder from the canons), and yet, one feels that everything is alive.... It is like Schnittlingen when we were lying in the garden and dreaming. Spring!

During these wonderful days I sit in front of my hut and contemplate what I should write to you. You have probably heard the latest news from home. The wound is well healed, but unfortunately I was not assigned back to my old unit, but temporarily to a neighboring battalion. I am sure I will return to my old unit, but when is not clear. For the foreseeable future I am a few kilometers behind the front line and have the good fortune to be lodging in flea-infested quarters. One becomes modest on the front line. I heard from soldiers who returned from their fur-

loughs that you had had a heavy air attack in Stuttgart.

I hope you all are doing well and I am anxiously awaiting the first mail. Isa, Isa, my brain compartment is getting worse and worse since I have no smokes and therefore cannot send the smoke into the sky and collect my thoughts. Perhaps you can actively support me in this matter. A few days ago, I wanted to send a film home, but it came back, because no more packages can be sent from here. I hope to hear soon from you.

Letters from Karl to Rudolf on the Western front

April 27, East

How are your prospects of being promoted to sergeant? My prospects for the next two years are bleak, because somebody else occupies this position. My consolation prize is a higher salary for a noncommissioned officer (corporal) that will be due in December.

April 1943

And now the latest: effective May 1 I will be transferred to an artillery unit. I am therefore in the first line at the front; we'll see how long it will last before I'm attacked. For what reason, and why this transfer came about, I'll write about in two to three months. Till then you have to rein in your curiosity. I only wrote to the parents that I now have a field post number, and that nothing else has changed. You are the only one who knows about this. Mum's the word.

P.S. Robert and Hermann were both in the field hospital. Therefore don't be surprised if they don't answer your letters. Robert has only written to me once. Why he was in the hospital I don't know. Mother wrote about it to me the other day. Hermann returned to his unit a few days ago. And now, old boy, all the best and a healthy Wiedersehen at Christmas 1943.

May 1, Eastern front

This morning at 5:00 a.m. I celebrated my new assignment. Quite modestly and quietly. I have to learn a lot. Am now the group leader, but because of big losses the last few days, my group has been decimated: down to two men. We are in an extremely windy corner here. Extremely bad air. The River Pau has a lot of sharpshooters on the other side. Considering my height, that's an uncomfortable feeling. But I am hoping that I will get through this OK. Everything here of course is very primitive. One lives like the first humans. No natural light, no artificial lighting, no water, but knee deep in the swampy ditches. Are you getting a furlough soon? If everything works out, I am due in August. Many thanks for the cigarettes. They were strong, but they nevertheless tasted good.

I have told the parents only that I have a new number, and that everything else is the same. Do not tell them.

To his family, May 29, Eastern front

Thanks a lot for the kilo package. I cannot tell you how happy I was to

get it and how much I liked it. Lately, I am always hungry. That's be-
cause I am outside all night and during the day I can only catch four or
five hours of sleep. That's why the rolls and the bacon were a welcome
complement. Weather was terrible the last few days. Today is the first
normal day. Did you get decent workers for the farm?

To Rudolf, June 1, Eastern front
    …to be quite honest, things are miserable for me right now. My mood
is quite a bit below zero. I have big problems here, but I am hoping for
improvement during the next few months. At the moment, my star has
totally abandoned me. My one bright cloud on the horizon is my hope for
a furlough. It's a pity that it's a long time till then. My cache of smokes is
also depleted. Couldn't you send me a few lung destroyers? At the mo-
ment I am out in the foxhole almost all night. During the day I am
pressed into service (to rebuild our quarters), so that there is damned lit-
tle time for sleeping. When it starts raining, you want to despair. When
will all of this end? Well anyway, I will stay strong. After all, I haven't
been a soldier for the last five years for nothing.

Poem by Karl [freely translated]

Mutter / Mother
 Meine liebe gute Mutter / My beloved dear mother
Mit dem schlichten grauen Haar / with your plain grey hair
 Sicher sitzt Du jetzt am Fenster / surely you sit at the window
Das Dein Lieblingsplätzchen war. / Which was your favorite place

Und Du denkst an Deinen Jungen / And you think of your boy
 Während Deine Hände ruhen / While your hands are at rest
Während Deine Hände beten / While your hands are praying
 Wie es tausend Mütter tun. / Like a thousand mothers do

Bange schauen Deine Augen / Worry shows in your eyes
 In die Ferne zu mir hin / As you look toward me, far away
Immer quält dich eine Frage / Always one question haunts you
 Ob ich noch am Leben bin. / Whether I am still alive.

Und Du sollst doch ruhig schlafen / And you should sleep peacefully
 Und nicht weinen bei der Nacht / And not cry at night
Denn Du hast mich bald wieder / Because you will soon have me again
 Wenn der Kampf zu End gebracht. / When the battle has come to an end.

Meine liebe gute Mutter / My beloved dear mother
 Mach ein froheres Gesicht / Put on a happier face
Sieh, ich bin gesund und munter / See, I am healthy and in good spirits
 Liebe Mutter, sorge Dich nicht. / Dear mother, don't worry.

Ethnic Germans in Occupied Territories

My brother Karl Heinz's mother-in-law told me her story at Christmastime 2000.

Interview with Resi Paffenholz, Karl Heinz's mother-in-law, 2000

I lived alone with my mother. When I was five, my father drowned in the Rhine. He was a stucco worker, and was looking for work at the seminary in Bensberg near Düsseldorf. On the way back from the interview he jumped into the Rhine for a swim and he was pulled in by the undertow. He was born in Egerland in the Sudeten—the area that became Czech after World War I. We were asked to become citizens; we were told that we were Czechs. This was more than my mother could handle. So, at age sixteen, I applied for the documents of my grandparents and great grandparents in Klösterle in Egerland and sent them to the authorities. At the same time, I included the documents of my mother, who came from Westfalia. We received our citizenship papers and were personally congratulated by the governor [I don't know of which state].

On December 11, 1941, my mother also received her German citizenship papers which was possible since she was originally German. We lived at that time in a small garden cottage. During the air raids we all ran into the cellar and trembled and prayed when the bombs fell. We lived a very secluded life, no radio and no newspaper and we didn't hear much about the whole Hitler propaganda. At that time I was an au pair (Pflichtjahrmaedchen) in a family. When I rode my bike to work in the morning, I often saw the newly bombed out or burning houses, and sometimes dead bodies in the street.

Contrasts between Life at Home and on the Front

Mother's diary, May 1943

While we were on vacation for three weeks in Hinterzarten, Bernd was at Oma's and enchanted everyone in the family. He does not speak much, but all day long he chatters in a loud voice. He prefers to play with cars and trains. He lies flat on his stomach and moves them back and forth for hours, under and around the furniture.

Letter from Richard to my mother, June 10, Schnittlingen

[I was then staying in Schnittlingen with my grandaunts and granduncles].

Your package arrived yesterday without a problem. Margit is doing well and is becoming wilder by the day. The weather is pretty lousy so we can't go out much. But Margit has no problem making herself "useful" in the house. Lately she insists on accompanying me into the darkroom in order to see how the photos are developed. I was worried that she would be afraid of the darkness, but not a trace of it. She is interested in everything and wanted to try her hand at developing right away. And when I asked her to assist me with some activities and praised her for her skill and hard work, she was overwhelmed with joy. But soon her critique started: "Uncle, you did not lighten this long enough" and "this time you didn't pay enough attention." Lately, she spends a lot of time in my room. She wants to learn how to write down numbers. I showed her the easy ones (0, 1, 4, 6, 9) and she practices with great diligence. I am also in the middle of teaching her how to tell time. It is not so easy to explain this concept at a child's level. But some of it, she already understands.

One of her characteristics is that she wants to actively help with all kinds of work. She prefers it to playing. Somehow she is always active. But she also understands perfectly how to become everyone's darling. And she declares to the person from whom she just profited: "You are my favorite." That works wonders of course. Last night she told me with great seriousness: "Uncle Richard, I like you best of all, but now I am going to Franz." Of course, she can stay with us longer.

Letters from Karl to his family, June 16, Eastern front

The Russian allows us no quiet night anymore. Always a racket, oncoming troops, and attacks, etc. My nerves are becoming slowly but surely frazzled. And it looks miserable in regard to a furlough. Perhaps in three to four months, that is, if I am still around then....

* * *

Many thanks for the cigarette package. I was pleasantly surprised, especially about the good brand, because normally I smoke a bad weed. We expect a new Russian offensive any day now. All indications are there. If only this anticipation would be over. Last week the "lad" [Russian soldiers] broke into our foxhole twice. We, of course, ejected them, but still. At the moment I have a lot of bad luck. Nothing works for me. My furlough also fell through—into the water.

Letter from Richard, to his niece Isa, June 18, Schnittlingen

The farmers are really worried because the hay harvest should have started, but the constant bad weather prevents that. Have you heard that the army is building a big complex in Treffelhausen! [the village next to Schnittlingen]. No one seems to know what it is for. In addition to all the farmers in the area who have to help out they are employing a few hundred people. The farmers also have to provide housing for the employees. If no one from Stuttgart occupies our extra rooms, we expect to be asked also—and we won't be able to refuse. Just this morning a messenger walked through the village with a bell, shouting that whoever refused quarters would be punished. Most probably the danger of more air attacks due to the existence of this building will increase substantially. What more will this disastrous war bring to us? And what will happen after it is all over?

Again best wishes from Richard, with Marie, Bernhard, and Barbara.

This letter is interesting since two months later when my mother asked the relatives in

Schnittlingen to take in our family because we had to leave Stuttgart, they turned us down because they said that three little children without a maid would be too upsetting for their quiet life.

Letter from Richard (written as if by "me"), June 19, Schnittlingen

Dear Mutti and Vati,

You have given me great joy with the many presents for my feast day. The unusual doll house living room is very interesting. I can already construct it all by myself and then break it down again and put it away. Uncle Richard read me the beautiful fairytale book and explained the stories. I enjoyed my feast day. Everybody congratulated me. From Uncle Bernhard and Uncle Richard I received some coins. But first they didn't know what to do when I told them that they had to give me something. I put the coins in my purse. When I return to Stuttgart, I want to buy something with them. Perhaps I even have enough for Bernd. In the afternoon, the two aunts made a very big round cake just for me. You know it was so big—they only make it like this in Schnittlingen. It tasted very good.

Now, dear Mutti, I want to congratulate you on your feast day. My heartfelt wishes. May the good God always keep you healthy and may he be able to present us with a little sister. I am looking forward to her. I am sorry but I can't give you presents because I am still so small. But I will pray for you. And then I promise you that I will always be well behaved and obedient when I return to Stuttgart ("perhaps" as she added), to be a joy for you and Vati. I am overjoyed that you will soon come and bring me back home. I am very curious how Bernd is doing and whether he will still recognize me. I am also looking forward to seeing Oma again.

Many hugs and kisses from your little Margit.

Letters from Karl

June 27

The Russian sprays us with artillery to the point that I see black in front of my eyes. But otherwise, I am fine.

Last letter to his friend Alfons Geiger, who also served on the Eastern front, June 27

Sorry for just writing today, but as you know there is a lot going on here at the moment. Up till now everything has worked out all right. Regrettably, I always have losses in my group. At the moment we have the slogan "Hail to South France." Hopefully, it will succeed. Do you hear good news from home? For today, my most heartfelt greetings.

Letter to Rudolf, sent on June 28, the day of Karl's death

I just received your letter of May 24. Since I received your later letters sent from Stuttgart before, this letter from the field is obsolete. I am happy for you that you received your furlough. And you even had time to get married? —The Russian covers us with artillery to the point where you see only black in front of you. But we can still handle it. Many greetings.

On June 28, Uncle Karl Brühl was killed in action at the age of twenty-seven, near Orel on the Eastern front. He was buried at the soldier's cemetery in Kirejkowo. None of the fallen soldiers' bodies were returned to Germany. The cemetery area was recaptured by Russian troops shortly afterwards. It is therefore not clear what became of the cemetery or the soldiers' remains.

Letter from Rudolf to Karl, June 19

Sent by Uffz. Rudolf Brühl (no. L 17847), Lppa, Paris
To: Fieldpost Uffz. Karl Brühl (no. 28560 C)
   ...why won't you tell me why you were transferred? What do you mean about differences and how shall I interpret that? I want to know what's really going on—unfortunately I can't send you cigarettes, because I don't have any myself. I would have liked to sweeten your hard and difficult life with them. Perhaps later. I won't be going anywhere in the near future. Don't worry about me in this respect.
   What do you mean: "I have big problems here?" Explain a bit in more detail so I know what's going on. I haven't heard anything from my brother-in-law Arnulf since the fighting stopped. On May 9, he wrote that he expects to become a prisoner of war. They are completely surrounded—the enemy tanks being only a short distance away. On May 5 was the general end of the battle. His family and wife are naturally very worried. I am basically OK. I have to get used to the new surroundings and learn to fit in. Since almost all of the other men have been together for a long time, it is difficult for a newcomer to be accepted. There isn't much in common, everybody has his own interests. But I expect it to be all right when some time passes. Best wishes and many greetings.

This letter was returned with a printed message: "Return to sender. Recipient killed in action for Great Germany."

   My father wrote a letter to Uncle Karl the same day. It was addressed to Fieldpost Herrn UFFz. Karl Brühl 28560 C. It was also returned. The address was crossed out. The printed message read: "Return to sender. Recipient killed in action."

Letter from Robert, June 29 [he was unaware at this time of Karl's death]
   I am at the bridgehead of Saraskij [most letters are written in pencil, therefore difficult to read]. *Little time to write. But don't worry, I am doing fine. Only, have no expectation for a furlough. So much for today. Patience! In six to eight weeks more.*

The first news of Uncle Karl's death came by letter from a medical doctor to his father, Achaz Brühl:

O.U. 7/1 Military Doctor Ziesmer, F.Nr. 31 134
Dear Mr. Brühl,

I have to give you the sad news that your son, Sergeant Karl Brühl, died in the main field hospital [Hauptverbandplatz]. *Your son was brought in on June 28, 1943, at 2:00 a.m. in an unconscious state, dying from severe wounds from grenade splinters in the abdomen, lower right arm, and right side of the head and neck. There was an immediate blood transfusion and surgery, but all medical efforts were unsuccessful. On June 28, 1943, at 1:00 p.m. your son, without ever regaining consciousness, died peacefully. He did not manage to convey any message for his relatives due to the seriousness of his wounds.*

I want to express my deep sympathy for your painful loss. Even though this must be a dreadful shock for you, I hope you can take solace in knowing that your son was killed while fighting for the greatness and future of Great Germany.

The funeral was on June 30 in the soldier's cemetery in Kirejkowo. His best friend, Sergeant Alfons Geiger, who is in my unit, showed his last respects for his friendship and comradeship by placing his rosary into the grave of your son. Again my deep sympathy!
Heil Hitler! Military doctor and company chief
P.S. Your son's belongings will be sent to you by his troop.

Letter written by Karl's company leader, June 30

Unit of the field post no. 28560 C
Dear Family Brühl,

You will have heard the sad news from the military doctor of the triage station of the heroic death of your beloved son. As the commander of your son's troop I want to give you the circumstances that led to your son's severe wounds. During the night of June 27–28, around midnight, he was in a machine gun location when an enemy grenade landed in his immediate vicinity. A few splinters entered his arm and torso, but he still managed to crawl to the nearest medical first aid station with his last energy. The medics provided first aid for him. Shortly after a doctor came and had him transported to the field hospital immediately. We were all hoping that though he was seriously wounded they could save his life. Then how indescribably sad it was when we heard the news that in the afternoon of the 28th your beloved Karl died of his severe injuries. This afternoon at 1:00 p.m. we buried him in the presence of the army chaplain in the hero's cemetery in Kirejkowo, 110 kilometers north of Orel.

Your son was in our company only a short time, but in this short time he gained our confidence through the integrity of his character and his willingness to help others; he enjoyed comradeship and general popularity. Now he has joined his comrades who went before him and who were taken from us by the merciless fate of the war. He also gave his life for the future and the greatness of our Reich. Even though we buried his body in the earth, his name and his actions among us will not be for-

*gotten. He died as he lived: courageous and loyal. You will look for
some solace in your grief. Know that your son has given everything so
that the red flood from the East can be forestalled, that the destruction
of our fatherland does not happen. He gave his life so that Germany can
live! He fought for everything that he loved from home and died in his
strong belief of eventual victory. His death will serve as a reminder of
our responsibility to continue fighting and to work, because at the end of
the immense battle will be victory. The hero's death of your beloved son
Karl cannot be in vain.*

Deepest sympathy. Captain and company leader

Mother's diary, July 1943

*Margit's dear godfather Karl died in combat on June 28 and is buried
in Orel. He was always so devoted to his little godchild—asked in every
letter for photos of her and enjoyed my stories about her pranks. To
each of her special days, my mother was ordered to buy something special for her; last Christmas she received the beautiful doll "Carola," who
can close her eyes and has real hair. —Margit can remember her Uncle
Karl well and is pondering where he is and what he is doing in heaven.*

Letter from Barbara, my maternal grandmother, to Karl, July 4

[Since this letter was found in Stuttgart, I don't think it was ever sent.
Only one other letter she sent to her boys in combat has survived.]

*Today is Sunday and my free time belongs to my dear soldiers. Many
thanks for the letter of June 19 and the pictures, which gave us great
joy. At last I have seen you again, but you have lost lots of weight; I
have looked at the picture many times; it seems that you have two very
nice comrades! The other two are as thin as you. Tomorrow I am sending a package. We also got your letter with the pictures from the winter,
where you are going for water. In what container is the water? It doesn't
look like a crate. Or is it a tin box? If you could just come home soon,
then you could tell us all. I would like to spend Sunday evenings listening to you. Hermann always writes about an upcoming furlough, but
then he doesn't show up. Robert is again behind the front lines. His boils
broke out again, so that he is excused from driving. Rudolf wants to wait
with his marriage, at least till his next furlough. I think that's good. I
would prefer if he would wait till the end of the war. Nothing else new.
We are always grateful when we can sleep a whole night without an
alarm.*

Many greetings from your mother

Please turn over

*Monday morning, July 5, your letter arrived, which told us that you re-
ceived the Gesälz* [marmalade] *and the pipe. I am glad to hear it. Today
we are sending another package. Your checking account has 1,392
marks and 40 pfennig and in the next few days I will transfer 1,200
marks into your savings account. You will get more interest. Rudolf told*

me that and I believe that's right.

Sincere greetings, Mother

Every week I go to Rohracker a few times to buy berries. I know that you are a strapping soldier of whom I can be very proud, isn't that so?

Telegram to Rudolf Brühl, 2764 Stuttgart 23 10 1800, June 28

Party Office Regional Group Uhlandshoehe

To Sergeant Rudolf Brühl LG PA Paris L 17 845

Our beloved Karl was wounded and died without regaining consciousness. Letter follows. Mother

Excerpts from letters by Alfons Geiger, Karl's best friend from his youth, written to his own parents and siblings from the combat zone after Karl's death

[Alfons took a death photo that the family gave our family with his letter.]

June 29

…our good friend Karl has left us forever. The two of us who endured joys and sorrows together all our lives will not see each other after the end of this terrible time. I still cannot comprehend it. Neither of us thought on May 14 when we shook hands for the last time with a hearty "Auf Wiedersehen" that this would be the last time.

When I came to the field hospital this morning, the staff sergeant told me about his death. They were burying him at this hour and I hurried to the cemetery and got there just as they unloaded his body. In my thoughts I said farewell to him, but in the belief that I will greet him in eternal life.

It was painful for me to look into my best friend's face…. He will always live in me. His actions will be rewarded by God, and we will accept his early death that he gave up for his beloved fatherland as God's providence. My thoughts go to his dear relatives who still have no idea that their beloved Karl is entombed in foreign soil and that he will not return to them. How hard will they take the news. I therefore ask you not just to write a few lines to them, but to make a visit and give them personal comfort about their dreadful loss. Among his personal belongings was his rosary, which I took with the permission of his company chief and placed around his neck. And I placed the cross on his chest. I believe this is what his family would have wanted.

Now I want to give you a short description of his injury and death. During the night June 28 around 12:15 a.m. he was wounded. He had been ordered to clean an area of high grasses and it can be assumed that the Russian who was only a few meters away noticed the action. One of the 12c grenades that the Russians shot off was a direct hit into the machine gun position where Karl and two of his comrades were working. It was a grenade thrower, which has a devastating explosive potential. The guy next to him was killed instantly, while the other guy next to him was only slightly wounded. Despite his own severe injury, my dear good friend crawled back to the first aid station where he collapsed. After a few heart-wrenching painful minutes he was bandaged and by 2:00 a.m. he was transported to the field hospital where he received immediate care…but with his injuries—grenade splinters all over his body and a severed aorta with very high blood loss, severe tears in his right intestines and liver, grenade splinters in the back of his head and neck—there was no way to save him. He did survive the surgery, but his general condition deteriorated very fast and his pulse was very weak. He immediately received blood transfusions, which made his pulse stronger and allowed him to wake up from the anesthesia. But in the morning he exhibited great restlessness and cramps, which led to a rapid decline in his heart rate and circulation. The heart medication and the oxygen that he received had no effect, and he died at 1:00 p.m. I have talked to the medic who was in charge of him and he assured me that Karl was never fully awake. He talked to him, and Karl tried to say something, but it could not be understood.

…I will be at the funeral tomorrow. My comrades made me a wonderful flower wreath with the inscription: "To my dear friend as a last greeting."

June 30

I have just returned from the funeral…. I feel his loss very deeply since a part of my memories of being a young boy have been taken away from me…. The pastor praised his healthy attitude to the military profession, his noble character…. His company chief and his troop leader summarized in military words with what courage, energy, and faith in the eventual victory this popular soldier conducted himself. His sense of duty, which was described as exemplary, allowed him to be a leader for his comrades and a fighter for his beloved country…. His comrades will never forget him. We turned him over to the earth with the song "I had a comrade." I greeted my good and loyal friend from his parents and siblings and told him "Auf Wiedersehen" in your name….

May he rest in peace! He was a really good friend and I will never forget him.

In Germany it is customary to print official death notices that are sent to all relatives and friends and printed in the major newspapers. They contain the name of the grieving relatives, the address where condolences can be sent, and details of the funeral arrangements.

> According to God's Holy Will
> our beloved good son,
> brother, brother-in-law,
> uncle, nephew
> **Karl Brühl**
> Sergeant in a grenadier regiment
> Recipient of the Iron Cross 2 and commendations
> Was killed in action on June 28, 1943 at the age of 27
> in fulfillment of his faithful duty on the Eastern front.

He is buried in a military cemetery.

This notice was signed by his parents, his nine surviving siblings (out of thirteen), and their spouses, including his three brothers, all on the battlefield.

Letter from Thea to the uncles and aunts in Schnittlingen, July 9

We have to tell you the sad news that we just received. Our dear Karl was killed.… We will write as soon as we know when the Mass will be. I cannot write any more at the moment. We will pray together.

My father added: "Funeral service July 16 at 8:00 a.m. in St. Nikolaus in Stuttgart."

Letter probably written by Thea, Karl's youngest sister, before the memorial service in Stuttgart

The news of Karl's death struck us like lightning. He was the last one that we expected to be killed since we believed that he was one lucky one. How many times was he close to death and came out of it unscathed. A message was sent out once before that he had died, but it did not reach us till he showed up for a visit. How much did God protect him when he received three shots from a machine gun not twenty meters away that just grazed him on his upper lip, chin, and neck. That could have been deadly. He told me then that due to shock and loss of blood, he was convinced that this was his last hour and he thought, "poor mom, poor mom." He found cover and even after a while had the energy to drive his moped to the first aid station where he was restored and everything healed in a few days, after only a few stitches. This incident filled us with thanks and joy, we were all convinced that God was with him.…

Excerpts from letters written later by from Alfons Geiger to his parents

…it breaks my heart every time I realize the truth, that my best friend will neither see his home nor his beloved family anymore. I go by his grave every day and talk with him. It seems to me that he wants to talk to me and my one solace is that I can decorate his grave in the name of his loved ones. I haven't been able to plant a lot of plants yet, since three wreaths still remain. Today I planted marigolds all around the borders that will hopefully bloom soon. Since I am at his grave every night between 7 and 8 p.m. to ask the Almighty God to take his immortal soul into eternal life, I ask you to join me some evening in prayers and thoughts. He has done so much good for his fellow humans and helped them out in their times of need.…

* * *

…the longer the war continues and the more its brutality is evident, the more difficult it is to find the meaning of death. Why the destruction of so many wonderful young lives? And how precious these young lives are becomes evident when we think of the loss of our dear Karl. Everybody who knew him knows that he was an upright and honest man, with

many gifts of character and heart....

God has found him deserving and accepted his sacrifice and Karl was prepared for it. He once asked his mother "how do you pray for your sons?" and she answered, "I pray to the Trinity: if it is your will, please keep my sons for me; if however your plan is different, please give them a good death." He then put his hand on her shoulder and said, "You pray correctly; that's the way I pray also." He therefore accepted his sacrifice and said "yes" to it. That's why his life and death is a precious gift on the sacrificial altar of God. The blood of our best ones is atonement for the guilt of the people—a grain of wheat sown in the field of the world.

Letter to Rudolf, Karl's brother, from Sergeant Werner Haller, Eastern front, Fieldpost- Nr.- 28 560 A, August 2
[Rudolf had inquired about the problems with Karl's transfer and asked why he had been transferred]

...we are at present involved in heavy fighting, but since we have a day off today, I want to answer your questions. Due to time constraints, I have to keep my notes short. I will later explain in more detail.

I know the following about Karl's transfer to another company: Karl was very popular with his bosses and his comrades. Supposedly a former adjutant, who has in the meantime been killed, suggested to our battalion commander that Karl should be trained to be an officer. Our commander, who got along very well with Karl, then asked him whether he wanted to be transferred to another company to become an officer. Karl did not warm to this offer because he was willing to forego officer status to stay with his old buddies, with whom he had been together for a long time.

He answered therefore that he had concerns whether he was capable of doing that job if he was away from the company for lengthy training and that he had little knowledge of the different weapons. The commander trusted Karl to gain the necessary knowledge in a short time. Karl asked for a few days contemplation. When the commander later asked again, Karl agreed. He would have preferred to stay with the old gang, but as a soldier he could not say "no" since that would have been interpreted the wrong way. I am telling you as it happened, because as a soldier yourself, you understand all the angles that come into play and you will understand Karl's actions. That Karl didn't tell you about it at the time stems from his worry that he might not be able to pass the tests and become an officer.

Karl was transferred and started officer training. At the beginning he had a hard time with the rigorous demands of that company, but he soon got used to it and never lost his sense of humor. When he wrote to you that his lucky star had abandoned him and that he had great difficulties, it was because he developed differences with his bosses and therefore was convinced that he would not become an officer. Shortly after that he was severely wounded and died the same day.

Letter from Robert to Rudolf, July 20, in the field

...I heard on July 16 that our dear Karl died in combat. It hit me like a punch in my stomach. Because of my skin condition [psoriasis] I had to go to a regional unit because our battalion has no medical help. The disadvantage is that we only receive mail if by chance a messenger comes by. That's bad luck. But I will soon be well enough to return to my old gang. July 7, I was working for the infantry because the Russian broke through and managed to get within 100 meters of our foxhole. But then you should have seen what kind of a firefight broke out from our machine gunners and artillery. They did a good job. After a few hours the left flank was weakened. Some of their men were able to escape into the forest that extends all the way to the Donez River. All the others were either flattened or taken prisoner. I will never forget that day.

The flies, snails, and other little critters are very sassy. They live mostly in the quarters since it is too hot for them outside. Lately we are living in houses again, but the artillery is in bunkers. Where are you quartered? I would gladly change places with you even if it is in the furthest peasant village. Here in Russia everything is shit. I hope the war is over soon.

Official reply to a letter written by my father on July, 14, 1943
[My father had written to Karl's unit in the name of his parents-in-law seeking more details about Karl's death and to get the photographs Karl had promised them a few days before his death.]

Office of the Unit 28 560 C, on the front, September 6

We have received your letter at the company. It was not possible to write before. The comrades who were with your brother-in-law, Sgt. Karl Brühl, are no longer in the company. Private P. was killed by the grenade launcher. Sgt H. was seriously wounded and is on furlough. Perhaps you can contact him at his private address in Stuttgart. Your brother-in-law was brought to the field hospital immediately after the attack, but died after a few hours without ever regaining consciousness. A Sgt took a photo during the funeral at the soldier's cemetery in Kirejkowo. He was wounded later, however, and at this point we don't know the address of the hospital where he is being treated. As soon as we receive his photos we will send copies to you. We don't have any information about the photographs that were supposedly taken a few days before the hero's death of your brother-in-law. Most probably they were taken by the same Sgt who took the graveside photo. We will send you more information soon.

Heil Hitler! Greetings, Ltnt.

My grandparents and other relatives received many letters of condolence that stressed Karl's good qualities. They also did receive the above-mentioned photos of the grave, which helped them achieve closure.

Excerpts from one letter to my parents from
a fellow Neudeutscher, a pastor, July 23, 1943, Stuttgart

I want to express to you, Mrs. Paulus, my special sympathy for the tragic loss that the hero's death of your brother has inflicted on the whole family. My wish is that his sacrificed blood will bring blessings to our nation! How lucky that during this difficult time you have Heinz at your side! I will include your beloved soldier in my daily Mass. Perhaps on occasion we can celebrate the holy sacrifice of the Mass together. In true solidarity, E.G.

Mother's diary, July 1943

When Margit returned from Schnittlingen after three months, Bernd's joy was unbounded. We were all surprised that he remembered his sister, and Margit became quite shy and overwhelmed with this stormy greeting. He rolled on the floor, ran to Margit all the time, and caressed and embraced her. It is good to watch how joyous he is. Oma told us that he enjoys each dirt heap when they go for a walk.

It is nice to observe the relationship between sister and brother: Margit, dominant and motherly, Bernd, attentive, imitating, and often jealous when he thinks he is being discriminated against or can't keep up with Margit. They present a united front, however, when it comes to being naughty or mischievous and when they want to prevail against the outside world.

Letter from Robert to Rudolf, August 1

Your report on the funeral service for Karl gave me great joy. I believe you when you say that it was very festive and I envy all of you who could participate! The news hit me very hard—in the midst of enemy territory. You can imagine how hard it is for me since I can't talk to anybody. Nobody understands what I am going through. The lancers are all too stiff for me to share my grief with them. When I received the telegram, one of them said to me: "Don't get excited, he is not the first one, and he will not be the last"! With such remarks, I get dismissed. Please believe that I would like nothing better than to see no one. The front is quiet at the moment. Considering the circumstances I am doing alright. I hope the same is true for you.

Letter from Robert to the family in Schnittlingen, August 23

Many thanks for the package from August 3 with the bacon and the rolls. Everything was fabulous and I enjoyed it so much. Of the six small 100-gram packages from Aunt Barbara, none has arrived yet. I hope that they will make it.

I have already written to say how hard the news of Karl's death has affected me. Most difficult was that I couldn't find anyone who could have understood me at that moment. I could only do one thing that brought me solace, and that is to pray for him daily. Only after I had been hit that hard could I understand how much strength a prayer can give. Did you get your [Polish prisoner of war] *back, or who is helping out with the harvest? By the time this letter reaches you, most of the crop will have been harvested. I would like to help you so much. I would do any work with pleasure if I could only escape this damned Russia. The people, the environment, and the climate are so unpleasant for me—like nothing else. But considering the circumstances, I am doing fine.*

My youngest brother, Karl Heinz, was born August 1 in the middle of air attacks on Stuttgart. Everything had become scarce in the meantime, so his birth announcement was only a printed postcard:

> Sunday, August 1, 1943
> 2 black/red candles
> GOD'S
> GRACE
> Gave us
> today
> Red Star Black Cradle with Red Heart Red Star
> The Third Child
> Karl Heinz
> *Heinz and Isa Paulus*

Karl Heinz was named after my mother's brother, who had just been killed, and my father.

Before the birth of my youngest brother I was sent to one of my mother's sisters, Minni, in Bregenz, Austria, to spend some time. Since my mother had many siblings, they often took in each other's children for lengthy periods of time.

Mother's diary, August 1943

In the middle of June, Margit went with Aunt Minni to Bregenz. This trip brought many new impressions for her: Lake Constance, the little boats, the mountains. She got along more or less with her one-and-a-half-year older cousin, Günther. In any case, she learned a lot from his independence. She returned well-tanned, with big cheeks and a true Bregenz Forest accent. Bernd greeted her enthusiastically, but her whole attention was on the "new" brother. She looked him all over and patted him often. She declared to us that in descending order the following are allowed to tend to him: Frau Mutsch [the midwife], *sister Fidelis, Mutti, and then she herself. She is already looking forward to when she will be responsible for him. Of course she had again wanted a little sister, and she advised me to order a little sister as soon as possible. When later I picked her up from a vacation in Ellwangen, at the train station in Ulm, her first question was "Do we have a little sister now?"*

Letter to Isa from Hermann, on the Eastern front, August 14

I have a burning desire to hear about any changes in Stuttgart. Hope that you did not have an air attack since I have been gone. Even though, don't become careless. The best is always to expect the worst, then you won't be disappointed and are well prepared.

My trip back here was quite nice. Have again tried to look at this land and its people not from the point of view of a soldier, but from the point of view of a researcher who is interested in things. I am quite aware that I have only been partially successful in this. Now I want to describe to you my impressions. From this aspect, Russia is not so despicable. I want to claim the opposite actually: it becomes ever more attractive. The situation is of course fundamentally different from what we are used to. But the country offers infinite possibilities and perhaps that is the attraction. It is obvious that a country with such dimensions includes truly charming corners. I could mention a few places, but where they are located is not important. The main thing is, they exist. Perhaps the real seduction stems from its immense vastness. The collective farming practices, where all the fields and meadows are huge, adds to this sense of expanse. I always have to return to the idea that you can only learn about a country during times of peace. At the moment we are on the Black Sea, and of course go swimming a lot. Such an opportunity needs to be used.

Letter to his family from Robert, Eastern front, August 14

Many thanks for the nice cigarette package. It's been a while since we have received brand name cigarettes, so it was very welcome.

How was the birth? Did Isa recover well? Was it a boy or a girl? I hope to get a birth announcement soon. I am as tense as an umbrella for news. The front has calmed down a bit. We are receiving first-rate equestrian training, jumping and all that was shown on "the day of the army."

Morgenstund hat Gold im Mund [Early morning is made of gold]—*that's the motto here. So, we rise every morning between 5:00 and 6:00 a.m.*

The following excerpts of congratulatory letters on the occasion of Karl Heinz's birth show the ravages of the war that was dragging on.

Letter from Richard to my parents, August 2, Schnittlingen

May Karl Heinz be the harbinger of a speedy peace and may his growing up fall in a time of blessed rebirth, for himself and for the re-strengthening of our beloved fatherland that has endured for so many years the most terrible burden.

We wish for mother and child God's protection from the looming dangers. The hard fate that your beloved Oma has to endure [the bombing of her house in Aachen] *has moved us deeply. It is very hard when all of a sudden in old age, one faces total loss. It is doubly hard since it is not possible to replace any of the most basic items. We express our deepest sympathy with the one who has lost so much.*

We just lost our Polish farm laborer. Totally unexpected—he was ar-

rested and taken away with an accomplice. We don't know what he was charged with or what has happened to them in the meantime. We are now left without any male help shortly before the beginning of the harvest. A few days ago, however, two soldiers were quartered with us, probably for a lengthy time. They are of the opinion that they will be allowed to help out occasionally with the harvesting chores. We hope for the best. Incidentally, it is still possible that the Polish fellow will return to us. We were very satisfied with him. He was very hardworking and willing and also had a good disposition. At the same time we received a letter from Maria [a niece] who told us that she and her whole family would come to us in the middle of August. She has already sent all of their luggage. We gave the two soldiers the room of the Polish fellow so that the other house is still available for guests. But it is high time that somebody occupies them soon, otherwise we will be pressed to take in non-family people.

Uncle Robert became Karl Heinz's godfather, but I doubt he ever saw him.

Letter from Robert to Isa, August 18

I have now received the birth announcement of Karl Heinz. Who represented me at the baptism? If possible send me some pictures. I don't want to miss congratulating you on your upcoming birthday and hope that you still celebrate many of them with joy.

This letter was sent to Stuttgart and forwarded by my mother to Ditzenbach, where we had moved in the meantime.

Letter to my parents from Aunt Lilli and Uncle Willi Suth
[This must have been written after the birth of Karl Heinz, but before we were evacuated. My aunt and uncle had already been evacuated, either voluntarily or involuntarily.]

Thank God that you were not in Stuttgart today, but you should leave—at least Isa and the children. Our landlady is really nasty to us, because she is angry that she has to rent out a room because her daughter in Berlin is not coming back. Lilly can understand her feelings, but she is really too dreadful.

Our heartiest congratulations; we hope that the small child who saw the first light in the world in these dark times has a happy and sunny life. We hope it is not too long till we have peace. In Cologne we lost everything that we had acquired with great difficulty during the last year and that we had stored in eleven places. I really don't care anymore; we are both so tired and exhausted that we can't go on much longer. Uncle Willi checked in on his sisters in Frechen, close to Bonn. It took him eight hours for the return trip [normally a two-hour trip]. Tomorrow he will go to Cologne, and I will go to Bonn, which was hit even worse. But we have to register our damages. Everything that we should have gotten from Aachen also burned at the carpentry shop including the material for the furniture. Now, take care, one is quite confused, what can you expect?

We didn't really relax or recover on our trip; we were always hungry.
Aunt Lilli

Also all the best for Karl Heinz and good wishes, including your
mother, if she should still be with you.
Uncle Willi

The enclosed twenty marks are for Karl Heinz.

Letters to my parents from Neudeutschland and Heliand friends

From Erich, Berlin, August 8

Congratulations on the birth of your third child. That's life: some have
to go and then others come; an eternal dying and being born. I will send
a toy that he can perhaps use in a year, but that's all I could get in these
times.

Berlin is in the process of being evacuated. The whole town is crazy,
really crazy. The action is so chaotic and furthermore, so severe, and
was announced so unexpectedly, you have the feeling that only one slo-
gan counts: "If you can, just save yourselves." They act accordingly. We
who are employed have to stay and hold down the fort. The mood is
very depressing. In my opinion it won't take much more and the Berlin-
ers will revolt. I haven't seen Elli since she returned from Hamburg,
where her mother has been totally bombed out. My sister is not coming
to Berlin considering the situation. A bitter disappointment. I hope to see
you happy and healthy in September,
Maria

I also wish all the best for KH and that you don't have to deal with the
same frenzy we do here.

From Elli and Max P., Berlin, August 8

...all the best to the little man who is born in such difficult times.
Thank God that he came early! We didn't hear anything about alarms in
Stuttgart during that time.

Please do not be angry that I write so late, but we have had a lot of
work and excitement since we returned. First we were worried about our
Hamburg family—till we could reach them by telegraph and found out
that my mother and grandparents lost all of their possessions, but sur-
vived. They both live with relatives temporarily. What happened in Ham-
burg has to have surpassed all the horrors that overcame other towns.
My sister Hilde came on Monday on a special furlough from Russia.

Eight days ago Goebbels proclaimed that all persons who are not em-
ployed have to leave Berlin at once. Immediately a mass flight started; it
is perilous at the train stations. I have decided to stay here for the fore-
seeable future—in spite of all the dreadful rumors, but I regret I didn't
leave my son in Hagenbuch. My sister-in-law wanted so to keep him.
Are you experiencing similar things? I haven't had time to see Maria yet.
Mrs. T. left yesterday for Silesia with their four sons. I must admit that I
have a heavy heart; it all seems so hopeless. Write soon.

Letter from Ernst, Allianz colleague, Breslau, August 9

How should I start this letter? Should I grieve or rejoice? We hope that the death of your brother-in-law was at least a small contribution to a happier Germany. Our sympathy cannot heal, but I hope it can soften your grief. The birth of the baby son gave us great joy. Is the boy happy to be alive and does he shout it out or is he worried about the future? Perhaps you can tell from his voice what emotions are uppermost. I am afraid that the second promised furlough for us soldiers has been cancelled, but we are hoping for a time when the furlough gets reinstated and we can descend on you.

What do you hear from Aachen? Do many of your relatives still live there? One of my colleagues just returned from Hamburg and told horror stories. Yesterday we received Goebbels's pamphlet in which he ordered the evacuation of everyone who is not working. The nervous Berliners got very upset and are now confused. We are expecting people from Berlin to stay with us for some time.

Letter from an unknown relative or friend who called my grandmother "Aunt"

August 12, 1943

Dear Aunt Thesa [family name for my grandmother], *Dear Heinz!*

Thanks for the congratulations for our second son and congratulations to you on the birth of Karl Heinz. Hopefully we don't have to train our boys for a third world war. Dear Aunt Thesa, our heartfelt sympathy on the loss of all your belongings and your house in Aachen. We observe things here in quietness and will bear the loss of our belongings with the same courage as you Rhinelanders. The main thing is that we stay healthy so that we can devote ourselves to rebuilding after the war.

Many things that we feel emotionally cannot be expressed on paper. But we think alike. Dear Aunt Thesa, take solace in the inexhaustible joy of your many grandchildren, who I am sure bring their Oma much sunshine.

Greetings, also from my wife, yours, Heinz

Uncle Richard's diary, with an overview of the first half of 1943

January 29

E. Deininger (Donzdorf, 32) died a hero's death, and the oldest son of the farmer on the Kuchalb (21) died near Woroschilowgrad.

March 3

Isa comes for a visit with Margit and Hans Bernd. Margit stays till June 24. As of March 3, private photography is prohibited. No films, plates, or photo paper may be sold to private people. This edict had to be relaxed soon.

March 3

The Polish farmhand Roman Kowal [not his real name] *came to us. A*

short time later he and an accomplice were arrested. Both had run away
from their previous boss. After his punishment, he had to return to his
original boss.

April 7
  I joined the NSV [Nationalsozialistische Volkswohlfahrt, a social welfare organization during the Third Reich].
* * *

  During the night of April 14–15 a severe air attack in Stuttgart dam-
aged the Nikolaus church, partially burnt the Haus Löhle, hit the city's
gas boiler, and leveled the surrounding area. Very much affected were
also the suburbs Münster, Mühlhausen, and Hofen, in addition to
Cannstatt, where there were many fires. Gerhard Baumgartner [my
mother's sister Wilma's husband] *comes for a furlough.*
  During the night of June 29, English/North American fighter bombers
attacked Cologne and the cathedral.

[Note: The Allies took special care not to hit the two tall spires of the cathedral, because
they used them for orientation purposes. They did however hit the rest of the cathedral many
times; the first attack was on May 31, 1942, and the last major attack was on March 2, 1945,
a few days before the American occupation of Cologne. After the war when the excavation
under the cathedral started, many bombs that embedded themselves in the thick walls, were
discovered. An official report written by the cathedral priest stated: "Thousands of Americans visited the cathedral shortly after the occupation to look at the edifice. They behaved
very well. Nothing of value was stolen during this time."]

  Just now, July 12, we were informed that our nephew Karl was killed in
Russia on June 28. He is buried in the hero's cemetery in Kirejkowo;
born June 12, 1916.

July 19
  An English/American plane's formation (about 300 planes) bombed
the city of Rome. The famous St. Lawrence Church was among the
buildings totally destroyed.

July 25
  Il Duce [Mussolini] *resigned, and was replaced by Marshall* [Pietro]
Badoglio. The reasons for this became known in Germany much later.

Aunt Thea's Reflections on the War Years

The house on Kernerplatz in Stuttgart into which we moved in 1938 was
inhabited by a motley group of people. The ground floor had two small
shops, a grocery and, next to it, a drycleaner and dye shop. One of the
women had a grandson who was half Jewish. I am not sure whether his
father or the second husband of the woman's daughter was executed
during the war, supposedly because they slaughtered animals on the

black market (illegally). The first floor was occupied by the Nazi regional group; there was constant coming and going, and we could see mountains of paper in the rooms, very much to the annoyance of the renter next door who was a very prim and proper Protestant fundamentalist. She was also our air warden [luftschutzwart], and when the sirens went off, she ran—despite her old age—from apartment to apartment and rang the door bells, if people didn't run immediately into the bomb shelter. Then we started to have blackouts at night. I always loved Stuttgart in the evening when the city was all lit up and I couldn't imagine how it would be with everything dark. I thought about it, but had no idea it could actually happen. But then I managed to navigate the streets in the dark as well as during the day. It was often dark when I returned from my job from the Keppler House [a Catholic publishing house and bookstore], and I sometimes ran home. Down off the curb to cross the street, and then up the curb on the other side to the other walkway. I knew where every stone was. And now when I think back to those nightly walks, I must admit that it often gave me the creeps when I walked by the state courthouse. My workplace was near the Marienplatz, so I had to cross almost all of downtown, to pass the Allianz [company] and the courthouse.

After a few years of the Nazi regime, we knew that there were weekly executions, mostly on Wednesdays, early in the morning. We heard this from a vicar who was a client of my father's and who ministered to the condemned in Stuttgart and in the Hohenasperg [prison]. I imagine that he accompanied the unfortunate people till the last minute and aided them. He often came to our store on Wednesdays, and always looked extremely pale. We had two other vicars in the parish. One day we heard that they were both arrested for listening to "illegal international radio broadcast" [probably the BBC]. Who reported them? Did they themselves gave any hint? During this time, denunciations were commonplace. In any case, the two vicars disappeared over night.

The Nazis were always happy when they could find something against the Catholic Church. During that time in our parish we formed a small youth group. Our bishop, Johannes Baptist Sproll, did not vote in 1938 when two of the questions were whether Austria should be asked "to come home" into the Reich and whether Adolf Hitler as führer and reichskanzler was wanted. Because he opposed the second question, he did not vote and consequently his windows were broken. Members of Hitlerjugend [Hitler Youth] were incited against him, etc. He was prohibited from living in the Württemberg region. First nobody wanted to take him in till the Bavarian gauleiter (Ritter von Epp) granted him asylum. He then lived till the end of the war in Bavarian Swabia, in Bad Krumbach. We had planned to have a service for him in the little chapel of the Antoniushaus, but when we heard about the two vicars, we dedicated the service to the two missing vicars. [Aunt Thea never said whether the vicars ever came back.]

132

It reminded me of the war, when the oldest bell of Stuttgart was ear-marked to be melted down—to become a cannon ball. It was a bell from the Stiftskirche. The people of Stuttgart were allowed to view the bell for some time in the Schiller plaza. It was engraved: AVE MARIA 1245. (I still consider this a cultural disgrace.)

My Reflections on the War till 1943

I was just a year old when Germany invaded Poland in 1939 and started the Second World War, which destroyed millions of peoples' lives and lifestyles. Therefore I have no recollections of the period of peace between the two big wars or the time when both sets of my grandparents where relatively wealthy.

Most of my first memories are of the war itself, and since I was only three or four years old when the war came to Stuttgart, my memories may not always be accurate. Almost my first recollection (around 1943) is of the sounds of sirens, followed by the sound of planes. Sirens led to instant blackouts of all dwellings and a scramble by about thirty-five other residents in our apartment house, running down six floors to spend the next few hours huddled together. We sat on benches with other apartment dwellers in our unheated potato cellar, two stories below ground level. It seemed that sirens only blared at night and shook us out of bed, so that we would throw on a few clothes, and half asleep, be ready for our flight down. Every so often a courageous soul would venture up to the back door of the apartment building to see whether the all clear had been sounded and the American/British planes had left. We were lucky that our building had more than one exit from the cellar. Many people died after a bombing raid because debris closed up their only exit and rescue troops could not get there in time to keep them from suffocating. During the last few weeks in August 1943 before we were evacuated, we slept with our clothes on.

At this time, my mother had her third child, my younger brother, Karl Heinz, and from then on I was responsible for getting my two-and-a-half-year old brother Bernd and myself ready for the cellar.

My second recollection is about sleeping on the floor in the inner hallway of the apartment, and not being allowed into the front rooms, because their windows faced the street where an unexploded bomb (*blindgänger*) was embedded in the pavement and could explode at any time—before the bomb disposal experts could get to it.

Every night the order was: black out. All shutters had to be tightly closed; no ray of light could emanate from any building; no streetlights were on. This was supposed to make it harder for enemy planes to find Stuttgart. Anybody who violated this order was severely punished.

It turned out that our apartment building was the only one in about a five block area that was not bombed out. One bomb did hit the building, coming through the roof, the ceiling and floor of the fifth-floor apartment, the ceiling of our fourth-floor living room, and embedding itself in a leather chair, where it did not explode. This was after we had evacuated and only my father was still living in the city. The bomb squad defused the bomb and removed it. The hole in the leather chair stayed as a reminder of the war for many years till my parents could afford to reupholster it. I still own the chair. Though it is not very nice looking and is old and unfashionably overstuffed, it is a most comfortable chair.

I have no recollection of the concept of "Jews" or that the couple who lived below us were different from the other inhabitants of the building. I also cannot remember being conscious of people wearing the Star of David. From the time I was five till I was almost seven, we lived in a very Catholic village. I am certain that no Jews were living there. Therefore I became aware of the atrocities against the Jews only after the war.

From Our Evacuation
to the End of the War

Recollections of Our Evacuation to Bad Ditzenbach, Schwäbische Alb

Three weeks after the birth of Karl Heinz, my mother and the three of us little ones were evacuated to Bad Ditzenbach, where we spent the rest of the war. Our father stayed at home in Stuttgart, working for Allianz, and visiting us on weekends.

Two of the most delightful years in my young life, 1943–1945, were a nightmare for my mother. Bad Ditzenbach is a small village, with a spa, in a secluded valley of the Schwäbische Alb. The people there speak a German that is still based on Celtic elements and cannot be understood by outsiders though it is only about fifty miles outside Stuttgart, the capital of the State of Baden-Württemberg. I do not remember how we got to Bad Ditzenbach, or our way to the involuntary evacuation out of the city, but my mother often told the story of how we came to choose Ditzenbach as our refuge. And every time she related her search she would choke up with emotion:

> By August 1943 the air attacks in Stuttgart had become so frequent
> that the regime decided that all nonessential people had to be moved
> out of the cities. If you could not find a place with relatives, you were
> evacuated by force and put with whomever the government could find to
> take you in. Everyone living in villages was forced to take someone in. I
> contacted my father's family in Schnittlingen first. There were four
> adults, a married couple, and two unmarried siblings living on a big
> farmstead, which had at least four empty rooms. But they refused be-
> cause three little children would upset their quiet lifestyle (my youngest
> child had been born three weeks ago). My mother's family were all very
> poor and lived in crowded quarters as it was, but in desperation I called
> the wife of my mother's half-brother, who herself had nine children. She
> immediately said, "Yes, we'll find you something."

So, we moved in with great uncle Xaver, great aunt Walburga, and their six daughters, Maria, Christel, Klara, Rosa, Paula, and Ellie (their three sons, Anton, Karl, and Otto were serving in the war).

At age five I loved the idea of open empty spaces. I loved the house, which seemed enormous to me (it had a big carpentry shop attached), the creek, 100 yards away, the forests all around us, and the friendliness of the villagers. Everyone knew everyone else. It didn't matter to me that my mother, two brothers, and I all slept in the same room during the week and shared the room with my father as well on the weekends when he came from the city. The room was divided by two wardrobes behind which were our five beds. The front part of the room served as a kitchen, dining, and living room. I remember an easy chair and a little cabinet on which there was a water heater with a heating coil that was used for cooking everything—including spaghetti. If there was a table, I do not recall. Of course we children spent most of our time outside. Our paternal Oma, Thesa, usually occupied our one easy chair. She had rented a very nice room in the spa, but she was lonely and spent every afternoon and evening with us. This was great for us children, because she played with us and read us stories, but it was a burden for my mother, since she could never put her feet up after a hard day: the only easy chair was already occupied.

In the winter, the entire family of my great aunt and uncle, six of their nine kids, various adults who worked in the carpentry shop, and we three Paulus children often spent time in the kitchen. That was the only place in the house that was heated. We all seemed to fit around the large table, or perhaps my great aunt fed us at different times? The big wood stove and oven was used for cooking and provided plenty of heat. It had all the human smells of a confined place. Only at Christmas and when the parish priest came for a visit was there a fire in the living room. How and if our quarters were heated, I do not recall. Water for our little family had to be pumped on the ground floor and carried up one flight of stairs. We did not have a room with running water. I do not remember a bathroom or how we washed (apparently not an important detail for a five-year old). There was only one toilet in the house, so lingering there was not an option.

The only time we children realized there was a war on was when our parents became desperate over the scarcity of food. Some incidents come to mind: Our mother's family gave us a small plot to plant our own vegetables. Both of my parents, raised in the city, had a hard time deciding when the vegetables were ripe for the picking. They pulled up the carrots and radishes every day to check on them and then replanted them "for continued growth." During one of the summers there was a flood (we were only about 100 yards from a creek). All of our potatoes, which had been harvested for the coming year, were stored in the root cellar. They rotted and were lost. I remember the desperation of the adults, but we children were happily rowing about the cellar in a tin bathtub having a fine old time. At the end of the war, food rationing became very strict and our family of five got enough ration cards for a quarter loaf of bread a week. I remember that every day for breakfast we ate *schwarze brei* (black mush), probably millet, though my mother claimed we only ate it about twice a week. Occasionally we were given a dab of butter. The big decision of the day was: Do you have one terrific spoonful of mush with lots of butter, or do you let the butter melt into the mass to trickle through it all but only a little. I still shudder at the sight of oatmeal, because it has the consistency of that black mush. The only fat we had was "schmalz," or goose fat, which we thought tasted wonderful. Many years later my husband and I and a colleague who had emigrated from Slovakia went to the Maukenestle in Stuttgart and ordered schmaltz and bread. Susan and I relished this "delicacy" from our childhood, but my husband's stomach churned after the first taste. I still reject red beets, because we got them when we were sick, for their source of vitamins.

My grandmother combined her ration tickets with ours, since she ate lunch and dinner with us. At this time she coined a phrase that we have often used since. Though there was never enough food to go around, if there was a bit left in the serving dish, she would offer, with a practical tone, to polish it off: "just to clean the plate." Later, whenever something delicious was served, we would all compete for it: "I'll take that, just to clean the plate."

My father, who had in the meantime been diagnosed with tuberculosis (as mentioned) and was thus not redrafted, stayed in Stuttgart those two years and worked for the Allianz insurance company. Few insurance policies were written then, so his job was to secure the building and to check the whole place out after each air raid. He had enough time between attacks to read the German classics: Goethe, Schiller, and Lessing. One volume of Goethe is missing in his collection because during one of the attacks he ran into the cellar and forgot to take his book along. Upon his return his office had been demolished and with it, his volume of Goethe. He came to Ditzenbach almost every weekend and most of the time he carried heavy suitcases, full of books. His books were more important to him than anything else. Our mother took the train to Stuttgart every month to clean the apartment and to cook a decent meal for our father. Since we had no refrigerator she could not prepare food ahead of time.

In 1943–1944 my paternal grandmother, who stayed with us, received a phone call that her house in Aachen had burned down after one of the frequent aerial bombardments. Now she was without a home.

Toward the end of the war, in September 1944, Stuttgart was heavily bombed. We stood in front of our house in Ditzenbach, about fifty miles away, and watched the sky during the evening and late into the night. It was fiery red. My mother kept saying: "Oh, Stuttgart is burning; I wonder whether our Vati and my parents will survive this attack." They all survived, but my grandparents and their youngest daughter, who still lived at home, lost their apartment and all their possessions. My grandmother recalled that after the attack people were so confused and stressed that when they wanted to salvage something from their burned-out apartments they carried bedding down the stairs, but threw jars of jam or vegetables out the window.

After my maternal grandparents were bombed out of their apartment in Stuttgart, they moved to Schnittlingen into the house that we had hoped to occupy in 1943. We went to visit them a few times from Ditzenbach. One New Year's Day, my parents, who were worried that they had not heard from them in quite a while (there were no phones in the farmstead in Schnittlingen), decided to check on them. So they walked from Ditzenbach to Schnittlingen, a distance of about eight miles, some of the way, quite steep. I accompanied them. According to my mother, while my parents sank into the deep snow with every step, I could walk over the top of the snow like a sprite.

When I was about six years old I spent some weeks in Schnittlingen in the summer. Because it was difficult to get farmhands during the war, everyone had to help out on the farm. A nasty job was to rid the potato plants of the potato bugs that had infested them that year. We crouched on the ground for hours, and examined every leaf, picked off the bugs and drowned them in a bucket of water. They looked like yellow ladybugs.

But often, rewarded for our work, we were allowed to ride home on the very top of the hay wagon. Once Bernd, my brother, was even allowed to ride the horse. When he fell off, right in front of the wheels of the wagon, the villagers who saw the accident scolded my great uncle Bernhard loudly: "What were you thinking? He could have been killed." The horse, however, had stopped immediately, and everything was fine. I watched this scene from my throne on top of the hay wagon, and never again wanted to ride a horse.

For me, a most unpleasant experience in Schnittlingen was the trip to the bathroom. The outhouse was inside the stable. To get to it I had to walk past a row of cows. They were secured in their stalls—or so the adults maintained—but how could I be sure? It didn't help that the two horses in the stable became agitated whenever people entered. These beasts looked enormous and quite threatening so I always covered the distance between the entry and the outhouse in record time.

To get to my grandparents' apartment on the other side of the farm you could take either the "inner way" or the "outside way." The inner way involved walking through the stable between its two rows of cows and horses, the hay barn, and the chicken and swine coops. Rain or shine, I preferred the outside way through the courtyard. Cows were milked by hand of course and the smaller animals were fed by hand. My great aunt Marie was in charge of the chickens and pigs. She would feed them by calling them in chicken talk: "kikerikee, kikerikee," or the pigs in pig talk, which wasn't "oink, oink," of course: she grunted at them in German. She would toss them their food from a pail and could always remember which hens were laying and which pigs were fattening up.

A whiff of manure today still brings back memories of Schnittlingen. There, the manure of the stable was shoveled onto a big manure pile just outside the farm buildings. It reached almost to the second floor. The more manure you had, the richer you were, because it showed you had a lot of animals. Every Saturday afternoon the pile was worked on and the surrounding area in front of the whole farm was swept clean for Sunday. No chance the visiting priest would step into manure! Once a year, the pile was disbanded, its contents shoveled into a manure wagon and spread as fertilizer over the fields. Since our relatives had one of the largest farmsteads and one of the sisters had married "a gentleman" (*Herrle*)—our uncle Richard—from Stuttgart, the priest had lunch at their house when he came to say Mass in Schnittlingen once a month. The other three Sundays, Mass was said in the larger neighboring village, Treffelhausen, and all the population of Schnittlingen walked about two miles over to Treffelhausen, rain or snow, sleet or sunshine. At that time, villages were either Catholic or Protestant. The village in the other direction of Schnittlingen was solidly Protestant and our young people were not encouraged to socialize with their youth.

Another Schnittlingen memory: When a thunderstorm was brewing, everyone on the farm, including the farmhands and visitors, assembled in the big front parlor (*die gute Stube*), faced the cross, and prayed for the duration of the thunderstorm: "Our Fathers" and as many rosaries as were needed. Had lightning struck the house, barn, or hayloft, it would have meant the financial ruin of the family. Sometimes whole sections of a village burned down before the volunteers (all the inhabitants) could quench the blaze with their bucket brigades to stop it from spreading. The nearest city with a fire station, Geislingen, was six miles away and at that time there were no telephone connections to Schnittlingen.

But the food! This is one pleasant memory of Schnittlingen. Till the end of the war, the farm produced enough to feed everyone and also to make some profit. Besides the cows, hens, chickens, and pigs, my uncle planted many fields with various grains, and my aunt had a large vegetable garden right behind the farmhouse. When we visited we received wonderful meals, which was a most-appreciated change from our daily diet.

In Bad Ditzenbach, at the beginning of our evacuation when foods could still be purchased, and when my father came from Stuttgart on Sundays, we'd walk to the next village, Gosbach, to eat at a restaurant. Ditzenbach itself did not have a restaurant. Both of these villages did not have more than a few hundred inhabitants. I was surprised when I met a German from Gosbach years later in the United States. She told me first that she was from Stuttgart, but when pressed for details she said, "Well, I actually come from a small village outside of Stuttgart. You wouldn't know it, Gosbach." Oh, but I did know it. The woman had married a GI after the war and now lives in Connecticut. Nowadays we love to exchange memories of our young lives in this secluded valley.

I remember the last months of the war quite well. Every few days, low-flying military planes flew over our playgrounds. Our house was on the main road of the narrow valley and we children automatically jumped into a ditch as we had been instructed to do. I do not remember whether these were German or American planes. My mother also tells the story of a trip with her mother-in-law to visit a doctor in Geislingen, about six miles away. Because train service was sporadic, they walked. On the way back, they were interrupted at least five times by low-flying planes. As soon as they heard them in the distance, they threw themselves into a ditch or into the bushes, because if they were American planes they shot at anyone who moved.

My mother had sewn pillowcases for us, into which she stuffed some clothing, a flashlight, dried fruit, and some crackers. We were told to run into the woods if the enemy was overrunning our village and we had a marked meeting place. I was responsible for my four-year-old brother. The inhabitants of the village started to bury their valuables in the gardens. We buried my mother's cutlery and very expensive camera (which still works). Stories are told that many people couldn't remember where they buried their treasures and thus lost them to the soil rather than to the occupying forces.

When the Americans came to the village in 1945, a white flag had been put up at the village entrance as a sign of surrender without resistance. However, one person was shot and killed, a peasant who was deaf and therefore could not hear the command to stop. Also, some Nazis barricaded themselves at the corner of Ditzenbach/Gosbach and Ditzenbach/Aulendorf, where our house was located. Because the house had no cellar and the inhabitants were afraid that the Germans would start shooting when the Americans arrived, we all spent a few hours in the cellar of a nearby farm until it was all clear. Our mother had pinned a note on our door in English: "Please don't hurt us, I have three little children." When the first soldier came to our door (they did search every house), he told my mother: "That's the reason we are here: to liberate you, so your children do not have to suffer anymore." These soldiers, who were all young—a lot of them students no doubt—drove into the village with tanks, new all-terrain tanks, wearing clean uniforms and looking well fed. This was in stark contrast to the German soldiers who had marched through the village a few weeks earlier, the so-called Volkssturm, the "people's army." When it was clear to everybody that Germany had lost the war, Hitler made a last-ditch effort to stop the advancing foreign troops. All males from age sixteen to well over fifty had to report for army duty and were marched toward enemy lines. These old men and young boys wore ill-fitting long coats and boots. They looked haggard and malnourished, because by that time, food was really scarce in Germany, including for Hitler's troops. I do not remember the young boys, but the shuffling old men made a deeply sad impression on me.

After the American occupation began, our little neighborhood gang of children sized up the situation promptly. We went to the American troops, who were quartered in the spa, to see whether they had something for us to eat. We sent in my two-year-old brother, Karl Heinz, first to charm them with his button nose, blond hair, and blue eyes. And, indeed, the soldiers gave us candy. We took these home to our parents and told them where they came from. Our parents, filled with mistrust, took them and threw them in the creek because they could have been poisoned. Of course we went right out and begged again. This time we knew not tell our parents. And we all survived.

Not too far from the village was the major super highway, the famous autobahn that Hitler built to move troops. When the French and then the Americans came along this highway, people lined up on both sides, and the Americans would often throw their packaged food rations to the starving people.

While we seemed to lead a fairly normal childhood in Ditzenbach, the war raged around us and become increasingly difficult for the soldiers and civilians who had to stay behind in big cities. The letters and diary entries below describe this.

Letters from Family and Friends on the Russian Front, and One Family Member Serving on the Western Front

My maternal grandparents were greatly affected by the war. By 1943, besides their four sons, three of their sons-in-law were at the front.

One was Dr. Paul Ludwig, a lawyer, who was married to their daughter Gertrud. He returned from the war and became a federal judge in Karlsruhe. Considered for a seat on the German Supreme Court (Verfassungsgericht), he declined because as an expert in criminal law he preferred to become judge at the highest federal court in Germany. With this new legal court, which was unprecedented in the German legal system, he perhaps felt that newly trained lawyers would be better suited for this high office. He was state chess champion in 1937 and again in 1946. He died of cancer in 1954 at the age of forty-four. His letters also show how he had to suppress his anti-Nazi feelings.

His daughter Dagmar summarized the letters that he sent between June 1943 and March 1945.

Though he was inducted into the army in 1940, none of the letters before June 1943 survived the bomb attack on Stuttgart of October 8, 1943, when his apartment completely burned. He was the only son of an officer who had been killed in the First World War. As such he had the right not to be sent to the front, a privilege, however, that could be rescinded any time. Sometimes his letters were delivered directly by a comrade on furlough and it is only in such letters that he could write openly, telling about his whereabouts, his unit, and details of his work.

From Russia: Because of the bombed-out apartment, he received a special furlough in October 1943. He writes from forty kilometers outside of Leningrad, near Novo-Lissinow. He is working for the general command, which is under the 18th Army of the Northern Army group. He works on requests and orders for the officers and the enlisted men. He is the first one to be informed about troop movements. In many letters he writes vaguely about work, but always hints that he can't say anything specific. He writes many times that he is a paper pusher. He also tells about the progress he is making in learning how to type and take dictation in shorthand. He is proud of his progress, but can't fulfill every demand and is afraid of a transfer. He detests cleaning jobs and is always glad when he shares his lodgings with practical mates.

He gets along well with his bosses, a university professor of art history and a federal judge. Once a week he has sentinel duty. They work in a log cabin, which is warm even in the winter. He has not volunteered for his job as legal field scribe. He plays chess and talks with visiting artists about music. A new boss speaks to him about his "problematic attitude." He writes: "Russia makes you numb. I will not have inner peace till this war is over." His inner conviction is not affected by anything.

The allusion to music and how important it is for him is a thread that runs through all his letters. He also tries to play chess as often as possible, but this makes him suspect in the eyes of the others. He is always surprised to find other good players, one a sergeant, and a lieutenant with whom he exchanges one move at a time either by telephone or by letter. It becomes clear that this activity distinguishes him from his comrades, and he recognizes that it is best not to draw attention to himself. He writes that "neither his disposition, his education, nor his profession make him suitable for the practicalities in life." Increasingly he writes about fallen comrades, including lawyers, and about air raid damages.

His wife sends her furniture to her sister in Austria for storage.

At the end of 1943 he writes that the cancellation of furloughs was extended from three months to six months if you had already received a special furlough. He is afraid of a total ban on furloughs due to the increase of Russian attacks. Many of the comrades were "shoved aside," "were involuntarily transferred to another unit," or "had to take up a nomadic life," meaning they were sent to the front lines. He also hears about the renewed attacks on Berlin and Stuttgart, and he hears from his brother-in-law, Hermann, that he had been wounded in Odessa.

A common theme in all letters is the exchange of packages. He sent smoking materials and marketenderware (goods that were brought along with the army and could be purchased by soldiers) in exchange for fruit, which he craves.

Letter to my father from a fellow Neudeutschen, shortly after our evacuation

September 10, 1943, on the front, FieldPost from Sergeant H.E. 24612 [printed underneath is the warning: "It is prohibited to mention the troop unit. Service functions like marksman, pioneer, airman may not be written. Use words like soldier, private first class, sergeant, etc.]

Three weeks ago I was involuntarily transferred to the communications unit of our division, and only managed a few days ago—during a march of my unit—to get a small bundle of mail, which informed me that great joy had come to the Paulus family with the birth of their second boy. My heartfelt congratulations, a bit late (as is understandable for us at the edge of civilization). And my sincerest hopes that the cradle of the children will be spared the horrors from the air. Do you have a place of refuge for your wife and children? I heard that Stuttgart is taking preventive measures. What do you hear from our friends? If you send a newsletter around, I would be grateful if you would send something to me occasionally. The need for contact with friends is strong. Excuse the informal letter, that's what happened to us. H.

Sending such a newsletter around would have meant punishment for my father, if the Gestapo had found out.

By now Uncle Robert had also been deployed to the Eastern front. While Uncles Karl, Hermann, Robert, and Paul had to endure many hardships and difficult situations on the Eastern front, Uncle Rudolf—my grandparents' fourth son—was having a much easier time on the Western front, as the following letters indicate.

Letter from Rudolf to Isa, September18

I appreciate the congratulations on my birthday, which came in such a timely fashion—considering the enormous distances they had to travel.

Interesting that you write that you see your two oldest only twice a day for lunch and dinner when the weather is nice. Your solution to the forced evacuation of women and children is not bad, even though it cannot be considered 100 percent. But it is bearable for you, the children, and Heinz. I am looking forward to the picture of your youngest since the data of height and weight that Heinz gave me with good intentions are rather meaningless for a [childless] layperson like me.

You asked how I am. Thanks, quite well. This, however, has become my standard answer. Service is rather demanding, but bearable. Also, I have survived attacks without injuries since no bombs have fallen close to us. During the last attack I could observe how three enemy machines were shot down in a very short time. All crashed in flames and one exploded in midair. It was a terrific sight to see the parts flying through the air. A lot of damage has been inflicted here. I went into Paris yesterday and saw a completely destroyed railroad station. A few direct hits crushed everything, the rails were bent, the cars of the train were toppled and crushed, and five- or six-story buildings had caved in on themselves. It looked a real mess.

Due to various circumstances, we can no longer visit Paris as often as before. I am glad I bought a guidebook right when we got there, which allowed me to stroll through the city. I have seen all the major attractions, and I can navigate quite well in the city. The city is really very wonderful and unique. You know, everything is laid out on such an imposingly large scale. The large buildings don't appear to be overwhelming, but fit harmoniously into the whole picture. I haven't been to a theater yet. But a few days ago, I visited a big French cinema. Not only do they have a newsreel and a short film, but before the feature film, a 25-30–person band plays live music for entertainment and they put on a variety show at intermission, which is quite risqué. Decorations, of course, are the best. I loved it. These shows are not only in the one cinema, but also in all the big movie houses.

I am glad that I did a lot of sightseeing at the beginning of my tour, because now, with the winter approaching, the dusk is coming before I have free time and the buildings will not look as good as they do in the summer's evening light. How can I not feel good, even if the service is hard, since I have these distractions?

Relocation of People from the East

At this time, when Germany was beginning to lose the war, ethnic Germans who lived in the occupied territories to the East were being relocated back to Germany.

Reminiscences of Gisela Brühl

[Gisela is the wife of Franz Brühl, my mother's cousin.
Franz took over the family farm in Schnittlingen.]

I was born and raised in Slovakia, near Bratislava. Since our parents were German, beginning in 1943, we were slowly evacuated to the west since Germany was no longer winning the war. First, the children, then the women. After the war the men were deported. In 1943 I was sent to camp first, then to foster parents. My three sisters all went to different foster parents. We established contact again only after the war.

[Note: In 2009 I met a woman who corroborated the stories of relocation of ethnic Germans. She lived with her mother and three siblings in Stettin, now Szczecin in Poland.]

Because the Russian troops were advancing from the East, and Hitler wanted to make sure that the youth survived, he started a movement whereby school-age children were separated from their parents and sent with their teachers into rural areas farther to the west. My older sister (14) and I (12) were sent to this camp, while my two younger siblings stayed with my mother (my father was in the war). We continued our education there. At the end of the war, when everyone started to flee from the approaching Russians, our group of students was abandoned by the teachers. For weeks, we roamed around the country side in small groups, begging and stealing food from the fields, sleeping in barns on straw, till we were picked up by the Caritas people and eventually reunited with our mother and two younger siblings, who had also become refugees. Without the moral and physical support of my older sister I would not have survived because at some time I had developed dysentery and had lost a tremendous amount of weight.

Life in Bad Ditzenbach

Mother's diaries

September 1943
Since the end of August we have lived in Bad Ditzenbach. It's a great time for the children. The gorgeous weather allows them to be outside from morning till night, and the wonderful fruit harvest assures that they always have an apple or a pear in their hand. Bernd can really romp. His loud demeanor is hardly noticed outside, but is often a catastrophe in our one-room apartment.

October 1943
Bernd is very good with his little brother, though for the longest time

he did not understand that he was not a little girl. In his uncoordinated and loud way he crowds the baby, sometimes a lot, but he shows so much emotion. I loved to watch the other day when he stormed into the room with his beloved teddy bear and held it up over the side of Karl Heinz's bed. Though he couldn't see over the side of the bed, he tried to show the baby his beloved toy. His speech is getting better. To his first words, which surprisingly included the difficult words "Butzi" and "Mutti," he now adds short sentences. His first one of course was "choo-choo comes." I don't think he has missed a train that comes through the intersection.

[Note: The Täle Bahn (little valley train) was about fifty meters from the house and ran frequently during the day. There were no buses and very few private cars connecting all the villages of the valley.]

In 1944 my mother began a diary about Karl Heinz.

Mother's diary

KH [Karl Heinz] saw the light of the world in very hard times. We were in the fourth year of the war. Every congratulatory letter or card included wishes for a more peaceful future. This is also my dearest wish for you, my little boy. He was baptized on August 4 in St. Fidelis (very soon after the birth, because of the constant fear of air raids). The little one was named in memory of his uncle Karl, recently killed in the war, and to carry on the Paulus family tradition of Heinrichs.

When he was eight days old, he had to go into the air raid cellar for the first time, and then almost every day after that. But when he was three weeks old, he went on this first trip when I took the three children to Bad Ditzenbach. During the first weeks of settling in, KH followed a very irregular routine. But his many aunts spoiled him, which probably explains why his obedience nowadays leaves much to be desired. The stay in the rural setting seems to be to his liking, because he progresses well. He looks very handsome when he lies in his pram with his sparkling blue eyes and his pink cheeks. He laughed for the first time after five weeks, returned our laughs after seven weeks, and started to form sounds. This is the third time that I have experienced this, but it is always new and wonderful with each child.

More Letters from the Front

Letter to Isa from Hermann from the front, October 6

A few days ago I received your letter of September 2. It is miserable how long the mail takes. Soon I'll be satisfied if the mail just arrives. I was glad you took the advice of an old experienced man. Safe is safe, and everybody has the duty just to survive this war the best they can. Well, what does duty mean, certainly everybody has the desire and the wish to be present for the final victory. Yes, when the war is over and ev-

144

erything gets back to normal, those are the times we all hope for. Now, however, we have to do things that we don't like, like you being in Ditzenbach and Heinz in Stuttgart. I am here and I wear someone else's clothes while at home, I have suits waiting for me for the last four-and-a-half years. But there is nothing that can be done about these things and therefore we want to exercise patience until better times come. The times we dream about. We always have to do our duty fully and completely, because a Fairy Tale World is just a fairy tale. If one doesn't expect and desire too much from the future, then one won't be disappointed.

    Now, I'll write something about myself. I have turned my back to the Kubau-Bridgehead and have disappeared into the vast flatlands of Rus-sia.... I am mired down in the south and during the first days I dug into the earth like a vole. It cost many drops of sweat, but two days ago my castle with all its comforts was finished. From the outside it distinguishes itself from the surroundings only by a mouse-high mole hill that is of course so brilliantly camouflaged that the enemy can only recognize it from a few meters away. The furnishings, however, are marvelous.... As a progressive person you know how you can change the furniture to make the finest living room from a bedroom, and then a music room (the bathroom is housed in the piano). Now, I used these concepts exclu-sively in my decorating and it looks fine.

In general I am a happy puppy and a soldier through and through, but these furnishings make me question myself, because they have no mili-tary flair. They remind me of the luxury home of a single woman. In the meantime, I am a person, and why shouldn't I have some beauty for once.

From a letter of Hermann's brother-in-law, Paul Ludwig, and from his own letters, I surmise that he had been severely wounded near Odessa, then transferred to a field hospital in Glatz, and finally taken as a prisoner of war in Germany. He limped for the rest of his life. After he returned from the war, Hermann became an artist who into old age always made the best of any situation.

Letter from Robert to Rudolf, November 16

For many days we have been marching and this is the first time that I am able to write. At the moment our situation is dire. You know yourself how good you feel when you receive mail and we haven't gotten any for three weeks. Who knows how long it will take before we receive some. I have sent stamps for a package home and I hope it will get there so that the family can send me a package. My mood is completely down. My letters and diary notes show something about our daily life [the diary did not survive]. I have to wait at least another four months, even though I have already served for thirteen months. What is the talk in your area about the general situation? We don't hear anything. I only know that we are sliding from one cauldron into another. Personally I am doing well, but I am angry about no furlough and no mail. Hopefully the war will be over soon so that we can pursue our dreams. If you are in Russia, you are damned and there is no easy exit. I hope that we will see each other again soon and I greet you with these sentiments.

Letter from Robert to his family, December 15
(written on small, torn piece of paper)

At last I have time to write. I am at a communication's training with the division since December 6. At the beginning I had to study hard to keep up, but now it's easier. But, alas, the course will be over December 21. I am enjoying the beautiful days where one can really relax. We are not on sentry duty and also the food is acceptable. What else could you ask for in Russia? Please excuse the stationery, but my toiletry bag caught fire and I could only save a few pieces of paper and envelopes. I wish you a Happy Christmas Season and a blessed and healthy 1944.

Letter from Robert to his family, end of December 1943

Thank you very much for the Christmas package with the bacon, which tasted wonderful and was such a welcome change from the monotonous military rations. The rolls and the rock candy were also balm for a sweet tooth. I am doing fine. Since we received replacements again for the communications people, I became a truck driver again. This means that I am farther behind the lines, with the disadvantage that I can no longer lead my cozy life, but have to do sentry duty and foot patrol. I don't expect to get a furlough till at least February or March.

On Christmas 1943 Uncle Rudolf sent a card to my parents. On the front was a yellow swastika surrounded by a yellow-and-black wreath over a sword that was encircled by a twig of pine. On the inside is a colorful picture with pine twigs, a steel helmet, a town seal of Paris with a ship with a white sail on the ocean, and a lit candle. The text reads "Frohe Weihnachtsgrüsse Aus Frankreich 1943" (Happy Christmas Greetings from France 1943). And in handwriting: "I wish you a Good New Year, Heinz, Margit, and Hans-Bernd. Your Rudolf. Please let me hear from you."

Uncle Richard's diary, 1943

September 7
We received the news that our neighbor's son died in action in Russia on August 12.

September 8
We learned that Badoglio had already signed the unconditional capitulation of Italy on September 3. Mussolini was arrested September 8, but already freed by the Germans on September 12, under difficult circumstances.

September 29
Three crates with linens and clothing arrived from our relatives in

Hamburg for safekeeping. Our niece Maria sent us three wooden crates with clothing from Hamburg for storage.

October 4

Maria and her two children spent a week with us before they moved into the house in Donzdorf, where an acquaintance had given them an apartment for their evacuation. The two children, Armin and Elinor, will go to high school in Geislingen. Our niece Wilma and Wolfgang and Suse were forced to evacuate to Griesingen near Ehingen.

December 6

Ober Gefreiter Karl Hruschka from Vienna leaves us and returns to his hometown. He was quartered with us for some time

1944 – The War Continues into Its Sixth Year

Letter to Isa from Hermann, Glatz (Klodzko), January 16, 1944
[then under German occupation, Gltaz lies southwest of Breslau (Wroclaw), Poland]

Today I received your letter from January 9, 1944.... I want to write you honestly about my condition and there is not much to report, because time will tell. At the moment everything is healed with the exception of the left foot and I am writing this letter, sitting at the table. I am getting around on two crutches and by moving the right leg forward inch by inch. It's not possible for longer periods, because then the blood shoots down into my left foot. When the wounds are completely healed, I hope that the foot will also be restored. Whether the foot will stay paralyzed or not, that no one can tell me right now. The instep of the left foot was shattered. Whether I will ever return as K.V. [?], I don't know; I am hoping that I don't have to go back to the front. A transfer is not so easy. If at all possible I will ask for a transfer to Lochau or Beuron. The days drone along and all spiritual guidance is totally lacking. Every day Thea sends me books and I will try to read.

Letter from Robert to Rudolf, January 16

At last it worked out with your furlough. The air force is still the better bunch. We have another total furlough prohibition, even though we are about thirty men who haven't had a vacation for thirty months. I would be so grateful if I would get my leave during the time of my birthday, so that I could celebrate it at home. Then I would drink the bottle of champagne from you. During the last few weeks there has been a lot of action. We always receive tobacco as combat pay. I sent a package to Father with nine packages of tobacco and eleven cigarettes. I was transferred to the communications tower since we are short of communications experts. I am the one who connects the phone calls in the trenches. But soon I will transfer to the B-Stelle. I like the job quite well even though it is harder than being a driver. Don't tell the parents anything about this.

Letter from Rudolf in Paris to Isa Paulus,
Bad Ditzenbach im Taele, c/o carpentry shop Priel, January 29

The first "bitter" days have passed and I have settled in well again. There is a lot of work at the moment, but other than that there is not much going on. I mean, on the personal level. But perhaps I can see "La Boheme" next Sunday. I have wanted to see the opera for a long time and I would love it, if it happens. I am still thinking back on that nice furlough day in Ditzenbach. I found it very nice there and loved seeing you again. As you gave me so much joy during these hours, I want to try to return the favor by sending you a small package. Please write if it arrived and when—and whether you can use the wild conglomeration of items. Enjoy your new "home" and its wonderful environs,… And many thanks for all you did during my stay there.

Letter to my parents in Ditzenbach from Hans Pardun, a priest in Düren,
near the Dutch and Belgian border, an old friend of our father's and godfather to Bernd

February 3, Düren Ahrweilerplatz

The hell hound has been loosened. One can definitely say that. You will be surprised to hear from me—yes we are still alive. My mother is with me yet. My youngest sister had to go to Bielefeld because the Deutsche Bank was evacuated there. My twin sister showed up unexpectedly from Gütersloh. She had to flee from Luxemburg head over heels [Hals über Kopf]. The situation is thus: there are constant alarm sirens—without interruption. For the last fourteen days there have been no all-clear sirens. At night we sleep in the damp cellar (which however has nothing "moist [Feuchtes] to drink"), because the artillery shells the city every half hour or so from the surrounding hills without any specific target. This beast has one good characteristic, it does not penetrate the basement, but makes a very nasty noise when it hits the ground. One does therefore sleep with interruptions, thinking of the noise of Judgment Day. I think of this often now because every day could be my last. However, sometimes during the day we hear a great tremor out of left field, probably because a gunner had the bright idea to shoot us harmless civilians.

Because we have to live and carry on with normal activities, many people get killed. So far, we have been able to say Mass in the early morning hours. You will have heard, in the peaceful fields of Ditzenbach, that the railroads here are destroyed over and over with these charming carpet bombs. So this is my report about my mood—no joyous news—but it mirrors our still-intact nerves and the strong will not to leave the field before we get forced to. May God grant it!…

Boy, I had to run into the basement. Four shells in the immediate vicinity. I was lucky again. This night was especially bad, because many planes were overhead. How is everybody…? Write in detail and soon because otherwise it could be too late, and then we wouldn't hear from each other for a long time. Gottfried [another priest and good friend] was

*here three weeks ago and picked up an application for war damage
compensation. Yesterday this application was brought to my house without any mention of Gottfried. When he left here, his leg* [which had been
injured in an attack] *was pretty bad. Yesterday an old friend showed up
to search for his mother in Aachen. You can still get to Aachen through
the Krefelderstraße, since the city is not yet occupied by the Tommies,
but that, only under threat of death and if one can find a ride with a military vehicle.*

*The Schuls's house was destroyed; the family evacuated to Linnich,
but their son Josef died in combat. Josef Schreiber is missing in action
in the Crimea and his wife died during the air raid on Aachen. I could
prolong this sad litany ad infinitum. However, there are still a few humor-
ous occurrences that you can only relate in person. Quietly we should
enjoy the few beautiful things of every day. I do hope that you experience many good things in Ditzenbach, and that I will see you again,
healthy. Be good and behave yourselves.*

May God grant it, with lots of love, Your Hans

While the war was raging in the cities on the Western front in the Rhineland with British and American troops advancing and on the Eastern front with Russian troops advancing,
life was still fairly normal in southern Germany and especially in our hidden valley.

Letter to me from my father, who was then in a TB sanatorium

*Many thanks for your letter. Were you sad that I didn't come last
Sunday? From now on, I will come every Sunday. I was very pleased to
hear that you are such a good eater and that you help Mutti so well. You
know, little Margit, you are our big daughter who can help Mutti with
many chores. Mutti also writes that you always put your things away and
that you obey when she tells you something. That is great and makes
me happy. That's why the Easter Bunny will surely bring you the things
that you wished for. Stay just as good. I am looking forward to Sunday.
Count how many more days.*

Mother's diary

February 1944

*We have been in Bad Ditzenbach for half a year and enjoy an involun-
tary country stay with its sunny and shadowy sides; that is an advantage
for the children's life here. If it doesn't rain, snow, or storm, they are out
all day. We have a sand box right outside the house, a slide made of two
planks, a garden and two play benches—what more could a child's
heart desire? For Margit, our little quicksilver, this stay is of great bene-
fit. She is heavily engaged in household chores. She does the shopping
in the village and takes the baby on a walk with the pram. She protects
and defends Bernd energetically against the village youth.*

*I especially value her work here in the room since she folds the dia-
pers and puts them away, keeps the toy drawers in neat order, etc. She
plays with him totally in his language, using the diminutive by adding "le"*

after the words. When Bernd, who had been warned repeatedly, still jumped up and down in his bed and fell out, I had to laugh, which brought this rebuttal from Margit: "Mutti, you shouldn't laugh! That hurts; it has happened to me before." Lately Margit shows great interest in learning poems and songs, and thank God her singing has improved so that one can actually recognize the melody. A few days ago she surprised me reciting her 2s, 3s, 5s, and 10s. Elli taught her that. How very receptive and curious is a child: it absorbs impressions from the whole environment—for good and for bad.

I notice this in my "two big ones" because they use idioms, pictures, and thought connections that are alien to me. Now we parents have the task to evaluate and order everything that goes on in their small heads.

There is Bernd, the beloved brother, but often enough an "interrupter." She often flatters me with the remark: "After God's mother and the mother of Dornröschen ("Dornröschen" is one of her favorite Grimm's fairy tales), you are the best Mutti."

Some of her sayings: Her friend Eva was almost born the same day as Margit, which led her to declare: "If we were born in the same house, we would be twins." When we went to the grocery store and Frau Gall opened instead of Frau Bruder, she remarked dryly: "It is Frau Bruder, just with another head." We told her that during a church procession Jesus himself walks with us. She was very interested and asked: "Will he be carried alive or dead?" When I scolded her the other day, she asked: "Later, will I also have children this wicked?"

Since the increased bombing raids killed civilians and destroyed property, extended family members, many of whom had been evacuated to distant places, informed each other whether they had survived an air attack, by express mail.

Telegram from Thea to Minni in Bregenz, Austria, March 17, 1944
[limited to ten words]

Sign of life: Brühl Thea from Stuttgart—East Kernerplatz 5.
All survived, nothing happened. Greetings, Thea

Remembrances by Aunt Thea about Robert, the brother she was closest to

On Holy Saturday, April 8, 1944, Robert appeared late at night in front of the glass door on Kernerplatz [where Aunt Thea lived with her parents]—without belt, rifle, bags, in an oversized soldier's coat from which he every so often extracted a louse during the meal that we quickly threw together. What a surprise! Mother dragged out anything edible in the house. After he had eaten a plate of Spätzle, jam, and all kinds of other stuff, he asked: "Mutterle, do you still have some cheese?" With incredible difficulties he dragged himself back from Russia, because the second lieutenant in charge would not give him sick leave. The lieutenant, himself, was in Krakow when Robert reached the field hospital. On his way to his Ulmer garrison, he disembarked for a short time to be with us, then because he was overtired he did not wake up in Ulm and eventually jumped off the slow-moving train in Günzburg. Eight days later he

received an official furlough for Rudolf's wedding. Even though the wed-
ding was a small, simple family affair, he seated himself next to me and
said with tears in his eyes: "I am dancing here, and perhaps I won't find
any of my buddies alive when I return." That's how it was. Another few
hours with parents, siblings, and his dear girl, and then at the end of
May the farewell hour arrived. What he and mother have suffered; God
only knows. In Him he is protected as he was when he was sitting inside
a straw bale that the Russians probed with their rifles.

Trudl Wintterle and Rudolf Brühl were married on April 15, 1944, in St. Nikolaus Church in Stuttgart. She wore a long white dress and a long white veil. However, since the wedding was in the middle of the war, she had to arrange for her whole trousseau. The white undergarment was from her aunt in America; the material for her dress that she and her mother sewed came from her brother who worked at the theatre in Rostock, where he bought materials for all the costumes; her veil came from France. A comrade on the front with her fiancé had a French girlfriend who found the veil. The shoes were from her sister-in-law, who used them for dance lessons. Since they fit her, but were used, she sent them to her brother to coat them with some silver lacquer. For her bride's bouquet her mother had to trade 4½ pounds of butter. Rudolf had to follow the law and get married in his soldier's uniform. In the evening while they were dancing, some of the silver lacquer on her shoes came off onto his uniform's pants. They spent some of their wedding night brushing the lacquer off his uniform.

Oma Barbara, my mother, Aunt Thea, and Uncle Robert, who was home on a furlough, attended the wedding. All the other siblings were either in the war or evacuated and couldn't attend.

When Rudolf had to get back to the front lines, Trudl stayed with her mother in their apartment. Someone in the apartment house listened to the radio day and night and as soon as there was a warning that enemy planes were headed for Stuttgart, he ran from apartment to apartment to warn the people to get out. According to Aunt Trudl, "We were lying on top of the beds, half dressed, anyway, threw on some more clothes and ran from the Werrastraße to the Hausmannstraße to the bomb shelter in the Wagenburgtunnel. We often sat there densely packed for hours before the all clear was sounded. In October 1944 we were bombed out and moved to the smithy at the edge of Schnittlingen."

Reminiscences of Aunt Thea

On April 15, 1944, [Rudolf] married his Trudl, amidst the unimaginable
chaos of the Second World War. The furloughs of all of my brothers
made a big impression on me. I felt the connection that our mother had
with her sons. And I saw how mother sat quietly next to her sons or
talked to them before they had to leave again for the front.

Letter from Sergeant Gerhard Baumgartner to Trudl,
April 22, on the Western front, F.P. Nr. 44 818 B
[Gerhard was my Aunt Wilma's husband; Trudl was his brother-in-law Rudolf's fiancée]

I received your wedding announcement today for which I thank you
with all my heart. I hope that Wilma has brought you my good wishes.
Unfortunately I had to go back to the front before the wedding day and

could not be part of your celebration. I hope the day was without air at-
tacks. I was concerned about Wilma and the children traveling to
Stuttgart. The large cities are no longer safe.

Could you send me Rudolf's address so I can send him belated con-
gratulations. I hope that the day on which we can all sit together in
peace is not too far off. Warm greetings.

Though Uncle Gerhard had written many letters to his wife, this is the only letter of his that survived. After the death of his wife, all the other letters were thrown out. He died at age ninety-six, but never talked about his war years or his long captivity.

Excerpts from Minni's Guest Book, Austria

Some German families keep guest books. At the end of a visit guests write a few reflections about their visit into this book. Even if people are shy about the idea, to be polite, they write a few comments. However, Aunt Minni's guest book during the war years shows that her family found refuge and some relaxation in her Austrian home.

Uncle Rudolf: "My first furlough after my more or less strenuous R.A.D.
service time (Reichsarbeitsdienst) was spent in Bregenz." January
24–29, 1940

Uncle Hermann: "Between R.A.D. and military service I spent my fur-
lough from February 27–March 4, 1940, in Lochau." [He also spent a
week in April 1942, back from Russia, in her home.]

Uncle Richard: "Saying farewell is not easy, but we leave with the hope
for a happy Wiedersehen next year. Our hope is that by then the bells of
peace will pronounce better days ahead." July 15–22, 1941

Oma Barbara Brühl: "Even in the war, I was granted the privilege to
spent a few gemütliche and beautiful days with you.... As God wills, we
hope that the hard and difficult days of the war will be over soon."

Uncle Karl: "I spent my first furlough from Russia in your wonderful
home." November 6–9, 1942

Uncle Robert: "After eighteen months on the front, I spent my first fur-
lough with you." April 18–31, 1944

Uncle Paul: "We spent two glowing holidays—the last ones in the war?"
April 22–23, 1944

Dire Situation on the Eastern Front

In letters written in early 1944, Uncle Paul often mentioned the fate of his brother-in-law Gerhard, from whom nobody had heard for a while and his cousin Max, who it turned out had become an American prisoner of war in 1944. It is clear that the communication and support of the whole family was very important for the soldiers. The weather also is constantly mentioned (cold, rain, and many colds).

Uncle Paul's daughter Dagmar cites from the lexicon of the Second World War:

"The army troop North had to abandon the Leningrad Front in January 1944 and withdraw behind the Narwa and to Pskow." Her father's letters from this time (some sent from Estonia) describe this retreat in detail. Starting in January of 1944 his letters sound more anxious. He has a new boss, new colleagues and the fear of Russian attacks increases. The soldiers also received terrible reports about the destruction at home from soldiers returning from furloughs. One of the soldiers lost his wife and four children in a sea of flames in Heilbronn.

At the end of January her father's unit was transferred. On January 27, 1944, he writes that in six days they changed their quarters five times. On February 2 they were in yet another location, in a castle, thirty kilometers behind the main line of fighting, which the bosses said had to be held at any cost. He tried to calm his family down by telling them that the "nerve center" of the high command was not threatened by enemy action. He writes about the retreat in detail: eight changes of locations, terrible scenes of refugees from the East. He praises his latest quarters in middle Europe, with running water, and real toilets. In Russia they lived in a log cabin. His fear of losing the exemption from combat, which he had because of his father's death in World War I, was lessened. A new edict gave him the assurance that he would be able to stay at headquarters and not be sent to the front. In all his letters about the retreat in January and February 1944 he tries to calm his wife. When he describes the retreat on the back of a flatbed truck, he writes in the next letter that he rode comfortably in the official bus. His mood is dependent on his bosses and comrades. He is happy when he meets a person who shares his philosophy. He writes often about the planned furlough, but also about the enormous workload that gets on his nerves. He goes on furlough on April 4.

He returns from furlough on April 28 and is happy that there are only alarms, but no attacks on the train. In the meantime, his wife is evacuated to the Lehrhof in Hausen near Rottweil, his home town. He is convinced that great decisions will be made soon and he slips into the role of "the great silent one." He believes in a landing of the Western Allies. His wife is afraid of gas attacks. He assures his wife that he is not in any danger since the new headquarters—a former farm—are far off the main road. He is convinced that "one day the door will open." This phrase is a good example of how he could only indirectly hint at his hope that the end of the war might become the threshold to freedom.
The rations of food and the extra rations for the people on the front are being reduced because his unit is not in the line of fire. A letter was censored and held back, but he thinks he "got away with it" this time.

His position in his company is secure now, since he is the only one who knows all the goings-on.

In letter number 20 he mentions the invasion of June 6, 1944: "Fantastic event." He compares the fighting in the West to a few rounds of chess. The Russians are progressing rapidly, but he hopes that, as in January, they can free themselves again. He is convinced that the war will end in its sixth year, but he is worried about the air raids on southwest Germany. He considers the fierce defensive fighting in the West a sign that the war is at its last high point, and that before long, it will all be over. He worries about the increase of air attacks. He trusts his wife to decide where to live. His location is secret, and since he is the deputy and has to substitute for his boss when he travels, he is convinced that he won't be transferred. This theme runs through many of his letters. He hopes to "stay with the old reliable bunch." He advises his wife on what to do in case of attacks. He mentions all the fallen comrades by name.

In letter number 47 of July 27, 1944, he mentions Goebbel's speech and goes on to say: "This is the fight for the end. You have to be there for the children. I will never give up hope that we will see each other again in happier circumstances." He repeats the theme that he will survive the war and that there will be a new beginning.

Dagmar adds this comment later: "How tragic to think how few years he survived in peace times."

Her father heard about the terrific attack on Stuttgart and that Oma and Opa Brühl "eventually were affected too." "One has to get used to accepting each day as it comes—thinking only from morning till that night." During boot camp he trained himself to think only a few hours ahead—no long-range considerations. He is afraid that the January retreat will be repeated. "Wherever I look, misery and more misery."

Tuesday, Thursday, and Sunday mail is delivered via airmail, the rest via surface mail. He writes every other day, and because he fears that his letters may get lost, he purposely repeats himself. He writes more freely and openly when he can give his letter to a soldier who is going home. Nonetheless, though some few get lost, letters and packages are sent back and forth until the very end.

"Live fully and with greater awareness. I have always had to fight for everything in life. But in the end it was all worth it."

On September 2 he received the war iron cross, second class. He took it as a sign that they were satisfied with his work. They all celebrated with dreadful schnapps. However, the threat from advancing troops for the soldiers' families is ever present. The front in the West is advancing at an incredibly rapid rate. He recalls earlier trips to the towns of Kolmar and Korntal and hears now that they are under attack.

The letters below from Robert show the different moods of the soldiers when they were home on furlough and when they returned to the front. The frequency of cards and letters from this day forward increase dramatically as though he has a premonition that his days are numbered and he does not have much time left to communicate with his loved ones.

Letters, notes, and postcard from Robert

While in transit to Karlsruhe from Ulm—where he had been treated in a field hospital—Robert sends a short note to Rudi:

> *At the moment I am on my way to the front again. Many greetings,*
> *Your Robert*

Postcard to Isa, May 9

Tomorrow I will be transferred. Wait for a new address.

The front of the postcard had Goethe's saying: "The world is empty when you think of it only as mountains, rivers, and cities. But occasionally, to know someone who thinks as you do and with whom you can live together in silence—that makes this globe into a living garden."

Mother's Day note to his mother

> *General march convoy: Quickly—I want to send you greetings. In two*
> *hours, we will march.*

Karlsruhe was the military mail center where mail was sent and from which it was officially distributed. This does not mean any of the soldiers where in this city, which is located about sixty kilometers from Stuttgart. However, the next letter is in fact from Karlsruhe at the end of Uncle Robert's furlough.

Letter from Robert to his family, May 13, Karlsruhe

> *It looks like I will be here till May 20, but it is useless to visit me. We*
> *are still in training and we have to do night marches. That's why I can't*
> *get away. I have no idea when I will be able to go out. If I find out more, I*
> *will call you. Please don't be angry with me, but I thought through every*
> *possibility and can't find a better solution.*
>
> *The few hours that I still have here, I will savor. Perhaps I can see a*
> *play or something. You can write to me and perhaps send me some*
> *black thread and some field postcards. Our barracks are very nicely lo-*
> *cated in the middle of a forest outside of Karlsruhe. Yesterday's trip was*
> *very nice. I had a ten-minute layover in Stuttgart and I walked up and*
> *down the platform hoping to recognize someone. But as expected, no*
> *success. Today I am on fire duty (Brandwache). I will shorten the time*
> *by writing letters. Affectionally, Your Robert*

Letter to Rudolf, May 14, Karlsruhe

> *I will be transferred to the front again earlier than I expected. I will still*
> *be here for a few days while our unit is put together. Unfortunately I*
> *can't allow anybody to come and visit. You know before I left Ulm,*
> *mother and Renate [his girlfriend] visited me. I am sure you can imagine*
> *how much I enjoyed their visit, but that meant saying good-bye again*
> *was that much harder. Now we are on the way again to the East and*

who knows what still awaits us. For today, many greetings, Robert

Letter, May 16, Karlsruhe

[addressee is unknown, but I presume it was sent to his sister Thea]

Now the few days that I will still be here are numbered. Today we had our first march. It was just a big stroll of eighteen kilometers. The next one will be twenty-five kilometers. Tomorrow we will have rifle practice. I am very eager to see how it will turn out. My mood has lifted a bit. During the first days after the furlough I walked around pretty depressed. This of course had the disadvantage that I constantly drew the attention of the authorities. But as an old soldier I don't get excited about these things anymore.

Things are better now. The reason was that I was very homesick, much more than the one-and-a-half years before. You must understand that when you return home after such a long time and always feel the love and care of your parents and siblings, that leaves a deep impression. And now after these wonderful six weeks at home, being back in the military—where you get screamed at and harassed all day long—that creates the harshest contrast. I was elated that mother could visit me one more time in Ulm, and I would have preferred if she could have come all the way here, but it will be better so. Otherwise I would have to say good-bye one more time and the old wound would have been torn open again.

Please don't be cross with me, because it would have been very complicated to arrange, since I couldn't avoid work during the day and could only go out for two to three hours in the evening. Do not write again till I send you my new mailing address. I expect mail from you tomorrow.

Letter to his parents and Thea, May 23

We have been on the move for two days already. The trip is proceeding smoothly. If it continues like this, we will have reached our goal in eight days. [Note: Most of the time, the soldiers had to march to their destinations because by then Germany didn't have enough vehicles. Trains brought them closer to the front, but from there they had to walk.] *I would like that because I can't stand this constant moving around* [Herumrutscherei]. *It would also help if I had my new mailing address. Mother, how was last Saturday? My thoughts were with you. I hope you celebrated your special day. And I hope I gave you some pleasure with the book and the flowers. Next year may we celebrate your special day in peace.*

Letter (written in transit) to his family, Monday after Pentecost

Soon we disembark. That will be followed by a march to the division and the battalion. I will send this letter once we have reached our unit; then at least, you will have my address since I don't know when I will be able to write again.

This region is gorgeous. Huge forests, green fields, large herds of grazing cows, horses and sheep. If the trip was not going to lead to the front, I would have been enthusiastic.

Letter to his parents and Thea, June 9

Yesterday at noon we disembarked. Then we had to march another twelve kilometers to the Division. This morning at 6:00 a.m. I used the opportunity to go to Mass and communion once more. I have and will again offer my fate into God's hands.

A few hours later we were greeted by a major who represented the Division.... Only a few...ten men are assigned to the artillery, all the others to the infantry, including me. Whether I will stay here, I am not sure. Dear parents, please don't worry too much about me, because I have great faith in God and everything will turn out alright. Up till now, God and Mary have always protected me, and I will pray frequently, because I know that I will then receive strength and mercy. I have learned now that you should not force anything, but that you should just do one's duty at whatever place one is assigned. With the help of God I will fulfill my duty in the future.

Letter to Rudolf

Now I have also landed at the infantry. I was able to go to communion yesterday morning. So, I put it all into God's hands. He will do right by me. Renate sent me a field rosary. I will enjoy it very much, because it will help me to overcome the difficulties that lie ahead.

Letter to Isa, June 18
[c/o Carpenter Priel, 14 Bad Ditzenbach, near Geislingen]

You will have heard from mother that I am now with the infantry. Some buddies I knew in my previous unit were also transferred here. At the moment I am attending a training course at the regiment, but it will end in the middle of next week. Please wait till I write the number of the new company to which I am assigned.

Letter to Rudolf, June 23

Was assigned to a company two days ago. It's a dog's life for sure. We have lunch at 11:00 p.m.; we sleep during the day, but at the most four or five hours. We can only wash ourselves every fourteen days when we return for a day. Yesterday it rained all night. I look as if I had spent at least a year in a foxhole. The Russian lies—every night—about twenty meters in front of our location. There is naturally a lot of action. Well, I hear it is not exactly quiet where you are. Greetings and much luck.

Letter [addressee unknown], June 23

Though I am not in a good mood today, since it rained all last night, I still want to send you greetings. Though I have been here only a short

157

time, I think I can say that I have accustomed quite well. My buddies are really fine. They are all old infantry people and they know very well that in the trenches everyone depends on everyone else. I never thought that I would be greeted and accepted in such a comradely fashion. Everything is upside down here, but I will get used to it; during the night we are all in the trenches and during the day we are on sentry duty for three hours and then can sleep for three hour. Otherwise I am doing fine. I only miss one thing, that is the opportunity to wash myself and my clothes. The way we look! There is no expression for it. Swine is still too mild. Nothing else new. Please tell everybody that I have little time and therefore cannot write.

Letter to his parents, June 26

Yesterday we were sorted out and tonight we will move to our positions. It is a pity that we were so separated, because during the training I got to know quite a few buddies with whom I got on very well. In my heart, I am still hoping to end up with one or two of them. I am anxious to find out how I will settle in here. Hopefully, fast and well.

Letter to Isa

For the last two days I have been at my new position: now for the first time I know what it means to be an infantry person. I have to agree with Karl, who always said that it was a dog's life. Every night the Ivan approaches as close as twenty meters from our positions. All night long then of course there are blind shootouts—I hope I get used to this nonsense soon.

Letter to his parents and Thea, June 28

Today a year ago our beloved Karl died in combat. I will pray especially for him and think of him. Already a whole year has passed and I can hardly believe it. I still feel as if I had just heard the sad news a week ago. In our belief in eternal life, God promised us so much that we can also master these hard fates. I have never had such a deep trust in God as now when I am sitting in my foxhole. Many times since I was transferred here, I prayed my rosary and felt power and grace. Especially during the hours of heavy fighting, when everything turns upside down, I feel an inner steely stillness because I know that God keeps watch over me. Be united with me in prayer since everything will happen according to God's will. Many greetings to all loved ones.

Letter to Rudolf

I come today with a plea. Could you send me cigarette paper? You see, we receive lots of tobacco as special combat rations and I don't want to smoke my pipe all the time. Otherwise I am doing fine. Last night I was on night patrol for the first time. In a hurry, Robert

Letters to his family

Today or perhaps tomorrow you will be able to write for the first time. I am already counting the days till I estimate that the first mail will arrive. You have no idea how much I look forward to mail. That is truly the only thing that gives some kind of diversion here. Otherwise I am fine. To-night I went on my first exploratory expedition. When you crawl around in no-man's-land you experience all kinds of emotions. But everything worked out, without any contact with the enemy. Now I want to ask you something. Please send me cigarette paper, a lighter, and a comb. You will find combs in my night table. You can enclose this in a letter. When you are allowed to send packages again and you find some fish paste, I would be grateful. But please don't run around for it.

July 2

In my thoughts I celebrated the Holy Mass with you just now. Now I will join you at the coffee table. A few pieces of first rate white bread, and from mother's kitchen, some jam. I start to salivate. For lunch then Spätzle and potato salad. I am already looking forward to my next, alas-so-distant furlough, hoping to get something decent between my teeth. And what are we getting here in reality? Perhaps barley or beans, possibly some dried vegetables (like barbed wire). Please send me field mail stationary, but not the small ones. I wish you a happy Sunday.

How is the mail? Did you get everything? I wrote on May 23 and 25, and June 1, 9, 12, 15, 18, 21, 28, and 30.

July 5

At last we have received some air mail stamps. We should have got-ten these at the start; that way the mail distribution would be functioning. We also received stamps for packages. Please keep them, but under no circumstances send me 100 gram packages with stuff that you have to give up ration coupons for. I am convinced that 100 gram packages are free again, because a buddy from my unit received four of them with ra-tion marks. Enclosed: six air mail and two package stamps. Please send me mail into the field with them.

July 8

Yesterday, at last, I visited the army welfare station. You probably don't know what that means. Let me explain. At five in the morning we left to take a bath and get rid of our lice. Then at about 8:00 a.m. we had breakfast in the barracks. Sugared coffee and a few slices of bread with cold cuts and a honey based Stollen. For lunch we had chicken soup, boiled potatoes and small meat patties and for dessert, cherry compote and a glass of wine. For dinner butter, cheeses, five eggs, cherry com-pote and a glass of wine. Pretty good, isn't it? At 9:00 p.m. we marched back to the trenches, freshly shaved and in good humor. So, I can start

*the work again. Otherwise all is as before. I am wondering whether I'll
get mail soon. I am expecting some today. Many greetings to all.*

July 10

*Today I have reason to be in a bit of a bad mood. I still have not re-
ceived any mail. I don't know what the problem is. The mail from my
comrades takes normally eight to nine days. Nothing much new here. I
am only writing so that you receive a sign of life from me, so that you
don't accuse me again on my next furlough that mail from me is so
scarce that you celebrate it like a feast day.*

*Thea please send me a novel or a magazine to read occasionally.
Then I want to remind you again that I could really use cigarette paper,
fire flints, fish paste, and large, double field mail envelopes. Did you receive my letter with the air mail and package stamps? Greetings to all.*

Uncle Robert's next letter admits for the first time that the German troops are in retreat.

Letter to his mother, July 13

*Many thanks for your letters of June 21 and 29, which I received yes-
terday. I was very pleased to read that you enjoyed the Mother's Day
bouquet. But know that the idea was not mine but Renate's. Important
news that you will want to know: tonight we will be transferred. Where
we are going is not yet determined, but probably just a few kilometers
back as the division's reserves. Naturally there will be more training and
pressure, but it counts toward service in the war.*

*Now to the case of Gauss. I can't write to his mother since I have no
address. Her son Werner was still at the battalion when I left. Some
comrades told me that he was brought to the field hospital a few days
after me and since then nobody knows what happened. Most probably
in the hurry of retreat the hospital could not be evacuated in time, or
there were no more vehicles available for transportation—or they got
bogged down in the mud and dirt. No other option seems possible, except perhaps that they were attacked by planes. It's up to you whether
you want to write to her. She has to accept the sad news that her son is
missing in action. Your son, Robert*

Letters to his family

July 16

*As I have already written we were transferred on July 13 and are en-
camped on the other side of the* [border river between Ukraine and
Moldavia], *relatively quiet. Does this peace mean anything? Tomorrow it
will probably be all over, but we did have a few good days. Today is a
good example. Besides a few hours of guard duty and two hours shelling green beans I didn't have to do anything. At 4:00 a.m. an apricot
search party was sent out. They had to pick a truck load of apricots.
Each man received 10 M* [an old-fashioned German weight] *so that I ate
well and still my steel helmet is full. But tomorrow the heavenly days will*

be over. We have to build trenches even farther back to defend against advancing troops. But things are good here, so don't worry, greetings and good wishes, I would love to send some apricots to you, but unfortunately that's not possible.

July 17

Unfortunately, mail from your side is very scarce. Here is the newest from me. In the morning we build trenches, in the afternoon we have arms training. This is all we do. Today I went to de-lousing. Even though I have no lice, I went anyway, because an occasional shower is so wonderful. I am recovering quite well since I am getting more sleep. Unfortunately the weather is already turning. One could call it autumn.

If I could only send you some apricots, I really have eaten a lot. Hopefully the juicy pears will ripen soon. How are you doing? Do you have enough this year to can preserves? Greetings.

My maternal grandmother, Barbara (Robert's mother) wrote a letter to him on July 17, 1944. Since I found this letter in my mother's house, I presume that it was never sent. But it could be that it was sent and he returned it for safekeeping. This would make it one of the few letters that survived from the families at home.

Letter to Robert from his mother, July 17

Today your letter of July 8 arrived. You were in the military service tent. I imagine they treated you well. I was astonished that you could eat so much, but father said immediately that a starving soldier can eat a lot. If such a meal could be repeated often, that would be good. Your airmail letter with the enclosed stamps from the fifth arrived on the fifteenth. If we could only send you some packages. Also the previous letters from the second and the letters from June arrived, but we couldn't write, because we had to wait for your new number.

Robert, I am always with you in spirit and thank you for thinking of Karl on the twenty-eighth. Pastor Schuster said a Mass for him, as did Assistant Pastor Geidel the next day.... I am convinced that Karl has been in heaven for some time.... You can pray to him even if it is only a short prayer: "Dear Karl, I am asking for the necessary strength to be with me." You can also pray this way to your guardian angel.

Nothing new here. We are healthy and like to work. On Sunday, the sixteenth, at 8:30 in the morning, there was an attack on Stuttgart. Nothing happened in our neighborhood, but Cannstatt, Münster, and Oeffingen were hard hit. Also, in the vicinity of the Bismarcktower, Relenbergstrasse,...also in the vicinity of Isa's apartment there was damage. For weeks it has been quiet, but now for three days, constant alarm. In Munich all the train stations have been destroyed, and even in Stuttgart no trains or street cars can operate to Fellbach, because they have all been affected. Hope that God will soon change this.

Hermann [third son at the front] wrote elatedly that he will be trans-

ferred to Gmünd. He is allowed to travel alone. We are anxiously await-
ing his coming and are overjoyed. It is only hours now till we see him
again at home. It's 4:00 p.m., and later I will go to Rohracker to get cher-
ries, so that I have something in the house for him. How much I would
like to give you some. But we are in spirit and prayer always with you. I
presume you are still doing okay. Many greetings from all, but especially
from your loving Mother.

Armin and Elinor [her two oldest grandchildren] *traveled two days ear-*
lier to see Minni in Lochau; I don't know how long Armin [sixteen years
old] *can stay there. He has been assigned to harvest duty in the coun-*
tryside, but because he will serve in Schnittlingen, it is not so urgent. Isa
is also here [in Stuttgart] *at the moment to can some fruits and vegeta-*
bles. Wilma [another daughter] *and her children were also here for a*
week; Gerhard [Wilma's husband] *is still doing okay; Rudolf* [the fourth
son at the front], *also; we are concerned about Paul* [Gertrud's hus-
band], *and are wondering whether he is surrounded by foreign troops.*

[Note: Robert was obviously serving in an area that was still controlled by German troops as
the sortie to the orchards shows, either in southwest Russia or in Romania.]

Letter from Robert, Sunday, July 23

Today I have a whole day to myself again. If you look at my life it
couldn't be better. We have no concerns and what we need, we get:
fruit, potatoes, beans, and everything else. We make a sortie, pick out
the biggest, juiciest, and ripest fruit and take what we want. We are told
where to go so we don't have to worry about a selection. We get our
room and board. Every two weeks we can buy special goods from the
army. What more could one want? And still I don't like it. And even if ev-
erything was great here, I would rather be at home, even if we didn't
have much to live on, than to live here in this abundance. In addition we
keep on hearing about the large air attacks and so one never knows
what's going on at home. You should hear what the common soldiers
talk about when they don't have much to do. Everyone tells everyone
else about their concerns and hardships. But we do have people here
who have lost a great deal already in this war. Not just houses and furni-
ture, but also spouses and children. If you talk with these people about
religious topics, and they say that there can't be a God who allows such
horrendous happenings, it is difficult to counter their argument. What so-
lace can I offer somebody who has turned away from God? It is really
bad and it is high time that the war comes to an end. Greetings.

Stuttgart was bombed in a very heavy air raid at the end of July, 1944. My maternal grandmother, Barbara, wrote a description of the event to family members who were not living in
Stuttgart.

Letter from my maternal grandmother

You will already have heard from Isa and Maria that we were totally bombed out in an air attack. It was during the night of Tuesday/Wednesday, July 25–26. The constant tremors and bombs for three quarters of an hour without interruption were dreadful. The whole Kernerplatz is one big heap of ruins: our house, the house across the street from us, and two houses to the right and left of us—all demolished. Behind the garden, four houses were all ablaze. The fire flowed like water and in between there were explosions. The houses to our right and left burned down first. Their cellars also collapsed; our cellar remained intact. Through a hole in the wall, the people next door came into our cellar. We first sprayed water on the two rooftops, but a very strong wind made the fire jump onto our house. No help came, no fire engines; we carried beds and mattresses into the cellar. Thea was very courageous, but then the heat was too strong and there was danger of the building collapsing. We could grab only a few pieces of clothing and hurriedly flee to the cellar. Electricity had already been cut off. It was about 4:00 a.m. Father was hit during our escape by a burning piece of wood from the neighboring house. I went with him to the house of another neighbor where he could sit down. Around 8:00 a.m. I went with him to the hospital; we had to make the whole trip on foot, because no street cars were in operation. The electric lines were all hanging down from above. Father was x-rayed and diagnosed with a broken shoulder blade. They put a splint on him and we walked back. We went to a friend where father waited, while I went to the ward office to get an identity card. At 2:00 p.m. we were loaded onto a truck that took us to the suburb of Cannstatt, from where we boarded a train that was specially put together for people who had lost their homes in Stuttgart. It was dreadfully crowded. At 9:30 p.m. we were in Schnittlingen. [The train ride to Geislingen normally takes forty-five minutes, and the bus to Schnittlingen another thirty minutes.] *Father still has to be in bed. Hermann was discharged to the army hospital in Gmünd. He could only spend half a day with us.*

If the cellar had not been completely burned, we could have saved quite a few things. Four suitcases and four boxes were filled with the things of the boys who are in the war. Also all our winter clothes were in there. I spoke today by telephone with the owner of the house; he will go to Stuttgart today and see whether there is anything left in the cellar. We could not save any furniture; the pieces I miss the most are the big wardrobes with the mirrors from the bedroom; they were made of mahogany and came from New Castle. [I presume that the furniture was auctioned off at the end of the Württemberg monarchy in 1918.] *Thea has lost a lot. She is visiting Aunt Katherine in the Black Forest for a few days. As soon as father is able to we will move into the other house, but first we need some furniture. This involves lots of bureaucratic running around.*

We are presuming that you are still healthy and in good spirits and that you are safe from more air attacks. I am sure the sirens go off every so often. Many greetings with love, Your Mother and Grandmother

P.S. I am enclosing different stamps and hope that this letter will reach you safely and soon.

Addendum written by Thea on June 28, 1993, fifty years after Karl's death

As far as I remember, a burning beam fell on father's shoulder. After the attack the house was still standing, but the roof and attic were on fire and we were in danger because of all the paper stored in the first floor apartment, which was rented by the local Nazi group. My biggest challenge was to unhook the large painting of the Dotzburger "Madonna with Child," which was hanging by a cord over the beds in the parents' bedroom. I climbed onto the beds with a broom, to unhook it, but I couldn't do it....

Because I kept on going back and forth, I think I carried the whole closet with my wardrobe into the cellar; mother called out to me pleadingly to come down immediately because the building was liable to collapse. I ran out just in time. Everything that was kept in front of the iron fire door in the cellar burned. That included the four suitcases and boxes with the boys' stuff, my wardrobe and a small suitcase in which I kept my most important documents. Every apartment had their own cellar room, in addition to a second cellar, a few steps deeper behind the fire door. These were the rooms into which the passage from the next house led. The house next door was also destroyed, but one could still crawl through the passage. Our parents were absolutely composed during the whole ordeal. Trembling, I tried to pray the Hail Mary. I can't remember to which hospital father went. Karl-Olga was the nearest one, but we generally went to St. Mary's Hospital. I still remember that I carried a small chair—nowadays it would have no value, but it was valuable then—down the many steps from the Kernerplatz to the Neckarstraße to Mr. Haug. He was a good man, an electrician, a "Wames" brother of father. During the Great War, many Catholic craftsmen/businessmen formed the Wames Club; they all wore the same outfits for public events.

At noon, cars with microphones drove through the streets to announce that old people who wanted to go in the direction of Plochingen, Göppingen could board trucks that would bring them to the edge of the city (perhaps, they also offered it for other directions). I helped my parents climb onto a truck and kept on thinking: "the poor old parents."

Now I am the same age.... I presume that this was also the time that the wife of the mayor Günther was spotted on the way to Cannstatt. Her husband was sitting on the curb because he could no longer walk.

I did not go to Altensteig as mother wrote in her letter; have been there only once, in 1942; perhaps I couldn't get through. My only thought was: "not another night in Stuttgart." I lined up at a ticket window, perhaps in Feuerbach, to get a ticket to Weil der Stadt to my colleague because I figured that I could easily get back to Stuttgart for my job. With incredible difficulty, waiting and stumbling over railroad tracks that were partly bombed out, I arrived at my colleague's house. Her father was a butcher; her mother had died. They lovingly gave me room and board for two weeks. In Stuttgart, I asked Uncle Xaver to allow me to store in his house whatever I could still salvage from the cellar until I could find somebody who could transport it for me to Schnittlingen.

I went into the hallway of the cellars, which was incredibly hot and dark,...my colleague, who was waiting outside, screamed for me to come out because there was another alarm. Eventually I managed to get everything to Uncle Xaver's house with his help. Then I stood in line for a whole day at the central point where people could book transportation. A man with a dour face offered to transport my things. Thank God, a young family from Kaltenbach was assigned to the same truck. We arrived at midnight at their destination in Böhmenkirchen. Thank God, they said that it was too late for me to go on to Schnittlingen, and they allowed me and the driver to stay with them overnight. We left about five in the morning, because later on the low-flying airplanes would be buzzing overhead. Though the trip from Böhmenkirchen to Schnittlingen took only a short time, it was still enough for a lot of foolish talk by the driver. In Schnittlingen, Aunt Barbara offered him a good lunch and I thought: "If you only knew!"

It is true that one is most vulnerable in a moving vehicle, but I had good protection on all my trips. Let me add here that once I became very frightened. I took a shortcut from Schnittlingen to Geislingen, not along the highway, but on a field path through the forest. That's when at 5:30 a.m. I encountered a Frenchman, a prisoner of war, who was allowed toward the end of the war to walk around freely. I was all alone and forlorn. Mother had accompanied me as far as the hill overlooking Schnittlingen and then said good-bye. But the Frenchman just said: "Guten Morgen" and walked by.

From the time of their being bombed out till the end of the war, I visited my parents frequently. At that time, my daily prayer was: "Dear God, let me sleep just once without fear of death." Often at night there were more air alarms; we ran to the underground bunker where Frau Bolz and her daughter sat in front of the iron door. [Mr. Bolz was the governor of Württemberg before the Nazis took over; he was then imprisoned and later executed by decapitation.] We were allowed inside; then I tried to find an early train in the direction of Schnittlingen; afterwards I continued the trek on foot from either Donzdorf, Weissenstein, or Geislingen [all of about six to seven miles], and on Monday very early the trek in reverse.

Our parents were bombed out one year after Karl's death, three months after Rudi's wedding, one month before Robert was missing. A few days after the attack my father traveled back by himself from Schnittlingen. He walked from the train station to Hauptstätterstraße in order to check on his brother Xaver; then he made the long trek to Upper Birkenwaldstraße where I had been living with Inge in the meantime. Then he slept there.

After they were bombed out, my grandparents moved to Schnittlingen, into the small house adjacent to the stables and the barn of the family farm. In Schnittlingen my grandparents were given two rooms: a kitchen and the adjacent chamber, where they lived till Achaz died in 1954. The two rooms were on the second floor in the back of the house for which Achaz had at one time given the biggest part of the purchase price to his father. At the same time, Richard Fischer, Achaz's brother-in-law, who contributed only a smaller amount toward the purchase price, claimed the use of the two bigger and more beautiful rooms toward the front of the house.

After their total loss in the bombing raid our grandparents received an identity card on August 7 for "Damage Due to Air Raids." Their apartment was certified a total loss.

- Extent of damage: Destruction of the whole apartment (four rooms): one living room, three bedrooms, one kitchen.
- Furniture and equipment saved? No
- Clothing and linens saved? No
- All agencies are asked to grant extensive relief help
- First payment for damage: 1000 RM, August 10, 1944, in Göppingen

They also received a card for their move from Stuttgart to Schnittlingen.

Beginning on September 1, 1944, they received the following payments [it is impossible to decipher what the payments were for]: 142.-; 92.50; 30.-; 74.50; 339.-; 69.-; 34.50.-;20.-; 8.- ;30.-; 52.50; 15.-; 94.- from the county board of the County Göppingen.

Due to the move to Schnittlingen, my grandfather also lost his earnings as his brother's employee in Stuttgart. For the rest of their lives till they died (one in 1954 and the other in 1955) my grandparents lived on a very small pension for the loss of their two sons and their apartment.

I found the following "indulgence card" in Aunt Thea's belongings after her death:

Plenary indulgence due to air raids
A decree by Pope Pius XII of December 23, 1942
Grants all believers who are exposed
To air bombardments in danger of losing their lives
A total indulgence during the duration of the present war
As long as they are pious and pray with a repentant heart
The quick prayer
My Jesus
Have mercy
The repentance over past sins
Has to be sincere, that is,
It has to result from the love for God

At the same time, Aunt Trudl, Uncle Rudolf's wife, was evacuated to Schnittlingen. She and her mother had one room and a kitchen in the Smithy, a house at the edge of the village. When Rudolf came home on furlough, her mother slept in the kitchen on a mattress; she shared the room with her husband. A few times a week Trudl had to take the milk on a little wooden cart from the farmer to the dairy in the village. Once when she started off, it snowed a little, but by the time she had to return home, it had snowed so much that she

166

couldn't find her own way back. No one had walked along the road, so there were no tracks to follow. She wandered far out of her way to another house, which had a weak light shining through the window shades. Generally, all houses had to be completely dark.

At the time my grandparents were bombed out, my Uncle Robert was missing in action and the other sons of the family were still at the front; our life in Bad Ditzenbach went on without much upheaval.

Mother's diary, 1944

June

The last half year was so busy that I have neglected to update the children's' diaries. This is especially regrettable for Karl Heinz, because in the first year a child makes so much progress. I will try to summarize the main events. One has to admit that Karl Heinz is receiving a rough upbringing, lacking the care that his siblings enjoyed. Since there is no running water in the house and therefore water has to be treated like a precious commodity, and since I have little time, he did not receive a daily bath. And since we live in one room only, he can't enjoy the silence that a baby needs, since his older siblings are very loud and not very considerate. I am often desperate, but he seems to be thriving. This winter he caught whooping cough from Bernd, but that would have happened in normal circumstances also. His coughing wasn't often, but quite severe. I nursed him till January, but I couldn't offer him any vegetables in the winter. The apple crop was plentiful, however. He spent some weeks with the family of the au pair, where he had regular meals, got his daily bath, had his quiet naps and plenty of private attention. They took him for rides, which he still insists on today. When we picked him up, he immediately recognized me, although didn't want to have anything to do with his siblings. But he greeted Papa, who visited us over the weekend without hesitation.

August

On August 10, [Karl Heinz] took his first steps, not at home, but at the Weilands, where he plays the guest role quite often. Now nothing is off limits for this little nomad. He loves this new mode of moving about; it gives him the needed freedom to investigate the world under all chairs and tables and outside in the big meadows. This means much work with the little "nomad"; nothing is safe from him.

In his diary Uncle Franz continues to chronicle his family's nomadic life, showing that other family members did not share the peaceful life we experienced in Bad Ditzenbach.

Uncle Franz's diary

[describing the frequent moves of his workplace and his family's home]

With the intensification of the air raids, life in the city during the day became more uncomfortable and eventually dangerous. My office was completely destroyed: part of it burnt down, the rest collapsed, which forced us to find other offices. We moved into an industrial park in

Dellbrück. We built a bomb shelter underground and temporary office barracks on top. Till the last months of the war, the defense commando was housed on these premises. The growth of the military combat activities made an expansion of the defense industry necessary. We needed to build more offices, and I convinced the boss that a second floor should be added to one of the buildings in Overath as our apartment. I received permission for this since I had been bombed out. Again Italian prisoners of war dug out the foundations and built the walls of the buildings. Our five-year-old son Walther got into the act by drawing plans for a house: an apartment with bathroom and toilets for his beloved stuffed bear family. [Walther grew up to become an engineer.]

Our new apartment had a living room, two bedrooms, a bathroom, and a kitchen. It was completed at the end of 1944 and we moved in with great joy. Staying in Cologne during the day became almost impossible because now the increasing air raids also came during the day. I rode a newly acquired motorcycle from Overath to Dellbrück to work while the family stayed in the new place in Overath. We did not enjoy the stay there for long, however. We celebrated one Christmas there, but during a morning raid in January an enemy low-flying plane dropped a bomb into our garden, right in front of the house. It was only a small bomb, but the walls in the cellar, which had to withstand most of the pressure, buckled in part. The glasses that we had collected with much effort for preserving fruit and vegetables lay in shards on the floor and the living room was partially destroyed.

The daily attacks on Overath made us conscious of the fact that Germany was obviously losing the war. We first thought that our apartment near the railroad station would be safe, especially since a secure bomb shelter that had been built into the mountain was only 200 meters from our house. The road from our apartment to this bomb shelter led over the train rails and with the sudden attacks by low-flying planes my wife and children became more and more nervous and afraid. It is true that we had figured out the secrets of the warning alarms: Germany was divided into squares and radio broadcasts could determine in time whether the approaching planes would hit Cologne or its surrounding area, but all of this was not much help. In short, our stay in Overath became more frightening and I started my new search for another apartment.

Mother's diary, July 1944

It is difficult to say whether Bernd is the most well behaved or most naughty child. He does everything in excess. If one can give him attention he is the dearest and most creative child. He is a big cuddler. When he is out of kisses, he goes to a wall and shops for more and showers us with his endearments, especially his beloved Vati when he comes on the weekends. He can play for hours alone and one has only to admire his work occasionally. He stands in front of his creations, admires them

168

*by saying "heijeiheijeheije." But when he wants your attention, whether
you have important things to do or not, he nags so long and loud that
you have to interrupt all work. He has a good nose for the time when
you are under time pressure and need him to do something. He stub-
bornly refuses to listen to any arguments. How often has he driven me
to the brink of desperation in these tight quarters! For example, when
Karl Heinz is supposed to sleep, and he wants something, he continues
with his demands so long that KH wakes up because of the racket. It is
really impossible to do justice to all three children, crammed into one
room,...and this first winter was exceptionally long and snowy.*

Reminiscences of Erna Kink, my brother Bernd's mother-in-law
[Erna shared these memories in conversations with me]

*In July 1944 Munich was bombed for five days straight. I was married
and living in rural Bavaria, but I was in Munich to visit my parents when
the first attacks occurred. During a short respite between attacks, the
people who were sitting in the bomb shelters were ordered to come up
and help put out the still-smoldering small bombs. While we were doing
that, I heard a voice: "Attention, new attack," and then the first sirens.
But before I reached the entrance of our house a bomb hit that was so
powerful that a heavy oak door was completely ripped out, the floor underneath me disappeared, and the wind suction threw me into the
house. But I made it to the bomb shelter before a second powerful bomb
destroyed most of the area. Since the attacks on Munich were continu-
ing, my parents suggested that I return as fast as possible to my rural
home. While on the train, which moved very slowly, we were bombed
since we were in open land, but no bomb hit us directly. As soon as we
reached the forest the train stopped and the conductor ran along the
train and told everybody to run into the woods as fast as we could.
There we spent a few hours on the ground till the attacks subsided. We
then moved slowly to our destination. These attacks lasted five days
and in January 1945 most of the surviving houses were leveled. The
Allies found the city even though it had been completely blacked out.*

Uncle Robert did not hear about the bombing in Stuttgart till August, which becomes
apparent from his letters, which were increasing in frequency.

Letters from Robert

July 28

   *At last I have convinced the authorities that I need to see an ear spe-
cialist. It is complicated to get to him because he is quite a few kilometers from our position. That's why I am in a first aid station at the
moment, waiting for a truck to take me to the doctor. I have been on the
road since yesterday and hope to reach my destination tonight. I don't
know of course whether I will only be examined or get treatment there.
But I am hoping that they can do something for me. Greetings in a hurry.*

Sunday, July 30

It turned out as I expected. I was examined, given a prescription, and am going back to my troop this afternoon. Unfortunately the medics are no longer in charge of my transportation, I have to see for myself how I can get away from here. Jolly is the gypsies' life! Here in Russia there is a wonderful invention! At the end of the village there is a "hitch-a-ride-station" where every truck is obligated to stop and take soldiers who want to go in their direction. I will sit in that place this afternoon and wait patiently. If I am lucky, I will be with my troop tomorrow afternoon, but most probably not till evening.

In the meantime, greetings from Robert.

[Note: The following letter was sent to Stuttgart, but forwarded to Schnittlingen, since Robert's parents had lost their home in Stuttgart and moved to Schnittlingen.]

August 1

When I left the field hospital on July 30, I was lucky to catch a truck from our division quickly, which took me close to our camp. The last eight kilometers I marched back on foot and so could join my unit by the evening of July 30. Before we drove off, I had a look around the village. It was a gruesome picture that presented itself to me. Ruins and nothing but ruins, because almost every night the Ivan comes here and bombs. In the midst of this destruction is a lively market life like a fair. However, you have to eliminate the beer tents, the booths, the roller coasters, but from the smallest Dadel [?] to the biggest wurst you can buy everything here dirt cheap. Groceries, wine, eggs, chocolate, pancakes, sausages, knives, harmonicas, etc. Unfortunately I could only buy two hard-boiled eggs and an ice cream cone. I didn't have any more local money, and you can't get anything for our money. Today mother's letter arrived. And I am sending it back; please keep it with all the other letters. Tomorrow we have another training session. I am dreading it already in this fierce heat. I live by the motto: this too shall pass. Thank God, this war as well. Greetings to all.

August 6

I am so glad that last week is behind me. On Wednesday we had battalion training and on Thursday and Friday we had to dig trenches and build earth walls all day. From 3:00 a.m. to 8:00 p.m. we were on our feet continually. To start off, we had to walk ten kilometers till we came to our work site, and then we had to build reinforcements for ten hours at a stretch. At night I was completely exhausted and could not write any more. But I am still relatively well and that is the main thing. Our food consists of up to 75 percent fruit. But I feel alright and strong.

August 10 (to his family)

There is no news from here, but I want to send a short sign of life. No changes other than that we have so damned much work. When will we be on the front again? We don't know, but I don't believe soon. I am sure not this month anymore. During the last few weeks, all mail stopped. The connection is probably interrupted because of the air raids on Stuttgart. Affectionately, Robert

August 13 (to his parents and Thea)

Finally, after a long time, I received mail yesterday. Unfortunately no mail from you, but Renate wrote that now for the second time a major blow has hit you. My dear parents, I am so sorry that you are being tested so in your old age. But I know of your unwavering trust in God, and I know that you will master these major setbacks. The main thing is that you are all healthy. As far as I am concerned the news depressed me immensely at first. But I have developed a strong will to live and the will to establish a new existence has been growing in me. I am convinced that with this will and my trust in God I can master any blows coming to me in my later life.

If I had had a telegram from you saying that we lost everything in the air raid I could have asked for a furlough right away. This way I have no official document—even though I tried everything and talked to my boss right after I got the letter from Renate. If it was up to him, I am sure I could have gone home, but since we have a furlough prohibition at the moment, the division would have to make an exception. He said to give it a try, but thought that it would not work because bomb furloughs are only given in cases of death. Under these circumstances I am willing to give up my home leave. However, the application is in progress, perhaps I'll be lucky. If I could enclose a telegram, that would be better. I am still relatively satisfied. Could anything be saved? Did my diploma and my grades survive? I think I kept them in the little cabinet.

August 15, to his parents [the envelope was decorated with fresh Edelweiss]

Today I received Thea's letter of August 4, 1944. I heard from Renate that your house had been totally demolished by bombs. Though I always expected such news, it did hit me hard. In addition I couldn't understand why there was no telegram. I talked to my boss right away and when the telegram arrived I had him add it to my application. I had written to you last Sunday, but to Westerheim, because Renate said that's where you were going. [Westerheim was the village where my grandmother was born and her family still lived.]

My good mama, don't fret too much that everything in the storage closet in the basement is burnt. The main thing is that you are alive. But one thing I care about, my grade books and my trade certificate (Gesellenbrief). I think I kept it in the little box. Can it be saved? If not, please try to get me a copy of the certificate that was issued by the chamber of trade and industry. [The certificate would allow Robert to prove that he had finished a three-year course and internship and allow him to get a skilled job.]. *My dear father, how did it happen that your shoulder was broken? Were you struck somewhere? I have only been informed about the rough details of the whole sequence of events, and I would be so interested in each little detail. If it is possible, please write to me in more detail. I have almost no hope that my furlough will be granted, especially now when so many soldiers hear about bomb damage of their loved ones and we have a ban on home leaves. I am so glad that now you are in a quieter place. That will be good for you, since your nerves, I am sure, are all shot. How is Hermann doing? I don't have an address for him. I am enclosing some stamps. But you don't have to send me anything. They would expire here.*

This is the last known letter from Robert. Shortly afterwards he was listed as missing in action. Other than one time, when he talked about Dnestr, he never mentioned where he was. In some of the early letters Russia is mentioned and in one later letter he writes about "the Ivan," a reference to Russians.

Many years later Thea wrote a kind of obituary about her brother, who was only two years younger than she and was her best friend in the family:

Our Robert, who was born March 11, 1924, has been missing in action since August 15, 1944. In Fall 1942 he was called up into the military (after having volunteered because all his brothers and buddies were already in the army) and after a six-week training course in Ludwigsburg and in Marseille he was shipped to the Eastern front in Russia. His unit participated in the fighting in Woroschilograd. He would still enjoy one home furlough, because of illness, in April–May 1944. After he returned to the front, his unit was completely wiped out. The German troops were in retreat; therefore the last letters came from Romania [possibly from the Russian/Ukrainian border, but very close to Romania].

These are Robert's few dates as far as we know; we do not know how the fighting went or how long it lasted. In 1931 he started school in Buxheim and he and I lived in the new large house that our parents had bought. My oldest sister Maria, her husband, and child, my second oldest sister Gertrud, Uncle Joseph, and Aunt Vero all lived there and on the weekends our parents and various other siblings came for visits. [This house was so big that later it became a children's hospital.] *After eight years of elementary schooling, at age fourteen, he started an apprenticeship as a tool and die maker. He passed his examination after four years, which allowed him to do skilled labor. I often thought that his life was one "under the cross." He was the thirteenth and last child of our parents and while they accepted him without hesitation, it seems to me that he sometimes didn't think so. To be a "Benjamin" is both a gift and a trial. He was a naturally happy child, perhaps a bit slow in his development. We were in school together in Buxheim, he in second grade and I in third grade, but all together in one room. I always felt a bit sorry for him, because he had a hard time with school work, but in general we had a good time together; also later when we attended a Catholic school in Stuttgart. Only once I got really upset when I saw that bigger boys had bound him to the school gate. I ran past him very fast so that he would not think that I had seen his humiliation. I was too cowardly to scream or fight for him against the boys.*

Whenever I took a train ride, mother, who was pretty relaxed, wouldn't let me go alone. Robert had to accompany me till I was sixteen. One summer, mother, Robert, and I were going to visit Minni. This was a special treat because of the 1,000 mark fee for any travel across borders. I can still see mother in front of the government official purchasing the tickets. Very condescendingly he said: "Good woman, you have to pay 1,000 marks. You can't do it." His eyes widened when she showed him the paper from the Interior Ministry allowing her to visit her daughter without any fee, because it would be too heavy a burden for her large family.

I think the apprenticeship was very hard on Robert. We were the only siblings still at home and we divided up the household chores. Because the other boys were all in the military, he fetched coal from the cellar—three and a half stories down—and cut wood for the stove. Mother or I had to make the same trek to fetch butter or milk from the cellar, where we had to keep it during the summer. Butter was kept in cold water, since we did not have a refrigerator. I did most of the shopping.

He and I joined the parish choir and he taught himself to play the mandolin. He was quite musical and loved records, especially melancholic songs. He loved his circle of friends, but became lonely when they left for the war one after the other. When he enlisted, father was really angry since he already had three boys at the front. But Robert wasn't fanatical about Germany or the government, he was just a big child who was lonely and bored. Very soon after he was sent into combat, and especially in Russia, he was very homesick. He joined the artillery and because of the constant loud noise soon experienced permanent hearing loss.

Mother's diary, August 1944

Bernd uses all kind of slang words that he picks up from the village kids. When we are in a restaurant or on a train, I am always wary about what will come out of his mouth. But he can also be amusing. He got an angel medallion from Aunt Minni that he keeps under his shirt. The other day he put it outside his shirt and when I wanted to put it inside again, he protested, "The little angel wants to see too." He played a grocery salesperson and I had to be the buyer. When I said, "Thank you, honey" his angry answer was, "Don't say honey, I am Mr. Salesperson." His cousins made him a wooden rifle and saber and a paper hat and when he appeared in front of me, I said, "Now you want to go into the war and shoot the soldiers dead," but he said very seriously, "I don't kill any sol-

diers, just little mice."

When he was asked why he didn't admit something bad that he had done, his answer was: "Because I have such a small mouth," and when he dropped the wood chips that he had to fetch for the stove, his laconic answer was: "The bucket threw the chips out." When he expresses his many, many wishes for toys, we always comfort him and say we will buy them for him when the war is over. "Is the war still going on? Mutti, please promise to tell me right away when it's over." One of his threats that has taken on proverbial properties in our family is "I'll throw you into the creek." If he wants to flatter me, he says, "You know, Mutti, I won't kill you." He values my good mood enormously. When he angers me, or when I scold or ignore him, he insistently begs: "Mutti, smile again," and if I smile, he himself grins like a ladybug over his whole small face.

While Margit plays most of the time with her friends, he sticks close to me: "Aren't the two of us good to each other!"

Starting School in All the Chaos

Mother's diary

August 1944

Margit loves to learn poems by heart and recite them. She is quite sensible and is a great help to me. She knows it, too, when she says to me: "Mutti, if you only had me, we could have a great time"; but she is nice to her brothers.

September 1944

Margit attends school since the fourth. The first school day to which I accompanied her was devoted to telling the teacher their names and the teacher admiring their school bags. The second day included a one-hour air raid alarm. But generally school is held without much interruption. Margit likes it, but the first few days she had a hard time understanding that homework had to be done. So far, it has all been fun and games. Now serious life begins, my child! She is being taught the Latin script. She seems to understand that there is another script and when I told her that I first learned the German script, she asked: "Why do I have to learn Protestant?" She cannot understand that her girlfriend Hilde goes to another church and another religious class. And I have no answers for her.

The school was a typical one room village school, where all eight grades of the primary school were taught by two teachers. The village was traditionally Catholic. At that time a whole village might be entirely Catholic or entirely Protestant. Hilde, who like us was evacuated from a bigger town, was the only Protestant in our little gang. I have no recollection whether and where she went to church, because there was no Protestant church in our village or in any of the surrounding villages at that time.

Letter to me from my father, sent from Stuttgart to Ditzenbach, September 9
Now you are really my big daughter, since you already attend school.

Papa is very sad that he could not be with you on your day. I would have liked to know how you enjoyed the first day.

You have to go to school every day and pay attention to what the teacher says.... I hope that when I visit the teacher and ask about Margit I will only hear good things. I hope you will be as obedient, hard-working, and accomplished a student as your Mutti was. [My father was not the best student in elementary or secondary school.] *To give you some joy I am sending you this book of fairy tales that shall always remind you of your first school day. On Sunday you have to tell me everything. Remember everything well. My best wishes, dear little Margit, for all the years of learning ahead. Many kisses, Your Vati*

Shortly after I started school, the biggest air raid on Stuttgart started in the night of September 12 to 13. Hundreds of British planes dropped 73 heavy air mines, 4,300 exploding bombs, and 180,000 fire bombs on the city. The inner city was leveled, including Stuttgart's landmark, the medieval church, the Stiftskirche. One thousand civilians were killed.

My mother, with my brothers and I, stood in front of our house and watched the skies over Stuttgart, which was about fifty miles away. With us, many of the villagers stood at the intersection of the roads leading from Wiesensteig to Geislingen and from Ditzenbach to Göppingen watching the heavens. For hours, the sky was a fiery red. My mother said over and over: "Will Vati survive this pounding of Stuttgart?"

From an interview with Resi Paffenholz, my brother Karl Heinz's mother-in-law

I heard from a friend that with a graduation certificate from a professional school you would be accepted into the professional school of nursing assistants and caretakers. I passed the test and was accepted at this Nazi school, though I was never a member of the Hitler Youth. The school was a horror for me. The female teachers were mostly good, but three times a week we were instructed by an SS officer in political science [state science], *where we learned that the pope and the Jews were responsible for all our miseries. Most probably they realized how upset I was, because after a short time an SS person appeared at our house with a questionnaire. He remarked that nothing was right in the house: we read the wrong paper, and the cross had to be taken down from the wall and a picture of Hitler had to replace it. I was very afraid and prayed that a bomb would fall into the school. My prayer was answered in October 1944 when bombs destroyed the school and our house became uninhabitable. With a few belongings we fled to Westerwald to acquaintances whom I met while in training to become a children's caretaker. When I arrived there, my eyes were opened. In a small house lived an old Jewish lady, whom I had met in 1939 and loved. When we arrived there we were told that we could live in Hannah's house since she had been picked up. Up to this point I believed that the Jews were rounded up for work, but Hännchen was old and weak.*

From Westerwald I took the daily train to Limburg/Lahn to work as an

*intern in the county office. Often the train could not go because of bomb
alarms. Then I had to walk about twenty-five kilometers, but the time in
the country with nice people was very relaxing.*

In another interview, Resi told me about her very hard childhood. After her father died, her mother received a Czech orphan's social security check of six marks monthly for her daughter Resi. She had to pick it up every month at the consulate. After her return to Cologne, her mother cleaned houses, because they were so poor.

Letter from my mother in Ditzenbach to O'gefreiter Hermann Brühl, 14 Schw. Gmünd Reserve Hospital St. Josef Room 14, October 17

*Thanks for your three letters. The first one took twelve days. I am re-
lieved that your condition has improved that much. It is very disappoint-
ing that your furlough was cancelled. We were looking forward to it. I
talked to Aunt Walburga right away and you will get a wooden suitcase.
But how to get it to you? If I have the time, I will visit you again. How
long will you still be there? Today I expected the parents, but in vain.
This week I will go to Stuttgart to do a rudimentary cleaning. My furniture
is now all here with some exceptions. Our quarters are quite nice now,
but there are too many people in it. Till we see you again, many greetings.*

Letter from Hans Pardun, Bernd's godfather, to our parents, Düren, November 1

*It is astonishing how much a person can endure. Since September 19
we have been sleeping in the basement. Since the bombers also attack
during the day now there is no light or water. Of Düren's 40,000 inhabitants 28,000 have already evacuated voluntarily. The Diocesan Office
has ordered that priests have to go with the evacuees. I assume that I
have to leave next week. Having to leave everything behind again that
one has just newly acquired in such difficult circumstances is very bitter
for my mother.* [His mother had been bombed out in Aachen.] *We have
refurbished our home with borrowed furniture. We don't know where we
will be sent since the political office determines the location. We discussed Oldenburg, but we have another possibility for our family.*

*The cathedral in Aachen was only slightly damaged. H.B. must have
stayed in Aachen. Is he still alive? F.S., who was looking for his parents,
has also not emerged; if he is still alive, he is in Aachen. It is said that
the bishop is in Eupen. Greetings to Isa and the children (remind Bernd
of his godfather!) and your mother. Stay well!*

*P.S. So you don't think I just give empty promises, I will tell to you
what my present for my godchild will be. I have commissioned a very
fine artist in Krefeld to paint a picture of St. Bernhard preaching in the
cloister of the Aachen cathedral. The artist has been bombed out twice
and was a soldier. I don't want to push him too much and therefore it
could take some time before delivery.*

On November 28, my father commented: The painting was never delivered because before Hans could be evacuated, he was killed in a bombing raid.

Retreat of the German Military Headquarters from the East

Excerpts from Paul's letters, summarized by his daughter Dagmar

From Kurland. Dagmar cites from the lexicon of the Second World War: the army troop North managed to escape in October 1944 from Estonia to Kurland, but was then surrounded there. Uncle Paul describes this retreat.

September 25

"Driven for many kilometers. The mothers are lamentable creatures in the refugee caravans with two or three children."

The retreating soldiers are all happy to have left Estonia. They are quartered in a small, not too clean town, on the border. Uncle Paul assumes that they will be there only two or three days, but he is glad that he is in the East and not in the West under the carpet bombings. In the middle of the night they escape from Riga. He paints deeply moving pictures of the refugees that the troops encounter on their retreat. He advises his wife, not to start wandering in the streets with no known destination.

October

They have left the town and he is glad to leave because of the constant bombing. He is convinced that retreat into rural areas will succeed as planned. He writes to his wife that it is really a triviality that in another bombing raid in Stuttgart more furniture and appliances were lost, and he tells her: "The war is in its deciding phase." This sentence can be understood in two ways; his wife knew that he hoped that Germany would be defeated.

He is starting to get concerned about the increasing air raids in and around Stuttgart: "I am convinced we will be cramped in our living quarters with others after the war is over. Sometimes we think things can't get any worse, but without a doubt, the worst months are still ahead of us. May God bless and protect you. I can't write anything else."

Dagmar writes: "How will they escape? Via land or will father take his first sea voyage?"

October 15

They cannot send packages anymore because before their retreat they burnt all cartons. "The Ivan smokes all our good cigars." The situation is serious, but not hopeless, especially for the "old reliable bunch." They escaped via the long land route from the location of their encirclement and he therefore expects to see the promised land short of a shipwreck. He won't write a "precautionary farewell letter" since "you know what to do if I do not return."

October 18

He hears that his brother-in-law Gerhard was taken as a prisoner of war. Letters from Robert have stopped.

End of October

He uses the words "Wirbeltage/Wirbelzeiten" [turbulent days/turbulent times] repeatedly in his letters, indicating that the situation is getting dire. "But we will also master these last rounds. It can't be that we will die like dogs during these last 100 meters. Without my children, what would life be for me?" He is not allowed to tell where they are stationed, but he wants his wife to have an approximate idea. He believes that a "second miracle" would soon occur. [The first one was probably breaking out of their encirclement.] He is afraid that the last phase of this "most terrible of all wars" would be like the previous war where poison gas was used. He tells his wife to check her and the children's gas masks.

Beginning of November

Winter is approaching with wet, unfriendly weather. He often thinks with great joy of the children, though he cannot picture Bille anymore.

November 14

"Wirbeltage. Watch out for low-flying planes." He can send packages again.

Retreat to Holland: Uncle Paul and his unit have successfully broken out of the encirclement. They drive to Liebau, then cross the Baltic Sea and proceed through the Reich to Holland.

November 9

"Landed on German soil. The crossing was uneventful, only my stomach was upset. We have now permanently shed the fear of encirclement, but it is getting more and more uncomfortable every day. Tell me whether you received the chocolate packages."

November 10

"We are rolling through Germany. The freight car is rolling and swerving, I can hardly write. Though we'd heard rumors for two weeks, our retreat came very suddenly. The twenty-four-hour sea voyage went without a hitch. Not a single air raid or U-boat alarm. We arrived in the harbor with a huge escort. Our 5,000-ton ship's lower deck is full of wounded soldiers, covered with lice, and many vehicles—so we are crammed in like herrings. I hope to find a mailbox somewhere to send this letter from. The first one I gave to a comrade who was transferred to Breslau. The train has just stopped for a few minutes so I can write the address."

November 14

"The journey will continue to the West. Where to? We'll see. At the
moment opinions vary whether the West or the East is better. However, I
am glad to be out of the cauldron [Kessel] encirclement. Come what
may, I trust in God. That theme runs like a thread throughout my life. I
believe in Him."

November 19

"Arrived at our destination without incident. The main thing is don't be
afraid for my sake. Don't be concerned. It will all turn out. Main thing: we
are out of the cauldron, and there is work here galore."

From Holland, November. He is outside the combat zone; even the air raids are not in his region. But he is very stressed because of the enormous workload and he often thinks he can't last much longer. They lived royally in wonderfully furnished rooms. In contrast to the East, it is like War and Peace. He is hoping for one more miracle and the war will be over.

November 17

He could buy apples, a rarity. They live a very normal life, but he is upset about the soldiers who were attacked on an accompanying boat and
all drowned.

End of November

While he is personally safe, they are getting terrible reports from the
East. The heaviest fighting was around Libau: great misery. How lucky
he is that he is in the West! "What power determines our lives? We only
do our traveling at night." He is thinking about whether his family should
go to Schnittlingen or "should start a nomadic life, by moving from one
friend to another" [auf die Strasse gehen].

There is heavy fighting in the cauldron of Kurland. He is thankful for their escape. The Allies are already in Strassburg [Alsace-Lorain, now France]. What should his wife do: stay where she is or flee if the fighting gets closer? Every day there is a conflict with his bosses. "The only reason I don't react sharply is because I am thinking of you." They are in new quarters close to the German border. "Any concern about me would be a betrayal of other soldiers' wives."

November 29

Air attack on Freiburg. "I often think this can't be happening, this terrible destruction of everything that had been built up by our ancestors
over centuries in hard and detailed labor."

He wants to hear about the children, their progress, their funny sayings, their mischief.

December 1944

His biggest worry is procuring heat. Everybody is in charge of one stove and getting the necessary wood can only be done by "semi-stealing." The third son of a befriended family from Rottweil, who went to school with him, was killed in action. He asks his wife to send him fruit and socks since his socks are full of holes. He wanted to buy a doll for Bille, but couldn't find any. He hopes a comrade whose family owns a toy factory will be able to secure toys for his five- and two-year-old girls.

He still hasn't heard from Robert. "The Schnittlinger family, especially Uncle Richard, has no compassion." [They probably turned his family down as well when they wanted to move there.]

His expectations of survival are rising. He advises his wife to go to Schnittlingen, but not to spend too much energy and time on it, because the times will get worse and one has to reserve one's remaining energy. After the war, he will move heaven and earth to find them somewhere in Europe. He needs socks, and he sends a pair home without heels.

He remembers in 1940 when the first plane was sighted over Stuttgart; now there are hundreds. "Eighty-seven bombers were shot down over Liebau. Somewhere a grenade explodes and destroys all on impact, but a bit farther away everything is untouched. Fate or coincidence?"

December 19

"What a travesty this war…the biggest tragedy of modern times…the Schnittlinger [family members] lack any kind of Christian love."

He describes his quiet life here, where two local girls do the housework and where they can get goods by trade. It is like a fairy tale. They even have their own bathroom for the first time since he left Estonia. His comrade, who returned from a furlough, could not find the place where his parents lived in Frankfurt, because of the widespread destruction; the people live like cave dwellers. Again he talks about the miracle of their escape. One hundred Russian bombers shot down over Liebau. Three major offensives south of Frauenburg, where he was stationed just a little while ago. "What the young men endure there, nobody at home can appreciate. Every time I hear about the death of my comrades' parents in air raids, I feel like someone has pierced my heart."

December 25

During their Christmas festivities he heard the humming of the fighter planes that fly toward the enemy, but then he heard a report about the incursion of fighter planes into southwest Germany. He muses that it can't be long now till it is over. He regrets the bad mail connection because of the war activities—even telegrams can take weeks—and that he cannot tell where he is. They are in telex communication with all major service units in the country. In an emergency, he could telephone via Uncle Max. Patience and more patience. His thoughts are with his family in their bomb shelters. He admonishes them to dress warmly and asks his wife to write in detail about the bomb shelter. In the meantime the temperatures have dropped so dramatically that the running water froze, but still no comparison to Russia. He hasn't played chess since he left Estonia and his chess club wrote that next year there will be no more newsletter. German chess life has ceased to exist. As have sports and cultural activities. "I pray that you will stay alive for me; the loss of the property we can handle; we are not going to fall apart over that."

December 31

The soldiers are forbidden to celebrate New Year's Eve. He expects the war to end in 1945. "Should we not see each other in this life—a possibility I don't believe in though we have to consider it—you must know that we are in no way guilty of this development. My life since my twenty-fourth year [the year of Hitler's seizure of power] has had only one idea. Now what is important is to get over the last 100 meters. The sun will shine again, the children will laugh again, and life will go on as long as we have each other; life will be worthwhile." He listens to Beethoven's violin concerto on the radio—from an American broadcast [totally illegal].

Last Months of the War on the Home Front

Aunt Resi's diary

I became pregnant again in 1944. Kurt was sent through his company, Bosch, on vacation to Bad Steben. This had something to do with "Kraft durch Freude" [strength through joy, a Nazi slogan about the importance of a strong body and how it could be developed through relaxation, vacations, etc.]. *I also needed a vacation. So, we decided that I would go with Ingrid to Zwiesel. That was a terrible and adventuresome trip. One could only travel with military furlough trains. All the seats were reserved for soldiers, while the other travelers had to stand in the aisles. You could hardly get into the train. Everywhere were boxes and crates. We were crammed in like herrings. I managed to seat Ingrid on a crate.*

The year 1944 was very turbulent. My parents returned to Aachen for a short time. They write in a long letter that they want to be killed by the incoming troops. That would end their persecution by the Nazis. It would be written in the stars when we would see each other again. I was very sad, but in the middle of the night, one day after I received the letter (September 13, 1944) the doorbell rang. For years we have had a secret signal for ringing the bell. This way I always knew who was at the door. I screamed for joy when I saw my parents coming up the stairs. They had packed their backpacks with a few essentials to go to Höfen, where most of their belongings already were. They wanted to wait there till the end of the war. But they couldn't get on the train to Monschau and the Gestapo pushed them onto a train that was going south. It was the time of forced evacuation. Fortunately at the station there was such chaos that nobody checked papers otherwise it could have been dire for my parents. In Würzburg they changed to a train for Bamberg. They only had their backpacks and the clothes on their backs. They stayed with us for the time being. But soon they found their own quarters, two small rooms in the coal trading business of some friends. They were always warm and they got on well with the owners. When my sister, who was studying in Greifswald, was evacuated, she was able to move into a third room next to them. A little while later the parents of a friend also stayed with us a while, till they found another place. I was happy to know that my parents and sister were safe and that my mother would be with me during the upcoming birth. At that time Bamberg was still very peaceful; no bomb attacks.

So I prepared for Christmas. The purchase of presents was very difficult, since there were almost no goods in the shops and the few things that one could buy when a shopkeeper knew one well was "UtT"—under the table.

Winfried's birth: I went to the clinic in the night during a complete blackout. Since there were no taxis any more, I wanted to ride my bike because I felt safer, but we walked. Instead a bicyclist ran into me from behind and caused me to fall. Thank God I was almost ready to give birth anyway. I had ridden my bike till the day before. But in the clinic it did take a bit longer till Winfried decided to join this world. Mother was ill with hunger and wanted to go home to eat something, but the idea of giving birth without her was abhorrent to me. The custom was that a pregnant woman received an extra ration of one glass of milk and one roll. I ordered it and gave it to mother. She stayed and Winfried was born in the evening.

Though the maternity ward was transferred to Schesslitz, I received permission to stay in Bamberg because I had to supervise the care of my two daughters. As it turned out, a woman that I befriended when Ursula was born gave birth to twins and she shared my room. Since her husband was a butcher, he brought sausages every day. She shared these with me, which was very much appreciated because the hospital food rations were very meager.

My sister Christel was now also pregnant. Her child was expected in May 1945. Her husband, Josef, was terribly excited. We sent very simple announcements for Winfried's birth, including to Josef. Unfortunately his answer was the last letter that I received from him before he died. In it he complained that we didn't reserve the name Winfried for his baby. He never learned before his death that his baby was a girl.

Reminiscences of Aunt Thea

I discovered a little book on my desk, "Christmas 1945." I mused how fast one forgets these times! I must have been at Isa's. We gave each other negligible presents, yet it was wonderful. Perhaps I made a cookbook "for Mrs. Isa," with wartime recipes. And Isa did everything possible for me. On Christmas 1944 I sat with my friend Inge in an air raid shelter in Canstatt. She wanted to visit her four beloved family members in the mass grave in the Steinfelden cemetery. At that time we were living with her near the Kriegsbergturm; we left from there to go to Christmas Mass at St. Nikolaus, which at that time was said at 5:00 a.m. Afterwards we wanted to visit the cemetery, but ended up sitting in the wet and dripping shelter for hours, after being freezing cold earlier. Inge ended up in the hospital for a lengthy stay. On New Year's Day 1945, I knocked at my Aunt Gertrud's door in Westerheim—melancholic—and looked up at the stars over the snow-covered village.

Reminiscences of Aunt Minni

Because of my marriage in Austria my experience of the war was different, but communication with the rest of the family was limited, mainly letters and the occasional phone call. Very occasionally, a visit.

I know little about the years of the war that were very hard on my parents and siblings. Our parents were bombed out and lost everything. They spent the last twelve years of their lives in Schnittlingen in abject poverty. The loss of their apartment was also a big loss to all the children who lived far away; we had lost our home. That's when Heinz and Isa opened their apartment to all of us "visiting relatives." They opened up their home, especially to me and Thea, even though the children had to move out of their bedrooms. Isa did all of the cooking, even invited our school friends over and went shopping with me and Thea, very patiently. Their apartment and later their house became our home.

Uncle Richard's diary, 1944

January 1
Isa, Heinz, and Margit were here for a three-hour visit.

January 16
Our relative Bernd Kottman was killed in Russia.

January 31
We heard that the only son of the church architect, Kaiser, was killed during the fighting in Italy.

April 15
Our nephew Rudolf is married—during a short furlough—in the emergency Church of St. Nikolaus.

April 22–June 7
Margit stays with us. Her mother picks her up to take her back to Ditzenbach.

April 27
Alfons, the youngest son of our neighbor Karl Gold, was accidently killed. Born in 1931, he was then thirteen years old. He was playing with an oil drum that had been jettisoned by English-American terror planes.

> *The drum exploded and hit him in such a way that he was killed instantly. Most probably he struck a match.*

[Note: This is one of my most horrible memories of the war in Schnittlingen. Though Alfons was quite a bit older than I, we often played together. As was the custom his wake was in the living room of the Gold's farm and I accompanied my relatives to express our sympathies. While we were there, they removed the sheet from his face and, at age six, I saw in horror that half of his face had been blown away.]

> *Between May 16 and May 26 we hear of the death of the following men from Schnittlingen: At the age of twenty, the oldest son of the Hirschwirt; the third son of the Eiseles [two of his brothers had been killed earlier]; the son of the letter carrier. All died in Russia. A second son of the letter carrier and his son-in-law are missing in action in Russia.*

June 4

> *The English–American troops marched into Rome.*

June 5–6

> *During the night the English-American troops invaded the continent via the English Channel.*

June 16

> *During the night (starting at 11:40 p.m.) and the next morning German pilots dropped the "new rockets of heavy caliber" for the first time—the "new weapon" that had been announced a long time ago—over southern England and London.*

July 20

> *The radio announced an assassination attempt against the Führer. Some men close to him were severely hurt, others only slightly. The Führer himself sustained only slight injuries, so that he was able to continue his activities right away. It was a mutiny by some officers, which was immediately put down. Some of them committed suicide, others were eliminated.*

July 25

> *We heard that during the last terror attack on Friedrichshafen three members of the Frank family, our relatives, were killed. The tragedy occurred in a bunker that should have given them protection.*

July 24–25

> *During the night, around 2:00 a.m., there was a heavy terror attack on Stuttgart. The following night there was another heavy attack. The house of Achaz at Kernerplatz 5 was totally destroyed. He lost everything. On the way out of the house, he was hit on the shoulder by a*

piece of wood that came loose from the neighboring house. It broke his collarbone. He arrived with his wife on July 26 at our house.

July 29

We found out that on the Eastern front Paul Brühl, the son of the daughter of the owner of the Hirsch, was killed in action, and Reinhold Brühl, a cousin, is missing on the Eastern front.

August 8

The officers who were involved in the assassination attempt were convicted and sentenced to death by strangulation:

> *Graf von Stauffenberg, who is already dead;*
> *General Fieldmarshall von Witzleben;*
> *Generaloberst Erich Hoepner;*
> *General Major Stieff;*
> *First Lieutenant of the reserves Von Hagen*
>   *(not sentenced to die);*
> *First Lieutenant at Headquarters Bernadis;*
> *Hauptmann Karl Klausig;*
> *Lieutenant von Hase;*
> *Lieutenant of the Reserve von Wartenberg.*

August 1

Florian Brühl, the oldest son of the tile installer Gregor Brühl, was killed in action on the Eastern front on August 1; thirty-seven years old.

August 14

Invasion of the enemy in the South of France between Toulon and Cannes.

October 1

Frau Bulling died at the age of 99¼ years. Until the last she was surprisingly healthy, physically and mentally. The news of the tragic death of her son and his wife in Stuttgart, who became victims of a terror attack, upset her so much that she died after not feeling well for a few days.

November 5

Josef Nagele, son of the Scheck farmer, was killed on November 5 in the Vogesen mountains in France. He was twenty-four.

November 18

Our nephew Rudolf left us after a two-week furlough from the army (his wife was evacuated in Schnittlingen).

The Last Year of the War Begins

Paul's last letters, from the beginning of 1945 till his capture as a prisoner of war
[in his daughter Dagmar's words]

The photos of their wedding have all burned. "Wedding, how long ago that was.... War years count double, and in this war probably three times." His need for socks has diminished, because the girls who clean will darn them in exchange for cigarettes. "I still have one more chocolate bar that I want to bring home to you from the war. Barter blooms here and our well-being depends on the stomach. I'll turn into a cook yet. I don't have time anymore for a birthday letter for Dagmar, and I have nothing to send her anyway. She'll get double in 1946."

* * *

His wife, Aunt Trudl, must have written many letters of complaints about the family in Schnittlingen, their control and the lack of her own apartment. He knows how hard it is for her, but asks her to "think of the hundreds of thousands of Germans who as soldiers have to give up all forms of personal freedom completely and who in addition are constantly in danger of losing life and limb." Aunt Trudl informed him that she has moved to a cousin in Ottenbach where his salary as judge gets sent. Obviously his salary was paid during all the years of the war. He thanks her for the wonderful socks, and sends more news of comrades killed or missing in action. He is worried about his in-laws, Wilma and Erich, and thinks that Erich will be drafted into the Volkssturm. (Erich, the husband of the oldest Brühl daughter, was not drafted for the ordinary military because he was the administrator of a big farmstead in East Prussia, in what now is Poland, and an expert on cheese quality.)

* * *

In a letter to his mother, Mrs. Ludwig, he writes that he is glad that his wife is in Ottenbach because her nerves and her resistance were being strained under the constant air attacks. He can understand her wish for her own home, but he cannot visualize his kids anymore. He is convinced that the war will be over soon. He is physically okay, but suffers because of the attitudes of his boss and his comrades. He also thinks a lot about the present battles in Kurland in which many units from Baden-Württemberg are involved. He still considers it a miracle that he escaped. They hear about the bombing terror in southern Germany and he is glad that she left the house in Rottweil, which is close to the train station and had been hit by bombs. He talks about a new spike in this pitiless, two-front war and the Russian major offensive. He is glad that they found a place in Ottenbach because he reckons that a lot of refugees will come to southern Germany. He is eagerly awaiting news that his family was not attacked during the move. He is hoping to share some of his war experiences so that the war years will not be a total waste. Thanks to a sergeant with whom he plays chess, he telephoned an aunt who told him that his family did arrive safely in Ottenbach. His wife no longer has a radio. He is glad that they were not in the area during the attack on Reutlingen.

He thanks them for the wonderful socks, which he will keep till he is "on the move again." His wife writes that the new place is safe, but they have problems with the heat. He has great pity for his comrades whose families are in the East, but he expects it to get worse again in the West with a Spring offensive. He is sending cigarettes that his wife can use for barter to get new furniture for her new home; however his rations have been halved to sixty a month and two a day as bonus. The earpiece of his glasses was repaired in exchange for twenty cigarettes. It is winter in Holland.

February

He asks his wife not to despair even if they don't hear much from each other: "We have to get through this terrible bottleneck to get to freedom." He doesn't want to write a farewell letter. His only wish is for his girls "to grow up to be good Germans who believe in the goodness of humanity and the beauty of the world." His family is happy in their own apartment with no sirens and they now have enough wood. His cousin is a prisoner of war in Oklahoma. He is convinced that the last war winter is upon them and he hopes for the next miracle, the end of the war. He endured five hard years.

The family has no radio, and cigarettes are lacking, which makes barter difficult. However the neighbors voluntarily give them butter and goose fat. He is proud of his Schwabian "tribe." He is concerned when he hears reports about the attacks on South Germany, but even more concerned about the East. Comrades are telling of horrible scenes of fleeing refugees from the East. Communication is becoming increasingly difficult. They are not receiving any more cigarettes and only once a month one-and-a-half packages of tobacco; he can send moisturizer, however, and he has lots of worthless money.

He plays two sets of chess with two people, one via telephone and one via mail: each day just one move, but it is good brain exercise. "Auf Wiedersehen, will the war last till letter Nr. 100?"

End of February

"The progress of the 'Tommy' is pitiful considering their overwhelming power. What if he really gets into it?" He can't say anything about the general situation, but his wife knows his attitude. In military reports he hears about the bombing raids on Lake Constance and is afraid their furniture in Lochau will also disappear. Again: "courage, trust, just a bit longer."

March

He is glad to hear that his wife can go to Schnittlingen to beg for some food, since the situation is getting critical. Armin, a nephew, has a skull fracture and so can come home again instead of serving in the Volkssturm. "Only a few more weeks and we will have survived the last and worst war winter. A new day dawns on the other shore." He lives in a cold hovel, not enough coal. All the cigarette factories have stopped producing. He prefers to stay silent about the coming defeat: "This silence is not due to a Pollyanna attitude; on the contrary, I have my eyes wide open, but it is a requirement of reason. Silence is golden."

He is very concerned about the fate of hundreds of thousands of soldiers and civilians during the next few weeks. The Americans have reached the Rhine in the North. He hears the news before the ordinary citizens, but has to keep silent. Unexpectedly he receives a letter from his wife through a comrade in which she writes: "We have talked about everything together, and I will wait and hope that we will see each other again somewhere." He is getting concerned about his family's hunger and urges his wife to ask the Schnittlinger farm family to help her.

The war has started a new phase with the battle for the bridge over the Rhine. If the battles get close to his family, he thinks they should not flee to the center of Germany but endure what comes their way. His mother has taken in a woman from Armenia with two small daughters. No more packages are allowed to be sent. Mother should go into the woods and have Dagmar help collect beechnuts. It's springtime in Holland, but that means good weather for planes and certain death for many comrades. On his wedding anniversary he muses: "What will happen?" The question of millions. Soon, we'll see major offensives. He regrets that he can't talk to anybody, because they don't share his philosophy, but he is getting used to his emotional loneliness.

March 20 (last letter from the field: Number 65)

"We went out again in the fresh air. Now it is only a Sunday walk to the fatherland."

The next message is via the Red Cross on June 6, 1945, from Sergeant Ludwig, c/o Farmer E. Kurth Landwebel, near Nortorf/ Holstein: "Dear, survived and am well. Hope desperately the same for you. Am in good spirits, still with the old comrades, not yet in the prison camp. Hope for an early release. Happy Birthday wishes, Petz" [his nickname].

From the Doerr interview, referring to events either in 1943 or 1944

M.E: "...the situation was as follows. I was working for a firm that issued ration cards. I had been granted a leave of absence because I was expecting a child, but when I miscarried I had to go back to work. Then the firm was bombed out and we were evacuated. First we were quartered in a bed-and-breakfast inn and then in a private house in Weissenstein on the Alb [the second village over from Schnittlingen—pure coincidence]. Our offices were in the castle on the hill. So everybody collected firewood on the way home. And one person stoked our little stove.

188

One of the women had a bigger radio and she listened often to the foreign radio stations, but I considered that too risky. Every morning we went to her room and asked her to tell us the news. You cannot imagine how much we hungered for news. But then it happened that our mayor received a complaint that so-and-so was listening to these prohibited stations and he was ordered to investigate whether he wanted to or not. Whether this was the mayor or the regional official, most of the time they were harmless people, but they had to investigate, when somebody complained."

The War Affects Every Part of Germany

Aunt Resi's diary, which still moves easily between past and present tenses

In the meantime we have had frequent alarms. Bombers flew over Bamberg on their way to Nürnberg in order to drop their bombs there. It happened in January 1945. The family was sitting down to eat dinner and I got up with Winfried because during an alarm I didn't feel right in bed by myself. And the first bomb was dropped on Bamberg. One of the bombers had lost a bomb on the way to Nürnberg. It hit the ground with a tremendous force, exactly in front of a friend's house, which was severely damaged. In our house all windows break, the stucco ceiling collapses in the dining room onto the dining room table. The bed in which I was minutes before was covered with glass splinters. We flee into the hallway, where Ursula has a major crying fit and in the confusion she destroys the porcelain head of the heirloom doll. Kurt organized everything perfectly and in a few days we had new window panes and the ceilings were newly stuccoed. But we then decided to spend the time during the alarms in the cellar. However, that wasn't much safer. The windows were above ground and not protected. We had warned the authorities about this and now some action was taken. Bricks were delivered and were lying in the driveway. The workmen were hired to brick up the windows. We moved Winfried's bed into the cellar and moved some other furniture. The individual cellars were divided by concrete pillars. In between was lattice work. We stood the baby crib in front of a concrete pillar. Kurt had been ordered to serve in the home air spotter brigade. The firm, Bosch, had a tall tower where the anti-aircraft artillery was posted. Kurt often had night watch, and day watch during alarms.

We prepared the cellar with care, by stocking it with food and drinks, wash clothes, and garden tools. A radio was supposed to alert us about the local situation. The little suitcase with papers and jewelry is always ready in the hallway. February 22 is another alarm at noon. All three families in the house run into their own cellars. We sit in the cellar when the radio announced: "Incoming airplanes to Bamberg." This time we took—because of the extreme cold and for protection—our two eiderdowns and the bedding from the children's beds. Winfried lies in front of me in the clothes basket. The two girls lie in Winfried's little bed. When the first bombs fall, the two maids and I snatch up a child and we cower under the eiderdowns, each one of us leaning instinctively over a child. And the bombs are starting to fall all around us. The children were only out of the bed a few seconds when the concrete pillar breaks, falls into the bed and destroys it completely. Terrible to think what would have happened if the girls were still in there. Stones and earth hail down on us through the windows onto our blankets, which protect us from the worst.

One bomb hit directly next to the house and took part of the wall down. Where there was a nice stone garden before, there was now a big crater into which a small house could fit. The children's bedroom was uninhabitable. The floor was uneven and the wall leaned. The rest of the apartment also looked terrible: debris and shards. But one thing was not touched. Kurt had given me a Rosenthal lamp, which stood on the desk and was plugged in. It was knocked off the desk and hung in the air from its electric cord. Kurt, who was on air spotter watch at Bosch, saw that the bombs hit in our area. As soon as he could, he ran to us and we were all safe. The next morning brought another alarm. Kurt, who had gotten the day off to help with the cleanup, was at home. What to do now? The house and cellar did not offer protection anymore. So, we started to run. Kurt and I had Winfried in the clothes basket between us. Mali and Gisela held Ingrid's and Ursula's hands. The next public bomb shelter was on the other side of the Regnitz. It was built into the mountain under an old beer and wine cellar. Since the bridge over the Regnitz was destroyed, the city had built a primitive wobbly emergency bridge. Just when we ran over this bridge, the first bombs fell in the old town. We reached the entrance and were guided into the poorly lit cellar over slippery steep stairs, and then assigned to different rooms and hallways. We landed eventually in the room: "Mother and Child," but by then Gisela and Ingrid were missing. There was a lot of shoving and pulling. Everybody experienced mortal fear; it was a panic. After a while Gisela appeared, but she had lost Ingrid in the pushing and shoving. This was the only time I saw Kurt crying. I stayed with the children while Kurt went in search of our "escapee," whom he soon found. Then Mrs. W. appeared with her two girls. She sobbed and sobbed and told us that her father dropped dead on the emergency bridge while the bombs were falling around them and she had to leave him there in order to save her two girls and herself.

Fortunately not as many bombs as yesterday were dropped, otherwise the destruction would have been more widespread. In upper Hain Street the villas are widely separated and surrounded by large gardens. Still, a lot of terrible things happened and a lot was destroyed. Our neighboring house, the most beautiful on the street, was not damaged at all, but the one just across the street was totally demolished. After we surfaced from our shelter, we saw only a smoking pile of ruins, with eleven people buried underneath and dead. It was a single-family home that belonged to an elderly couple whose son was married in the

Rhineland. He had seven children. When they were bombed out there, they took refuge with his parents. An aunt, who was also bombed out, came with them. The son had to go back to the front. The idea that he lost his wife, his seven children, his parents, and an aunt in one day was terrifying.

Another house in the neighborhood belonged to a doctor. His son was also a doctor and lived with his family in Bonn. He was drafted into the army as a military doctor. When his family was bombed out in Bonn, he moved his wife and three small children, exactly the age of ours, to his parent's house. While I stood in front of the pile of rubble and watched the rescue workers, they brought the baby out last. All the others were brought out already dead, including the household assistant. The baby was still alive, but then died suddenly. It was terrible to see that. It could have been us. Now the war had also really reached us with all its force.

Kurt talked to the Bosch people the next day before the second attack to arrange for a car that would evacuate us. We decided that Gunzendorf was the only alternative. It was off the beaten track, not too far from Bamberg; it was the home of our au pair, Mali. When we got "home" we packed the most important essentials and all of us were packed onto a lorry to bring us to Gunzendorf. We knew Mali's parents and their farm because we had visited them a few times. I do remember that the first night I lay under a heavy eiderdown with the kids in one bed. Sleep of course did not come after all the previous excitement.

The principal of the school was also the local Nazi group leader and Kurt managed to convince him, since the village had taken in few refugees, to assign us the teacher's lounge as our "home." Kurt cleaned out our uninhabitable apartment in Bamberg. We used the beds to furnish our new room. The other furniture came into a temporary storage place, which of course was broken into. The principal lived in a large apartment at the school. In his large kitchen was a big stove in the middle, but when I asked whether I could cook there or at least warm the baby's bottle, I was turned down. We had—I can't remember who gave it to us—a small hot plate, with exposed wires. On it I had to prepare all our meals with Gisela, who had a tiny room on a farm, for our six people, and warm the bath water for Winfried. Afterwards you wonder how you survived that ordeal.

A few days later a refugee caravan with horses and farm carts from Jauer in Silesia arrived—a picture of misery. During their long trek, three babies were born. Quickly all the classrooms were emptied and mattresses were put down. How good we had it; we slept in our own beds. A huge water kettle was put up in the courtyard in which pea or lentil soups were cooked. The principal's kitchen was also off limits for these babies. How and where could they bathe their babies? Most of the babies and toddlers had diarrhea due to the bad nutrition. Where could they boil water for tea? Because of our dilapidated hot plate we were seen as kings. Between meals I made tea and then the babies were bathed one after the other. And then the wash was done in cold water, all in our baby bathtub. Before the capitulation we and the people from Jauer were moved out, because the school had to be readied as a field hospital. The "happy times" were over for us. Where could we go? In the meantime Gunzendorf had had its fill of refugees. We found a new "home" in a cow stable with a small chamber next to it. Two friends also found a home with a farmer. At least we had an outhouse, but the others had to sit in a stable on wooden beams. There was hardly any room between our beds, our clothes closet, and a little sideboard. But in the little chamber we could put up our kitchen cabinet and the children's table. A little stove allowed us to cook more normally. In the field hospital there was an epidemic of paratyphoid. I caught it somehow and was in bed with a fever and diarrhea. The doctor ordered that I stop nursing immediately. First, my milk would not stop, even by breast binding. Then, where would I get milk for Winfried? The farmers were not giving any milk away anymore. After a few days I was better, only to get sick again. The doctor said: either the child or you. I decided that the child was more important. But I did recover as well, though I was very weak.

The fight for survival now was to get food. Almost every day I rode my bike along the railroad track to the neighboring village over a hill, because Gunzendorf was in a valley. This was the only place that still had bread. Once during a return trip there was a warning about incoming planes. I discarded the bike and jumped into the ditch and lay very flat. The low-flying planes strafed all along the rural road—shooting at anything that moved—and into the houses on the side of the road. I was not hurt, but the shock went deep. Every time low-flying planes are in the area I become afraid, and I duck my head. No wonder your nerves got destroyed during those times. In January before the second attack we received the sad news that my sister's husband had been shot down in his plane and killed. She had just received a letter from him telling her not to believe everything and that often false death notices reach the relatives. So, of course, she did not believe it. But the death was confirmed and a Requiem Mass was said for her husband and his brother, who was also killed about the same time.

My first handwritten letter to my father [then in a TB sanatorium in the Black Forest]
January 1945, from Bad Ditzenbach
Dear Vati,

How do you like Schönberg? I am going to send you a little package soon. You have to write to us soon.

A little kiss, Margit greetings, and a kiss, your mother

Field post, to my father

Dear Vati,

Yesterday I saw a beautiful film; it showed a farm from the Black Forest where you are. And then the hard coals, young lions, and the

192

fairytale about the one who went out to learn what fear was.

A little kiss, Margit

Mother's diary, February 1

Today Karl Heinz is one-and-a-half years old. He spent the last three months with the Weilands, where he learned a lot. He can give kisses and is quite generous with them, and he is starting to say his first words: auto, mama, puff (for the noise that the train makes), hoppa (for his horse). Margit and Bernd treat him like a little prince who can do whatever he wants. He loves the noisy life of the family, but does feel hemmed in by our close living quarters. He wants to go with anybody who leaves the room. For hours he moves the pots and pans around in the kitchen [in the meantime, the Priel family gave us a second room that we used as a kitchen/ dining area] and tries to find the right lids for the pots. When I have to get water or potatoes downstairs, he sulks when he is not allowed to carry the pail or basket.

Oma Paulus spends a lot of time with him. She is enchanted by him though he is a lot of work for her, because he constantly climbs over all the furniture. I am sometimes amazed how so much impishness can be in such a small person. He loves any antics. Vati, who is again in a sanatorium in Schoenberg, misses his little boy very much.

Letter to my mother from E.M., my father's colleague, February 6, from the Eastern front
[Writing shortly before the end of the war, the colleague predicts that they will have parties again in our parents' apartment.]

Thank you for your letter, which arrived at the same time as a letter from my wife, Isa, who informed me that she is evacuating our apartment in Breslau and will move in with my brother in Hirschberg. For days I have been writing to his address in the hope that she will check for mail there, even if she had to move somewhere else. Whether or when the mail will arrive there, is uncertain, but I am hopeful. Unfortunately, I am starting to have doubts. I agree with you that seeing your children alive every day makes you happy. I hope to see your Swabian offspring soon and I hope that their father will be as healthy then as we all wish. I am here in a small Hungarian village and am relatively happy, and that should mean something. If I didn't have to worry about my wife and home, everything would be fine. Since I was on furlough a few months ago, I can't expect to get another furlough for helping with the evacuation. Many good wishes

Letter to my father in the sanatorium from Monsignor Gottfried Dossing, a friend of my father and Hans Pardun, February 6, Paderborn

I am enclosing a death prayer card of G.L., and two of Hans Pardun. R.B. is pastor in Krefeld. I visited him in January. All residents of the house sat in the basement. Three meters away from the door of the house and fifty centimeters in front of the house a dud was embedded in the ground. It took eight days to defuse it. My visit was exactly three days after the big raid on Krefeld. They all survived this attack. From the reports of refugees, Krefeld surrendered to the Americans without much of a fight. If Hans were still there, he would probably have survived. Now he is dead, but I feel in a way he is still with us, and is a part of our future work.

In November 1944 the Americans started their offensive with a strong air attack on Heimsberg, Jülich, and Düren. The bombardment of Düren is indescribable. Continuously, waves of new heavy machines plunged onto the city, which already had suffered for weeks from daily heavy artillery bombardment. Düren was completely obliterated. Hans was at home. Shortly before that he was planning to meet with a vicar who was supposed to come to Hans. On the way there, the vicar was caught in an alarm, which made him turn back. Right after the attack he ran through the ruins to Hans's house. But this house was totally razed. More than half of it is a large bomb crater. Over the other half lies the spire of his church, St. Anna. The only thing that survived of the church is a staircase into the sacristy and a part of the choir wall. The custodian of St. Dyonysius Church in Krefeld, who rode his bike to Düren on the third day after the attack to look for Hans, told me that one could no longer be sure where the altar and the spire of the church had been. He said that only a well-equipped rescue team could move the massive stone piles to search for Hans and his mother. This custodian is used to ruins in Krefeld and does not exaggerate. The number of dead must be extremely high. The coadjutor and another vicar are also dead. The third vicar only survived because he was outside of Düren during the attack.

A few days later Hans had planned to evacuate to Thüringen with his mother to serve the refugees there. A suitcase had already been deposited on the Cologne road, where refugees saw it days later in the ruins of the house with a tag that read: Property of Pastor Pardun, St. Anna. A few valuables are still entombed in a wall in a house in Düren. Perhaps one can find them after the war.

I spoke to him in October by telephone and he told me that the decision to stay was one of nerves, not of courage. During the last few days before the attack, he vacillated between staying and going. If his coadjutor had not ordered him to stay, he would have left a few days earlier.

I never thought that Hans would die before me. His death has deeply affected me. We were close friends and classmates and we were close in the seminary. His death is also a big personal loss for me. I will not write an obituary here, because it would be too personal. I hope that from heaven he will support the things that he so ardently supported here on earth. Now to the others that you asked about...two of them are still in an area that is being fought over. The next few weeks will tell whether they can survive. I don't know whether I already wrote to you that I was injured during an air raid in Gummersbach, splinter injuries in the head, internal brain bleeding, buried under debris. My foot will never be completely *healed. For the future: I will have a limp.*

Now I hope you will improve your health and survive till better times ahead. I hope this letter reaches you. I will also write to Isa—it may be impossible to write in the future. W.K. did not return from Rumania. I hope he is still alive. We also have not heard from A.S. from Silesia, but that might be due to the bad mail connections. Greetings to your loved ones and to you. Hopefully we will see each other in the not too distant future.

Gottfried Dossing had a pronounced limp for the rest of his life and often walked with a cane, but he became world renowned as the founder and long-time director of Misereor, the German Bishops' Conference effort to fight hunger and disease in the world. He died in the 1990s at more than ninety years. I worked for Misereor from 1965 till 1968, before emigrating to the United States.

Letter from Isa to Heinz, February 7
[sent from Ditzenbach to the sanatorium in the Black Forest]

Many good wishes for your birthday. Do you remember how we celebrated that first birthday together? Your twenty-first. Those were the days. My sincerest wish is that we can spend the next feast days in peace and together again. We will be thinking of you especially on your special day. And you of us. Today I am enclosing a package with butter cookies again. I hope you receive it in time. I won't be able to bake again soon, but Trudl had sent me a half pound of butter in exchange for an old dress of Margit's. Thea will send you a book from us. She sent me stationery today. We can't buy anything anymore.

Heinz, if I were you, I would stay there as long as you can. You will be better off there than here. And it will help improve your health. Don't you think it's better that I do not come and visit you, but stay with the children? The enemy has already reached Alsace. One hears so many terrible things about Berlin and the refugees from the East. That confirms my plan to stay here as long as possible. The children would be squeezed and trampled in the overstuffed trains or separated from their parents. I would rather stay here and embrace them so any bullet would kill us all together. If I would lose one of the children, I could not go on living. I will put little name tags around their necks. Please don't laugh. It is sad that one has to think of these things.

Do you know what happened to Regine, Max, Elli, and Hans? Where might they be if they are still alive? I wrote to you already last time that I have absolutely no more cigarettes. [My father was not a smoker, but at the end of the war, when commodities were scarce, cigarettes were used as money.] *I sent the last ones to you.... And I am not getting new goods. What do you want to trade for cigarettes? Perhaps I will go to Göppingen....* [The rest is illegible, but has to do with my father's salary from Allianz.] *We are very pleased that you have gained weight. Hopefully it will continue. Tomorrow morning I have to go with Margit for a medical examination for school. Now, celebrate your birthday with eat-*

ing, drinking, reading, and relaxation! All of us greet you and send you our heartfelt wishes.

Mother's diary

February 1945

  Margit asked me today: "When this war is finished, when will the next one start?" I told her, "I hope not for some time, because otherwise Bernd would have to become a soldier and go to war." Butzi got very upset and answered: "What? I am supposed to go to war alone? No, I am going to take my Oma, my Mutti, and my Margit with me."

  He loves rhymes and knows his rhyme books by heart, especially "Struwelpeter" and "Max and Moritz." He recites them to friends outside, he regales all visitors with them, and he loves to "read" his books from front to back. He did have a hard time understanding that these were two ragamuffins. He called them Max, Mohr, and Ritz. He amazes us by using the sayings in his books quite correctly in everyday activities. When Oma was looking for her needle the other day, he recited: "Wo der Wind sie hingetragen, das weiss kein Mensch zu sagen" [where the wind carried it off, no one can say].

  But his big loves are cars and trains. Picture books are checked immediately for these items and evaluated accordingly. The Christchild did bring him many trains, carriages, and cars. All, old recycled toys that were repainted or spruced up like new.

March 1945

  Bernd and I looked at photo albums. When we looked at the photo of Margit with the large dog, Hector, he declared, "That's not Margit, that's me. You know, little girls are afraid of large dogs like this. Boys aren't."

  He attended the baptism of a cousin's daughter and watched everything with great interest. But he took exception to the anointing with oil: The way this priest did it was not correct. One is not allowed to put lotion on children if they don't have a wound. When he is grown up, he would baptize differently.

Air Attacks on Dresden

While our little village was still untouched by the advancing Allied troops, the same cannot be said about the eastern part of Germany. Maria Hayer, a family friend, in an interview with me described the night of the American-British air attack on Dresden.

Interview with Maria Hayer

February 1945

  I was on night watch at the train station as a registered nurse, but because my mother was old—and had a small baby who was born eighteen years after the other four children—I received permission to go home after the first sirens sounded. I ran through the streets to my home—into the cellar in which my grandmother, my mother, one of my brothers, and my baby sister had already fled. Our father was a prisoner of war, as was another brother; the third brother was missing in action when his U-boat went down. After a while we crawled out of the winding hallways of the cellar into the night, when we believed that the attack was over. We could get out because our house was attached to a school and therefore had various exits and we found ourselves in the school yard. Most of the exits were sprayed with phosphorus. The baby had to be covered with wet blankets and clothes because the flying ashes singed her skin and left pock marks. The whole family ran to an acquaintance in a suburb, where we spent the night on chairs since the family had already given refuge to people from the East.

The third attack came in the morning. Our house was totally demolished. We wandered—with many others—first toward the south, then the west. (A man we asked en route for advice—which way we should go—told us that he would be put against the wall and shot if he told us anything. But he suggested we go west since the Russians were already at the shore of the Elbe.) We then proceeded with the pram, no other clothes, no change of underwear, one toothbrush for all, toward the West till we reached Rittershausen. Occasionally we received a cup of tea, a piece of bread, but we were not hungry, we just wanted to move on. First we were put up in a camp where we slept on cots. Then we were assigned to a farmer where my brother and I helped out in the field, and my mother and grandmother sewed and did knitting.

We had a small wood stove, on which we cooked everything. Instead of wood we used roots, there was no running water; the warmest place was the stable where we also had the "indoor" outhouse.

After the first attack, people who had fled their houses toward the Elbe were shot down systematically by low-flying English/American planes. It was the night of carnival 1945.

Last Months of the War in the West

Dr. Doerr's interview with my mother and M.E.

M.E.: *At the end of the war my husband was in Hall-Hessenstahl, at the air base where I still visited him on Good Friday. While I was on the train there were air attacks and a bomb hit the train directly. Not our compartment, but the one next to ours was hit and everyone died. Three of us escaped, ran out of the train, and up the embankment. I must say that I still feel guilty today that I didn't stay to help. Paramedics materialized immediately—I will say, they were very organized, it was amazing. They were the trained personnel who looked after the people, but I can still visualize it in front of me today. And what still weighs on me is that I did not stay and hold the hand of a dying person. I have to admit.*

Then the three of us, a young girl, a soldier on leave, and I climbed up the embankment, but as soon as we reached the ridge, the planes came back and we threw ourselves in a ditch. When we eventually reached the next village, there was an alarm again. So, into a cellar.

The train was hit in the morning between eight and nine; I finally ar-

rived at the air base in the late afternoon. There was an alarm and the soldiers came pouring out. I told them my name at the entrance gate and my husband greeted me with a steel helmet: *"Das ist Gott versucht"* [this is terrible]. *That was his entire greeting. We stood under a ruin with steel helmets on our heads. I thought I would like to see how bombs come down, since we were always in the basement during the air raids. My husband said: "Come, rush, you have to leave here immediately." He accompanied me to the train station and on the way there we encountered a whole gathering of people in blue-and-white-striped suits. That was a Jewish troop that was being marched to a camp in the area. My husband didn't know that. But I worked in Weissenstein in the agricultural office and every day I issued ration cards for camps, which were called "labor camps"; I had no idea that they were concentration camps.*

Actually I thought they had a pretty good life. But it seems that the rations never reached the inmates. We had always heard that people who listened, for example, to foreign radio stations (i.e., enemy stations) were assigned to work in a factory and had to work for the war effort. In any case, I thought they didn't have such a bad life.

I often get asked: "Didn't you notice that your neighbors disappeared?" You know, these times were so topsy-turvy, we had to work like crazy—almost every night we had to get out of bed because of air raids—one was only half alive.... Then someone's house was destroyed here, and someone else's there—one had to take in people who had lost everything. There were glass shards everywhere....
It is true that the low-flying planes swooped down on individual people while they walked in open fields. Every time one heard them, one had to lie flat on the ground. I always tried to walk near bushes and throw myself down there.

Doerr: *Did that make you furious?*

M.E.: *Yes, we were very angry, but we also had a strong will to survive, so we always got up and continued till the next planes came. But later the rage did surface. To me this was the biggest conflict of my life. We had heard that when the Americans came we would be liberated and we could talk freely again, but how many people still had to die before that happened? What did the destruction of Heilbronn look like? Where is my husband? Is he still alive—or dead? When we said good-bye in Hesselbach he had to leave because as he told me, "The Americans are only ten kilometers from here." He was an officer and when the troops retreated he marched via Stuttgart on the way to Austria, but did not stop in Stuttgart because he had a whole troop of people with him. He felt he couldn't tell them: "Find your own way home." So he was captured by the Americans and then became a French prisoner of war.*

Doerr: *Did he experience the terrible conditions of the prisoner of war camps on the Rhine?*

M.E.: *No, some of his comrades who didn't march with him were not able to avoid those terrible camps. They dug themselves into the ground and put their coats over themselves. That was all the protection that they had for sleeping. My husband was still in combat—the Americans shot people like rabbits—but on the other hand they were the liberators. From then on one could speak freely again. I am sure you cannot iden-tify with this, but for me it was like I could breathe freely again.*

We were living in Weissenstein, which is at the bottom of a valley, and shortly before the Americans rolled in we, the women, because nobody else was left, had to put up tank barriers—so they could not proceed to the top of the hill and roll their tanks into the village. Before the village surrendered three young boys, children really, tried to stop the advanc-ing troops with anti-tank grenade launchers. They were shot to death. You ask why nobody took the weapons from them, but if somebody had done that the Nazis who were still there would have shot their houses to pieces. It is unfathomable that people actually believed in victory till the last minute.

Reminiscences of Armin Tietze, my oldest cousin (born 1929)

Since the beginning of 1941 we had been living in Prussian Holland (Preussisch Holland) in East Prussia. My father was exempt from mili-tary service because he was classified as an indispensable expert on soft cheese. From about the middle of 1943 one needed special permis-sion to travel out of East Prussia. A fake telegram about the serious ill-ness of our grandmother was enough to get us this special permit for my mother, sister, and me. In the autumn of 1943 we voluntarily evacuated and lived with distant relatives in Donzdorf. First I went to school in Geislingen, and after the war in Göppingen.

About every four weeks, my mother and younger sister Elinor went on foot to Schnittlingen, especially during the harvest times where we al-ways had to help. We also collected beechnuts, which we took to the oil mill to get oil for cooking. During the summer of 1944 we had to help with all the harvest activities at Schnittlingen. Toward the end of the year, hunger started to become severe. Once, for a whole week, we had only bread soup. Since the people we stayed with were small farmers, my mother and sister and I occasionally got some food from them. Ap-ples and apple juice were available when the juice and alcoholic apple cider was made. They also had milk, but shoes and clothes were no lon-ger available, and there was no soap or soap substitute.

In 1943–1944 our mother, sister, and I occasionally visited our grand-parents in Stuttgart on weekends. I still remember that after the air raids there was no electricity. To announce the "all clear," a car with a siren drove through the streets. One of the necessities was to replace the bro-ken windows. Often we used an opaque man-made material because glass was no longer available and would have to be replaced at the next attack anyway. At least three times after an attack we had to get right back to Donzdorf. Since the streetcars were no longer in operation, we had to do everything on foot. On the way to the station we saw many roofs on fire. The trains could not come into the station, that's why we walked along on the rails till we found a train that would go in our direction. At the next visit electricity, water, gas, streetcars, and the train station were all restored, but the bombed-out houses were still in ruins. In the Fall of 1944 I was drafted into service by the army [Arbeitsdienst]. Most of us were between fourteen and sixteen years old. Under the supervision of the Wehrmacht, we had to dig long trenches at the Westwall between Bühl and Karlsruhe, wide and deep enough so that soldiers could walk in them undetected. Low-flying enemy planes were always close by. Every day the food consisted of pasta that was boiled for hours, sometimes with some other ingredients.

Toward the end of this assignment a hoe that was thrown out of the trench hit me in the head. No first aid service was available. I wasn't even allowed to rest. Eventually at the hospital in Geislingen and then later at the university hospital in Tübingen they determined that I had a skull fracture, a dent in the head, and brain damage. It was decided that an operation was not advisable, so the damage was allowed to heal itself. I suffered from terrible headaches for the next twenty-five years, but kept quiet because I was afraid to jeopardize my job. [He went to the University of Cologne for a physics degree, worked for IBM all his life, is the owner of many patents, and emigrated with his wife and five children to the United States in 1969.]

It must have been around January–March 1945 when, due to the constant bombings by low-flying planes, the railroad service between Stuttgart and Ulm was halted during the day. As students we had to take two trains from Donzdorf to our high school in Geislingen and often had no way of returning after classes were over. Three female classmates and I undertook the return journey of fifteen kilometers on foot every day. We walked alongside ditches and houses and through forests that gave us protection when the planes came. We had to avoid shortcuts that led through open country. In April 1945 the school was closed—indefinitely.

About half a year before the end of the war, fourteen- to fifteen-year-old males were ordered to be prepared to be sent to a safer region [sixteen-year-olds had already been called up for the Volkssturm]. The real reason one could only imagine. And two days before the Americans occupied our area, we were called up. I "got lost," which was possible since the administration had broken down. The ones who heeded the call were given rifles and grenade launchers. Two days after the occupation I would have had to go with them. During this time, we lived in constant fear. On one side was the Nazi threat and on the other, the advancing American and French soldiers. In the end, the Volkssturm was not called up in the region of Schnittlingen and Donzdorf. Also, two days before the American invasion the reserve depots were opened up to the general public. Donzdorf had the warehouse for tobacco leaves. Farmers and other civilians took whole cart loads, as much as they *could carry. The plan was to use these goods for future trading, because other villages had warehouses of different goods. When my mother, sister, and I left for Donzdorf in 1943, my father stayed behind and was drafted into the Volkssturm in 1945, and shortly afterwards became a Russian prisoner of war. I remember many Sunday trips to Schnittlingen. Since this was a big farm, they had enough to eat through all the hard times. On Sundays they served pork roast, potato salad, and Spätzle covered by a sauce of pure fat. It was heavenly (no one else had meat at that time). Then around 1:00 p.m. Uncle Richard brought his radio down and we listened to the news and half an hour of music in the big dining/living room where everyone was assembled. In the afternoon we returned to Donzdorf. Aunt Barbara and Aunt Maria always gave my mother some food to take home.*

Other family members recall that they were not as lucky. When they asked for food, they were told by my great aunt Barbara Brühl that she didn't have any to spare.

Reminiscences of Bernd's mother-in-law, Erna Kink

Many Polish people, either carried off by German authorities or taken as prisoners of war, had to work on farms. At one point a young woman was pregnant and when time came for her delivery the farmer's wife told her to walk to the nearest hospital, about eight kilometers away. Many hours later, she came back and said the child was born in the forest and died.

A little outside of our village there was a house whose inhabitants were always well stocked with all kinds of goods that no one else had had in a long time, like chocolate, liquor, wine, and coffee. Rumor had it that this house had a telephone connection to Obersalzach [Hitler's headquarters near Berchtesgarten]. It was the only house in the village that was bombed by the Allies and totally destroyed. All inhabitants, the owner, his wife, three of his nine children, and a friend who was visiting and her children died.

The last band of German resisters put up stone barriers over roads to stop the advancing Allied troops from entering villages because Hitler had called for that resistance. At the end of the war when the low-flying planes strafed the area, the peasants stacked themselves on the ground on top of each other—to look like manure piles. They bent their bodies in such a way that they could be mistaken for dung heaps. But sometimes the planes did not shoot, but dropped things for the population, like once when a plane flew very low over a peasant and dropped a bundle of tobacco and other times when they dropped leaflets reading: "Deutsche, nicht schanzen, sondern pflanzen" [Germans, don't put up barriers, start planting your crops]. Later they gave sweets to the children.

Uncle Franz's diary from when he and his family decided that they had to leave Overath

A business person whom I had befriended had erected an alternative plant in a closed mine in Mühlhausen and we were able to rent a room in one of the buildings. We moved immediately. One of my jobs was to find new locations for businesses threatened by the air attacks. This included building barracks for the employees. This work was carried out by French prisoners of war. We stored part of our furniture in one of these barracks and moved into it together with another family in March of 1945.

After the American occupation of the left side of the Rhine we had to abandon our offices in Dellbrück especially since the impending encircling by the enemies of the Ruhr Valley was progressing slowly but steadily. We received the order to move to the Bergisches Land. Part of the office moved to Kotthausen, while my technical department was relocated to barracks in Berghausen im Tal because the main office did not have room to accommodate us. In this valley was a minor railroad line that provided materials for the smaller steel industries. This railroad became the target of low-flying planes and one day our barracks and the abutting barracks of Italian prisoners of war completely burnt down. Our office was moved to Bickenbach and I myself commuted by motorcycle between the different offices and the businesses that we supervised. At night I rode over the hills of the Bergisches Land to our barracks home in Alpetal. This is where the war ended for us. The encirclement of the Ruhr area became tighter and tighter and after a night spent in the mountain bomb shelter—because the Americans had blocked our through street to Alpetal from the surrounding hills with fire power—the first scout troops of the "Amis" [Americans] appeared on April 10, 1945. I had shed my uniform and hoped that as a civilian I would survive the end of the war happily. This did not work, because two hours after the incursion of the Amis in Mühlhausen a jeep with four heavily armed Americans drove up outside our barracks and asked for the managing officer. This could only mean me, and after some give and take during which I was repeatedly threatened with their weapons, I admitted who I was and put on my uniform again, all under the watchful eyes of the soldiers.

The French prisoners of war who had built our temporary quarters had given me away. They explained to Marie Therese afterwards that they were of the opinion that the German side should also experience the prisoner of war conditions that they had endured so long. The jeep convoy transported me with pride that they had captured such a beautiful prisoner: first, to Mühlhausen from where we marched on foot with ten other prisoners to Oberwiehl where we spent one night lying on a stone floor in the basement of a villa that the Americans had occupied. From there we went to Oehlschlag. Here they collected the few remaining German troops in the area and also the numerous relatives of the employees in the diverse defense agencies. In an adventuresome night trip in an American lorry we were brought to the Rhine, which we crossed in the vicinity of Andernach over a brightly illuminated pontoon bridge. We were then unloaded in a huge prisoner of war camp. This camp was put up in the area of Andernach in a big field. There was fresh new dirt, temporary fences, deep ditches for "the necessities," rain, occasionally some food—like small tins with precooked meals and cookies.

After five days some of us officers were loaded into a closed freight car and the trip to our real imprisonment began. Via Aachen, first to Namur, unloaded there and paraded through the town—amidst the loud shouting and scolding of the population. Housing in a big industrial plant, sleep—or not—on a stone floor, meals in a big hall, American style, standing up at long tables. The next day on to Reims, to Mailly de Camp. Here there was a huge "prisoners" camp among rolling hills. The floor, a thin meadow, clay underneath, in the Champagne. I want to forego writing in more detail about my time in this camp: deep depression, complete isolation from the outside world and its events, very minimal food rations, lots of hunger, great homesickness.

Reconstruction of German Cities before the End of the War

Toward the end of the war, in January 1945, when the Americans and British had already occupied the western parts of Germany around Aachen and Cologne, they asked the Catholic Church who should become the caretaker of Cologne. The Cathedral Chapter, the dominant Catholic authority in Cologne, recommended Konrad Adenauer, who as mayor in the 1920s had done much for the city. When the Allies contacted him, he turned them down because he still had three sons in the army and he was afraid that the Nazis would kill them. He recommended his brother-in-law, Willi Suth, my grandmother's brother, because he did not have children. Uncle Willi accepted and was city manager (Oberstadtdirektor) till his retirement in 1953.

Mother's diary, written in 1946 about the last months in Ditzenbach

We returned to Stuttgart almost a year ago, where the children easily made the transition into city life. The end of the war was exciting and interesting for Bernd. I had sewn a little backpack for each child with the most important items for survival. He tried his out proudly and paraded it in front of people. When a few foreigners stopped in front of our house, Bernd came running in breathlessly to get his backpack: "Mama the tanners [Americans] are coming. Are we fleeing into the forest?' During the occupation we spent three hours in the cellar of a brewery and then returned to our undamaged house. The American jeeps and tanks rolled into the village endlessly, an indescribable spectacle for the heart of a little boy. Shortly afterwards we prepared for our return to Stuttgart. At the end of August we drove in a truck piled high with furniture, with Bernd sitting with me in the driver's cabin.

This first auto trip of his life made a huge impression on him. In Stuttgart he loved the broad spaces of the apartment.

Mother's diary, February 1947

*Since it took me two-and-a-half years before I could take up writing in
the albums again, I can only mention the most important events in
Margit's life. I deeply regret it because each of the children is so unique.
School in Ditzenbach was very irregular during the Spring semester of
1945 due to the constant interruptions of low-flying enemy planes. At the
end it was almost impossible to go for a walk with the children or to allow them to play outside away from the house. The low-flying planes
surprised us at all times of the day. In the neighboring villages of
Wiesensteig and Gosbach they damaged quite a bit.*

*The preparation for the invasion of the enemy troops was exciting and
interesting—only for the children. We sewed little backpacks for them in
which they carried a few pieces of clothes and underwear. Margit
showed great interest in these preparations. Also the actual invasion of
the Americans and the times of the occupation fascinated her: the new
uniforms, the many vehicles, the endless tires of the big tanks—these
things kept the children breathless for days. Margit also participated
happily and busily in the packing and the move back to Stuttgart. She
traveled, perched high on top of the furniture, in the back of an open
truck into Stuttgart.*

Uncle Richard's diary entries describe the last few months of the war

January 12, 1945

The big winter offensive of the Russians starts.

February 23

*Around noon enemy planes strafed the radio tower on the Stöttener
Hill* [this tower overlooks Schnittlingen and explains the many attacks on
the town]. *Katherine Geiger from Schnittlingen, who works there as a
cook, was badly injured. Also a soldier was injured. The planes flew very
low, very close to our house. Katherine died of her injuries during the
night.*

April 4

*We received the official news that our nephew Robert is MIA on the
Eastern front* [he had been missing since August 1944].

April 12

President Roosevelt died of a brain hemorrhage.

April 19, between 2:30 and 3:00 p.m.

*A heavy terror attack on Schnittlingen took place. It only took about a
minute, but its effect was devastating. The buildings of the following
people burned to the ground: Kaiser, from Roessle (restaurant); Brühl,
from the Hirsch (restaurant); Geiger; Küchle; Kümmel; and Bulling.
Partially burned down were the houses of Achaz Brühl* [not my grandfa-

ther]; *Riepert (Junghans); and Eisele.*

The roof and the tower of the church were damaged, though not very badly. On April 21 the two radio towers on Stöttener Hill were blown up.

April 22

Sunday was a black day. The weather showed its worst mood: storm and snow showers. In addition, in the afternoon a short thunderstorm. From the morning till the late afternoon—not far away, but without reaching us, almost without interruption—there was shelling by the enemy artillery. In the night, from 10:30 p.m. till 3:00 a.m., renewed bombardment, so that nobody could think of sleep.

April 24

In the evening enemy soldiers [Americans] entered our village. The village capitulated without resistance. All weapons had to be given up.
April 30

The Russian Maria Murashowa, who had been in our service since 1942, left us.

May 1

For the last ten days we have been totally isolated. No electricity, therefore, no radio. Newspapers have ceased to publish. No mail service, because rail transportation has stopped. Every so often a neighbor stops by with "news" that is mainly exaggerated or blatantly false or freely invented. We hear nothing about how the war is going. How long will this continue? Life is becoming harder and harder. Joy or even serenity are alien to us. Every day brings a new difficulty.

* * *

In the evening of May 4 Master Teacher Dürr was fetched by American occupation troops. Where to? Why? He was released after a few days, however, but given ninety days house arrest.

In the night of May 3–4, Russians, who were armed with army pistols, plundered the Linden farm and Steig farms. A few days later the Scharf farm as well. During this assault a farmer who resisted was shot to death.
May 8.

Cease-fire.

Reminiscences about the Postwar Years

The significance of the end of the war for me lay in a ride on the back of a truck. A few months after the capitulation of Germany in May 1945 our carefree stay in Bad Ditzenbach came to an end in August when we had to return to Stuttgart.

The smaller pieces of our furniture were piled high on the back of a flatbed truck; my mother and Bernd were riding in the cabin with the driver. (Karl Heinz stayed behind with the family of our au pair.) One of my older cousins and I made the trip in the back of the truck. I can remember very well that I was sitting on a little bench from our children's set of a table and chairs, which to my recollection was perched on a big crate. Every few kilometers we knocked on the window of the front cabin and asked the driver to stop because the furniture was shifting and we were in danger of sliding off our furniture. I can't remember how long the sixty-kilometer ride took, but it was a very, very long time. In retrospect, it also seems to have been quite dangerous. But that kind of transportation was normal for the time: people would jump on and off slow-moving trains and as youngsters we often jumped on and off the moving streetcars.

Our Return to Stuttgart

As we returned from our idyllic village where none of the houses had been damaged or destroyed, the sight of Stuttgart was overwhelming. In a large square block, no other house besides ours had survived. All the surrounding apartment buildings were bombed out, which meant that only the walls were standing. For us children this meant exciting places to play games in: like "Hide and Seek," "Cops and Robbers." We were repeatedly warned that the walls were unstable and could collapse on us, but I don't remember that we paid much attention to these grave warnings.

Surprisingly the cleanup of the debris and the ruins was accomplished in a short time and the old buildings were restored or rebuilt.

In the recently published book *Weisst du noch? Stuttgart in den 50iger Jahren,* author Jochen A. Veeser writes that "about 400,000 truckloads of debris were transported to a hill on the other side of the city. The new hill, which can be seen from everywhere in Stuttgart, rose by over forty meters and is lovingly called 'Monte Sherbelino' [mountain of shards]."

I belonged to a group of boys and girls who roamed the neighborhood at will since there were no cars on the road. In the summer we played on stilts and in the winter we used our sleds to slide right down the middle of the sloping road. I do remember, however, that Karl Heinz's sled slid right under a parked mail truck, one of the few cars on the road. The driver was just about to drive away, but the screams of the assembled horde of kids told him that something was amiss and he waited till we had gotten Karl Heinz out of harm's way.

Our free and wild outdoor life was possible because most of the adults were preoccupied with the chores of rebuilding and surviving. Since many men had been killed or were still prisoners of war, much of the immediate afterwar rebuilding fell on the women. They moved the debris lying round on the streets, cleaned out their apartments, if they were still livable, replaced windows with whatever materials they could get to keep the elements out, painted over war-damaged walls, cleaned bricks that they found in the ruins of houses and traded them for other goods, and so forth. They also tried to find out the fate of their missing husbands, sons, and brothers.

Though I was only six years old when the war ended, I have very vivid memories of the first few postwar years. The most pronounced memory is the hunger we experienced, which actually started during the last years of the war but became more severe in the postwar period. Each person received ration cards that allowed roughly the purchase of about 1,000 calories a day. Meat was unheard of. We had to stand in long lines for a piece of fish (wrapped in newspaper) or a pint of skim milk, and it happened more than once that the merchant came out of the store to inform the waiting line that he had run out of fish or milk. Much of what we ate could be made with just milk/water and flour, or millet: Pfitzauf; Windbütel; Dampfnudeln; Griesschnitten; and of course the Schwabian staple of Spätzle (hand-made noodles) and lentils. Kohlrabi is the vegetable that I remember the best. Though most of the recipes asked for more than one egg, we were lucky when our mother could find just one egg. Milk was bought in large tin pails. We all tried to swing the cans in a complete circle as fast as possible so that no milk would escape. We weren't always proficient in this skill, and lost a lot of milk, which made our parents very unhappy and angry since milk had to be purchased with ration cards and no replacement was possible. When we had pancakes or waffles, it was considered a feast. My mother, as her mother before her, would take me with her on the street car with our little baskets. We walked a few kilometers to a suburb that had many gardens and small farms. We would go from gardener to gardener to see if we could buy fruit and potatoes. Sometimes we got enough for a week, sometimes we came home with nothing. Some of the gardeners had known my grandmother and so gave us something when they had it. However, we were often told that they would rather keep their merchandise than exchange it for money, which was fast losing its value. Before the currency reform in 1948, bartering was very common.

To augment our scarce foodstuffs, we regularly took walks in the surrounding forests to collect blackberries, elderberries, and beech nuts. Berries were used to make jam and juice and the nuts that my mother rescued from our hungry mouths were turned into cooking oil. When my mother, very occasionally, baked a cake, we were allowed to lick the bowl—a special treat. Everything put on your plate was eaten. No picky eaters! As mentioned, the only fat we knew was goose fat (*Schmalz*). Real coffee was also unknown for some years. We had a substitute coffee, called *Muckefuck*. It was made from roasted grain, mainly barley. When coffee from coffee beans reappeared in Germany it was called "little flower coffee" (*Blümchenkaffee*), because it was brewed so thin you could see through it to the flowers on the bottom of the cup.

Because of his tuberculosis, my father received one egg a week as an extra ration. A family story circulates that when he ate it: I looked at it longingly, but said nothing, while Bernd said: "We don't beg!" This led the youngest, Karl Heinz, to say: "But we'll get a bit anyway." And we always got one bite each of the egg.

Besides feeling hunger, we also suffered from a lack of any number of vitamins and minerals. For weeks, my youngest brother tore at the wallpaper next to his bed, to scrape at the underlying plaster wall to eat it. Threats and pleading didn't stop him, till the doctor diagnosed a severe lack of calcium in his body. Thereafter our diets were amended with a daily spoonful of cod liver oil—a nasty taste and texture that I can still feel in my mouth

Another strong memory concerns the profound cold. Apartments did not have central heating. The rationed allocation of coal or wood was such that only our dining room as the smaller of the two living spaces could be heated, and all activities took place there during the winter. In addition, the winter of 1945–1946 was especially severe and long. The bedrooms and the kitchen were not heated and each morning there were thick frost flowers on the windows. The floor of the kitchen was stone and when I had to wash or dry the dishes I stood on a little wooden stool to get off the penetrating cold. We had knit gloves and stockings that had to be diligently mended every night. Ration cards did not extend to new purchases. If people did not manage to repair and recycle their winter clothes during the war, there was little they could purchase to protect against the fierce cold. Materials for staying warm were all terribly scarce, and so the cardinal of Cologne, Cardinal Frings, coined a new verb, "fringsen." He told the congregation that it was not a sin to take some pieces of coal from slow-moving trains as long as it was only for one's own use, and not for resale. So people snuck up on the coal cars and carried home whatever "fell off."

This was also a time of creative recycling. Every knit piece of clothing was mended and re-mended with the help of a wooden darning egg. When the item was beyond repair, it was unraveled and something new was knit with that wool. Dresses and shirts were recut and styled to fit younger siblings. One of the most durable pieces of clothing was my brothers' leather pants: lederhosen. They lasted a long time, and grew rather disgusting, when the leather started to shine with grease. Shoes were re-soled and re-heeled, and carpets were made from rags that were cut into strips, sewn together, and woven or braided and sewn in a coil. We had one of these carpets in our hallway for many years. I believe the boys and men wore knee-high socks.

Newspapers were put to many uses. They were used to start fires, to wrap things, to clean windows, and, most importantly, they were used as toilet paper. Every Sunday my father cut the newspaper into the appropriate sizes to be used all week. Leftover paper was sold for a few pennies—together with scrap metal and rags—to an itinerant merchant who came around about once a month with a little wooden handcart. He rang all the house bells and shouted: "rags, paper, iron." Another itinerant salesperson was the knife sharpener.

After we returned to Stuttgart I entered second grade. Children in the elementary grades used individual framed slates that were written on with slim chalk-like instruments and wiped off with a sponge and a rag. The rags were attached to the slate and fluttered outside the children's backpack as they trotted to school. The styluses were kept in a small wooden box that was often self-made. Paper, pencils, pens, and ink were in short supply. When I attended school for three months in Switzerland at age ten, the teacher reprimanded me for writing in very small letters—using every inch of paper so the whole page was covered. Later we had pencils and fountain pens with ink, and an inkpot on each desk. Many tears were shed when I had to redo a page because somehow I had smudged the ink. It was years before pens were introduced that didn't have to be dipped or even refilled. Working on computers today makes us forget the frustrations of reaching the end of a typed page, discovering a typographical error, and needing to retype the whole page.

During these first postwar years, our school received packages from the United States

(I believe from CARE). This well-meant gesture didn't help my—and so many European's—natural aversion to peanut butter. The high-protein food was often an ingredient in chocolate bars, but the brown/orange color was a giveaway.

Transportation during and after the war was rather chaotic. As soon as the air raids in the cities started, the orderly transportation system broke down. After an air raid, which often destroyed apartments and houses, people who had relatives in a more rural area went to the train station where trains leaving for different destinations were announced. Often railroad stations had been destroyed so the trains could not come into the station; people had to walk over debris to find a train that was going in the general direction of their destination. The trains often went only part way and then you waited again for another train to come. My family's destination was either Schnittlingen or Ditzenbach, and we often had to walk the last ten miles or so because no transportation was available. After the war, train travel was avoided if at all possible.

Streetcar travel within the city was a necessary convenience to get to school or work, since no one had a car or motorcycle. The streetcars did not follow a timetable, and at every station a great number of people just waited for one to come by. The streetcars were so full that you had to scream at the top of your lungs to make sure that the conductor did not leave before you had pushed your way through the crammed cars to disembark. We didn't have to worry about falling when the car had to break unexpectedly, because we were stuffed in like sardines, but we all competed to reach the overhead leather strap to hang on to, because that showed that we were growing up. Often I rode the whole way on tiptoes to show how big I was! Many a time, we jumped on or off the car while it was still moving. Because the trams were so overcrowded we often had only one foot on the running board and one hand on the handle of the door. The other foot and arm was hanging free. More adventurous youngsters even rode on the couplings between two cars. It took some years till transportation was normalized and these practices stopped.

After the monetary reform in 1948, motorcycles started to appear on the streets. I have often heard people say Adenauer was reelected in 1953, because for the first time people could buy motorcycles and then cars, which was considered a sign that he followed the right economic policy.

I cannot remember any birthday or Christmas presents in the period immediately after the war, because there was no money for luxuries or there were no wares in the stores. However that didn't stop our neighborhood gang of girls and boys from having a good time: we entertained ourselves with hopscotch, hide-and-seek and other games, crafted whistles from elderberry twigs, which were hollow and made high-pitched squeals that drove our parents crazy, especially when we put together an "orchestra" and blew our whistles in the narrow alleys between the apartment buildings. The acoustics were thrilling and these games didn't cost a thing. Later we spent hours on stilts, often just leaning against a wall and jabbering. The time came when we got very loud roller skates, and we played a noisy game of dodgeball (*Völkerball*). I remember we were shouted at quite often for our raucous behavior.

The only indoor toy I remember getting in 1945 was a doll that a friend made out of an old silk stocking, stuffed with straw. I can't remember whether there were movie theaters then, but I know that the first movie I saw after the war was a romantic comedy that my Oma took me to at age ten. I felt so adult!

Since my father had developed tuberculosis during the war, he was sent to a TB sanatorium six times, sometimes for as long as half a year. My mother used to visit him there.

While we lived in Ditzenbach, our cousins and aunts looked after us three children while she was away. (The concept of "babysitters" was not known then.) But in Stuttgart we didn't have any more relatives, since they all had lost their apartments through bombing raids. When my mother visited my father, generally all day Sunday, she precooked some meals, which I heated up and I was in charge of my five- and three-year-old brothers, when I was just eight or nine. The only adult who looked in on us during the day was Mrs. K., who lived in the apartment next to ours.

Mother's diary

...my husband's illness was a burden for the family. He had to be in a sanatorium every so often, sometimes for half a year, even when our children were still very young. He waited so ardently for my visits twice a week, and I had to leave the children by themselves during these times. I tried to keep them occupied by telling them that they could open a particular drawer at 3:00 p.m. if they behaved till then, and another one at 5:00 p.m. I had put treats in the drawers. I often stayed the whole afternoon and didn't return till evening when it was dark. While I was visiting I knew that my children were at home alone, but my husband relied on these visits so much.

This lack of babysitters started only after the war. During the Nazi regime every young man had to serve in the army and every young girl had to complete one year of community service. Most of the girls were assigned to families with children; they received a small stipend from the government. Three girls were assigned to our family. No consideration was given as to whether they were in the middle of their education or already had a job. Families were not free to choose a particular girl, but we were fortunate with the first and the third girl. The second girl, however, did not like this enforced assignment and didn't put any effort into the job. Once she put the safety pin of Bernd's diaper right into his skin when she tried to pin it up. In the case of the third girl who was assigned to us during our evacuation, a lifelong friendship ensued with her family. Her family "adopted" Karl Heinz in a way and he spent many nights with them, especially when enemy planes flew over the valley, because they had a better cellar than the one in our house. After the war, they brought him back to Stuttgart only after the rest of the family had settled in.

When the father in this family died, my mother and Karl Heinz wanted to attend the funeral. They boarded the train to Geislingen where they had planned to change to the "little valley train" (*Taelebahn*). But the train from Stuttgart was delayed so often that they knew they would miss their connection. My mother convinced the conductor to telegraph to a special fast train that was not supposed to stop in either Göppingen or Geislingen and ask them to make an exception and stop in both places. During the stop in Göppingen, they switched to the fast train, which stopped for just a minute. In Geislingen this train made another unannounced one-minute stop and they managed to catch the right local train to Wiesensteig. In Göppingen a man in a black suit and with a wreath disembarked in a great hurry and switched to the same train. He was on the way to the same funeral! I doubt very much that a conductor nowadays would stop a train for such an occasion. The au pair who later had children and grandchildren of her own always said: "Our year of community service was a good preparation." Hitler did not introduce this year of community service out of the goodness of his heart, but because he wanted to promote big German families: he wanted families to have many children. For the same reason he awarded every woman who had at least seven children the Iron Cross, the highest honor.

After the war, the population decreased dramatically and population growth was threatened, thus the subsequent German administrations introduced incentives for families to have children: tax breaks, subsidies, discounts for transportation, and education vouchers for any family with more than two children.

The Prisoners of War Return

All of my relatives who survived the war as soldiers became prisoners of war of the Americans, French, British, or Russians. The war came to an end for them only after they were released from captivity. It made a difference whether they were captured by Western Allies or by the Russians. The Western prisoners were sent home during the first postwar years, 1945 or 1946, while the ones captured by the Russians spent longer times in Russian camps.

Of my relatives, the ones imprisoned in the west were Uncle Hermann, Uncle Rudolf, Uncle Gerhard, Uncle Paul, and Uncle Franz.

Uncle Hermann, my mother's oldest surviving brother, was the first one who returned from the war, on June 16, 1945. He returned from the front and spent time in various military hospitals, where he had been treated during the last months of the war for his wounds. One of these hospitals was in Schwäbisch Gemünd; the other was in Konstanz. I don't know in which hospital he became a prisoner of war.

While a prisoner he managed to obtain civilian clothes and amidst the confusion and chaos of the last days of the war he made his way to his sister Minni in Lochau, Austria. He was there when the French troops marched into Lindau and Bregenz (Lochau is midway between these two cities), even as German soldiers were still trying to defend these cities. His brother-in-law Peppi was away, hiding in the woods to escape the Volkssturm and living in a barn on the mountainside. During a pause in the fighting, Peppi sent a Ukrainian woman—who had been captured by the Germans and was also trying to escape—to his house to fetch his wife and son. But because Hermann was wounded and could not walk up into the mountains, Minni decided to stay home with him in the house. She sent her son Günther to spend a few days with his father in the woods, while his mother and uncle hid in the cellar of their home. One evening two nuns who were unable to return to their abbey (about two hundred meters from Minni's home) because of the shooting appeared at the cellar window. They were literally dragged into the cellar through this small window. Because the Germans were using a neighboring property as a base from which they fired their cannons and exchanged fire with the French, Minni's house had many pockmarks from shrapnel. But the four of them survived in the cellar until the fighting ceased.

After some time in Austria, Hermann returned to his parents' new home in Schnittlingen.

The next one to come home was my mother's youngest surviving brother, Rudolf Brühl. He was discharged to Schnittlingen on August 15, 1945, as a British prisoner of war. His wife, Gertrud, comments on his release and about her last months with her mother in Schnittlingen before she was reunited with her husband.

Comments by Gertrud, Rudolf's wife

He spent most of the war in Paris and later in the Bretagne. After the Normandy invasion by the Allies, German troops began their retreat. His company marched from France, across Belgium, all the way to southern Germany. When they were in Kirchheim/Teck, near Stuttgart, he borrowed a bicycle and rode to Schnittlingen for a short visit. The retreating troops then marched to northern Germany, where he was captured near Husum by British troops at the end of the war. He remained a British prisoner of war till August 15, when he was loaded on a freight train that went south. He met with his brother-in-law, who was supposed to be a French prisoner of war, but whose wife had connections and managed to smuggle civilian clothes into the camp and this allowed him to walk away from the camp. Rudolf and his wife's brother took a train and bus together to Schnittlingen where they expected to find me and my mother. In the meantime, however, we had returned to Stuttgart, where we lived at my sister-in-law's apartment in one room.

My brother, who had fled the French prison camp, desperately wanted to reach the American zone. At that point Stuttgart was still occupied by the French, but Schnittlingen was in the American zone. Later Stuttgart was also transferred to the Americans. A few weeks earlier, my mother and I had gone to Stuttgart to check on our apartment. The house itself and the outer walls withstood the raid, but the interior walls were partially destroyed and there was no glass for windowpanes to be had anywhere. We returned to Schnittlingen where we had spent the last few war years in the smithy.

The train that was supposed to take us to Geislingen stopped in Goeppingen and all the passengers were asked to disembark since the train would go no farther. We started to walk to Schnittlingen and reached Donzdorf—where my sister-in-law Maria Tietze had been evacuated—around 9.30 p.m. Curfew was at 10:00 p.m., so my mother went to the French occupation agency and asked for a permission paper to allow us to be out at night. We climbed over fallen trees and parts of ruins till we reached American-occupied Schnittlingen in the early morning. After the war we returned to Stuttgart, where my mother and I first moved in with a sister-in-law. After Rudolf returned from captivity, the three of us exchanged household goods for windowpanes, paint, and stucco and restored our apartment by ourselves.

According to his wife and his son, Rudolf mentioned that they had been taken to a peninsula where they waited to be discharged. He never had a bad word to say about his time as a prisoner of war.

My aunt Gertrud's husband, Paul Ludwig, was released on August 18, 1945, by the English. His release papers, which were signed by F.F. Mosley (Royal Air Force), classified his general health as "fit." (He died nine years later of kidney and liver cancer, a condition that he may already have had during the war, judging from his letters.)

Comments by Dagmar, Paul's daughter

Maja Sonntag, whom I visited regularly and who still lives in the house that we stayed in in 1945, told me that my father returned in August and

that mother embraced him on the open street. We lived in Ottenbach till
December 1945. My father was astonished at the strong Swabian ac-
cent of his two girls. The house in Ottenbach is the Ausdinggut [gener-
ally a small addition on a farm to which the farmer retires after turning
over the farm to his heir] of the Sonnentags from Schonderhof, where
our great grandmother Brühl came from originally.

About the same time, my aunt Marie Therese's husband, Franz Heinrich, was sent home. His diary describes what happened after he was captured by the Americans, then turned over to the British, and finally released.

Uncle Franz Heinrich's diary

On August 15 I was transferred with about thirty other officers to an
English prisoner of war camp near Ostende; about five weeks later I
was transported on a truck to Bonn, where I was discharged in the big
park in front of the university. From Bonn I took a ferry across the Rhine
and a small tram to Waldbröl; from there I walked home to our barracks
in Mühlhausen. I found the place empty, however.

Marie Therese and the children succeeded in moving back to Cologne
where, with the help of her Uncle Willi Suth, she found an apartment in
Köln-Deutz. A truck from a company that I had helped to relocate at the
end of the war finally brought me into the arms of my loved ones. I had
lost a lot of weight and was very weak, but recovered fairly quickly. Then
I could start looking for a job. I began to work at the Cologne Utility
Company in November 1945 and worked there till my retirement in
1969.

The last one to be released from the West was my Aunt Wilma's husband, Uncle Gerhard, who was a French prisoner of war. He returned on August 23–24, 1946, more than one year after the end of the war. Nothing more is known about his military service, his captivity, or return, since the family has destroyed all wartime correspondence.

The one problem the released prisoners from the West had was that they didn't always know where their families were after the families had been bombed out. In our big family that was not a problem, since somebody always knew where the other family members were. But in less communicative and smaller families it sometimes took a bit longer for a reunion. As far as I remember, the Red Cross played a major role in uniting families as soon as possible. Even many years later the Red Cross was broadcasting the names and ages of people who were still looking for their families.

The relatives captured by the Russians were Uncle Erich and Uncle Guido. My Aunt Maria's husband, Erich Tietze, was released from a Russian prison camp in September and returned to Schnittlingen on September 22, 1945.

Comments by Armin, Erich Tietze's son

He had been exempt from military service due to his job, but was
called up during the last few months of the war to serve in the Volks-
sturm. He was captured by the Russians somewhere in East Prussia

[today Poland]. He was assigned to a camp about 200 km east of Moscow to dig for peat. He was discharged at the end of 1945 in Berlin when he collapsed from serious weight loss due to constant diarrhea. He had endured a transport from Russia on which about a third or half the prisoners died. He arrived in Schnittlingen emaciated: he was about over six feet tall and weighed one hundred pounds. He recuperated there for a while and then joined the rest of his family in Donzdorf. He started his first job after the war around the end of 1947 in Osnabrueck, and then in 1948 in Cologne.

I can still remember that I was in Schnittlingen when a very bedraggled and emaciated man in an oversized coat came shuffling slowly toward our house from the direction of Geislingen. But I cannot reconstruct whether this was Uncle Hermann, Rudolf, or Erich.

The last prisoner of war from our family to be released was Guido H., my father's cousin, who was married, had two daughters, and had been drafted into the army when he was in his thirties. He became a prisoner of war in Russia in one of the Siberian camps that did not allow the prisoners to communicate with anyone outside. The German government knew that these so-called silent camps existed, but they had no idea who was in them. In 1955, ten years after the end of the war, Chancellor Adenauer went to Moscow and arranged with the Soviet Union that the Federal Republic of Germany would recognize the Soviet Union, if among other conditions, they opened all the silent camps and allowed the prisoners to return to Germany. One of them was Adenauer's nephew Guido, who returned with him in 1955.

Besides Uncle Franz's short remarks about camp life, no written notes were found by any other family members who were prisoners of war. Their children also do not remember that their parents ever talked about that time. They took their memories to their graves.

Missing in Action—and the Efforts to Discover What Happened

My mother's youngest brother, Robert Brühl, twenty years old, went missing in action (MIA) in August 1944.

Achaz and Barbara, Robert's parents, later his siblings, Isa, Rudolf, and Minni, and after the death of Rudolf his wife, Trudl, and much later his nephew, Johannes, all wrote to many official agencies and former comrades to find out about his fate after he was declared missing in action. They wanted to know whether Robert died in combat or whether he was taken prisoner and died in a camp. They often included a picture of Robert in order to jolt someone's memory. This searching started in 1945 and continued through the 1950s; the search was started again by Johannes Baumgartner in 2004 after the Russian and Romanian files were opened. Following is a list of agencies that were contacted and excerpts from letters that the family received back. Some are from former comrades who had been in silent Russian camps themselves for years.

- The list of search agencies that the family contacted was extensive: fifteen different agencies, including the Red Cross, government agencies, and radio and newspaper search agencies.
- Excerpts of over 100 letters sent by the Brühl family to agencies and fellow soldiers (here only the letters from 1945 to 1950).

Most of the letters sent by the family read as follows:

I received your address from...and would be very thankful if you could give me information about my son (brother), Robert Brühl, born on March 11, 1924, in Stuttgart, assigned to the unit 095 45 C, private first class, who has been missing since August 1944 in Romania. We received notice in March 1945 that he was missing in action. His last letter was dated August 1944. Since then there has been no communication.

The Romanian Red Cross to which we sent an inquiry told us that Romania has no more prisoners of war since they were all transported to Russia.

In the hope of a speedy and favorable answer, we remain,

Sincerely...

All inquiries received a negative response, starting with the first one from March 16, 1945, while the war was still going on.

High Commission of the Army
(15) Rudolstadt, (Ob d E) Prinz-Eugen-Kaserne
AHA/Abwicklungstab, Tel. 754-756 Sachgebiet: 335
Herr Ochag Brühl(14) Schnittlingen
*   The conclusion of our inquiries into the fate of your son, private first class Robert Brühl, born March 11, 1924, in Stuttgart, 8 Kp.Gren.Rgt.663, Fp. Nr. 09545 E, has not resulted in a clear outcome. He is missing in action since the battles near Kishinew (Romania) in the period August 22–25, 1944. Heil Hitler!*

From: Barbara Brühl, November 14, 1947, 14a Schnittlingen Krs Goeppingen Haus 13
To: Search agency for missing Germans 1 Berlin W. Kanonierstr. 35
*   I am requesting inquiry into the fate of my son, private first class Robert Brühl, formerly from Stuttgart-0, Kernerplatz 5. His last field number was 09545 C. His last letter was stamped August 17, 1944 (Eastern front). My address is Frau Barbara Brühl, 14a Schnittlingen, County Göppingen, House 13.*
Sincerely

Excerpts from letters from Robert's fellow soldiers—who were not known to the family—show clearly that they knew nothing about his fate after the battles in August 1944

Mr. P (November 7, 1948): ...August 23, 1944, was for us the fateful day. I was a Russian prisoner of war for four years and have lost a lot of memory. The name Brühl rings a bell, but I can't really remember who he was. The best thing would be for you to send a picture, because I don't want to make a mistake....

Mr. P (November 15 and November 28): I recognized Robert in the sec-

ond picture. When we retreated we marched back in two groups, planning to unite in Kishinew. But just sixteen kilometers out of Kishinew I was taken prisoner, the only survivor of a five-man unit. I therefore did not see what happened after that to our company. The next day I was marched back as a prisoner to Kishinew. During this march I saw many dead soldiers on the side of the road and also saw field correspondence with our number strewn all over. In the camp in Odessa I met the only member from our company, second lieutenant A. Fiedler, who told me to be happy that I did not see the end. He had been shot through the hip and abandoned by his own soldiers because they were being chased by the Russians. He developed dysentery and was probably transferred because I never saw him again. I presume some of the others made it....

F.D. (1948): I also have not heard from my son since August 19, 1944, and do not know whether he is dead or still living.

K.M. (February 14, 1949): Yes, during August we were in action near the capital, Kishinew, in Bessarabia. We already had bitter battles behind us because the Russian was constantly on our heels; had great losses as prisoners of war, wounded and dead; whole companies and regiments were wiped out; the enormous number of losses cannot be ascertained.... Knew the company, but not Robert.

A.G. (June 1, 1949): I did not know him well because he joined our company shortly before we were involved in the last battles. On August 19, 1944, we were in action again and started our retreat on August 22. On August 23 we were fighting near Kishinew, where we were attacked in a fierce battle by the Russian. Toward evening we were still together on the western outskirts of Kishinew. There were only fifteen men left of the whole company. A few days later lieutenant Fiedler was wounded.... Our company suffered a lot and made great sacrifices. In the end, when I was captured, I was alone, but that doesn't mean that others were not still alive and became prisoners. Myself, I was in captivity for four years and had the good luck to survive that difficult fate....

P.K. (June 13, 1949, Frankfurt): I can give you the following information: your brother joined our company at the end of June as a last addition to our unit. On August 20, we started our orderly retreat according to plan toward Kishinew. After we had crossed the Pruth River (August 25–28) we were engaged in heavy fighting, during which our company was completely defeated. More than 70 percent of the soldiers were captured between August 28 and 30. Among them was also the group that was led by Fiedler. According to information that I received during my captivity, the soldiers that were captured at this time were transported to the Krim peninsula and the Donez basin.

Personally, I strongly believe that your brother still lives and like my-self will return unexpectedly. My relatives were also without any commu-nication from me. They only received a notice from my division that I was missing in action. Do not give up hope, because I believe that he will return some day. Surely, it is an enormous mental burden, to live with this insecurity, but how much harder it must be for the prisoners who in their captivity have no communication with the homeland, be-sides all the physical worries. However, hope and the will to survive al-low people to endure all kinds of hardships.

Wishing you and your relatives all the best.

I am returning the enclosed photograph.

O.B. (January 10, 1950): I am afraid that I have to disappoint you. It is impossible for me to have known your brother because I was captured by the Russians shortly after the defeat of the bridgehead position Nikopol. Your brother joined our unit many months after I was already a prisoner.

W.E. (1950): At the beginning of 1944 I was wounded and after my re-covery I was sent to Denmark. There I heard that our units had been sent to Romania.... In 1947, I was discharged from a Russian prison camp where I contracted a disease and am presently in Freudenhall in therapy.

Though the family pursued the search for some information till 2004, no news about the fate of Robert was ever received.

The Allied Occupation of Places Where Our Family and Friends Had Been Evacuated

Doerr interview about the American occupation of Weissenstein

M.E.: *Right in front of our house, a tank parked and a soldier came into the house and said "eggs, eggs." We had a big tiled stove to which they went to get warm. I was the only one who spoke a bit of English, only school English. On the sideboard was a photo of the daughter whose husband had been killed in action and a small bouquet of Vergissmein-nicht and the soldier said, "Oh, forget-me-nots." Then I thought he can't be bad if he notices a flower bouquet, and we started to talk. The sol-diers were students.*

Doerr: *I heard that there were also bad experiences with Americans.*

M.E.: *I believe the one that I talked to was a student. They had mando-lins and violins and played our old hiking songs! I cried! And the next morning I heard that the owner of a little hole-in-the-wall shop where you could buy everything was the cousin of the commander of the troop. He knew that she lived in Weissenstein, had asked where she lived, and so they met. Isn't that a coincidence? We had a lot of advantages in Weissenstein. The first Americans who entered were the scouting* group. Then there were none for a while. Finally, the occupation troops came: they were Texans; they were different; they were fiery. They always looked for people who would wash and sew for them. I always said: "Don't give them alcohol." And then they always looked for hidden weapons. I did know that there were weapons hidden in an adjacent room under a wood pile. The owners hadn't had time to bury them yet.

I observed nice character traits among the Americans. A woman whose daughter worked for us had to give up her apartment for the occupying troops. Occasionally we all sat down together and the Americans provided us with coffee and Nescafe.... They were looking for some ordinary talk, a bit of communication. It did happen that young women were raped—it seems that happened everywhere—but this seemed to happen more often with French troops. In general the Americans were decent, especially the first troops who were told to continue on. When the occupying groups came, their behavior depended on what part of the country they came from. I had a small room halfway up the hill, and the back door of the building had to stay open, so the soldiers could come in freely. I was often afraid and locked my room, but nothing ever happened.

Reminiscences of postwar Munich by Erna Kink, my brother Bernd's mother-in-law

The way we got our first apartment in Munich was very interesting. A man was convicted of shooting his lover to death. She was a nymphomaniac and when her husband found out that she had quite a few lovers, she didn't see a way out and asked the lover to shoot her. During the Nazi regime he was convicted and did long-term jail time. My father found out that the Nazis transferred inmates with long prison sentences to an agency that conducted medical experiments on them. So, my father asked the authorities to release him after ten years, which was possible because the Nazis did not follow the law but reacted to personal interventions. The prisoner heard about my father's intervention, and he gave our family two rooms in his apartment after the war till we could raise the 5,000 marks that the building owner requested for restoring our old apartment. Before that my husband lived in one room without water while I was still in the countryside.

The American officers were all quartered in the most elegant villas. They all had an aide. One of these young aides would often go for a walk on the lake and when he heard me play "Lili Marlene" on the piano, he would ask me to repeat it. He said that he could listen to it all day long.

The birth of my daughter Christa was also an adventure. Christa was a breach baby; that's why I wanted to deliver in a hospital. But to be able to have the doctor drive me to the hospital in Rosenheim I needed a gasoline coupon that my father secured for me. When my labor started, my father rode his bicycle to the doctor's office; the doctor then drove me to the clinic. At this time, in August 1947, there was an electric

*blackout in Rosenheim. The delivery had to be done with emergency
lighting from tiny tea lights. Today my daughter would have been delivered by caesarean.*

Postwar reminiscences of Resi Paffenholz, my brother Karl Heinz's mother-in-law

*When the Americans marched into our village in 1945, everything was
quiet. They searched every house thoroughly, but encountered no problems. In a very short time, I made my way to Cologne, on foot, which
meant long hours of trekking. Cologne was completely devastated. In
Lindenthal, the area of Cologne where we lived, I gradually met more
acquaintances. During the first days, I slept anywhere in the ruins. I
managed to slide down a board into the cellar of our destroyed house, in
which we had kept our potato bin. The potatoes were already sprouting,
but they were a precious find. We cooked them in a friend's apartment,
which had not been destroyed. We continued to search for and found a
pot with fat. It was like Christmas.*

*After two weeks, I was offered two rooms and fetched my mother and
we slowly found some furniture and settled in. People's readiness to
help was great, but improvement only came after the monetary reform in
1948. I lived with my mother in these rooms from 1945 till 1949 when I
got married. The rooms were cold; we warmed our feet by opening the
door of the wood-burning stove and putting them inside the door. The
toilet was outside of the apartment, a few steps down. It was shared
with other families.*

Germans Fleeing or Being Expelled from the East

Toward the end of the war and after the war, Germans in the previously occupied territories
either fled from the advancing Russians or were forcibly expelled from the territories that
Germany had illegally occupied, like Poland, East Prussia, Czechoslovakia, Hungary, and
Romania.

Nobody within our immediate family fell into this category, but my Uncle Kurt's second wife, the wife of a cousin of my mother, and a friend left or were expelled from their
homeland or what they considered their homeland.

M.H. and her family were among them. After they had been bombed out in Dresden,
her grandmother, mother, younger brother, baby sister, and she started their trek to the west.
They landed first in Rittershausen near Würzburg, where they made their sleeping quarters
on straw and stayed for months above the horses' stable. They had to cross the farmyard to
get to a toilet and to pump water. The mother and grandmother received some groceries for
sewing and washing for the farm family. Maria, who had been trained as a nurse, tried to get
a job in the west. Since she was a Heliand sister, my mother offered her room and board in
exchange for help with us children till she could find an appropriate job. She slept in our living room and became part of the family. She later supported her mother, baby sister, and
grandmother by becoming a city employee who would be sent to families where the mother
was sick or otherwise incapable of caring for her children. This was a low-paying job, and
she never recovered her old high-paying position as a nurse. Her mother decided after her
father was released as a prisoner of war to return to Dresden with her little sister. After the
Berlin Wall was erected in 1961, they were not allowed to visit the west.

Maria is now ninety-five years old and we are still in touch.

Mother's interview with Dr. Doerr

The bombardment of the German cities was a cruel means to exert pressure on the Nazis. Otherwise, they would not have given in. Some of it was too much, like the total destruction of Dresden during one night at the end of the war.

Gisela Brühl's relocation from the occupied territories of Czechoslovakia in 1943 was described above.

Reminiscenses of Erika Paulus, Kurt's second wife

My father was the director of a big tobacco company. After the Germans took over Czechoslovakia, he became the director of a tobacco firm in Karlsbad. He was a member of the Nazi Party. My first husband, whom I married at age nineteen, was a soldier. I myself was a member of the BMW Maedchenjugend. I was a kindergarten teacher in the firm's kindergarten, where both Czech and German children were cared for. In 1945 all Germans were ordered to come to the main square to view the public execution of a German SS officer (who was our wedding witness). My family was given special permission not to attend since we had good relationships with the Czech authorities through our work. Shortly after that, we were ordered to pack a few things since we were going to be expelled. On a handcart we transported our belongings and clothes on foot to the border. I managed to save some money by sewing it into the hems of dresses. I put old clothes on top in the suitcase and told the customs officials that they had already checked the suitcase, which to my amazement they believed. After three weeks on the road from one camp to another we arrived in Bamberg. My father and I had to go through the process of denazification (Entnazifizierung) before we were allowed to work again.

Denazification

Denazification brings us to another chapter on the road to normalcy after the Nazi years. After the end of the war, every German adult had to prove to the occupying Allies that s/he was not part of the Nazi regime. There were four classifications: (1) Innocent, not guilty of supporting the Nazis in any way; not part of any Nazi organization, engaged in anti-Nazi activities. (2) Part of some Nazi organization, but under duress due to professional reasons, like teachers, lawyers, state employees—found not guilty. (3) Hangers-on or fellow travelers, (Mitläufer)—found guilty and sentenced to small fines and community service. (4) Nazi supporters or members of the official Nazi Party, NSDAP (Nationalsozialistische Deutsche Arbeiterpartei), sentenced to fines, prison, or death.

Our family and circle of my parents' friends had members in the first three categories. The role of many family members during these years is not known to me because the older generation wouldn't talk about this time.

First Category: Anti-Nazis

My parents, my maternal grandparents, my paternal grandmother and the wife of my father's brother (and her parents) fell into the first category. We have official cards that testify to their anti-Nazi background.

My grandmother Barbara Brühl's official card (below), which shall represent the cards sent to both my parents and grandparents in November 1946, proves her innocence.

To Barbara Brühl

Public prosecutor

Date: October 28, 1946

On the basis of your information on the survey/questionnaire (Meldebogen) you are not affected by the law of March 5, 1946, for the liberation of national socialism and militarism.

Mother's interview with Dr. Doerr

Isa: *Neither my husband nor I were in any Nazi organization. For us the family was the top priority. Since my husband spent months in TB sanatoria, we had a very restricted social life. But our friends in our two youth groups, Neudeutschland and Heliand, stood by us. This way one could have open talks, and every night we listened to foreign radio broadcasts (though this was strictly prohibited and punished).*

...individual bishops and priests spoke openly from the pulpit, but they were then persecuted by Goebbels.... Yet these were the persons we relied on. When Neudeutschland was disbanded by Goebbels, we met just the same in individual apartments.

Doerr: *Was that dangerous?*

Isa: *Yes, very much so. Anti-Semitism was widespread...but then all of a sudden we had a Secretary of Propaganda, which Germany had never had before. And Goebbels understood how to take advantage of this anti-Semitic sentiment and make it into a huge issue. And then the Jews were made the main enemies of the nation. The basis of course was there, but nobody could have imagined how the Nazis exploited the situation. The appointment of a Secretary of Propaganda shows how they planned and manipulated the situation.*

M.E. (in the same interview): *And during Hitler's time, we came together in small circles at the home of the Paulus family to discuss the latest news. I remember how somebody who had been in Switzerland brought back newspapers. We had no access to news from other countries. Woe, if somebody listened to foreign radio stations.... I remember very well that toward the end, just as the start of the war put an end to our meetings, we always left your apartment in small groups, never all at the same time.*

Isa: *In our big house there lived a very old woman who was an ardent Nazi. We had to really be careful around her. She watched all the comings and goings and when the Jewish families went by her door, she berated them and threw things at them. This ended any freedom of expression. You couldn't even carry out a normal conversation in a streetcar because someone might overhear and denounce you.*

Nowadays you cannot understand how we longed to talk to people who thought the way we did, because you always had to watch what you said. When I was at the Gestapo office on one of my "visits" there, they brought in a very simple man and interrogated him. The Gestapo officer kept on screaming at him: "What did you mean that there is no difference between Moscow and Berlin?" This man must have said this while on his job in a factory and somebody reported him to the authorities. He was a very ordinary man, who kept on twirling his hat between his fingers, and of course had no answer to the question. I don't know how this situation ended, but I am sure they kept him for a few weeks.

The judicial chamber of the commission the Allies established after the war to conduct the denazification process had to decide on the punishment for the people who were not high in the party hierarchy. They could acquit them, fine them, take their possessions away, or hand them over for trial and subsequent imprisonment. My father was appointed chairperson of the Stuttgart West fact-finding "Commission for the Liberation from National Socialism and Militarism."

Mother's diary

This Commission's process was an impossible and unfortunate task. My husband was immediately assigned to this commission because they could find so few uncompromised lawyers. We have never received so many visitors. Many compromised people tried to influence the procedure through the intervention of an uncompromised friend, mostly a well-known personality. Of course, the Nazis forced the population to align themselves with the party by forcing them into party membership. Their methods backfired. The judges had a hard time: they didn't have to judge the facts, but had to seek out motivations. I still remember how glad my husband was when he was committed to a TB sanatorium during this time.

As mentioned, my father was a conflict-avoider, and he was afraid that he would have had to judge friends and acquaintances.

I have my own opinion about how my father was appointed to this commission. One possibility was that his Uncle Willi Suth, who had been appointed by the Allies to a leading position in Cologne, recommended him. The other possibility is that as in Cologne, the Allies asked the churches in Stuttgart for recommendations. Since my father was active in church circles and through Neudeutschland, he was in contact with many priests. One of them might have recommended him.

Unfortunately, none of these suppositions can now be verified, since I only learned about my father's appointment to the denazification commission after the death of both my parents in the 1990s.

My great-uncle Willi Suth had the full support of the Allies after the war since he was known to have been an anti-Nazi through the whole period of the Third Reich. As mentioned above, he was appointed city manager (*Oberstadtdirektor*) by the Allies to help in the reconstruction of the city.

Obituary of Willi Suth by Fritz Schlockermann

He did not push for that position. In March 1945 after the Americans had occupied Cologne they searched him out in the Siebengebirge, near Bad Honnef, and made him the acting mayor of Cologne, a city that had been devastated by the war. The rebuilding of the city involved great troubles, stress, and even danger. Only recently, the Werewolf, a Nazi organization, murdered the mayor of Aachen, whom the Allies had also appointed.

During this time those wards of the city that lay to the left of the Rhine had already been occupied, but on the other side of the Rhine, battles continued. Absolute chaos reigned in the city. He brought law and order into this chaos with a very small army of helpers. The main task was to restore the infrastructure, electricity, and water, for the remaining 40,000 inhabitants from an original total of 750,000. He was experienced in this area since he had been in charge of the city government during World War I.

My father supported his uncle who served on the City Council of Cologne till Hitler dismissed him. From the day of his dismissal throughout the entire war, when Uncle Willi was in semiretirement, my father met with him clandestinely at various times. All the while, though, the Gestapo was watching Uncle Willi.

Much has been written about Willi Suth's public life, but I would like to add a few personal reminiscences. As a child, I had no concept of the role of mayor or similar positions, but I did understand that Uncle Willi either had an important job or was well off through some other means. When he visited my parents in Stuttgart in the late forties, he would arrive in a long limousine (or what looked to me like a long limousine) and a driver, whom he would instruct: "Take the children around the block a few times." This was at a time when there were very few private cars, so this was a special thrill. He also always had loose change in his pocket, which he generously doled out to us. This struck me as the height of wealth!

When I visited him in Cologne in the fifties, I was of course impressed with his villa (I now know that it belonged to the city) and his tropical garden. He introduced me to my first figs and dates.

Uncle Willi's funeral in 1956 was memorable because of Adenauer's attendance. Since he was then the Chancellor, he arrived with a host of security personnel. I was riding in a car with my cousin Walther (we were both teens) and my cousin managed to insert himself into the funeral procession a few cars behind Adenauer, so that we flew through the streets, red lights flashing, protected by Adenauer's motorcycle brigade, the famous "White Mice."

At the private family lunch after the funeral, Adenauer looked distracted and his face seemed frozen. At one point he told my mother and me: "Today, I have buried my last contemporary friend who was with me during the long dark times of the Nazi regime." (Adenauer was then eighty years old and would live another eleven years).

Second Category: Involuntary membership in Nazi organizations due to their professions

My uncle, Paul Ludwig, married to my mother's sister Gertrud, was a brilliant lawyer who had been caught in the Nazi web. In 1937, he had involuntarily joined the National Socialist Volkswohlfahrt (NSV), a NSDAP welfare organization founded in Berlin in September 1931. The NSV was put in charge of welfare and later of the racial policy of the Third Reich. After the war every civil servant like Uncle Paul had to go through the process of denazification. In April 1947 he received a document that labeled him as "less guilty" (*Minderbelastet*). Uncle Paul objected to this verdict because he felt that he should be classified as "not affected by the law" or "innocent." If the authorities refused to change the classification then he insisted on a trial. It should have become clear from his letters during the war, that he did not share the Nazi philosophy.

Paul's defense paper, written to support his position

It is correct that I acted as NSV Blockwalter [the person responsible for the political supervision of a city block, usually forty to sixty households]—*informally nominated, but never formally confirmed—from September 1937 till I was drafted into the army in April 1940. Therefore I fall legally under the law Nr. 104. As Blockwalter I had to collect the fees of the NSV members in my block every month and forward them. However, I was only Blockwalter in name, since my mother did most of the collecting. Because of this neglect of my duties, I was ordered to appear—in the summer of 1938—in front of the regional group and was warned by Dr. Koenig that further neglect of responsibility would lead to consequences. After this warning, I still tried to avoid the collection of fees as much as I could, and I never carried out any other functions for the NSV. I therefore deny that my activities in any way supported National Socialism (Art. 12).*

Like any astute lawyer, Uncle Paul then mentions a precedent involving another Blockwalter, who had been exonerated because he did not belong to the NSDAP or any of its other subgroups, since it could be shown that he philosophically was opposed to any Nazi ideology and only carried out the job of a Blockwalter under the pressure of the local group [*Ortsgruppe*].

He introduces his character witnesses along with a letter from Gauleiter Murr [Gau: territory of NSDAP divided districts. Gauleiter: leader of a Gau, who had to swear personal loyalty to the Führer], who had blocked his appointment to the state judicial system, as he explained to the panel:

"National Socialism [NS] *and the NSDAP, with their glorification of the Nordic person, the fight against Judaism, the suppression of personal freedoms, the expansion of police power at the costs of the legitimate judicial system, the degradation of women to baby factories, and the uniformity and equalization were always abhorrent to me."*

He mentions more witnesses from the *Stuttgarter Zeitung* and from the local and regional courts who will testify in his behalf.

With regard to my attitude toward the Wehrmacht [the armed forces of Nazi Germany], *the other pillar of the NS regime, I can categorically say that I have always been against the war and a military system. My father* died in World War I, which robbed my mother of her life's happiness. She educated me in a non-militaristic sense and I have acted accordingly. I did not, like most young civil servants, apply in 1936–1937 for a short-term, state-led military course. Neither did I later apply to become an officer. I served the duration of the war as a noncommissioned soldier. I would also like to point out that my wife shared my sentiments and attitudes. She was not a member of any Nazi organization, not even the women's auxiliary. I became Blockwalter only under constant pressure from the human resource person at the state attorney's office, when I didn't see any other way to earn a living.

After four years in law school and three years as Referendar, which exhausted my mother's savings, I passed the bar examination in the Spring of 1934. Because I didn't want to become a civil servant in the Third Reich I applied at various private law firms as a law clerk. With no success, however, since hostility toward the judicial system caused their work to become more and more limited. I could not afford to start my own law firm, so therefore I decided to enter government service in November1934. I was of the opinion that the Third Reich would collapse sooner or later. Later, around 1936, after I had unsuccessfully applied at Bosch, I was hopeful that my good grades and evaluations—summa cum laude and worthy of praise—and my work as Gerichtsassessor, would lead to my appointment as a civil servant without my having to join the NSDAP or one of its subgroups. This hope was destroyed when a decision of the Oberlandesgericht München in 1937 denied my application. I was also afraid that I would be dismissed from the government service. I tried again to find a job outside the judicial system and applied at Allianz, but again without success. At this time I decided—with a heavy heart—to ensure my financial existence by working for the NSV as a Blockwalter. Then and always, I remained determined not to become a member of the party under any circumstances, and I have not wavered from that decision even under enormous pressure.

It is common knowledge that the pressure of the NSDAP bosses on the civil servants was strong, encouraging them to become a member of the NS Party and participants in Party activities. The pressure increased on young employees who were still in their probationary period. As proof: after 1934, for four years, I withstood constant and repeated requests to enter the NSDAP or at least the SA [Sturm Abteilung, or Stormtroopers] as a young lawyer, even after having been evaluated thus: "Shows absolutely no interest in the movement." This shows—I believe—that I have actively resisted the Nazis, to the utmost of my ability. I am of the strong opinion that fewer than ten out of every one hundred young lawyers received such a negative evaluation in 1937. And only with the intercession of my immediate superior could I keep my job. Even after having taken on the job of NSV–Blockwalter, I have persistently refused repeated demands to join. As late as during my furlough in 1943, the regional boss of the Gau pointed out to me that young law-

yers especially are expected to join the Party. From then on, I did not visit him again.

Had I, like almost all the working judicial employees in Stuttgart, given in to pressure to join at least the SA, I would have been employed after two years as a permanent civil servant like most everyone else, since I fulfilled all the qualifications. In fact, I was only appointed to a state's attorney position in 1939—after a four-year waiting period. This meant considerable financial disadvantages, since I had no other income. Furthermore, the psychological burden was great. My plans to marry in 1938 had to abandoned, since I had not yet secured a permanent position.

I agree to this process in writing only if the panel agrees to my request to classify me "as not affected by the law." If the panel rejects this request and classifies me as "exonerated only," I respectfully request a written/oral trial in which I and my lawyer and my witnesses shall be heard.

Excerpts from the document finding Paul "not guilty under the law"
[no trial was thus required]

Law chamber, Göppingen, May 7, 1947
Judgment

On the basis of the law for liberation from National Socialism and Militarism of March 5, 1946, the panel [Spruchkammer, which was made up of one lawyer and four ordinary citizens who were known anti-Nazis: a baker, a craftsman, etc.] *decrees that the accused, Dr. Paul Ludwig, lawyer, state judge, is not guilty under the law. The proceedings are terminated. The costs of the proceedings are born by the state.*
Reasons (excerpts)

2. The accused was neither a member of the Nazi Party nor any of its subcommittees. Since 1937 he was a member of the NSV and since September 1937 he was a committee member till he was drafted into the army, where he became a member of the Nazi-Rechtswehrverbund.

3. and 4. Because of these memberships, it had been assumed that he fulfilled parts of law F II, nr. 2, and according to Article 10, part of article 7 to 9.

5. The proceedings have proven that this assumption could be totally repudiated.

6. In addition, the proceedings have shown the following: nothing incriminating is known about him. The [U.S.] military government has therefore retained him as a judge.

Witnesses were called to testify to his character and activities during the Nazi regime.

Excerpts from the testimony of two witnesses

My father:
Any compromise with the Nazi regime was not compatible with his character. He refused to join the party many times, even though it meant

disadvantages for his job as a lawyer. [He was not named prosecutor for many years because of his political leanings.] *He joined the NSV and became a committee member only after his attempts to either become a state's attorney or to switch to the private sector were unsuccessful and he found himself in a financially precarious situation. His attitude did not change after he was accepted into the state's service. He did not sympathize with the Nazis. He was not a member of the NSDAP.*

From the official trial document:

This witness was not a member of the NSDAP or any of its subcommittees. He was director of the examining committee D for denazification in Stuttgart-West, under the committee that had been established by the mayor of Stuttgart according to the military regime's law Nr.8. He was the director till the committee's dissolution.

The next witness was another lawyer, Dr. K., who had known Uncle Paul since 1924:

The accused is a thoroughly liberal person, very open to the ideals and rules of law and democracy and an enemy of the suppression of human rights. He was opposed to National Socialism and militarism and expressed his opinion to his friends. In 1933 and later he rejected the idea of becoming a member of the NSDAP, which led to discrimination against him in his professional life.

Though he was one of the top graduates in his PhD class, his appointment as a state prosecutor was continuously postponed. When he saw that he could not keep his job as an assessor without being a party member, he tried to get employment at Allianz or Bosch, but did not secure a job, because at that time the companies were under pressure to hire as legal counsels only persons who were totally loyal to the party. It was also not possible for politically suspect people to go into private practice. He contemplated emigrating or finding a compromise that would allow him to be hired by the state. He therefore accepted the role of committee member for the NSV, which meant he had to collect member's fees. Because this was repellent to him and he did not carry out his duty conscientiously, his mother feared for him and took over his duties. He did get reprimanded by the party for neglect of duty, and therefore his promotion was delayed.

Five years after his PhD examination, or three-and-a-half years longer than others in his class, who were much less qualified, he was appointed to the state court in Stuttgart. Even after his appointment, he waited for the end of the Nazi regime. His behavior in the war was consistent with his attitude: he refused to become an officer and refused to become a state employee in any war court, or to become the scribe at a war court. Though he served five years in the army, he remained a simple soldier and was released as a British prisoner of war as private first class.

...In 1937 the former Gauleiter Murr considered him unworthy of pro-

motion since he showed no enthusiasm for the movement: "We ascertained that his inner conviction was anti-Nazi and that he accepted the committee chair under pressure."

Excerpts from an official document introduced on December 17, 1937, to verify Dr. K's testimony in Paul's support

To the Oberlandesgerichtspräsident, Stuttgart

Re: Political evaluation of the judicial assessor Dr. Paul Ludwig

Up to this point, Dr. Paul Ludwig has shown no interest in the movement. Since September 1937 he has worked for the NSV (upon the advice of a third party). This short period of time does not allow me to testify that he is politically safe. I therefore plead that the planned employment be postponed and that the candidate shall apply again at a later date.

Heil Hitler! Murr, Gauleiter

[Note: Mr. Murr tried to flee with some friends after the collapse of the regime, but then committed suicide.]

Third Category: Those generally supportive of the Nazis, hangers-on, "joiners," or "fellow travelers" (Mitläufer)

In my immediate family, my Uncle Kurt, my father's younger brother, was a supporter of the Nazis from the beginning. Since he had joined the SA, he had to go through the denazification trial.

Aunt Resi's diary

And then came the time of the denazification. I was born too early and therefore didn't have to join the Nazi Youth movement, but my sister joined two groups. She was enthusiastic, understandably due to her age, but it was a bitter pill for my parents. In 1945, Kurt and I were pressured to join the party. He was already a member of the SA [Sturmabteilung, a party militia that was not under the command of the army, but reported directly to party headquarters] and was told that there would be consequences if he did not join the party. He filled out an application, but due to the end of the war he never joined. I was often visited by a woman from the women's auxiliary of the party. When I continued to refuse, she threatened that there would be consequences for my husband and our family. I schemed to think up the most bizarre excuses and managed not to join.

Chambers were created. Everybody received a questionnaire with 131 questions. According to their answers, people were classified as innocent, as I was, or as fellow travelers like Kurt—or they were punished more severely. For Kurt's trial we needed an uncompromised witness. My mother agreed to testify for Kurt's character. This allowed Kurt to keep his job.

Atonement Verdict
By order of the military government, Uncle Kurt was sentenced to
short-term community service and to pay a small fine.

Confirmation
It is hereby confirmed that Mr. Kurt Paulus has completed the prescribed
service of seven Sundays. February 11, 1946, Municipal Engineering
Department.

After Kurt completed his community service, he was ordered to appear in front of a judge in Bamberg on February 3, 1947.

Atonement Verdict
Mr. Kurt Paulus, engineer,...at the request of the state's attorney of the
city Bamberg of February 24, 1947, the following verdict was pro-
nounced:
1. *You are classified as a "fellow traveler"* [Mitläufer].
2. *You are assessed a monetary fine of RM 300. The amount has*
   to be paid to the city of Bamberg by April 30, 1947.... For every
   RM 10 not paid, one day of service will be ordered.
3. *Court costs are assessed at RM 251.60 and will have to be*
   paid at the same time.
This verdict will be in effect if you don't appeal within one week.
[Signed] *Chairman of the Spruchkammer H.*

Reinstatement
Office of the Military Government, Bamberg, July 23, 1947
Subject: Reinstatement in Position and Employment
To: Mr. Kurt Paulus, Bamberg, Hainstr. 50
1. You are hereby notified that your appeal for reinstatement in the posi-
tion from which you were removed under provisions of Military Govern-
ment U.S. Zone Law No. 8 has been favorably considered.
2. The restrictions imposed on your employment under the provisions of
Law No. 8 are removed.
3. Note: reinstatement referring to Questionnaire appeal ata. 27.3.46
By Order of Military Government, Copy to Review Board Special Branch

Under military occupation, people could not move freely amongst the different Allied zones. Uncle Kurt, who then worked and lived in the American zone, was assigned to return to the French/British/Russian zone, but he appealed. (We do not have the document stating his reasons.) The Refugee Commission accepted his reasons and freed him from returning to the British, French, or Russian zones.

Aunt Resi's diary
Kurt was now able to work again for his old company.

Special Certificate as a Result of the War

Directly after the war my father, who had been discharged from the military in 1940 and was not re-enlisted because of his tuberculosis, was issued a disability certificate by the government. This verified that he was totally disabled and could therefore ride free on the local streetcar, receive priority seating near the door, and travel first class with a second class railway ticket—as partial compensation for his war-related illness. Every five years he had to undergo a medical examination to verify that his disabled condition still existed. Since his tuberculosis was never healed, the pass was always renewed till his death. He was classified as 90 percent disabled. His employer, the large insurance company, Allianz, also had to grant him a two-hour lunch break (instead of the customary half hour). He always came home in the afternoon, ate, and took a half-hour nap.

Slowly, Life Returns to Normal

Very slowly, people started to get back to a normal life as their diaries show.

Aunt Resi's diary, after the war

After the capitulation I rode my bike every day to Bamberg, at times quite a dangerous trip. Once I barely avoided an attack. With a heavy heart I had to leave the children alone with our au pair. One evening when I returned home, it was already quite chilly, Winfried lay in his crib without any clothes. The girl had run off with a soldier—she ultimately fled with him some time later after she had stolen quite a few items from me. Musical instruments and sports equipment were stored in a Nazi warehouse. The peasants "cleaned out" this storage place and distributed the things. Many peasants received record players, but didn't have records. But one day I heard what sounded like one of my records through a window in the village and, sure enough, [I discovered that] our au pair girl before she ran away with the soldier had robbed me of all my records and jewelry, my underclothes, and a large jar of honey that I had hoarded. She exchanged these things for fat and bacon. The war destroyed any sense of morality.

Our apartment was made habitable again at the end of June.... My father rode his bike to Aachen in the summer [at least a two-hundred-mile trip]. *His house was still standing, but the roof had been ripped off and the front was gone. Everything was under water; everything was destroyed.*

The English occupation forces were looking for my father because they wanted him to help with the reconstruction. He had been offered the office of mayor of Aachen, but he didn't want to take on a political office. However, when he was offered a chance to rebuild the school system and become its superintendent, he accepted and started work in July 1945.

[Note: Shortly after the American troops occupied Aachen, before the end of the war, one of the few terrorist attacks against the Allies was carried out when the Werewolf assassinated the American-appointed mayor of Aachen.]

*We were all afraid of the coming winter. We had used up our coal ra-
tions and the new rations would never be sufficient to heat our apartment. Therefore we had to buy wood. Kurt organized a trip to the Steiger
forest and Winfried—who was still in the pram—and I rode in the back of
a truck with former Nazis who had been ordered to do community service. I had to get a ration card for the wood. I had to push the pram for a
long time, over a hill, to my forest destination. But when I wanted to pick
up the wood in the forest I realized that there were no branches to be
had that didn't need use of a saw and an axe. The next day I spent all
day in the forest and sawed and sawed, even young beeches. Many
times later I regretted that I committed such a forest sacrilege, but at the
moment I was preoccupied with thoughts of my freezing family.*

[Note: Aunt Resi takes a detour in her recollections and talks about one of her husband's
colleagues.]

*At the end of the war, they moved into an apartment and furnished it.
When they had to leave this apartment and turn it over to the occupying
force they were told that they could only take their beds, but all the rest
had to stay—so he took an axe and hacked every piece of furniture into
small pieces. Then they moved into a tiny apartment and used orange
crates as their main pieces of furniture....*

*1945–1946, we all suffered through a winter of hunger and cold. We
could not heat our central heater with wood, so we needed to find an
iron wood-burning stove. This allowed us to heat at least the living room.
The kitchen was heated with a combination gas/wood stove. We spent
most of our time there—eating, cooking, washing, and playing.*

*I lost a lot of weight and was very weak, but now had no help in the
household with the two girls and the baby. During an afternoon walk a
young woman approached me, a refugee from Silesia, who was all by
herself without a room and a job. A friend had taken her in for a few
days. We both came to an agreement and I hired her.* [The free au pair
service did not carry over to the new government. Resi must have hired
her and paid her out of her own pocket.]

*One morning the Americans put three layers of barbed wire between
one arm of the river and the other and patrolled the area. We couldn't
figure out what was going on until a soldier appeared at our door and
gave us a letter ordering us to vacate the apartment within twenty-four
hours. We were only allowed to take our beds and personal belongings.
Who wouldn't panic? But Kurt again showed his organizational skills by
finding a truck and people to help us. We took the furniture apart, put the
pieces in the bottom of the truck, and heaped our bedding and personal
stuff on top. Then we drove along streets that we knew were not yet being patrolled. We stored everything in the first place that we could find.
When the Americans found out that we had taken items that we were
supposed to have left behind, we put our things on a ferry across the*

Regnitz.

The Americans had confiscated all lamps, carpets, and curtains; we lit our rooms with cellar lamps that a friend gave us. We furnished our new apartment with simple closets and tables. If the Americans had actually wanted to move into our old apartment, we would have been in real trouble. The housing agency secured two little attic rooms for us on a street that had not been turned over to the military authorities. We all slept in one room and in a little chamber we had a closet and a table. Since we were not allowed to share the kitchen again, all our cooking had to be done on our old hotplate.

Every day I went to the housing agency; eventually we were offered a small apartment in a very old house: a small kitchen with a sink, next to a small bedroom, and behind a glass door the children's bedroom, without windows or fresh air. There was no bathroom in this place; the toilet was outside the apartment on the staircase. The house had landmark status, but we couldn't wash ourselves. So we mounted the bathroom sink we had taken from the old apartment—because it had belonged to us—in the bedroom. We planted a pail under the drainpipe and used another pail to pour water into the sink. We tried to make it as cozy as possible.

Almost every night we had potatoes and beans, but we were grateful that we had that. I did receive one egg, some butter, and some cold cuts as long as I was nursing Winfried, but I couldn't eat these in front of the others, who hadn't received these extra rations. So, it all went into the family pot.

Now the youngsters had no place to play. We had no courtyard, no garden, and no balcony. I went to the American authorities and received permission to return every day to our old garden with my children. The children could play and I could watch what was happening in our old apartment. The apartment was uninhabitable for the Americans, but they completely stripped it of everything they could use in houses that could be lived in. They took all the electrical installations, switches, plugs, etc. I managed to convince them not to take the bathtub and the boiler. I also had to get special permission to ride my bike with all three children, which was normally prohibited. When I came to the checkpoint every day, I heard them say: "Here comes the bus!"

Then I started negotiations to move back into our old apartment, which turned out to be rather difficult. After a three-way switch with families who all needed a place to stay and permission from the housing authority, we were allowed to move into our old apartment. In August 1946, we were one of the first families to move back into this occupied sector.

One day Kurt got a truck to take the children and me back to my hometown, Aachen, and pick us up again a week later. It was a strenuous five-hour trip, sitting on sacks in the back of the truck. And what a sight! The ruins! I could only get my bearings by looking at the base of the houses.

Things were getting better, however. One could sleep at night without fear of bomb attacks. The food situation was improving; one still had to fight for daily necessities, but we learned to improvise. We wanted to make up for all the missed festivities by giving personal and business parties.

One of our friends returned from being an American prisoner of war and told us the following story: Some of his fellow inmates told him that they spent the end of the war in a cellar in our house. Because they had nothing to do, they opened up a bundle of letters, bound in fine paper with a string around them. These were the numbered love letters that Kurt and I had written to each other every day when he was still in the army. When we returned to our house, we found the whole bunch of loose letters strewn all over. Unfortunately, they were no longer legible and we burned them. But at least they provided a bit of entertainment for some poor soldiers for a few days.

Winfried had a boil on his nose, which took quite a few days to heal. There was no medication available so Winfried laid in his bed completely apathetic. Someone suggested I give him coffee to stimulate his circulation. But where could I find even one coffee bean? Then a friend who sewed clothes for American officers' families in exchange for coffee and other foodstuff, presented us with some coffee. And lo and behold, Winfried was his normal self again in a short time. Our children lost everything—I mean everything. Gloves, hats, aprons, shoes, and their toys; some of these cost a fortune because they were so difficult to get. When they came home from using their bottoms to sled down a sledding track, their play suits didn't have a rear anymore. This wouldn't have mattered if they had been replaceable.

Which brings me to the clothes situation. Every family got a certain amount of points, which were just enough to buy a few small pairs of pants and some coats. I sewed the dresses and coats for girls' first communion myself. I also sewed nightgowns, because that material used up fewer ration points than ready-made clothes. I unraveled my dresses to make two children's dresses out of them. I also saved up my special "pregnancy" points. I cut a dress of mine in the middle and inserted a piece of cloth rather than buying a new maternity dress. My dark blue "maternity" coat later became two coats for the girls, which I spruced up with a light fur collar from our rabbit. I sewed dresses out of old sheets and curtains for all of them. Kurt had the habit of rubbing his ring finger over his knees, which meant that soon his pants were worn through. When we got married he had quite a few suits, all with two pairs of pants. I combined the materials from the two pants that were still like new to make a single pair of pants. If the collars or the wrists of the shirts were worn out, I took the back of a shirt to make new parts and took the material of a still older shirt to replace the back. That worked because he always had to wear a suit coat and nobody would see the back of his shirt.

Yes, the war and the postwar times were a constant fight for survival. After the denazification trials, the next operation began: the de-Aryanization. This was to determine how much money the Jews should receive as compensation or whether they should receive their companies back. Kurt's boss had bought his company from a Jewish owner, of course for a song. We spent hours every night calculating, typing, and adding till the right amount of compensation was determined.

Resi's oldest daughter, Ingrid (my cousin), adds to her mother's notes

When I was a little girl I experienced the Americans' Independence Day celebrations. When I returned from kindergarten, some Americans shot wildly into the air. I ran home screaming, convinced the war had broken out again. I couldn't watch fireworks for years, always afraid of another war. In our neighborhood the many Americans who were living there were very friendly to children. We occasionally received presents from them: Ursula, for example, got a little suitcase. And sometimes they gave us sweets, always a great treat for us. But still we were hungry for sweets. I remember distinctly that we picked up the discarded pieces of chewing gum that the Americans had spit out and continued to chew them. We also loved to rummage in the Americans' garbage cans. For example, we brought orange rinds to my mother, who cooked them and made orange marmalade out of them. Once we brought home toothbrushes that looked like new, but when we tried to clean them with boiling water they lost all of their bristles.

A letter written by my nine-year-old cousin, Günther (Aunt Minni's son), shows that even in Austria, which had been spared the worst effects of the war, times were difficult.

Letter from Minni's son, Günther, Advent 1946

To the dear Christchild in heaven,

You will visit us soon. For quite some time, we have been looking forward to Christmas. However, this year you won't have many presents. That is why I am writing to you early enough. Perhaps you can go to Switzerland first and buy some presents there. Now, here is my wish list: the small stuff, I leave to you to decide. A pair of skis and for my altar, different things: a monstrance, a thurible for incense, a golden chalice, a little bell, and anything else one needs for a proper altar. As for the rest, you know what I want and need.

I don't know whether he got any of these presents, but he did receive a piano for which his father traded a large wheel of cheese and an old typewriter. In hindsight this was just the right present. Günther Fetz became a professor of music and is a well-known harpsichordist who gives concerts in Europe and the United States and has produced many CDs of classical music.

Uncle Richard's diary describes the personal and political occurrences in the first months after the end of the war. He vacillates between criticism of the Nazi regime and its atrocities and criticism of the Allies, who are not treating the Germans the way he deemed fit. He has a hard time accepting Germany's defeat. He is of the staunch opinion that the non-Jewish Germans suffered as much as the Jews and other nationalities. Clearly he lacks insight into his own behavior and attitude. He seems to have forgotten that after an initial hesitation he went on to support the regime wholeheartedly. This is reflected in his earlier diary entries.

Uncle Richard's diary

June 2, 1945:

I handed over my camera to the American occupation troops.
On the night of June 12–13 our cellar was broken into. Goose fat (about fifty pounds), meat, and bread were stolen. In the same night there was a break-in at a farm in Stoetten. The perpetrators are probably the same and most probably foreigners (Poles or Russians).

June 14

Our bishop, Dr. Johannes Baptist Sproll, returned to his diocese from a seven-year exile (1938–1945). In 1938 he declined to participate in the Reichtagselection, which in reality was not a real election, but a shameless farce. One might pose the question: Couldn't the rest of the bishops have acted in the same way as our courageous and sincere Bekennerbishop [a bishop who stood up for his beliefs]. *Just remember that with the dominant psychological attitude of the German people—even some Catholics—severe persecution of the Catholic Church would most likely have followed. The result would have been the total elimination of the church and its institutions. Today, it has been proven that the destruction of Christendom in Germany (including Protestantism) was an important goal of the Nazi Party, which would have become reality after the Final Victory. Pope Pius XII declared a little while ago, that he has trustworthy documents in his hands in which this intention is obvious. The total defeat of Germany prevented this. That Germany's enemies—by pointing to the Nazi's atrocities, for which they now blame the whole nation—dealt with Germany in such cruel ways, says little for their own views, based on peaceful Christian principles. If there isn't a change for the better, one can only look forward with the greatest anxiety to any future development. The level of misery is already extremely high and the occupying troops, especially the French, add to it with insane actions.*

There has been no improvement in transportation and communication. There are almost no trains—with a few exceptions; mail is totally prohibited so that we have not heard about the fates of various relatives in many months. The press is also destroyed. We have to rely on what the "radio stations of the United Nations" broadcast in German about the situation. Nazi crimes—especially by the SS—were indeed monstrous.

However, the Germans had to suffer the most under them. I shall mention only

- *the concentration camps, in which many thousands of sincere, responsible Germans were exposed to insane ordeals and lost their lives;*
- *the irresponsible, yes sadistic, crimes against the countless Jews;*
- *the innumerable people liquidated without trial and often after terrible torture (like our former governor, Bolz);*
- *the total suppression of freedom of the press and the total secularization of the still-existing Nazi press;*
- *the prohibition of all religiously oriented literature;*
- *the limitation of freedom for the clergy and the church in general;*
- *the suppression of all church activities (processions, pilgrimages);*
- *the de-Christianization of the schools and the pressure on the teachers to accept and teach the National Socialism philosophy.*

It was the teachers, especially in the rural areas, working for the Propaganda, who wreaked havoc.

Now this destructive movement has broken down abruptly and radically due to the German defeat. The prominent leaders mostly fell into the hands of the enemy like Ribbentrop, Schirach, Schleicher, Göring, Frank, Forster, Rosenberg. Others committed suicide and have thereby evaded responsibility (Hitler, Goebbels, Himmler). Now the ones still alive are languishing with thousands of their supporters (SS) in the very concentration camps in which they tortured their adversaries in such gruesome fashion. And for many the death penalty will be the last verdict of the judge. So ends this movement that from the beginning was based on lies and illusions. That a large part of the German people became ensnared by its leaders will always be an enigma. The period 1933–1945 will be entered into the book of history in black letters. Is the history of Germany finished now forever? According to the will and the opinion of its enemies, one has to assume so. But the ways of Providence often take a completely different turn from that of the people who think they are so wise and clever.

June 16

The first of our relatives, our nephew Hermann, returned from the war. He had been in different military hospitals for some time due to his injuries, the last one in Konstanz.

Saturday, June 21

In Schnittlingen, as in the other towns they occupied, the Americans conducted a house-to-house search to look for hidden weapons. Early in the morning the town crier informed us that no one could leave the house all day. Armed guards were posted at all access routes to the village. At about 9:00 a.m. they came to us, six men, heavily armed. The searches took over an hour. All closets, desks, etc. had to be opened and were subjected to search. The result was negative, since we had no hidden weapons. In house number 13 they rummaged through the three

suitcases we were keeping for our relatives from Hamburg; two they
pried open, because there were no keys. Otherwise the teams behaved
properly. They did not take anything—at least in our house. There were
a few discharged German soldiers who didn't dare return to their homes,
which were occupied by the French, because the French arrested all re-
turning soldiers and carried them off for restoration work in France. Now
the Americans were taking in all of these soldiers. After a few days they
dismissed them again and even paid each forty RM. They had only
taken them in to issue them discharge papers. They also wanted to in-
vestigate whether SS people were among them.

July 27
   The first issue of the Catholic Sunday newspaper in Stuttgart was
published again. The last issue had been published on May 25, 1941.
By order of the Nazi government its publication had to cease after that
date.

August 7
   Pastor Kucher told us today that he heard that H. had been shot in the
vicinity of Ravensburg. H. had been a teacher in Schnittlingen and was
a friend of ours. He joined the Nazis very early and was called by the
Party to Stuttgart where he received the title Regierungsrat, then
Oberregierungsrat. There he evolved into a spiteful and dangerous en-
emy of his church. In this capacity he hurt quite a few of his former col-
leagues. I was told by several sources that morally he sank to a very low
level. He also started to drink. He became the victim of his own unre-
strained ambition.

August 14
   In the evening, our nephew Rudolf Brühl returned home hale and well.

August 15
   We heard that Japan surrendered without conditions. Thus, peace
has been restored to this Earth. Whether the victorious nations are will-
ing and able to grant a peace based on justice and law will be decided in
the future. The difficulties that have to be overcome are enormous.

August 18
   Paul Ludwig, the husband of our niece Gertrud, returned from a pris-
oner of war camp.

August 29
   Mail service has been reestablished; at the present time, however,
only in the county Göppingen. And individuals can only send postcards.
If one uses old postcards, one has to cut out the old [Nazi] stamps and
hand over the new fee to the post office.

From September 3, mail can be sent within the American occupied zone, but not to the zones of the state that are occupied by the French.

In the afternoon of September 22 Erich Tietze, the husband of our niece Maria, returned unexpectedly from a Russian prisoner of war camp. But how utterly ragged he looked—reduced to skin and bones and looking very old. Of 1,400 in his camp 700 were still alive when he left. He himself came from a military hospital and was discharged only because he was no longer fit for work. Everything had been taken from him: clothes, shoes, money, watch, even his wedding ring and his glasses. What a situation! Outrageous!

October 15

The former French premier, Pierre Laval, was shot. He had collaborated with the German occupation administration during his term and was therefore convicted of treason.

On October 24, mail service to the French-, British-, and Russian-occupied zones was reinstated.

November 11

In the Federal Court Building in Nuremberg, the great trial against the so-called war criminals started: Göring; Hess; Von Rippentrop; Ley; Keitel; Keltenbrunner; Rosenberg; Frank; Frick; Steicher; Funk; Schacht; Krupp von Bohlen und Hallbach; Dönitz; Raeder; von Schirrach; Sauckel; Jodl; Borman; von Papen; Seyss- Inquart; Speer; von Neurath; Fritsche.

Of the 9.6 million Jews who lived in Europe before the war, 60 percent disappeared during the Nazi regime (circa 5.76 million).

December 28

We heard from Frau Oberpraeceptor Emma Eitle that her only son, Hermann, died in action on April 23, shortly before the end of the war. They had been our neighbors for sixteen years and we watched their son grow up.

Life on the Family Farm in Schnittlingen in the Early Postwar Years

Many of my relatives had to remain with other family members in 1946 and 1947 because their own apartments had not been restored or they had lost their homes permanently in the air raids. The Brühl grandparents had moved to the family farm in Schnittlingen and took in their sons and sons-in-law upon their return from captivity till they could return to their own homes.

The family farm was run by the siblings of Opa Achaz, Bernhard and Barbara. Till his death my grandfather worked on the farm. He was the first one up in the morning, cleaning out the horse stable, and the last one to retire at night. He was also in charge of splitting wood, which was needed for the various stoves for the families. Once he injured his knee so badly that he had to stay in the hospital in Geislingen for some weeks. Oma visited him there by walking back and forth five miles each way, since transportation was irregular and she didn't have much money for bus fare. Though he worked every day—without financial compensation—until shortly before his death at the age of eighty, he and his wife always received the shabbiest produce from the farm. The best produce went to "Uncle Fischer." I heard from more than one person that my grandparents only received the apples that had started to rot.

Though the great-grandparents received my grandmother graciously when she joined the family, the siblings (Marie, Barbara, and Bernard) and the brother-in-law (Richard) of Achaz did not care for her since she came from a very poor family. They did admit, however, that she was very pious. They treated her poorly and she left Schnittlingen the day after my grandfather's funeral to go back to her old homestead in Westerheim where she was warmly welcomed and spent a peaceful time with her relatives before she died six months later.

Unfortunately after the grandparents were bombed out they had nowhere else to go. They had lost everything and lived on a very small pension. In the meantime their children lived elsewhere, but in houses not big enough to invite them to stay overnight. They lived a lonely life—especially my grandmother who had no more responsibilities now—that lasted till they died in 1954 (grandfather) and 1955 (grandmother).

The loneliness of my two elderly grandparents was increased because they could not visit their children and grandchildren after the war, partly because of a lack of travel funds, partly because of government rules and regulations of the military occupation forces. This is already evident in a letter to their grandchild, Günther, who had invited them to his First Communion. He lived with his parents in Austria.

Letter from my grandparents to their grandchild, Günther, May 13, 1946, Schnittlingen

To the Bregenzer: We would have so loved to spend the day with you and your dear parents, but it would be impossible at this time. We don't know whether we would have gotten an entry visa.... Perhaps you can come to Germany some day with your mother. If one of you or perhaps all three of you could visit us, it would give us great joy. Especially on Sundays we feel very lonely.
Oma and Opa
We are healthy and happy. Our big worry is for Robert. If God wills it, we will receive news from him soon.

Most of the sons and sons-in-law who returned from prisoner of war camps only stayed a few weeks or months to recuperate before they returned to their own families. However, Uncle Hermann who was not married at the time, and had lost his only place to live when his parents' apartment burned down, moved into a tiny room next to his parents' rooms and stayed a few years. He had no job and was recovering from his war wounds.

He describes the situation that existed early after the war: restrictions on travel, ration cards for all goods, lack of basic necessities, and so forth. Excerpts from his letters follow.

Letters from Hermann to Minni, his married sister in Austria

October 6, Schnittlingen
The mailman passes our house every day, but no mail from you. We still don't know whether you are coming. Did you receive the doctor's

evaluation of mother that we sent at the beginning of August? Peppi, thank you for the promised cigarettes. For obvious reasons I am a non-smoker at the moment, but I hope to relish this enjoyment soon again. I am envious of you that you can travel to Switzerland. It must be wonderful to live in a country where you can buy everything. I am longing for the time when the bureaucracies, the trips to the official agencies and sub-agencies, the filling out of many forms, the ration cards, and so forth cease to exist.

Lately, I have spent a lot of time collecting beechnuts in the forest for turning them into cooking oil. Everybody else does it, too, and some have already more than 100 pounds. I wasn't quite as hard working, but together with mother I have about thirty pounds. Maria and Uncle Richard are also collecting. We are anxiously awaiting the beginning of the peace negotiations with Germany. We hope then the paralysis that permeates the economy can be lifted.

Our parents are doing all right. On mother's birthday, we even had one cup of real coffee. Mother is so fervently waiting for Robert's return and a visit from you. Every time we return from the forest, mother says that surely either Robert or Minni will be there or will have sent a letter at least. We wonder will anyone come looking for us in the forest if Robert returns? We imagine what it would be like to come home and find one of you actually there! But then, when no one comes, her yearning for all her children becomes obvious. I am glad that I can give her some support. Today it rained all day, which makes father very upset and edgy because he can't work on the farm. He paces up and down the kitchen with small steps, and claims that mother, who has to cook, is in his way. During such days, father's mind races. He gives suggestions to mother about simplified cooking, the advantages of coffee made from acorns, about hair treatments with tea made from burning nettles [Brennessel-wasser], and how one could rearrange the kitchen. In between he disappears to check if there isn't any work that he could do, and depending on the outcome he returns satisfied, smug, and hungry and sits at the table—or he starts pacing up and down again, complaining that mother is in his way. I am lying in bed and hope that you will come and keep me company soon and tell me all about your beautiful Bregenz corner.

Added on October 7

It is really terrible that we can't even buy the most basic necessities for daily life, like laundry brushes. You have to stand in line for everything in one office after the other, only to be told that nothing is available. I am wondering how long it will take till we can buy the most basic items that we need for our daily life.

Undated

We just received your birthday letter for mother. We regret very much that your travel application was denied. [At that time, you needed a visa

240

to travel from Austria to Germany or in between the German states]. *Too bad! It was not to be, we won't complain. A week ago, after some considerable time, I had blood in my stool again and visited a doctor, who said that I don't have to worry about my lungs because they would heal. However, I have to be careful about my digestive system. This was the most blood that I ever had. Today is the first day without blood, probably due to the many medicines that I am taking. So, it looks like everything will be okay.*

December 28, Schnittlingen

At the end of the holidays I want to write you a short letter. Thea is chatting with Aunt Barbara, mother is reading her Christmas book, and father is praying, so I have time to chat with you at leisure. We spent the holidays in harmony together. Thea came from Stuttgart on Christmas Eve. I walked to Treffelhausen to meet her and then we walked back to Schnittlingen in a pre-Christmas mood. Two or three years ago, you and I walked the same road, very early in the morning. You were on your way to Stuttgart and I on my way to the military hospital in Gmünd. Yes, Minni, one doesn't forget these hours together. And so, Thea and I walked the same road. When we reached the cemetery we stopped to pay our respects to Karl and then went home to the parents. Their joy was naturally exuberant, and mother had prepared wonderful Krausknöpfle. Between much talk back and forth, we ate to our heart's content. In the evening Thea read the gospel and then we went to the aunts and uncles for coffee and carols. We had prepared our presents of course on a little table in our kitchen. We even had a small Christmas tree. Even before Christmas we received some surprise packages with wonderful goodies. Father received tobacco and a few cigarettes and cigars. Mother got a few items for the household. I received a nice Sunday shirt. And we got some sweets and cookies. Our most prized possession was an orange. Due to her large circle of friends, Thea received the most. As you can see, we spent a few wonderful hours on Christmas Eve and remembered all our loved ones, especially Robert from whom we still have not heard. We have sent a few more requests for information to the Russian Red Cross, but have not received any answer as yet.

We now have many refugees from the East in the village. Life for these poor people is really not easy. Expelled from their homes and farms, they are now here with nothing. Oh, why doesn't the world listen to God's words and follow them? Or is it that everybody hears it, but thinks it is meant for his neighbor? It doesn't make much sense to talk about it, there is only one thing to do and that is to work on oneself with all one's might and to pursue the Good, even if we never quite reach it.

January 16

...for the time being I work a bit in my room and I receive a small pension for my war injuries and that's how I manage.... Mother received the two pears that you sent, and Rudolf also sent some goods.

Hermann was a very quiet man, who hardly spoke about his time in the war. His children remember only two incidences that he shared with them.

Uncle Hermann's reminiscences
[recalled by his children]

While alone on reconnaissance duty, I met a lonely Russian soldier. We both lifted our rifles in order to shoot each other. But then we looked into each other's eyes, and saw that we were not the enemy, lowered our rifles, turned around and walked away.

I was lying next to a comrade in a field when a shot rang out that hit my comrade and killed him. Because he screamed, I turned my face. I credit this movement for my survival, because the next shot did not hit me in the head, but only grazed my chin.

Thea and Hermann spent Christmas 1945 and 1946 with their parents in Schnittlingen. In 1946 Thea entered the Carmelite monastery and was no longer allowed to come home. Meanwhile, Hermann had moved to Stuttgart and he was also unable to come home. The other children lived all over Germany, married, many with small children themselves. The grandparents therefore celebrated Christmas 1947 alone for the first time since the birth of their oldest daughter in 1908. This is the reason for the following letter that Thea circulated among the whole family after the death of both parents.

Letter to Thea (Sr. Pia Theresia) from my grandmother, December 1947, Schnittlingen

Today I will break my silence, the thoughts of your parents and siblings have often been with you, but during Holy Communion at the Christmas Mass we were particularly connected to you. We ourselves in our loneliness received so much strength that we celebrated a real Christmas Eve. I have been anticipating this day with trepidation for some time. Father and I already offered up our sacrifices, especially Robert's fate and all the other difficult times that we endured, as gold, our faith, prayer, and trust as incense, and our wounded hearts as myrrh. We put it in the crèche and God has accepted it. We were not sad. First we were invited to Uncle Fischer, listened to the radio, and then all went down to Aunt Barbara, where the Christmas tree was lit. First we sang carols and then drank coffee. Around 8:00 p.m. we returned to our apartment. I read aloud from Katherina Emmerich—Uncle Fischer loaned us this book. Tietzes [daughter Maria and family] left on December 14 to return to Cologne: Erich and Armin, with a truck, and Maria and Elinor, by train. The train was overcrowded, but Maria could sit during the eight-hour ride; she is very glad that the trip is over. Elinor will start school at a school run by nuns near their house.

I am sending you stockings in a separate package, one pair from Isa, one pair from Minni, and the thicker one from me. I hope that it will arrive safely.

This letter shows one of the saddest effects of the war on my family: the isolation, poverty, and loneliness of my grandparents till their deaths. Though they had been relatively rich when they ran their own business they lost that business in the Great Depression and then they lost their apartment and all of their belongings in the air raid in 1944, and my grandfather lost his job with his brother in Stuttgart. And though they had thirteen children, eight of whom were still alive after the war, they never spent another Christmas with any of their children. Neither did any of their children visit them at Christmas. I asked my cousins about this and they verified it.

None of their children had an apartment big enough to accommodate two extra people. (Two of their children built houses the year after they died). While their children individually visited them at various times, none of them could afford to visit with their families. In Germany, Christmas is a family affair, so they spent their time with their own spouses and children. Also, the small place where my grandparents lived could not provide room enough for a family. Their daughter Thea, who was in the convent, was not allowed to leave for a family visit. These restrictions were eased only many years later.

Our paternal grandmother, who had also lost all her possessions in the war, first lived with her daughter and then with her son, before she spent a few weeks in a home before her death She therefore never experienced the same loneliness. She visited us for weeks at a time twice a year, since we could accommodate a single person (but not a couple).

Life in Other Cities Returns to Normal

Mother's diary, June 1946

Hans Bernd entered the kindergarten just across the street from us shortly after our return. He is learning a lot there.

He also is creative in his use of language. He calls me lovingly "my favorite food" [Lieblingsspeise] and he doesn't just use this expression when he wants to cuddle with me, but he tells people: "Favorite food is not home" or "Be quiet, favorite food is sleeping." Often he calls me "Mrs. Isa"; his younger brother is called "the very fair one"; and he and Karl Heinz are "the little men." And they are really a pair to behold, the dark-haired one and the blond one, and they are ready to make any kind of mischief together. They love life.

When he gets excited, he develops a fever. Last year at Christmas he was so agitated that we couldn't calm him down. I told the children that they had to pray and sing in front of the crèche first and that they should not look for their presents till later or the Christchild could take them back. Worriedly he told us, "but my head moves back and forth by itself."

He is elated when he doesn't get called on the carpet for a misdeed. He then tries to get on my good side. The other day he told me: "Mutti, you look gorgeous today; you look like Red Riding Hood." And once he said: "I know you are a young Mutti, otherwise you would have deep wrinkles in your face." On the other hand, he is our enfant terrible. He told Oma: "You are a hunchback," and to a visitor: "At last, you are leav-

ing."

He is starting to get interested in Vati's extensive stamp collection and maintains that Heinz started the collection for him and that he would inherit it later. He often tells us: "I have absolutely the best Mutti and absolutely the best Vati." And I am sure he believes it.

Mother's diary

Margit got used to the different way of life, since the situation was not new to her. She still remembered the time before the evacuation—a time that was a happy one for her. In October schools were opened again and Margit spent half a year in second grade at the Falkertschool and then moved into the year-long third and fourth grades. She made friends easily. The great excitement for the children was jumping rope and she became proficient in all kinds of difficult manoeuvers. During the winter, sledding and skating were her great joys. She used my (very old) skates that you have to screw on and that slip off often, but this did not deter her. In February 1946 she had to have her adenoids removed. Since our hospital had been relocated to Stetten at the end of the war she was operated on there. Because I had to look after the two younger boys, I couldn't accompany her to the hospital, but the surgeon offered to take her. She got into his car with her little valise without any fear. When I visited her the day after the operation, the nurse told me that they were amazed that she arrived alone, but that she moved into her room and unpacked without being told and fit in right away. She stayed in the hospital for six days without complaint.

A big event in Margit's young life was her first confession, on the last Saturday before Christmas 1946. When I checked her confessional list of sins, she reacted surprised when I told her that she had to confess all her sins: "Yes, but then I won't have anything to confess next time."

While I prepared for my first confession, I had to study a long catalogue of sins and decide which ones I had committed. I remember distinctly stumbling over the expression "I had lust in my heart" and asking my mother why that was a sin. I don't think I got a satisfactory explanation.

Mother's diary, 1947

January

Karl Heinz, as ever, still plays first fiddle in the family. He is our little darling. Bernd often remarks, "Isn't our fair little blond one most precious? There isn't another as precious as he."

He did not move back with us to Stuttgart in August. He stayed with the Weilands as he did at the end of the war when Friedl called us up and told us that they had heard the enemy was already in Gmünd. I then picked up our little sparrow at 9:30 p.m. because during the defining moments of the war we all wanted to be together. Vati had already returned to us three weeks earlier; he came with the last train that still ran from Schönbuch [sanatorium]. Saturday afternoon, April 21, 1945, we spent

in the cellar of farmer Moser. Karl Heinz did not understand the serious-
ness of the situation and drove me crazy with his constant moving back
and forth.

Thank God everything turned out all right. And the next few months in
Ditzenbach went without any incidents. For the first time in three years
Karl Heinz finally returned to his home in Stuttgart in October. We fell in
love with him all over again and spoiled him rotten. However, his favorite
is Olo (Mr. Weiland), after that, me, and only then, the rest of the family.
Every time Olo leaves after a visit, there are tears and loud bawling.
[Note: I still remember when Olo brought Karl Heinz back to Stuttgart.
When Mr. Weiland boarded the streetcar that took him to the train station and Karl Heinz was left with us, Karl Heinz bawled and cried so
loudly that some of the neighbors flung open their windows to see what
was happening on the street below.] *Mr. Weiland takes him everywhere.*
He can accompany him when he plays the organ in Ave Maria church.
Once when Karl Heinz fell down, Olo had a hard time extricating him
from the organ's pedals. "Once," he tells us with a grin, "I just touched a
key and it blasted a high-pitched tone."

After his return it didn't take him long to figure out that he played a
special favorite role in the family. When I give general instructions to the
children, he doesn't feel these are meant for him: "The children go to
bed, I stay up, okay?" On the one hand, he is afraid of things, but on the
other hand, he is a daredevil. I watched the other day with horror from
my window four stories up, as he drove his little car in the middle of the
street (strictly forbidden) and forced a car to stop. After he received a
paddling, I asked him "where are the cars supposed to drive if you are in
the middle of the road?" to which he answered "they should drive on the
sidewalk." He also surprises me with some original thoughts and say-
ings: "Where did you buy Vati?" and when Vati wanted to punish him for
a misdeed, he said: "Vati, don't spank me, I'll cry by myself." He calls
himself the "little man" and Margit and Hans Bernd "the kids" or the "big
ones."

February
Karl Heinz's favorite activity is playing at home, preferably close to
me. He wants to help in the kitchen and when I clean the rooms. And
when he draws or builds something, I have to praise his work many
times or find names and explanations for his creations. He often comes
and says, "Mutti, I want to cuddle." I sometimes find Vati's wild games
too much, but Karl Heinz cannot get enough and laughs and roars and
enjoys himself so that the whole family joins in. To be complete, I have
to mention that Karl Heinz, like his older siblings, had the German mea-
sles in December 1946.

Aunt Resi writes about the chaotic circumstances after the war before people really settled in and their families were whole again: "I often went for walks with a friend who was

happy to find a hiking partner. He didn't want to go alone and his wife couldn't accompany him anymore because during one of the air raids in Stuttgart she suffered a stroke."

Aunt Resi's diary entries about nannies and au pairs

After G. came M. The employment office had called me to ask whether I would accept a pregnant woman, who was very responsible and hard working. This proved to be true; she was a real pearl. Together with her mother she had fled from the East to Bad Steben and worked in an old age home there. She told me that when she was hanging up laundry in the attic together with the custodian, "it" happened. She wasn't the most beautiful woman, with very cheap steel-rimmed glasses. While she was on maternity leave she stayed with us. But L., a former au pair, had returned in the meantime from the Sudetenland in the Czech Republic. She had a young son, but her husband had made his way to Hamburg with another woman and did not want to return to her. She didn't want to divorce him. She came to us every day for the twelve weeks of M.'s maternity leave. The whole time she provided us with asparagus. After M.'s daughter was born, the custodian showed up at our house with his wife to visit his daughter and to ask M. whether she was willing to give up her daughter to the couple for adoption. But she wanted to keep her child. She returned to Bad Steben after her year with us was up.

Personal lives slipped back into normalcy and the Catholic groups that Goebbels had dissolved were revived, among them Neudeutschland.

From the Neudeutschland obituary of my father, 1980

Since Heinz managed to save the whole list of addresses of the members, even though his apartment was searched a few times by the Gestapo—he had kept the list in the false bottom of the big grandfather clock in the hallway—the group was able to be revived in a very short time. He called a general meeting in Heidelberg in 1947 and—mainly for health reasons—gave up his position as the leader of the group.

Compensation for War Losses

Starting in 1946, people could claim reimbursement from the new German government for war losses to their houses, their furniture, appliances, or personal belongings. Our family had only one minor claim, the damage from the bomb that lodged in our living room's upholstered chair.

Mother' diary

During one of the air raids, two bombs hit the house, but because the inhabitants had a good community and some men were still living in the house, a patrol was organized and all ten apartments were checked after every attack. If a bomb was found, it was defused and put into the water and sand buckets that were sitting in front of every apartment door.

Uncle Kurt, who had been bombed out various times, filled out a very detailed list of lost items, noting the date of the air raids, the original price, the replacement cost of furniture, china, silverware, glasses, linens, bedding, clothes, and appliances. He applied for 1,844 marks and gave a bank account number. How much he received, if anything, is not recorded. I am sure both sets of grandparents also filled out an application, but I don't how much they may have received in compensation.

Uncle Richard's diary

February 1946. In the Catholic Sunday paper I read that the Russians have carried off the famous painting by Raphael—the "Sistine Madonna"—to Moscow. Raphael painted it on canvas as the altar piece for the Benedictine Abbey of Saint Sixtus in Piacenza (1515). August III, the art-loving archduke and king of Poland, son of August the Strong, bought it for 20,000 ducats. That's how it came to Dresden in 1774.

In March, it was announced that mailing a letter or postcard would be 100 percent more expensive (twenty-four pfennige for a letter; twelve pfennige for a postcard).

The Stuttgarter newspaper of April 23 wrote that the former Reichsstatthalter of Württemberg [equivalent of a governor under the Nazis], *Murr and his wife were made prisoners by the French in April 1945 and committed suicide by poison on May 14, 1945, in Egg in Vorarlberg, where they were buried.*

On April 19, 1945, many of the Stuttgart Nazi administrators fled in ten overcrowded personal cars toward the South (via Ursprung bei Geislingen, Kissleg, Trauchburg, etc.).

On April 25, two ethnic German refugees from Yugoslavia, a thirty-six-year-old mother and her seventeen-year-old daughter, came to us. They are Protestants. Four months later they left us to join other refugees from their home region and to settle near Herrenberg.

During the night of August 23–24, Gerhard Baumgartner, the husband of our niece Wilma, returned from captivity in France. It had lasted one and a quarter years. But many millions of German soldiers are still in captivity. We know nothing of the ones in Russia, because the Russians will not publicize their names. They are listed as MIA, because we do not know whether they are still living. These are incredible conditions.

Because of the high taxes, one book of matches costs ten cents now. Before we could buy ten books of a much better quality for the same price. The cheapest cigar, whose value is at the most five cents, is now one mark twenty cents. And a liter of cognac is 140 marks.

On October 1, the trial that had begun on November 25, 1945, against the so-called war criminals ended with verdicts. Twelve were sentenced to death by hanging; three (Papen, Schacht, and Fritsche) were cleared of all charges; the others received prison sentences. In detail, the follow-ing were sentenced to death and executed on October 16: Goering, who took his own life by poison shortly before the execution; von Ribbentrop; Keitel; Rosenberg; Kaltenbrunner; Frank; Frick; Streicher; Sauckel; Jodl; Seyess-Inquart; Bormann (whose whereabouts could not be ascertained at this time). Hess, Funk, and Raeder received life sentences; Schirach and Speer, twenty, years each; Von Neurath and Dönitz, ten years each.

Hereby the epoch of the German history of terrible tragedy is finished. Whether the verdict imposed by the foreign judges can be fully justified from a strictly legal point of view, can be finally determined only when true freedom of opinion is reestablished. It is our ardent wish that this situation will occur in the not so distant future. Today, it is still true that the Germans are burdened with all the responsibility for these dreadful events, while the other side, the victorious nations, wash their hands in innocence.

Germans Helping One another Rebuild Their Lives

Shortly after the end of the war, Germans started to help their fellow citizens within the country. My mother established the Hilfsdienst (Social Outreach Service) of the Heliand in 1945. As mentioned above, the Heliand was a group of Catholic women who wanted to live a Christian life based on Christian principles of peace, justice, and empathic mutuality.

Providing Goods and Services

Mother saw the enormous misery of the people. Since no one had money, she based her project on the idea that people who were neither bombed out nor were refugees and who still had employment could give some of their possessions to those who were in desperate need of them. This service, which included the donation of goods and a referral service for jobs and apartments, was oriented to members of Heliand and their families. People dropped off items they could spare at our apartment on the fourth floor of our building. We repackaged the items, addressed them, carried them down four flights of stairs again, and walked them to the post office using a little wooden handcart. Just as valuable as the material goods was the idea that people not feel abandoned in their poverty. My mother always reminded her fellow "sisters" to watch and care for each other, since often the poor feel ashamed of their poverty and don't express their needs.

Mother's interview with Dr. Doerr

Many of our acquaintances lost everything during a bombing raid in a single night. It was very difficult to replace these items only with ration cards. That's why I had the idea to create a service within the commu-nity: we would share in a sisterly fashion. During the first months, I re-ceived goods exclusively, no money. It is difficult to imagine today, how people lacked essential goods.

My mother then started a newsletter that listed needs and asked for help.

Excerpts from the first newsletter

– a mother asks for feathers for her children's beds. She has the cover. Which family or group can sacrifice the stuffing from a few sofa pillows?
– a refugee family asks for some sheets and blankets and a few dish towels;
– a winter coat, size 44, is desperately needed;
– heavy curtain material;
– who could spare a grater for a family with many children?
– and a sturdy comb.

The second newsletter mentions some results and asks for further help

Running this service is a joy. The letters that I receive show real concern and warm interest, especially among the older members. On the other hand, there is so much gratitude, which increases our responsibility. My sincere thanks to all who have already contributed goods, services, and money! Through your help, many needs have been addressed.

And now an added request: Watch out for each other and see whether someone needs help. Many times people are too shy to ask for help, especially when they need money. Please help so that none of our families is forgotten. I still do not have the addresses from the members in Silesia, who have fled and are now living with their families as refugees among us. They will need our help especially. Also, please send me addresses of single women who do not have an official connection to our groups, but are connected to us by their principles and ideology.

Already by the next letter, the donation of practical goods had expanded to services. She is asking for a helper in a household of a mother who is exhausted and sick; an apartment for a young family. She also offered jobs for women.

Complete list of needed items that my mother circulated

Clothes closet, sideboard, and shelves for a family with five youngsters; a winter coat (large size), shawl, and gloves for the blind brother of a member; a carpet or rug for a damp garden apartment with two toddlers; pillows, blankets, sheets, feathers, cover (does anybody have relatives in the country, who could give up some feathers?); heavy material for curtains, twice 126 to 153 cm and once 126 to 153 cm.; shoes and stockings size thirty-seven, thirty-eight, or thirty-nine (I know we all need those, but this is for an especially poor family. Please see if you can help.); two winter dresses, size forty-four; a knit cardigan; children's stockings, sizes four and five; a warm dress for an eight-year-old child; children's' shoes, sizes thirty-three and thirty-four; fabric for children's' nightgowns; dark blue material (for patching and mending); white or multi-colored tablecloth; a large kettle; sieves (multiple requests); clothesline and clothespins; laundry and shoe brushes; an enamel bowl for washing dishes; a kitchen knife; an electric connection cord for an iron (Gerätestecker); a small tub for bathing a baby; a baby carriage; sheet music for piano and beginner's literature for the piano; a French dictionary.

A member in Lower Bavaria is looking for a girl to help with her four children. Help with cleaning is provided.

A helper is needed in a good household in Würzburg with three children, aged eleven, eight, and five. Because of occupation restrictions for travel and relocation, only a girl from the area or a refugee can be considered.

A well-run smaller factory in Untertürkheim is still looking for female workers for light work with good remuneration. The owner values a Christian attitude and sense of responsibility. Because of occupation restrictions for travel and relocation, only local or refugee girls can be considered.

A refugee from the East is looking for a position in a Catholic household, preferably on a farm where in-depth learning of household and garden tasks is possible.

A kindergarten teacher is looking for an independent job.

Can somebody refer one or two rooms to a young couple in either Frankfurt or Wiesbaden?

Third newsletter, in which my mother summarizes the actions

Please send all addresses of the "our far-flung Heliand" and needy sisters to me. Our service has one big problem: it functions too slowly.

The individual needs are mostly of a pressing nature and should be dealt with quickly. I tried to address the problems by forwarding the requests directly to the different local groups. And the groups have really stepped up. I want to mention this here specifically.

What cannot be solved in the immediate small circle or group is sent back to me and published in the newsletter. Many groups have also shown initiative by sending me a list of items that their members can spare, which I can immediately access when a plea comes in.

In the Fall of 1947, in her fourth newsletter, my mother directly addresses the younger members of the group and asks them not to leave the work only to the older members:

Fourth newsletter, addressed to the younger members of the group

My dear younger sisters.... Every group is asked to carry out charitable work. That is the requirement of the hour. We would lose our justification for existence if the work in groups were only for the care and education of ourselves. We cannot ignore the misery of our days. We have to fight against it even with our small resources.

She then gives a few practical examples of how the different age groups can help. Everyone received the following advice:

Give to the poor what they need and not just what you want to get rid of. Heliand should not be known just for "lovely parents' nights and festive occasions." It should live up to its name in a most beautiful manner—practical charity work in the real world. You know yourselves this means more than just making a monetary sacrifice.

You need to rekindle love among the people again. We cannot educate our girls early enough, that actions follow words. Now we need people who don't just make noise, but who act quietly. That, in my opinion, is currently the job for us women.

Mother organized a fund-raising concert for the services. She also pointed out in this newsletter that this service was supposed to be limited in time:

Our service should not become a snake without an end. That would be too burdensome and unsettling for the ones who are contributing and doing the work. It should be a project that can come to fruition in a short period of time. I hope that I can say at the end of the year: we have procured so many goods and services that we have done everything in our power. Every one of our members owns a warm dress, a warm coat, and her own bed. After this the service will continue, but only as a support for individual families, especially financial support. The newsletter will become unnecessary then.

Letter from Thea, my mother's sister, to her family
[Thea, who was also a member of Heliand, entered the cloister in 1947]

Isa saw the needs of people. When our choir director was killed in the war, she wondered whether his widow needed help. I still remember one incident. In 1947 I was in the convent, but I did not have a comb (I hope you don't think nuns have feathers on their head!). In my need I contacted Isa. She then wrote in a newsletter: "Help! A comb!" that's how I got a comb from a Heliand donation.

My mother had asked from the beginning for monetary contributions and had started a checking account. But she knew that most of the women were not financially well off and had to fight for their own survival and could ill afford to contribute monetarily. In letters to the priest Georg Kifinger, who was the spiritual leader of the Heliand, are lines like these: "I distribute money without much checking, because our members do not abuse it.... So far, I have only given monetary support to refugees, widows, or women whose husbands are missing in action or are prisoners of war."

She could say this with confidence because the women who received help were known to the other members of Heliand.

Providing Monetary Support

A few years after the establishment of the Hilfsdienst, the kind of help needed changed: more money and fewer goods were demanded. After the monetary reform in 1948 money took on new importance, since now it had value.

Greeting Card/Art Card Fund-raiser

In 1951, after it became clear that the need for help was still greater than the voluntary contributions, my mother started an art card operation, or a card fund-raiser that, with the help of the central committee, was extended to the whole country. Cards with photos and sayings and a collection of art cards were selected from the growing supply of cards art publishers were now printing again. She negotiated with the publishers, made the selection, and ordered the card designs; she then organized the shipments: an average of 25,000 cards a year in the 1950s and 1960s. These cards were to be sold by Heliand members to collect more money for the needy. The orders came in for individual cards as well as for packets of twenty and fifty. And this from over 250 city groups. Each of them had to be counted, packaged, addressed, and taken to the post office. The addressees stayed in touch with her, so that they could place their orders; meanwhile she collected the money.

In the 1970s Mother handed over this operation to Helene Moehler.

Helene Moehler's recollections

To understand the effectiveness and relevancy of this function it helps to understand the reality of life at that time. Young girls in the community were lacking greatly in their experience of art. The museums, the theaters, the concert halls, almost everything was in ruins; in addition the art that had been labeled "Entartete Kunst" (degenerate art) under the Nazis and therefore prohibited, was totally unknown to the younger generation.

Right after the publishing houses started to issue art cards again, Isa contacted the ones that also included religious topics in their selection and the ones that offered favorable conditions for a charitable enterprise of this kind. She first negotiated with them about a yearly card project during the Christmas holidays, in order to offer them to the individual Heliand groups who were asked to sell them in turn.

The task was to select fifty designs from the continuously growing supply, which were sent to over 250 city groups. Purchases and sales were about 20,000 to 25,000 pieces. The profit from the sales was then directly used for the Service [Hilfsdienst]. By doing this, Isa added another big task to her daily life, which could only be successfully completed with the help of her family and some local friends in Stuttgart. Imagine: for many years, one room in the Paulus household, from September till December, was dedicated to the storage, sorting, and shipping of thousands of these cards. They were sorted into piles of twenty and fifty for each design. Sometimes they were returned and other times, new cards were ordered.

Custom-made cartons were supplied by a firm for the different shipments. Stamps were put on by hand without a stamp machine, and the parcels were walked to the post office. This meant counting, sorting, making piles, comparing the order lists with the various assortments, packaging, stacking for delivery to the post office and then bringing them to the post office in a little hand cart. She organized and implemented this project for years.

Years later the members of the community began to realize the magnitude of this project for the financial help it extended to needy members—and what this meant for all of them. Art, reproduced on postcards by artists from every European epoch, including modern art, got into the hands of these young women. The artists included painters like Emil Nolde, Paula Modersohn-Becker, the expressionists in general, all of them, artists who had been shunned and censored by the Nazis. The cards added a tasteful and educational instrument to the surrounding world that lay in rubble.

In 1952, after the goods and services project was replaced with financial aid, my mother gave an overview to Heliand.

Mother's diary, 1952

We support mothers with many children whose husbands were killed in the war or who were still prisoners of war, refugees from the East, people with illnesses, widows and orphans and families with many children. The emergency cases are increasing and the lack of money is becoming dire. In many cases our help is a drop in the bucket. This could lead to burnout and despair. Yet we will keep the spirit of helping alive with a consciousness for sacrifice. My aim is to help—at least in many cases—in such a comprehensive way that our help leads to permanent and noticeable improvement in the quality of life. Our community only makes sense and is justified if it also encompasses its weaker members.

To help as a community, unbureaucratically and in an uncomplicated and discreet manner—that was her goal, according to Helene Moehler.

[Note: I still remember vividly that I sorted postcards for hours after I was a bit older, probably around 1955. Since all this was voluntary work, the budget of the Hilfsdienst increased, allowing my mother to support fellow members of Heliand in the West and send about fifty packages to the Eastern zone of Germany. I remember when Pope Pius XII was very ill in 1958, I sorted cards and listened to the hourly radio reports till he died.]

Helene Moehler's recollections (continued)

The recipients of these charities changed over time. Fewer and fewer young mothers whose husbands were listed as missing or prisoners of war, people who were bombed out or refugees, needed help. Now it was the older women with minimal pensions, single people who were sick, daughters of business owners who had lost their parents or their businesses in the war and never received a professional education, women with children whose marriages had crumbled and who needed financial help. Students with little financial help received loans and newlyweds were helped with their household purchases.

How were these needs identified? That was the beauty of the group, which had only about 8,000 members nationwide. Isa obtained informa-

tion through local group leaders and priests, who for their part treated every case confidentially. She trusted that the information was legitimate and she in turn was trusted to help the most serious cases. Later confidentiality became especially important when the help was extended to members who lived in the Eastern zone of Germany (the Russian-occupied zone). Help was given directly to those in need without a bureaucratic intermediary.

I haven't even mentioned yet the extensive correspondence that Isa started with the donors and the recipients of the help. Due to Isa's extreme discretion we don't have copies of those letters, but we know from other members of our groups how important this work was for her: to advise, to comfort, to negotiate on behalf of the ones who needed help, to help, and to include the needy in her prayers.

Before my mother handed over the Hilfsdienst and the card fund-raiser in the1970s to Helene Moehler, she had collected and spent about 75,000 marks in addition to the goods and services provided. Many of the donations came in small amounts since many of the donors had also lost most of their possessions and income and were only slowly becoming financially stable.

After the official handover of the services, my family continued to send about fifty packages per year to the people in the East till 1991, two years after the fall of the Berlin Wall, when people started to have access to goods again.

Other families also sent packages. I remember the most coveted items before the fall of the Wall were coffee (including instant coffee), chocolate and other sweets and cookies, canned fruit, pancake mixes, and also washcloths, towels, hose and later pantyhose, toothpaste, face cream, and dresses. Some of the recipients reciprocated with art books that were plentiful in the East and handmade straw stars for Christmas trees, which to this day decorate my own tree in the States.

Excerpts from letters show how long this service went on:

Isa to Margrit [me], February 3, 1987: "I have to say goodbye, because I have to go to the post office to send my packages to the East zone."

December 15, 1987: "Now at last I am done with the packages to the East. (I sent forty-eight coffee packages this year.)"

November 9, 1980, Finnentrop
Dear Frau Paulus,

Many thanks for your package with all the clothing…. I have sent most of the clothes to the monastery in Neisse. They can use every piece. Just a few days ago, I received a letter from the abbot, telling me that they can use clothes. They have 250 theology students. You can send everything there directly, from shoelaces to a heavy winter coat. I myself travel to Poland because I know some priests there who live in indescribably poor conditions. No priest receives a salary and they live on what the parishioners can give them. But their vocations are up. This year I have sent forty-eight packages to Poland. Everywhere there are grateful recipients. With good wishes.

U.S. Foreign Aid—Private, Nonprofit Agencies, and Government

General

One of the reasons Germans survived after the war was the generosity of the American people. (The British, French, and Russians had themselves suffered much in the war and were not able to help a great deal.) Much has been written about the Marshall Plan and its role in the rebuilding of Europe; I want to concentrate on private help. Many Germans who had either friends or relatives in the United States received regular relief packages. For example, the wife of one of my uncles had an aunt who had emigrated long before the war and sent food packages regularly.

But many people who didn't have personal connections also received official packages sent by the American agency CARE. In our case, the packages were distributed by the parish or in schools.

Another form of help was the person-to-person assistance that was given to Germans by the occupying troops.

Letter from Erna Kink, my brother Bernd's mother-in-law

When I was pregnant with my first child in 1945 and saw no possibility of getting to the hospital, I asked the American commander of the troops in our area for help. He told me to write a letter, which I did immediately. Shortly after my contractions started the commander sent a young soldier with a jeep, who kept on looking nervously at the pregnant woman next to him. When we arrived at the hospital, he gave me peppermint candy as a present. He visited me once more in the hospital during one of his patrols and laid more peppermint candy into the crib of my son.

I heard of other good deeds by the Americans. For example, an American pilot flew very low over the field of a farmer and dropped tobacco down to him (at that time a precious commodity). Often soldiers gave sweets to the children. I had to go into the neighboring village one winter day and on the way back was caught in a snowstorm. A U.S. military vehicle with a German prisoner of war drove by and gave me a ride. When I disembarked, the soldier gave me a large loaf of bread.

Aunt Resi's diary

After the Americans had moved out of our house and we moved back in, the highest American general, General Patton moved into a neighboring house. One day the girls returned home with chocolate that they showed me proudly. They admitted under questioning that they had begged the American soldiers for it, saying that all the children were doing it. I was upset: accepting sweets was one thing, but to beg for it, quite another matter. I strictly forbade them to ever beg again.

[Note: Begging was actually common. A friend of mine, who originally came from Gosbach, told me: "We would often walk from Gosbach to

Mühlhausen, where the autobahn from Stuttgart to Munich came through, and stand there for hours waiting for an American military convoy to come by, because the soldiers who saw the hungry people on the side of the road would often toss their military food rations to us."]

The children must have obeyed, because one day when we passed the house, General Patton was standing on the balcony. He spoke to me and said that our children were so nice, and that they never begged like the others. He asked whether he could give them chocolate occasionally. When he returned from a vacation in the United States, he brought back clothes from his grandchildren, almost new and really sweet. Unfortunately he was killed in an accident shortly afterwards in Luxemburg. Then two other generals moved into that house. One of the families had children about the same age as ours, which meant ours often got ice cream and cake. Once they were invited to a party for the officers' children. Their children often played in our sandbox. One day they asked me, whether I could give them some dark bread, but we had hardly enough for ourselves. I therefore suggested to them that they could get dark bread if they gave us their white bread in exchange. So, everybody was happy.

Help Given to the Family of My Husband, Warren Roth

My own family didn't have any U.S. connections, so I use my husband Warren's family as an example of the importance of American help. His grandparents, Adam Roth and Ottilie Spielman, had emigrated to the United States in 1891 from the same small village in Bavaria, Soden, near Aschaffenburg. They came separately in steerage because the ship's passage was cheaper for single people. Since Warren's grandmother was seasick the whole three weeks of the voyage, she had no desire to ever go back home for a visit. There had been regular correspondence between the families before World War I and in between the two world wars. This correspondence was interrupted, however, during both wars. The first timid inquiries into whether any family members on both sides of the ocean were still alive were made in 1947, after the Americans had again normalized the mail service. Warren's grandfather had died in 1938, but since mail service was interrupted during the war his relatives in Germany did not discover this till 1947. His grandmother also found out that of her nine siblings only three were still living, and of her husband's siblings, only one was still alive.

Till her death in 1948, Warren's grandmother sent packages of food and clothing regularly. After that her children followed her example. Excerpts of the thank you letters from the recipients in Germany show how appreciated these valuable shipments were. As far as can be gleaned from the few surviving letters, the packages were distributed among the families of the surviving brothers and sisters of both grandparents. They were mainly small peasants.

Excerpts follow of letters from Germany that were sent to my husband's grandmother in New York. (The letters sent *from* New York are not in our possession, if they still exist.) The letters from Germany deal with the human costs of a war and the misery and poverty that follows a war. They also demonstrate the dependence of the German relatives on the generosity of their American family members.

Letters sent to Warren Roth's grandmother from her siblings and their children

From a brother

I was not part of this war, but served in Russia in the last war. Those times when you were still here were the best years; they were different times from the ones that we now have. The ones who died happily are the lucky ones. When will better times come? We don't know. I am wondering which generation will experience better times.... So many are still prisoners of war. Some will be treated well, but not all. There are certainly many family fathers among them.

From another brother, who was a monk

Now I have to do cleaning jobs, which I like quite a bit. We have so few men now because so many were killed in the war. And we don't have any new recruits. Dear sister, if you want to and can send something, I would like to ask you for sugar and coffee. If possible! I don't know whether you can or not. But no money, rather nothing. I presume you have no cigars or cigarettes. I don't know whether the package will arrive or whether it will be stolen on the way. But no money.

From one of her nephews

I have three children. One son lost his right leg in the war.... You have written that your sons have clothes that they no longer wear. We would be very grateful if you could send them. Almost everything that we need for daily life we can get only with ration cards, including clothes and shoes. We hope that things will be better soon.

From the brother in the monastery

After a long wait, your package has arrived. I will tell you what was in it: 2 bags of flour; 1 tin of coffee; 1 package of sugar; 2 chocolate bars; 2 tins of margarine; 2 tins of dried milk; and 2 soap bars. The rest of the tins were sausage and...meat.

[Note: An American friend, after reading the paragraph above, explained: "We kept a journal of every item in every package. The recipient wrote back what they actually received because very often the packages had been opened and items taken from it.... The postman often bartered directly for the stamps or various contents."]

We are a conquered nation; we have lost the war and that has all kinds of consequences. For a long time, we have not had sugar or fat—not even enough for cooking. Then the...skim milk. Meat we only see once or twice a week and that's not much.... This summer was very hot and everybody suffered. We also have nothing to stoke our stoves with. Especially coal. Everything is lacking.... The children who are now growing up will have a hard life; they are undernourished.... Have already tasted the first cup of coffee from your package. And the canned sausage. And the chocolate. During our hard times, these are wonderful things. In former times, we wouldn't have asked for these things, because we had them ourselves. The saying is that the times are astonishing. But we have to get through them; there is no way around it. Anybody who has survived has to be part of it.

We have a beautiful church, but very many windows were blown out during the war. We cannot replace them because no glass is available. Reconstruction is a very slow process, because we lack everything. Again my heartfelt thanks for the package.

From another brother, October 28, 1947

It was a great surprise that we received a letter from J.H. [a nephew] to whom you had written. I have often inquired about you, and whether somebody had heard from you, but no one knew anything—so now we received your surprising letter.... Unfortunately we lost the war and are now poor people who have nothing to say because the other countries have their say. Dear sister, you want to know how we are doing and what we do. We have seven children, three boys and four girls. I will tell you about them in order of age.

1. Rosa is married with a husband who is a tailor, but lost his right arm in the war.

2. Ludwig is married, but is still a Russian prisoner of war.

3. Maria is married in Soden with a husband who became disabled in the war.

4. Franziska and her five-year-old daughter live with us; she had a husband who unfortunately was killed in Russia on October 7, 1943.

5. Hilbert also lives with us. He lost all of his toes on both feet, but can walk pretty well.

6. Anton is married in Gailbach. He is also a tailor and was drafted at age seventeen, sent to Russia, and still has about ten pieces of shrapnel in his body. I feel sorry for him.

7. Paulina is the youngest. She learned how to be a seamstress, lives with us, and is twenty-one years old....

...It is a long trip to America otherwise we would have visited each other. The planes fly too high, that's too far from the ground; I have never seen as many planes as during the war. You cannot imagine how it looked here. You would not recognize Aschaffenburg, just as you wouldn't recognize many other cities. They have started to rebuild, but all materials are lacking.... This year was very hot. No rain all summer, everything is dried out. The potatoes are very small and wilted; we had planted them all on the sunny side, we didn't harvest more than ten zentners and the wild pigs ate almost half of that; we have so many wild pigs, they come all the way into our farm.... The corn that we planted was being dug up by the wild pigs—there are still a few potatoes in the ground. The meadows are all burrowed into where they are not completely dry because the pigs look for grubs, but they destroy everything in their path; it's a great plague and we have no rifles to shoot them. If we could shoot them, we would have fat and meat; this way we are suffering from starvation [all rifles and the like had to be handed over to the occupation forces]. Our foodstuffs are so insufficient.... Also the bread, we receive one pound weekly per person and everything else is rationed.... When the Americans marched in, we billeted six men and I asked one of them who spoke German about your sons, but he couldn't give me any information, and so the time went on till they departed.

From a sister-in-law, November 9, 1947

...during this war I had to suffer a lot. Because of the bombing raids we hadn't a quiet moment day or night. The bombing raids were heavy attacks on the city and the surrounding areas; a few bombs fell in our village also. Every window in the house was blown out.... One cannot believe it.... Of my nine children, seven are still alive. One girl died and one boy was killed in the war.... My brother Lorenz died. He was in bed for eight weeks; I spent much time with him because only his daughter was with him. His son was still in the war, and by the time he returned both his parents had died....

Lastly, I want to explain that the situation in Germany is very bad. One has to buy everything with ration cards; you can't even think of a roll or white bread, because there is no flour for it. Dear Ottilie—the son in whose house I am living—has one son, who is still a Russian prisoner of war, and three girls. It is difficult with the girls since....one can't buy anything.... Now we'll shiver all winter.

From a brother in the German U.S. zone, March 15, 1948

I want to express my "may God repay you" [Vergelts Gott] for the wonderful packets you sent to us. I was present when the packages were opened. We were very astonished about their contents because we can't buy...any clothes. We distributed everything in a brotherly fashion from the biggest boy to the smallest child. Everything worked out fine. We have little fat because the cattle had to be slaughtered during the summer due to the extreme drought—and now we have nothing left.... Again many thanks, and thanks from my wife.

From a sister-in-law, April 18, 1948, Soden

I want to thank you especially for the beautiful and good skirt you sent me, because here we can't get any clothes. It's been eight years since we have been able to buy anything. Dear sister-in-law, that's why we appreciate so much anything we receive. You cannot imagine how many people are helped in their need when we receive that many packages from America. Now we have to experience misery and poverty again in our old age; I never thought that this would be the case.

From a nephew, April 21, 1948

I want to thank you and our dear cousins for the second package that arrived on April 14 with clothes for us men. The suits and coats that fit me and my uncles perfectly were still in very good condition. We were very glad to get them. We divided everything into three equal parts....

This year we received American potatoes for the first time to stick in the ground. We have a real plague with the wild pigs and last year we had the great drought—that's why in all of Germany there were hardly any potatoes. Never in my wildest imagination did I think that I would eat your potatoes; they are okay, but there is a big difference: yours are very thick, while ours are of medium size and beautifully mealy. We are awaiting more news from you and your pictures.

My daughter just now told me to ask you for something. While she was attending the household school in Aschaffenburg, from 1943 to 1945, she lost all of her clothes and undergarments during a bombing raid. Do William's daughters have something they don't wear anymore so that she might have something? She mostly needs stockings, size nine and a half and shoes size six and a half. I support her wish, but if you don't have anything, perhaps there is another well-meaning family of German extraction who hasn't sent any packages to Germany yet and who could spare some items. My daughter asked me to make sure to mention that she would not beg if she wasn't so needy. But misery forces us to do things we normally wouldn't do. I am closing with many thanks and thanks to God.

From a nephew or niece, April 27, 1948, Soden, German U.S. zone
Right at the beginning of this letter accept heartfelt greetings from your old home. It was a very, very big and unexpected and joyous surprise for all of us when we received the news that you loved ones from the United States had sent us two more packages. They were distributed in brotherly satisfaction. We want to thank you very much for these very valuable things. Special thanks from my father for the wonderful shoes, they fit perfectly, and he did not expect to get shoes.

Oh, there is so much need here, especially for clothes; one has to wait for months just to get an application for a coupon, then another long time to get the coupon, and then one hopes to be lucky to find the appropriate garment. These are really bad times, especially in these matters, but unfortunately there is nothing we unimportant people can do about it. Well, we just have to be content, do it, accept it. There are constantly small traces of the lost war that appear every day. I believe we don't have to pretend in front of you, I am sure you have heard enough about our way of life—what it looks like in Germany and in our neighborhood in the Spessart during these bitter times.

Dear aunt and cousins, it is devastating—yes, one has to say it—unbearable with the plague of the wild pigs. They come in packs of twenty, twenty-eight, thirty, even thirty-five—oh, a person who hasn't seen this can't imagine or see how much destruction these beasts leave in their wake: yes, they dig up more potatoes in one night than a peasant can *plant in three or four days. How can poor small peasants like us still have joy in farming when these beasts destroy everything. Yes, dear aunt and cousins, every night two or three of us go out in the fields and the meadow and protect our corn and potatoes so that we can have some crops to harvest.*

From a brother
In the USA it must be excellent. Food and other things without ration cards—we have not known that for ten years. We do not know how long it will be this way in Germany.

From a brother, June 15, 1948, Soden [written in English, obviously with help]
On the 8th of June we received your two packets of clothes, which we divided amongst three families on the same day. For this we thank you. Dear Otto [Warren's father], you cannot feel how many joy had our wives and daughters, if they saw the clothes and all of the beautiful things. My dear Otto, my wife said, "How to do them also enjoy, which have done us so many and how to thank them." God repay you all....
You cannot thank God enough, that you are living in the United States. It is bad that we are living separated by the great ocean. Otherwise we could visit you, this to-day is impossible and it will take a long time till we can get a travelling permission to the US. At this time I and my wife will never live in this world.

Children's Transports to Switzerland by the U.S. Agency, CARE

My first trip to another country came in 1948, shortly before the monetary reform, when my parish selected me to be one of about fifty children to spend some time in Switzerland—thanks to the U.S. agency, CARE. They selected undernourished or sickly children to spend three months with foster parents to improve their physical condition. This is how I came to spend three months with the Lüthi family in Muri, Canton Aargau. I was issued a children's passport that I kept around my neck for the whole trip. We took the train from Stuttgart to Schaffhausen and then changed to a train to Zurich, where the foster parents picked us up. I was picked up by the twenty-four-year-old daughter Annie, who took me to Muri where I met Mrs. Lüthi ("Aunt Lüthi"), a widow, and her oldest son, Koby. Her younger son was in the Swiss military (all able-bodied Swiss males have to serve some time in the military); I met him later on one of his visits. While some foster parents used the children as cheap labor, especially on farms, I drew the grand prize. The family owned a big house that originally belonged to the monastery in the village.

The first night I was very homesick, especially since I had a hard time understanding the Swiss German that the family spoke, but after that I never looked back. Adjacent to their house was a big vegetable garden and fruit orchard. Aunt Lüthi and her daughter spoiled me. For the first time, I remember having enough to eat, even getting some chocolate and tropical fruit. Since Annie was a seamstress, she sewed me nice clothes and Aunt Lüthi knitted a warm woolen sweater for me. I earned a few cents by knitting covers for clothes hangers. When I stretched my knitted work quite a lot to avoid having to knit more, the family normally accepted it with a smile. Only when I tried to get away with very little work, did they put their foot down. Most of my "hard-earned" money went, of course, for sweets.

When I first arrived in the village, there were people there who distrusted Germans. I was very proud of my "aunt" when someone said that Germans act poor so they can get more handouts. She answered: "That's not the case with our child. Her mother saved ration cards so that she could buy her a new dress in order for her to look decent when she got to Switzerland." I went to school for one month, but when neighbors noticed that a few times I vomited into the river on the way back from school, the adults decided that I should concentrate on just having fun and gaining weight. I don't know whether it was school that stressed me out so much: my teacher scolded me often for writing too small and using every inch of the paper. Or perhaps I unwittingly invited the envy of the other children. The teacher would assign work in class and when you were finished you had to go up and have your work checked. If it was correct, you were asked to stand in a line till the last kid had finished the assignment. Since I had been instructed in an urban school where every class had their own teacher while the Swiss pupils were in a typical village school with four grades in the same class room, I was always the first one to finish the assignment and ended up at the first spot in the line. This did not endear me to my classmates. I tried to slow down my work, but the teacher noticed it. After I stopped attending school, I became good friends with many of the children.

Two more firsts followed: I learned how to swim and ride a bike, which would have been impossible at that time in Germany. The family also showed me much of beautiful German Switzerland, all by train and bus.

But my biggest adventure was when I helped in the production of "Most," an alcoholic apple cider. I had already learned how to climb trees in Schnittlingen and this came in handy when I was asked to climb into the higher branches and either collect apples in a little basket around my neck or throw them down to people who held open a cloth. But the best part came last. I was allowed—with my bare feet—to pound and mash the apples in a big vat till only the skin was left and all the juice had been siphoned off. The cider was then allowed to ferment for alcoholic cider, but a certain amount was kept back for me to enjoy. This was called sweet cider. Very delicious!

After three months the wonderful time in Switzerland was over. I had gained eleven pounds. When my aunt went with me to her friends in the village to say my good-byes, I received many presents of food, clothing, and other necessities, all of which were difficult to come by in Stuttgart. I was really petrified that the customs people would accuse me of smuggling and confiscate my loot, but they left our children's transport undisturbed. My first experience with smuggling came to a good end!

This enormous "loot" led again to one of the famous family lists, written by my mother. What Margit brought back from Schwitzerland: 3 salami sausages; 1 slab of bacon; one package of cookies; one package of sugar (very precious!); 1 tin of cheese; 1 tin of sausage; 1.5 pounds of butter; 1 pound of cocoa butter (*kokosfett*); 12 chocolate bars; 2 oranges; 1 tin *Einmalzin* (maltpowder – when mixed with milk or water, it makes a sweet drink); 2 large bars of soap and 2 face soaps; 2 skeins of real wool; 3 knitted stockings and socks for me; stockings for Mutti and socks for Vati; 1 pair knee-highs; gloves; 2 skirts; 2 pullovers; 2 knitted cardigans; 3 aprons; 3 undershirts; 1 knitted cap; 3 underpants; 1 pair shoes; 1 blouse and pajamas.

My family treasured every one of these items.

When I arrived home, my brothers were interested mostly in the "goods," while my parents couldn't get over the fact that I had a very heavy Swiss–German pronunciation. (I can still speak Schwizerdeutsch.)

The family invited me back to their house in 1949 and 1951 for a month each time. These times I traveled by myself, again with my children's passport around my neck, went through customs and immigration, and switched trains in Schaffhausen. I was so afraid that I wouldn't be able to figure out which trains to change to, but the conductors were all very nice and there was no problem. Annie also visited us in Stuttgart.

Mother's diary

A big event occurred in Margit's short life. On August 17 she went with a children's transport, organized by CARE, to Switzerland, where she can stay for three months. She lives with the family Lüthi in Muri in Aargau.
November 1948

One has to say that Margit couldn't have had a more wonderful trip and a more wonderful family. She looks good, has put on weight, and came back with a suitcase full of wondrous and rare goods (twelve chocolate bars!) and with such a heavy Swiss accent that we could hardly understand her. This stay was invaluable for her. She was also given a whole set of new clothes; we cannot be grateful enough to the Lüthi family.

First Communion

One of the big events of 1947 was my first communion. This was a year before the monetary reform, which meant that everything still had to be bought on ration cards and few goods were in the stores because the money was becoming increasingly valueless. My white communion dress was a hand-me-down from my older cousin Elinor; I in turn turned it over to my next cousin, Dagmar, after two years. My shoes were my ordinary shoes, brown not white. My long communion candle was my baptismal candle. For my silver communion cross, my mother had to give up a silver spoon. But for the first time I was taken to a hairdresser who gave me lovely curls.

Mother's diary

The day of the first communion, April 13, 1947, was a beautiful day, the first warm and sunny day after this long and unforgiving winter. The church of St. Fidelis had just been rebuilt, so that the celebration was for the first communion children as well as the rebirth of the parish. The children were asked to offer special prayers. Margit prayed for her missing uncle Robert, her fallen uncle Karl, and the health of her Vati.

For us adults it was a real family celebration. We could only afford to invite her two grandparents for lunch, but many family members joined us for afternoon coffee. After the many years of hunger in the war and the postwar years, we enjoyed cups of real coffee and cakes and tortes. Of course, our family could not procure all the good things ourselves, so everyone contributed something to the feast.

Here is a sample of gifts that I received, some of which were not of particular interest for an eight-year-old child, but were very much appreciated by the family. It's interesting to see what one could buy then, like flowers and handkerchiefs: about eleven arrangements of flowers; two pounds of flour and some eggs; two cans of half-and- half; about five wooden boxes, some handmade or hand painted; handkerchiefs; two drawings made by the donors; a picture frame; a flute that I still keep in a drawer and sometimes take out at Christmastime; a silver napkin ring with my name on it, which I still have; a garnet necklace and some bracelets; and a special gift from my aunt in Austria: cocoa; currants; two lemons, and chocolate.

I also received thirty marks, but cannot remember whether I was allowed to spend them or whether they were saved for me.

A special treat were two telegrams from relatives in the Rhineland who couldn't come to the celebration. I do also remember receiving some children's' books, among them the Icelandic stories of Nonni and Manni, which I bought again years later on a trip to Iceland. My parents gave me a children's bible, a New Testament, and a book cover; one of my brothers gave me the Elfer Raus card game (from the look of the deck that is still in Stuttgart, this is the original deck from 1947!); from my other brother, the Kinderlieder Quartett card game.

Mother's diary

The next day we invited a few of Margit's friends. The following week, Margit and I accompanied Vati to Stetten. He then took a train on to the TB sanatorium in Schwäbisch Gemünd, while Margit and I went for a long walk through the Remstal during the cherry blossom time.

The following excerpts from Uncle Richards's diary give insight into the thinking of many Germans. Even after the war he did not grasp the magnitude of the German atrocities. He is trying to shift some of the guilt onto the Allies. He doesn't show much sympathy for the victims of the Nazis, but rather feels bad for the perpetrators, whom he feels were not treated fairly. An overdeveloped patriotism blinds him to the crimes committed by his home country.

Uncle Richard's diary, 1947

January 14

Preparations for the peace treaties with Germany and Austria were begun by the secretaries of state of the so-called victor nations. Present are also representatives of eighteen smaller nations. Characteristic of the spirit in which the negotiations will be conducted is the fact that representatives of Germany—whose fate will be determined—are not permitted to attend.

Representatives of Austria were inexplicably included. Austria was the country that in great part paid special homage to Nazism and from whence the "Führer" originates. The negotiations ended in February with almost no results.

March 3

We received eight liters of oil from sixty-four pounds of beech seeds that we collected in the autumn of 1946.

March 10

In Moscow (nomen est omen), the "peace negotiations" for Germany and the so-called State Treaty with Austria have begun. Germans are not permitted in either as delegates or as reporters. Therefore one can draw conclusions about the spirit in which these "negotiations" are being conducted. Doubts that a useful result will follow are therefore widespread.

March 21

I read in the newspaper "the mail committee of the Allies" decided at their last meeting that the weight limit of packages within Germany will be raised from half a kilo to one kilo.

April 24

The peace conference in Moscow, which began on March 10, ended. Almost nothing was achieved even though the secretaries met for six weeks.

May 30

Achaz was taken by ambulance to the hospital in Geislingen because of a knee injury. He was discharged as healed only on November 26.

July 4

Erich Tietze leaves Donzdorf and travels to Cologne to start his new job. Since he was discharged on September 22, 1945, as a prisoner of war [after seven months in a Russian prison] he spent his time either here in Schnittlingen or in Donzdorf with his family, recuperating.

For the second time, on November 25, the secretaries of state met—this time in London—to discuss the peace treaty for Germany. Again, the Germans are excluded from the discussion. The prospects for a successful result of the discussions are very bad.

November 26

We heard that a relative of ours had died in 1944 in a Russian prisoner of war camp. He was thirty-four years old and left a widow and three children.

December 2

The oldest inhabitant of Schnittlingen, Maria Anna Brühl, died as a result of an accident [she fell down some stairs]. She would have been ninety-three in January 1948. She didn't have children of her own, but raised her husband's children [among them pastor Georg Brühl, who died in 1941]. She survived all of them.

December 4

Our niece Thea says good-bye to the family. She is entering the

Carmelite Convent in Hoheneck near Ludwigsburg on December 8.

December 13

The Tietze family moves to Cologne, where Erich has been working since July at a cheese factory. Erich and Armin drive with the moving van, while Maria and Elinor take the train.

The Neue Württemberg Zeitung *writes on December 16 regarding the number of deaths during the aerial bombardment of Heilbronn on December 4, 1944: "The official number has now been released by the town administration. It is 6,504. Of these 5,140 persons are buried in cemeteries, while 1,364 bodies could not be recovered."*

Living Conditions Immediately after the End of the War

Aunt Resi's diary

And now I have to add something about nutrition and its procurement. What we received in calories through the ration cards was minimal. Occasionally our au pair would bring us some asparagus during the season, a delicacy, but no calories. The only things we had in sufficient quantities were potatoes, beans, and cabbage. I had a bit of fruit in the garden, and we could buy apples and pears, but no bananas. Once an announcement was made that there was a special offer of oranges. I stood in the marketplace in a long line with the children. People kept pushing into the line, till the salesclerk shouted: "Why don't you let the 'miss' with the kids through?"

The situation got worse after the war, and the time of bargaining started. Anything that one didn't need desperately was exchanged for groceries. Since one of my au pairs had stolen my jewelry, we had little to bargain with. The saying went around that the peasants ended up with so many Oriental carpets that they could decorate their stables with them. During a visit to Aachen, I begged a bag of sewing needles from a company that I knew. I kept a few for myself, but the rest I exchanged during my visits to peasants for eggs and bacon. Sometimes I had to resort to begging. The bread was very poor, made of cornmeal. The children could not eat it, since we had nothing to put on it. That's when I toasted the pieces of bread over the open gas flame, skimmed off the cream from the milk, and spread it over the bread. We also had no fish. When my father visited, we went for a walk along the Regnitz, where we were surprised by a violent thunderstorm. On the shore we saw an eel that had been thrown onto the bank by the wind and waves. We grabbed the fighting fish and carried it home in a rain coat, put it in a big bowl in the laundry room, killed it the next day, and had a delicious meal when my brother-in-law came to visit [my father]. Heinz, the lawyer, informed us that this was a crime, when we told him where we got the eel. But Ingrid just stroked her little stomach and replied, "yummy, yummy"!

Then there was the "meat bank." Once a week at the Kranen Square Market meat was sold from animals that had to be slaughtered. One could receive double rations for one's cards. I usually stood in line at six in the morning to garner some meat for goulash and sauerbraten. Once Kurt's boss invited us for dinner. When we complimented his wife on the good meal, she told us that it was horse meat. She had connections to the horse butcher.

I can't remember how we made the connections, but when we visited a farm one day, the farmer's wife admired my children's clothes. I told her that I had sewn them myself. She said that she had exchanged lots of foodstuffs for fabrics, but had no one to sew clothes from it. I agreed to sew for her and for a whole week, I went to the farm early in the morning every day and sewed clothes for her and her children. We got a substantial meal for lunch and at the end of the week I received eggs, bacon, good bread, and even a slaughtered rabbit. In my backyard I was also raising rabbits, which every so often graced our table.

Occasionally Kurt's company gave us light bulbs that I exchanged on my trips to the farms. That's how we got through the rough times. We were all thin, skinny, but generally healthy. Only our nerves were negatively affected. The children could play in the street, since there was almost no traffic. Occasionally a horse-drawn carriage passed, and when the horses dropped their "apples" I ran out and scooped them up with my broom and shovel—to the great consternation of my mother-in-law. But I needed it as fertilizer for my vegetable garden. We augmented our meals by collecting mushrooms. After the war, it was not advisable as a woman to walk alone in the dark. Too many crimes were committed.

During the summer we had raw tomatoes with bread, as a salad. I made tomato sauce, tomato soup, and tomato vegetable, and especially tomato ketchup. If I remember correctly, we had to cut them into small cubes and then mix them with salt, vinegar, and cubed onions. Then we poured them into jars. Our friends also profited from our cornucopia of tomatoes. Besides the potato, the tomato is the most versatile vegetable.

In February 1948 I wrote in my own handwriting into the diary that my mother had started for me shortly after my birth:

> *Last August I was in summer camp on the Mühlbach farm. It was very nice. They always had good food. In September I started fourth grade. My teacher is Frl. Korherr. I like going to school. My favorite subject is reading. I read a lot at home too. Too bad there are so few books. At Christmas I got a little oven.*

Mother's diary, 1948

February

I often think that it is good that my oldest is a girl. I don't know how I could run the household without her. She does much of the shopping, carries the wood and coal from six flights down up to the apartment, and goes into the deep cellar to bring up potatoes and apples. I often wonder that she doesn't express any fear. [Not true, see above.] She now gets 1 mark allowance a week.

February

    When it's cold outside, Karl Heinz says, "my teeth chatter." When Margit was being punished for something, he stated: "I feel sorry for myself on account of Margit." And he flatters me: "Mutti, you golden one, isn't it good that you have me?" When the children were debating how they could manage to get across the border to Austria to visit their cousin, he had an answer: "You know what, I'll jump into the mailman's bag; he'll bring me to Bregenz." And when he doesn't like our demands, he diplomatically tells me that "I would do it differently with my children." When, the other day, we had cocoa and I told them that we could only afford one cup for each, he finished his cup, then climbed on Vati's lap and said, "It's a pity," and when Vati asked: "What's a pity?" he answered with a sad face: "About the cocoa." What else could Vati do but give him the rest of his?

    Heinz's large stamp collection has not only captured his own heart, but also the hearts of the boys. When he was sitting next to Vati, he asked: "Will we get the stamp collection, when you are dead?" "Yes." And after a while: "Perhaps you could eat something poisonous." And still a bit later: "No, I know, don't eat anything, then you'll die."

    Last summer Uncle Willi and Aunt Lilli came for a visit with their large official Maybach car and driver, which created a lot of excitement in the neighborhood. The boys were driven twice to kindergarten. And once the whole family was driven to visit Vati in the sanatorium. Karl Heinz was so overwhelmed by this trip that he didn't say a word the whole time. He only pointed out each gas station. It's incredible what amazes children.

    Last summer he was in Schnittlingen for three weeks by himself. He loved all the animals, but I was astonished at how wild he has become. Yet, grandma and the aunts told me that he insisted whenever some good food was prepared that part of it should go to us in Stuttgart.

    He also spent some time with the Weilands again, and when he returned he told us proudly: "You don't have to buy me a watch, I'll get a gold watch from my uncle Olo."

Uncle Richard's diary, 1948

January 17

    We received a relief package from a relative in Rorschach [Switzerland], who sent it more than a month ago. Its contents: one pound of coffee; one bag of a concoction that was used to "stretch" the real coffee [Kaffeezusatz]; one bag of hazelnuts; one bag of raisins; three bags of sugar substitutes; five sewing needles; one safety pin; one skein of mending thread; one skein of wool; four white Christmas tree candles;

one package of laundry powder; and one calendar.

February 2
   *A general twenty-four-hour protest strike took place in the American
zone of Baden-Württemberg because of the dreadful food situation. It
also involved the entire transportation system, trains, and mail.*

February14
   *In February, Walter B. from Stuttgart visited us. He was the supplier of
my photographic equipment for many years. However, he lost his house
during a bombardment. The equipment he had in storage was stolen
during his absence, while he was serving in the war.*

March 8
   *Our farm helper, whom we hired only a few weeks ago, had to leave
us because he could not show any papers. He was without a doubt the
main perpetrator of the break-in in April* [see below].

April 28–29
   *During the night a break-in occurred in the basement of my house.
Sixty to seventy glass jars with stewed meat, fruit, various tools, and a
twenty-five-centimeter-long cable was stolen.*

The Monetary Reform and Germany's Economic Recovery

In June 1948 the real recovery of Germany began. With the help of the massive infusion of
money through the Marshall Plan and the monetary reform, economic progress accelerated
at a fast pace.

   One day, every family member received forty new marks by giving up four hundred
Reichsmarks; eventually people's savings were exchanged ten to one: e.g. for every accu-
mulated 1,000 Reichsmarks or Rentenmarks or for marks issued by the military authorities
they received 100 new marks. This was a real burden on the people who had saved money,
but it did stop the creeping inflation and started the new economic boom. Everybody had to
apply for this exchange and give the government the following information about each family member: first and last names; birthdates; relationship to head of household; profession,
if appropriate; name of the person holding a savings account; name of the bank; account
number; whether the account was blocked or not according to regulation fifty-two; amount
of money; and the amount of money the persons wanted to exchange.

   I do remember that my family of five was entitled to receive 200 new marks in exchange for 2,000 old marks. My father did not have that much money on hand and had to
borrow from his mother. I also remember that after the exchange our bakery, which had
closed its doors for a few days was re-opened and we could again purchase bread.

Diary Writers Described This Enormous Event

Aunt Resi's diary

*In 1948 the monetary reform took place, and now the shops were full
of merchandise. Everyone received forty DM* [Deutsche marks] *on June*

20, 1948, and another twenty DM in August. All savings accounts were devalued ten to one. It wasn't so bad for us; we had hardly any savings, but my parents had started a savings account for each of the children, which were now almost without value. We were still hungry in 1948. Only at the beginning of 1950 were the ration cards slowly phased out and on March 31, totally suspended.

Uncle Richard's diary

In the evening of June 18, at 7:45, it was announced that the monetary reform was going to be implemented. On Sunday, the 20th, each person will receive sixty marks in DMs after a one-to-one exchange of sixty marks in old money. The final accounting of one to ten [one DM for ten Reichsmarks] will be done later. Old money can no longer be used after June 21, with the exception of old money up to one mark, but only in a one-to-ten exchange. Old money has to be handed in at a bank, otherwise it is totally useless. Further regulations will be announced later. The law stipulates: in general old money will be exchanged for new money at ten to one, of which half can be put into a checking account or in cash, but half has to be put into a medium-term savings account. It will be decided later how people can use this money. Any account that exceeds 5,000 Reichsmarks is subject to an audit from the taxing agency. Therefore every person can only access half of 500 DM, or 250 DM.

July 1 sees the discontinuation of the egg supply control. Till June 30 every chicken farmer had to deliver to the authorities fifty eggs for each hen each year, regardless of one's own needs.

Despite the monetary reform, the high prices for rail travel and mail service (twenty-four cents for a letter; twelve cents for a postcard), the fees for radio programming (two marks per month) will not be lowered. However, on July 25, train tickets were lowered by 25 percent (to six cents per kilometer). However, considering the scarcity of money, that price is still too high.

August 18

We learned from a returning prisoner of war that Vitus Brühl, son of Gregor Brühl (at the smithy) was killed in Russia on January 1, 1945.

October 8

The private bus service from Geislingen via Stoetten, Schnittlingen, and Treffelhausen to Weissenstein and back has been reopened.

More and More Signs that Life is Becoming Normal Again

Mother's diary

[Margit] is preparing for her entrance examination into high school. The enthusiasm of this preparation is more on the side of the parents than on Margit who still treats homework as a burden and shrugs it off.

On June 28, she sat for the day-long examination to get into the Hölderlin- Gymnasium. Because she did so well, she was excused from taking orals.

So I started a new phase in my life—in a more normal country and a more normal lifestyle. I spent nine years in high school, from 1948 to 1957, from age ten to nineteen, when I entered the University of Tübingen. Upon reflection one thing astonishes me: though I was older at this time, I do not recall many memorable moments from my high school years, while I recall vividly the activities described above from four to nine years of age. Unusual events make an impression even on a very young child, while ordinary life just floats by.

The frequent and sometimes long absences of my father, the regular air raids and subsequent trips to the bomb shelters, the many long stays with great aunts, great uncles, and some strangers away from my parents and brothers, and the responsibilities that I had for my brothers at a very young age must have left an impression—even though I wouldn't go so far as some psychologists who maintain that all children born between 1932 and 1942 in Europe were traumatized as a consequence of life during the war. As mentioned many times in the story, parents all tried to shield their children from the chaos surrounding them.

Mother's diary

August 1949

Now we see so many lovely toys again that the children's desires are unlimited. The war and postwar years had their advantages, especially for Vati's wallet. Karl Heinz was so overwhelmed by the volume of Christmas presents that he told Vati, "Isn't the Christchild dear? Imagine if you had to buy all this!" He especially liked his little tractor [before the monetary reform there were no self-propelled toy vehicles] *and he rode it for hours without interruption, so it was already broken on Christmas day. This summer we gave him a scooter and I watch with sheer joy how he navigates on the street. He is a real street kid.*

Life Returns to Normal for Most—But Not for All

Though the war ended in 1945, the effects lingered for many years, e.g., the search for missing soldiers and the devastating economic situation with its accompanying suffering from hunger and cold. What hasn't been described yet is one of the longest lasting results of any war: posttraumatic stress disorder (PTSD) of the returning soldiers. This was never talked about or identified as a medical condition and probably not known by most until decades later.

Only a few years ago, around 2010, my cousin Paul handed me a diary—handwritten in pencil—that his father, Hermann, had written from 1944 to 1951, documenting his suffering from a severe war injury to his leg that never completely healed, a lung disease that wasn't diagnosed for a long time, and possible symptoms of PTSD, which neither he nor anybody in the family recognized.

I have elected to publish only excerpts from 1944 to 1947, a time when the soldiers either returned directly home or became prisoners of war, a time when unemployment was rampant, and homes had been destroyed and not yet rebuilt. During this time Hermann led a nomadic lifestyle, moving from his parents' rooms on the farm, to his sisters' apartments in different cities, while he tried to make enough money to get his own room.

He started a romance with a pen pal, but couldn't decide whether he wanted a committed relationship…and so the friendship faded away. He also took stabs at reclaiming his professional life, but couldn't decide which direction to go. His diary mirrors the symptoms of PTSD: his constant mood swings; his difficulty in establishing personal relationships; and his professional vacillation between his technical training and work experience and his desire to become an artist. Neither he nor anybody in the family ever considered whether or not these symptoms were a result of his war experiences.

Uncle Hermann's diary, begun in an army hospital, Gmünd

September 8, 1944 (nine months before the end of the war)

I believe that my time in the hospital is coming to an end. It's been a long time since I was wounded, and part of me is happy to go back to life…. On the other hand, I am happy that I am residing in such a remote place during these troubled times.

September 30

I was operated again for the ninth time. I am starting to get sick of it and I would be happy if I was discharged. After the last surgery, they are now suspecting that I have a new illness, one that I don't even want to mention in writing.

October

For a few days, I thought all was well, but yesterday I was informed that I again have tuberculosis…. The days pass by with an unshakeable sameness that is interrupted by only air-raid alarms. My main occupation is to wait for mail, mostly in vain.

I am happy because I heard clearly the word "negativ," which means without a doubt that the suspicion of tuberculosis is unfounded. Because of our clear skies, we often have air-raid alarms, especially when the fast fighter planes approach to shoot at trains. When they approach, no full air raid warning is given, since they target the transportation system only. But riding trains is dangerous.

…I am elated about my leave. I am looking forward to meeting my unknown pen pal after corresponding with her for such a long time.

November

Fourteen days ago, it was decided that I will not be discharged. Yes, I will also patiently endure this extra time. For the last few days I worked for four hours a day in a mechanic's training site. First it was mind-numbing work, but I asked the supervisor for more challenging jobs and am now happy.

December

I was discharged from the military hospital and visited my parents and three of my sisters, all in different places. It is wonderful, if one can visit ones relatives in this turbulent time, since one never knows, if or when one can see each other again.

Shortly before Christmas
  A few days ago, I finally met A., my long-term pen pal.

April 1945
  *I am again on vacation in Bregenz. Meanwhile I have been in the re-
serves and then again in the hospital. I had major surgery and scarlet fever. The fronts are coming closer and closer and I am hoping to see the
surrender here. There is great excitement everywhere and as I judge
the situation, the Third Reich is dissolving. Nobody wants to continue
this senseless fight. As soon as one recognizes somebody as having
the same political outlook, one can express one's feelings freely, but if
one doesn't know the person one is very circumspect. There are many
spies among the folks who make money by subjugating and selling others.*

End of April
  *I am super happy and the reason is that the end of this senseless war
seems near. One has to rejoice when the resistance will be completely
broken down....and I am in love.*

First days of May
  *The French have been in Lochau and Bregenz for a few days now.
We don't know how far they have advanced anywhere else, since we
have neither a radio or newspaper.*

May 23, after the end of the war
  *Now they have jailed me for a few days. I have no idea why. The only
accusation that they can levy against me, is that I am a
Reichsdeutscher.*

June 1 [as a prisoner of war in Lochau]
  *Time goes by and one hardly notices it. I have been here for six
weeks and am waiting till I can go home to my parents. I found out today
that we will be issued departure passes; tomorrow I will apply for one. If
there is no other way, I will hike slowly to Schnittlingen.*
  *I had imagined my days in Lochau very differently. I am now pretty
sure how I stand with A. And yet, I am a terrible person.*
  *I have not seen her for the last four weeks. I am longing to see her,
but then I am afraid that when I see her I will commit a stupidity. I am already so old and I still can't figure out what it means to be in love. Perhaps my mistake is that I use my brain to investigate situations and
thereby kill my emotions. Oh, to be able not to think...but follow the
heart.... Yes, A., I only know that you have roused me from my bachelor
life into a disquieting mood, which I love at times, and I long for this*

power over me that no woman ever had over me. If I could only see clearly. A., what shall I tell you when we say good-bye?

June 7

A., how I have waited for you. I had hoped that my thoughts about you would bring you here. Yes, since your visit last Sunday I have been happy and I see everything in a different light and I wanted to declare myself to you today. But you didn't come, and I keep my wisdom to my-self.

June 16

I am now at home…. How wonderful it is to sit with my parents.
And saying good-bye to you, A., was very hard on me. I love you! Yes, these words, how hard they are to pass my lips when one doesn't know how you would accept them. But I had to tell you, even if I did it so awkwardly. It does show how difficult it has become for me to disclose my inner thoughts and emotions. I can only hope that you understood what I meant. A., A., if I could only see you one more time. I would act very differently. Everything is really so easy, but humans make it so complicated.
Besides all my worries about a job, I constantly think of you, A.
Returned from Geislingen and Donzdorf. The first attempts at reintegration into the work world have failed. Now the fight for survival starts. Soon there will be masses of unemployed. And what then? I will try many things in vain…but something will come up. It has to.

June 24

Returned also from Gmünd without finding work. The expectations are bad. Everybody lacks materials.

June 25

At last, I will get work in Böhmenkirchen. One should never give up hope.

July 2

One should never rejoice too early. I also received a rejection from Böhmenkirchen! Alas!

July 26

I have now returned to Stuttgart. Six and a half years have passed since I was drafted into the army, on April 1, 1939, and I have experienced a lot since then. Yes, the memories of the peace years are so far back, the years when Stuttgart, my hometown, was still beautiful and untouched. And today, debris, misery, and unemployment! I have tried very hard to find a place of employment, but….during these days you have to live in the moment and trust in God, like we did at the front.

*If I could only see things clearly, especially my relationship with A.
How long will it take till the mail gets delivered again?*

August 4

*For a change, I have been back in the hospital due to my war injury.
Another splinter surfaced.*

August 8

*Lately, I have been thinking a lot of what I will do in the future. I am
sure the unemployment rate will skyrocket and of course I will endeavor
to keep it away from me. A while ago, I entertained the idea of becoming
a teacher, but then I rejected the idea. The idea of having to sit again on
a school bench and to go into a completely different direction is a bitter
pill. On the other hand, it would be a secure job and also a beautiful vo-
cation, which appeals to me. Yesterday, the government called on returning soldiers who want to become teachers to report to an agency.
But I can't decide; I am weighing the pros and cons: job security versus
a long training period at my age, in a completely different profession.*

August 14

*My thoughts continually revolve around what will happen in the fu-
ture? We Germans stand at the edge of an enormous abyss.... I see
only the awful, black, and profound depth. How will all these people find
employment? Industry is destroyed and it will be many years before
Germany recovers from this blow. Whoever cooked the soup has to eat
it too. The only good effect is that the German people have experienced
war in all its details on their own skin and will therefore not lightly start
another war—hopefully never again and so we want to use all our energy to work against it. It should and must be possible to solve all problems between nations in a peaceful way. Every war is a big evil for all
humanity.*

August 15, Mary's Assumption, in the evening

*This afternoon a man was wheeled into our hospital room...after a dif-
ficult stomach surgery. He can hardly breathe. His parents and wife visit
him. Hardly anything is spoken, because he is not able to speak. His
mother sits by his bed and occasionally wipes the sweat from his fore-
head or shoos away the flies. Looking at their clothes, one can immediately see that they are not from Germany. They are
Volksdeutsche...driven from the East by the war. They have lost everything, and wherever they are they are lost [uebrig]. How this war has
thrown people all over the world into misery. And who is responsible for
all that?... I could scream.*

August 17

Oh, I am again totally overjoyed, and see the world through rose-col-

275

ored glasses. It's not going to be as bad as I thought, like in the saying "Nothing is eaten as hot as it is cooked." The weather is marvelous and I had a sweet visitor at my bedside.

August 23

Have again been discharged from the hospital. It's only been a few days, yet it seems a long time ago. What yesterday seemed so important, is immaterial today; it just belongs to the daily routine, since I have now been successful and found a job. I will start in eight days. Life is beginning again!

...A., you gave me more grief than joy, yet I think of you with love. Was it right of me to leave you so abruptly? The most stupid thing was that I blathered so. I only wanted to clarify the situation and I created even more confusion. A., I would love to see you soon to create more confusion!

September 15

Germany is bleeding...and I have been—for the first time in a very long time—at my old business, helping a bit with the rebuilding of Germany.

Today I worked at my old job for the first time after six years, five months, and fifteen days. If I had any idea how long I would be in the army, I would probably have despaired right away. Only the hope that all would end soon helped me through the worst times.

September 29

For the last fourteen days I have tried to work at my old job, but my knowledge is too insignificant and I constantly stumble and, am insecure; so I left work to-day. It's a big leap into the unknown and yet I am content with my decision. With God's help I'll find the right job.

October 10, Schnittlingen

I am free, I can do or not do what I like and I have to live with the advantages and disadvantages of my actions. I shy away from applying for a job in various businesses since the possibility exists that I would be hired! Is this attitude right, to just float along? To await what the future will bring and to just soak up today's sunshine? Not to think about tomorrow! Or is it my laziness in not bringing my life under control? With all my heart I want to work really hard to uproot trees, and if I experience serious resistance, I will just lay myself under the tree and wait till it rots away and falls by itself.

December 19

For the last few days, I have been with my parents in Schnittlingen. I am home! I am elated and happy! There is only one home and only there is one completely oneself.

In the last four weeks I have undergone an inner change. After much back and forth I have decided to no longer pursue my technical/mechanical profession. With all my heart I hate this technical time. I want to find my inner self. I want to have time for myself. I am going to start at the beginning again. I was in much anguish before I reached this decision. But now I have a clear vision! It will be hard work, but I won't shy away from it and I will make any effort—to carve.

February 5, 1946

When I returned to Stuttgart, I got carving knives and started to work hard. The Christ head that I started in Schnittlingen is now finished and I have also carved a Madonna with child and other small carvings. I am working like mad and enjoy carving very much, especially when a piece is finished successfully. But what inner conflicts continue to plague me. Employment worries! What should I do? Carver or sculptor? I researched it and as a sculptor I'd have to do a long apprenticeship. It's not as I thought, that it is enough if my carvings are well reviewed to be able to sell them easily. Or even to get an apprenticeship. So far, I have no prospect of such a position.

February 20

Every day is different, yet the same. Since my last entry, I decided a few times to work in radio or then again to continue with sculpting. What a difference in the two professions! And now that I have made a definite decision, I will enter a one-year apprenticeship as a sculptor. I met with Mr. Lutz, a sculptor, and am full of hope.

March 10

I now work with Mr. Lutz. Work is very hard on me, since I have to stand so much. Lutz has warned me often against pursuing the profession of a sculptor because of the bad times, not because of my lack of talent. But my decision is now irrevocable.

May 1

I have now finished the portrait of my brother Karl. Physically, I am not doing well. I have a suspicion that I have tuberculosis.

May 25

Today, Stuttgart had its first normal election. As I thought, I do have TB. Always something!

July 23

I am happy to be in Stuttgart…one needs a certain air to be able to blossom. All the gloomy thoughts of Schnittlingen have disappeared. In short, I am happy and my sense of enterprise has awakened. I believe again and dream of the future.

End of September

I collect beechnuts, which can be pressed into oil—a welcome improvement in the kitchen.

December 31

Another year ends. I sit here and still don't have clarity about my future! Just failures!

January 5, 1947

I am afraid of the future, what concerns I have because my inner soul is sick, since I despise myself. It is probably the most terrible thing that can befall a person: to be constantly confronted with his own dreadful character. I constantly have my disgust with myself in front of my eyes. Shame on me!

It's all useless. It would be best if one would just drift. Both eyes closed, head in the sand and the stinking mud. There is something to say about wallowing in the dirt. One doesn't see the sun and doesn't have to pine for it. But woe, three times woe, to the person who gives up on himself.

March 8

Soon I will return to Stuttgart. There are good arguments for it and good ones against it, and I hope that my decision was the right one. If one could only correct some of one's old mistakes—but then one would have to lead a completely different life.

A new Spring has started, a new Hope, a new Longing—what will it bring?

March 12

For weeks I have been waiting for mail and it should have arrived a while ago, but I am still waiting. Life is so incredibly sad; I can't even talk about it. One could ask, what's the sense of it all, if one didn't have one's religion. I often think about shooting a bullet into my head—and yet I cling with my last fiber to life. Who can understand that? Oh, I am a miserable creature of small faith. Either to live or to die, but not this hermaphrodite existence.

March 15

Yesterday I was contacted by my previous employer at Ruh Radio, who wanted me to start working for him again. This was for me a real shock. What now? I have thought about it a lot but can't come to a decision. Yes, it's hard and everything has its lights and shadows. If I could be sure that I would become a halfway decent carver, it would be easy. But I lack the courage and courage is needed to start all over again at age thirty. And what does the position at Ruh give me? A middle-class existence. I wouldn't be hanging in the air or swimming anymore. Oh, if I only had clarity about my health.

April 6

Easter Sunday! Christ has risen! I am again making another attempt to change the direction of my life.

Soon I am going to Stuttgart, and I am really scared. Lately, I have had a fever again! Oh, if I was only healthy and could work to the point of being tired. Two years have passed since the end of the war and I am still waiting—but I don't know what I am waiting for—perhaps something that will allow me to lay the basis for the future.

Drawing is so important! It sharpens the sense of observation. It challenges a person mentally and spiritually.

April 8

The world is getting more beautiful by the day and I don't know when the blooming will end. Today the sun is out and Spring is really here, which does the heart good. And soon I will be in Stuttgart. What will the future bring?"

April 10

Tomorrow I am leaving and today I pack. Since I don't know whether I will return, I am quietly saying good-bye to many cherished things....

Hermann returns to Stuttgart to consider working in his old job, but then decides he wants to be an artist.... This indecision about his work and income goes on till he meets his wife in the Kunstakademie in Stuttgart, settles with her in Konstanz, manages the houses of his wife's family, and works as an artist in many media.

The diary gives little insight into the frequency of meeting between his pen pal/friend and how and who ended the friendship. After 1947, A. was no longer mentioned. Due to his nomadic life, his small war pension, and the fact that she lived in a French-occupied zone and he in the American-occupied zone, meetings were difficult to arrange.

Investigation Continues into Robert's Fate

Though the members of the family were trying to rebuild their lives and to put the war and the Nazi years behind them, the war never really ended for our family, because no certainty about Robert's fate was achieved. There was no grave, there were no remains, and so my grandparents never stopped mourning for their son till their own deaths. Though I have no recollection of this uncle myself, I still feel strongly that I would like to know how and where he died.

How very painful it must be for so many Jews and others who died in the camps who never heard from their loved ones again after they were taken by the Gestapo. Did they die on the way to the camps, did they die in a concentration camp? Ruth Kluger writes in her book *Still Alive* (Feminist Press, 2001, p. 80): "Where there is no grave, we are condemned to go on mourning." A cousin of my father married a German Jew who escaped to England with one of the last children's' transports organized by Rothschild and who came back to Germany with the British occupation forces. Their daughter told me that her grandfather was murdered in Buchenwald; his brother was transported first to Theresienstadt and then to Auschwitz, "where he probably died, though the family never received a definite answer."

As soon as the political situation in Germany and then in Russia and Romania changed, someone in the family tried to get information again about Robert.

Letters to my father from his parents-in-law in Schnittlingen

February 1950

Father read in the newspaper this morning that all soldiers missing in action should be registered between March 1 and 11. Please tell Rudolf and Hermann to do it: Private Robert Brühl 09545 C.

Replies to requests for information

January 12, 1954

German Red Cross: "On the basis of the March 1950 registration of MIAs, your brother was entered under his unit. This list is given to all returning prisoners of war and they are asked to identify anyone on the list. So far nothing has been learned about your brother. In addition two meetings of returning soldiers from his unit have taken place, during which the lists were distributed. This also did not result in any knowledge about the fate of your brother. We will continue to research...."

[Note: After the deaths of our grandfather and grandmother, Uncle Robert's siblings, especially Uncle Rudolf and my mother, continued their investigations.]

February 20, 1958

The magazine Deutsche Illustrierte: *"...to date we have published 4,530 fotos of MIAs. Through our effort "Help Us Search" we have found five missing soldiers alive who had been sought by their families for years. We have also received 275 clues from readers that we forwarded to the authorities. Unfortunately, we have a backlog of 1,660 unpublished photos and can therefore not accept any more....*"

September 17, 1958

Search Service newspaper: "...we can inform you that we have publicized the following search notice: Brühl, Robert, born March 11, 1924, toolmaker, last known field address 09545 C, Sixth Company Grenade Regiment 683 of the 336 I.D. Missing since the battles during the retreat on August 22, 1944, in the vicinity of Kishinew (Bessarabia), belonged to group of first Lt. Fiedler. After crossing the Pruth River the company was decimated. Who was with him then or who knows anything about his fate? Please contact VW 3091 at the Suchdienst-Zeitung."

June 8, 1961

German Red Cross: "...we have asked all the former comrades in your brother's unit who have returned. I regret that no information has been received...."

After many years of fruitless inquiries, Rudolf initiated the process of declaration of death on June 16, 1961. After seventeen letters between Rudolf, the lawyers, and the official departments, Robert was declared legally dead on December 1, 1961. His time of death was established as at midnight December 31, 1945, since no other date can be proven. Before the siblings could access his "estate," more correspondence between banks and lawyers followed. Since Robert had joined the army right after his graduation as a toolmaker, the only money that he earned came from the army. He established a checking account into which his army salary was deposited; he also withdrew some money occasionally. His total savings, including interest, came to 819.40 RM, which was transferred to Rudolf. Since all of his belongings were burned in the bombing raid in Stuttgart, there were no goods to distribute to his surviving siblings.

Red Cross report to my mother, February 17, 1969

With the information provided by you and your brother Rudolf, we entered your brother Robert in all Red Cross investigations conducted since 1950, most recently in the picture gallery of the missing soldiers, in the general and the special lists of his unit. These lists were given to all survivors in Germany, Austria, and other neighboring countries and they were questioned intensively. When we could not solve the mystery of many MIAs through these individual interviews, we researched in detail the last battles in which your brother was involved. We investigated whether his unit was captured and whether your brother had been taken prisoner.

The summary of all of these investigations leads us to the conclusion that Robert Brühl with a high degree of probability died between August 20 and the first days of September 1944 either during the battles or in the first days of his captivity.

Reasons: In August 1944 the Russians had completed their preparations for a major offensive: six tank units, one mounted corps, and ninety-four infantry divisions. In the area where the Germans were defending their position, Russia's Twenty-Seventh Division outnumbered them as follows: infantry, five to one; artillery, eight to one; tanks, ten to one. The offensive started on the morning of August 20. After an intensive barrage, the Russian tank and infantry divisions, supported by planes that attacked relentlessly, managed to break through completely. For three days the Germans withstood the offensive, but then their energy was exhausted and the unified front was destroyed. Without pause, the motorized units of the "2. Ukrainian Front" pushed forward to the crossing at the Pruth River. The "3. Ukrainian Front" approached from the East near Tiraspol and pushed forward to the Danube Delta. Already on August 24, the towns Husi, Leovo, Falciu, and Barland were in Soviet hands. [All of these towns are on the Soviet/Ukrainian/Romanian border.] This sealed the fate of the Sixth and part of the Eighth German army, because now the route to the West was cut off. Only small units still found some gaps in the encirclement during the first days; later only individuals escaped. In the night of August 24, the Romanian Army capitulated and thereby accelerated the Soviet advance, so that the Danube Delta, Galacia, and all of East Romania (including Konstanza,

Bukarest, and Ploetzi) became occupied by August 31.

In the meantime the encircled units tried to break out. During their retreat from Dnjestr they had to break through enemy barriers while constantly being shot at by artillery and planes. They therefore lost most of their tools and weapons. On the last remaining overcrowded but still open roads, the cohesiveness and the communications of their units completely broke down. During this chaotic and rushed retreat small groups of men came together haphazardly, but they had to find their own way back.

Everyone wanted to get to the West to the Pruth, but on the road between Sereth and the river the Soviets had put up many barricades, which made escape impossible. This is the reason for the encircled triangle Jasi–Husi–Kishinew in which most of the Germans were taken prisoner during day-long battles. Only a very few troops managed to cross the Pruth after having suffered great losses. They reunited on the other side of the river to march to Sereth. However, at the beginning of September they were surrounded again and were captured. A few units that had been pushed to the south by the Dnjestr front were surrounded by the enemy near Sarata. In addition, the units farther behind the front were defeated due to the rapid advance of enemy troops.

Twenty-one German divisions, independent army troops, artillery and marine units, and other organizations under the command of the army were involved in the battles. Most of the soldiers were killed in combat. The number of prisoners was estimated at 150,000.

Reports from returning prisoners tell us that many prisoners had already died during the first few weeks or months due to mental and physical exhaustion, because they lacked food and medical supplies, and due to an outbreak of dysentery and typhoid.

In regard to your missing relative it is known that he was fighting in August in Romania. He was part of the Seventy-ninth Infantry Division, which had to defend the area around Jasi. The center of the area was the village Stanca. Some of the comrades were in training or had served in special commandos outside the area of operation of the unit.

At that point the main action of the Russians was more to the West so that his division was not directly involved in this battle. On August 22, however, when the Soviets had completed their breakthrough, his unit was ordered to join the general retreat toward the South. During their attempt (August 25 to 27) to reach Musi and then move south they were pushed back and were surrounded in the great cauldron between Jasi and Kishinew. That sealed their fate. Individuals managed to escape the fighting near Husi and marched via Baradul to the West, but could not breach the barricades.

Mail service between the prisoners and the homeland was slowly established around the end of 1945. Your missing brother has never contacted anyone from prison, however, and none of his comrades have seen him in a Soviet prison. That's why we have to conclude that he ei-

ther died during the final battles or in the first days of captivity.

When Thea was in Rome for a month in 1967, she created a small prayer card for her brother and parents:

[Front:] *In memory of our dear parents and siblings in*
their eternal resting place
Brühl
[Back:] Small photo of Robert
As the youngest in the family
born March 11, 1924, in Stuttgart
and missing since August 1944
near Kishinew in Romania.
Loyal to his family and his friends in the parish,
he strived—like his older brother—to please his parents.
But both had a sad premonition.
In the trust that God has accepted his childlike soul
into his eternal life and that Mary protected his last months,
we remember him with love.

Letter from my mother to the Human Rights Commission, August 14, 1975

I have heard that a German expatriate living in Russia has contacted your commission to get more information about MIAs. This plea was forwarded to the chancellor. I would be interested to hear whether this plea has led to results. We have been missing our brother since August 1944, and all inquiries with the Red Cross were without results.

The last information is that he probably was killed during the battle in August of 1944.

Answer from the Human Rights Commission, August 19, 1975

...to our great regret we have to inform you that as far as we know the German government did not pursue this matter. According to the letter that was sent to us, the camp near Perm that was mentioned was not a prisoner of war camp, but a camp for political prisoners [ethnic German Russians], who were imprisoned during the years 1924–1925 and 1936–1938. The letter was not dated; it was therefore difficult to ascertain when it was written. However, we are trying to find out more about this camp. This is very difficult because the official Soviet agencies will not release any information. To this date, no international agency, not even the Red Cross, has gained access to any Russian prison.

In May 1995 the German Red Cross contacted Trudl Brühl, Rudolf's widow, and told her to fill out a questionnaire in case Robert was still missing, since Russia had opened up its files. The questionnaire was filled out in June 1995, but because I found a copy in Stuttgart, I don't know whether it was ever sent.

The last inquiry to the Red Cross was sent by Johannes Baumgartner, a nephew of Uncle Robert, in 2004, because by that time all the files of the Eastern bloc states had been opened.

Excerpts from the reply from the German Red Cross

Robert Brühl has been known to us for many years as MIA in World War II. Extensive investigations have unfortunately not been successful. In the early nineties we started to research the archives and registrations of the Soviet Union. Since then we have been able to study 400,000 MIAs' information and have solved 20,000 cases. We continue to receive new information from new sources. However, we have not been able to obtain information about your missing relative. We will continue our research till all possibilities have been investigated, including variations of names. In any case, you will receive a concluding report. We regret that we do not have more positive news for you.

Nothing has been heard since then from the Red Cross or any other agency.

Summary

The results of the Second World War on Stuttgart were as follows: In fifty-three air raids between 1939 and April of 1945, more than 4,500 inhabitants, including 770 forced laborers (prisoners of war who had to work in Germany) were killed. Fourteen thousand soldiers from Stuttgart were killed in action or died in a prisoner of war camp. The number of disabled or severely disabled cannot be ascertained. Of Stuttgart's Jewish population 4,490 were known to have been murdered by the Nazis. Today, a small plaque in front of all the homes of the Jews who perished is embedded in the sidewalk. This reminder of the Nazi atrocities has the following inscription:

> *First and family name*
> *Birth date*
> *Rounded up and transported to a camp on* [date].
> *Murdered in* [name of camp]… *on* [date].

Effects on My Family

Our grandparents suffered the most in our family during two wars and the Great Depression.

My mother's parents lost one son in 1943 in Russia and another son went missing in 1944. At the ages of seventy-one (grandfather) and sixty-five (grandmother), they were bombed out of their apartment and lost all their belongings. A third son returned from the war with a serious knee injury; two of their sons-in-law developed serious illnesses (TB and kidney disease) that stayed with them till they died.

In 1931, during the Depression, my grandfather lost his cheese factory and retail shop. In 1944 he lost his job after he had to move away from Stuttgart. My grandparents died poor, my grandfather in 1954 and my grandmother in 1955.

My father's mother lost her husband in 1915 in the First World War in France. This also meant that the very successful firm went to the next oldest brother of my grandfather and his descendants. One of her sons returned from the Second World War with TB, which stayed with him till his death.

In 1944, at the age of sixty-five, her house in Aachen was completely bombed out and she lost all her belongings. The firm that had been in her family for some time also went bankrupt during the war, and she lost any income from it. After the war, she still had two properties in Aachen: one on which her bombed-out house stood and one in the middle of the business district. Since she had no money, she had to sell both properties at a very low price. The buyer who paid in monthly installments often fell behind in his payments. She lived first with her daughter, then with one of her sons. She visited our family twice a year for three to four weeks each time. Shortly before her death, she went to a nursing home. She also died relatively poor in 1955.

None of my grandparents therefore lived long enough to partake in Germany's "economic miracle." None of their grandchildren were able to help them out financially.

My brothers and I lost our godfathers in the war: my uncle Karl Brühl was killed in Russia in June 1943; Bernd's godfather, Hans Pardun, was killed in Düren during an air raid in September 1944. Karl Heinz's uncle Robert Brühl has been missing in action at the Russian/Rumanian Border since August 1944.

The Second World War was certainly the most devastating and life-changing war that affected my immediate family, but it was not the first one. Europe has been a hotbed of military strife for millennia with devastating results for all involved.

Lest we forget this violent history, here is a short outline of my more distant family members' involvement with wars:

A maternal great, great grandfather, Georg Nagel, was the first known "draft dodger" or "conscientious objector," depending on one's point of view.

From the family chronicle

The following story still circulates today in the family. When the Napoleonic/Russian War erupted in the early 1800s he was of marriageable age. All unmarried men were called up to service. To avoid this draft, he saddled a horse and rode in the middle of the night—probably because he didn't want to be betrayed—from Kuchalb to the neighboring village of Degenfeld to fetch a bride who had been recommended to him. He reached Degenfeld safely. The two of them came quickly to an arrangement and in order not to miss the short time he had before he had to report he put his bride in front of him on the horse and rode back with her. However, it was still in the middle of the night and because of nonexistent street lights, the two of them did not see each other clearly nor had they ever met before.

During the communal ride to the Kuchalb, the sun was coming up. When the bride turned around to see her "lover," she noticed that he had a red beard. She got such a fright that she wanted to jump off the white horse and walk home again. But she changed her mind.

On the way to the church ceremony the bridegroom realized that the bride was also not perfect. She dragged one foot a bit. But he was not deterred. The wedding took place right away and the marriage was considered to be a long and happy one.

One of his descendants, Konrad Nagel, was one of six children. Two of his siblings did not survive beyond childhood, his three surviving sisters all became nuns (one in Brazil, one in South Africa, one in Isny). He was killed in 1915 in the First World War, before he had any children. His father had to sell the family farm because he had no more descendants.

My paternal great grandfather, Heinrich Paulus, was a professional soldier for twenty years before he started the family bridge-building business. He served in the war of 1870–1871.

Excerpts from the military pass of Heinrich Paulus
[six pages of rules and regulations; a list of every piece of clothing given him by the military; and a description of the battles he was in]

1870–1871 campaign against France
Battle near Gravelotte, August 18, 1870
Siege of Metz, August 20–October 29, 1870
Battle near Amiens, November 27, 1870
Battle on the Hallve, December 23–24, 1870
Fight near Lapignies, January 2, 1871
Battle near Bapaume, January 3, 1871
Fight near Tettry Poully, January 18, 1871
Battle near St. Quentin, January 19, 1871

Granted a leave of absence for a trip to the USA (New York) from 1872 till 1876. Decommissioned to the national guards in Aachen, October 8, 1875 [possibly in absentia]. Discharged from the guards due to fulfillment of his duties, November 2, 1885.

He had thirteen children. Of his five sons who survived to adulthood, two were killed in the First World War.

My grandfather, the oldest son of Heinrich Paulus, Eduard Paulus, was drafted in 1914 at the age of thirty-seven. He had three children ages nine, four, and a baby.

From the memorial prayer card of Eduard Paulus
The deceased was born May 15, 1877, and lived since January 23, 1904, in harmonious marriage with his wife. He was a loving husband and a devoted father to his three children. For the honor of his fatherland he went to war with much courage and in the knowledge of victory. But too soon—on February 22, 1915—a bullet found him when he was at the head of his unit during an intense battle, and ended his life suddenly.

He was popular with everyone due to his good-natured character.

From the memorial prayer card of my great uncle,
Alfred Paulus, youngest son of Heinrich Paulus
In Christian memory of the private Alfred Paulus who had volunteered for the artillery.

He was a student in the officer's academy in Bedburg, when the call from the highest war command [the kaiser, I presume] *came to defend the threatened homeland. He no longer could sit at a students' desk.*

He also wanted to join in order to protect Germany's honor and exis-
tence. Though he was turned back repeatedly because of his youth,
he insisted till he received permission to wear the king's uniform.

He proved to be worthy of this honor; he was always in the first posi-
tion when a new battle or a sortie had to be carried out.

During a reconnaissance trip a bullet hit him on September 26, 1916.

He was in a field hospital for eight days and even assured his parents
of his full recovery. However, he succumbed to his wounds on October
8—a young hero!

The grief of his parents and siblings is made worse since this is the
second son and brother who was lost, and he was the darling of the
family. However, they offer this sacrifice in the hope of a reunion in eter-
nal life.

He was seventeen years old.

The daughter of another of our grandfather's brothers. Though she and her husband did not serve in the military, they were directly affected by war activities. During the Second World War they lived for years in Indonesia, where her husband worked as a businessman. They were interned for some years by the Dutch. Because Germany was allied with the Japanese, who had attacked Indonesia, all Germans were put into internment camps.

My maternal grandfather, Achaz Brühl, was drafted at age nineteen into the infantry, and sent to the Sixth Regiment in Ulm in 1893. In 1895 he was discharged from the army, but transferred to the reserves. He finished one reserve tour of duty, but before he was ordered for the second one he was discharged from the reserves due to varicose veins and an en-larged heart. I guess this was the reason he did not serve in the First World War though he was the same age as my paternal grandfather. It could also be because he was an independ-ent businessman or because at the beginning of the war he already had six children. Three more of his children were born during the First World War and the last four of his thirteen children were born in the postwar period.

One of these children also became a victim of this war, though only indirectly. After five daughters, Achaz's first son, Richard, was born in the first year of World War I, 1914. To keep him safe from the war activities, he was sent from Stuttgart to Westerheim to live with my grandmother's relatives. Westerheim was a tiny isolated village with no easy ac-cess to hospitals or doctors. Richard developed diphtheria and died at age four during the last year of the war, because the family was either too poor to afford medical help or the re-mote area was not served by a doctor.

My parents' family members' military history is described in detail above.

From the obituaries of soldiers who were killed we can see that the young men went into the wars with great courage and ready to sacrifice themselves for Germany. The per-sonal miseries of the soldiers and the effects of their deaths and injuries on their relatives at home were never mentioned publicly. I hope the above history shows how devastating and drastic the effects of war were on everyone.

Researching the military history of a family, we can conclude that Europe was involved in a war about every twenty to thirty years for the last centuries. I consider it therefore a hopeful sign that for the last seventy years there have been almost no intra-European wars. The next generation after ours is the first generation for a long time that has lived without war.

May it stay this way, so that we can say with my Aunt Minni:

War no more.

About the Author

Margarete Paulus Roth was born in Stuttgart, Germany, a year before the start of World War II. She spent her first seven years under the Nazi regime, the last two years of which as an internal refugee in a secluded valley in southern Germany. She emigrated to the United States in 1968 and devoted her career to advocating for understanding different attitudes and behaviors worldwide as a professor of international economics and business at Catholic universities. She is Professor Emeritus at Benedictine University in Lisle, Illinois. She lives with her husband, Warren, in Naperville, Illinois.

Made in the USA
Lexington, KY
11 June 2018